A Guide to the Criminal Justice and Public Order Act 1994

A Guide to the Criminal Justice and Public Order Act 1994

James Morton, Solicitor

Butterworths
London, Dublin, Edinburgh
1994

Q

United Kingdom	Butterworths a Division of Reed Elsevier (UK) Ltd, Halsbury House, 35 Chancery Lane, LONDON WC2A 1EL and 4 Hill Street, EDINBURGH EH2 3JZ
Australia	Butterworths, SYDNEY, MELBOURNE, BRISBANE, ADELAIDE, PERTH, CANBERRA and HOBART
Canada	Butterworths Canada Ltd, TORONTO and VANCOUVER
Ireland	Butterworth (Ireland) Ltd, DUBLIN
Malaysia	Malayan Law Journal Sdn Bhd, KUALA LUMPUR
New Zealand	Butterworths of New Zealand Ltd, WELLINGTON and AUCKLAND
Puerto Rico	Butterworth of Puerto Rico Inc, SAN JUAN
Singapore	Butterworths Asia, SINGAPORE
South Africa	Butterworths Publishers (Pty) Ltd, DURBAN
USA	Butterworth Legal Publishers, CARLSBAD, California, and SALEM, New Hampshire

Reprinted 1995 (March)

The right of James Morton to be identified as the author of this book has been asserted.

A CIP Catalogue record for this book is available from the British Library.

ISBN 0 406 04585 2

Printed and bound in Great Britain by Antony Rowe Ltd, Chippenham, Wiltshire

Contents

Table of statutes

References in this Table to *Statutes* are to Halsbury's Statutes of England (Fourth Edition) showing the volume and page at which the annotated text of an Act may be found.

Table of cases

Introduction

GENERAL

'Lord Randolph threw himself on his horse and rode off in all directions' wrote the Canadian humorist Stephen Leacock.

> 'In October, I announced the most comprehensive package of measures to tackle crime ever announced by a Home Secretary. The measures rest on some basic, common-sense principles: that protecting the public is the first job of Government, that criminals should be held responsible for their actions and that the police, who are in the forefront of the fight against crime, should be given the powers which they need to catch criminals. Those are principles in which the Government believe, and they lie at the heart of the Bill . . . The Bill will enact a major reform of the criminal justice system, which needs reform. It is not providing adequate protection for the law abiding. It has not been able to cope with the small hard core of persistent juvenile offenders. Bail is too often granted to criminals who offend again and again. Too many obstacles are still in the way of the police. They must have the powers that they need to combat crime and to bring criminals to justice. The powers of the courts are inadequate. They are not able to deal as they or we would wish with the cases that come before them. The balance in the criminal justice system is tilted too far in favour of the criminal and against protecting the public. The Bill will help to put that right.'

So said the Home Secretary, Michael Howard, moving the second reading of the Criminal Justice and Public Order Bill on 11 January 1994[1]. Were the matter not so serious it would be tempting to apply the act of Lord Randolph to the Government's penal policy over the last decade. In 1987, we had a short Criminal Justice Act dealing with serious fraud cases. This was followed a year later by the full blown Criminal Justice Act 1988. Three years after that the whole of sentencing policy was re-arranged by the Criminal Justice Act 1991 and when, as had been predicted by many critics, this did not work, the Criminal Justice Act 1993 effectively changed many of the provisions and policies. In fairness to the Government, penal policy rarely seems to work for any length of time and certainly not for everybody.

The Home Office, in its handbook for magistrates and judges *The Sentence of the Court* sadly admits that it must be accepted that no single type of sentence can be shown to be more likely to prevent re-offending than any other—

> 'The almost invariable conclusion of the large amount of research which has been undertaken (in various Western countries) is that it is hard to show any effect that one type of sentence is more likely than any other to reduce the likelihood of re-offending, which is high for all. Equally, longer periods of custody or particular institutional regimes do not seem to have a significant effect. Studies comparing the reconviction rates of offenders given community service orders with those custodial sentences have also shown little difference.'[2]

In other words, as the American writer, the late John D MacDonald put it rather more succinctly, 'The only thing that prisons demonstrably cure is heterosexuality'..

The changes in sentencing policy may not, however, be wholly altruistic. It has become apparent that the cost of keeping a person in an open prison is about 10 times that of placing him on probation or making him work out a community service order[3]. By 1993, however, it was apparent that there was another wave of opinion in favour of sterner, if not harsher, treatment of criminals. There were stories of young boys racking up literally hundreds of offences without the youth courts being able to do anything about them. Earl Ferrers, moving the second reading of the Bill in the House of Lords, gave two examples—

> 'There are reports of a 14 year-old from Tyneside who has 28 convictions and who has escaped 22 times from local authority accommodation. Another 14 year-old boy in south London has admitted taking part in more than 1,000 burglaries of shops and homes in the past two years. On a single night he, and other teenagers, raided 23 branches of one particular store. He has stolen over 100 cars to ferry himself between burglaries, and the total value of all the goods stolen and the cost of damage is estimated to be in the region of £2 million. He has been arrested 40 times but is too young to be given a custodial sentence for the crimes he has committed. That is pretty hot stuff.'[4]

There were also well publicised press stories of youths being sent on character building holidays to Europe and Africa—ones which the majority of the public could never hope to afford even for their retirement trips—and subsequent cynical re-offending by the beneficiaries of such treatment.

So far as the prisons themselves are concerned, there are now three contracted out prisons and, if reports are correct, they seem to be experiencing all the problems of the so called designated prisons. Escort duty to magistrates' courts has resulted in a series of highly publicised escapes and the death of one inmate who drank too much liquor. As for the Government run prisons, there was a break-out by IRA prisoners in September followed by the discovery of explosives in the prison grounds. Prison after prison has been condemned by Sir Stephen Tumim, HM Inspector of Prisons, for overcrowding, lack of facilities, bullying, drug-dealing and the like. In the good old days, which may be deemed to be pre-1970, the use of drugs was not a menace in prison. A certain amount of alcohol was brewed or even smuggled in but any illicit dealing was in tobacco. All that has changed: the supply and sale of drugs has become big business inside prison as well as outside. The problems are the same, only magnified. Here is Shifty Burke writing in 1966—

> 'The debt could only be repaid if the men wrote to relatives outside to pay the money to a nominee of the baron. These letters were carried by the bent screws who had to be paid likewise. So some wretched woman trying to bring up her kids on what she could earn or get from the National Assistance Board was bombarded with letters begging her to pay up and save her husband from disaster. Those who had no means to pay became serfs of the barons and strong arm men. They slaved for them and prostituted themselves if required, but the debt still mounted up. Finally the wretched prisoner would be cornered by strong arm men and beaten up and that squared the debt for the moment.'[5]

Shortly after the 1994 Act received Royal Assent, a two year prison service study exposed the extent of the present market in drugs and how organised gangs from London, Liverpool and Manchester were running the trade. According to the report, the gangs make their profits by supplying heavily cut heroin at five times its street price. Inmates, often introduced to the drug in prison with free samples and encouraged to buy on credit, are spending up to £200 a week on their habits. The level of intimidation of the families of prisoners is such that gangs post sentries outside prison on visiting days and, at Wormwood Scrubs, women have been harassed in the visiting room[6].

The worries of the more liberal minded over the undoubted problems of the criminal justice system brought about by a series of cases where, after much goading and whilst beating their collective breasts, their Lordships in the Court of Appeal (Criminal Division) overturned long standing convictions and made public apologies to the defendants, had long since evaporated. By the time the Runciman Committee reported in the summer of 1993[7] there had been a law and order backlash. We were no longer concerned with miscarriages of justice and wrongful convictions; we were again concerned with the prospect of the guilty being acquitted. At the 1993 Conservative Party Conference Michael Howard, the Home Secretary, announced 27 pledges of action to be introduced into his Criminal Justice Bill. It was intended that the Bill would have passed through Parliament by the end of the Parliamentary year. It did not. First, it was attacked on all sides and on almost all grounds and then, when it finally wound its way through the House of Commons, it was repeatedly savaged in the House of Lords, where one clause after another was amended or defeated. By September 1993, only one of the 27 pledges, the new guide-lines to reduce cautioning of offenders, was genuinely up and running. Things perked up for the Government after the summer recess. The amendments proposed by the House of Lords went through the House of Commons without any real trouble and their Lordships second time around bowed to the inevitable. On the passing of the Bill, Mr Howard was able to say that 17 of his pledges were now on the statute books. Some of the 27 proposals were, however, lost to the Government. The extension of the Crown's right to appeal against lenient sentences under the Criminal Justice Act 1988, s 36, has been shelved for the moment but, more importantly, so has the setting up of the body to review miscarriages of criminal justice which was really the *raison d'être* behind the Runciman Commission in the first place. It was this omission onto which the opposition latched[8].

Critics of the Act point to a serious erosion of civil liberties in the sections which increase the police powers of stop and search, preventing gatherings on private land, curbing the right of silence as well as making squatting a criminal offence and giving the police power to move travellers. Its supporters believe that the creation of a central DNA database will assist in the prevention of crime and that the creation of secure training centres may actually put a stop to the wave of pre-and early teen crime which, they say, has become out of control. Perhaps one thing out of control was the legislative process. A bill of relatively modest proportions (117 clauses) grew to one of 172 clauses and 11 Schedules. Perhaps such growth is not all that extraordinary. The Criminal Justice Acts of 1987 and 1988, which were conceived as an entirety and split only because of a General Election, ended with a total of 191 clauses and 18 Schedules.

In some ways, the clauses left on the committee room floor are the most interesting part of the Criminal Justice Bill. The casualties of this Bill included proposals for the sale by post of weapons, assistance for the deaf in court or in custody, a compensation agency to enforce compensation orders, provisions against intimidatory begging, research into juries and the power of a judge to provide a multi-racial jury, stalking (people rather than animals) and unauthorised advertising in telephone kiosks, ie those cards which advertise the arrival of a new model in the locality and which, it is said, is now a £200,000 a year industry in some cities. At the end of the day at least Michael Howard appeared to be pleased—

'The Act includes 19 of the 27 measures which I announced last year to redress the balance of the criminal justice system. It will be an important weapon in the fight against crime. It will give the police the powers they need to catch criminals. It will also give the courts the powers they need to sentence the guilty appropriately and offers victims a better deal from the criminal justice system. It will help victims in a number of ways. It will give courts powers to protect them from persistent juvenile offenders who will be detained in secure training centres instead of roaming the streets, committing crime after crime. The abolition of committal proceedings will mean that witnesses, including many victims, will not have to endure the stress of having to give evidence twice. The Act also means that judges will no longer have to give a warning to juries in rape cases that it is dangerous to convict solely on the basis of the unsupported evidence of a complainant. This practice has been considered insulting to victims and prevented some of them coming forward. The Act also creates a new offence of witness intimidation. The Act will help the police too. The provisions allowing samples to be taken for DNA testing will be a major weapon for officers in their fight against crime and will pave the way for this country to have the most comprehensive DNA database in the world. The Act allows senior police officers to authorise stop and search operations in a limited area for up to 24 hours when they believe incidents involving serious violence may take place, allowing them to move quickly and effectively to stop problems before they get out of hand. They will be given powers to impose conditions on suspects granted bail and will be able to arrest those who flout bail by failing to report back to the police station when required. New powers will also be at their disposal for dealing with public order such as raves, gathering of new age travellers and mass trespass which can be a blight for individuals and local communities. There will also be enhanced powers and procedures for courts. Magistrates and juries will be able to take into consideration a defendant's silence when deciding a case. The courts will also be able to impose custodial sentences on juvenile offenders who have repeatedly committed certain offences. Greater sentencing powers will also be made available to the courts, strengthening their ability to deal with those who possess firearms or certain drugs illegally and those who trade in obscene material and child pornography. The Act also provides for mandatory drug testing of prisoners which will give the prison authorities a powerful tool in controlling drugs in prison and provide a better picture of the scale of the problem.'[9]

Cynics may say that much of that is pure rhetoric and ask, in particular, how some matters such as the scale of drug taking in prison have reached such a pass before the Government appears to have taken notice of them. The civil rights organisation *Liberty*, for one, was none too pleased. It believes that several of the new measures in the Act are likely to breach fundamental human rights as protected by the European Convention of Human Rights. In particular, it singled out the right to a fair trial, the right to privacy and family life and the right to free assembly. Andrew Puddephatt, the General Secretary of *Liberty*, commented—

'The ease with which governments can pass laws undermining basic freedoms is a disgrace to democracy. It emphasises the need for enforceable rights so individuals can challenge such abuses with greater effect than at present. Now more than ever we need a Bill of Rights to force the government to respect minimum human rights standards.'[10]

Liberty plans to challenge a number of measures in the Act in the European Court of Human Rights. It points out that this lengthy process can take up to seven years, by which time, if the past few years are any guide, there will have been a number of new Criminal Justice Acts. It is, however, an ill wind which blows no good. The Act would seem to be set to provide many a happy pay day for enterprising lawyers throughout the country.

---

1   HC 2R, 11 January 1994, cols 20, 23.
2   HMSO 5th Ed. (1990), p 7.
3   HMSO 5th Ed. (1990), p 110.
4   HL 2R, 25 April 1994, col 381.
5   Shifty Burke, (1966) *Peterman* pp 146, 147.
6   The Sunday Times, 6 November 1994.
7   The Royal Commission on Criminal Justice (1993), Cm 2263.
8   See, for example, HL 2R 25 April 1994, col 386, *per* Lord McIntosh of Haringey.
9   Home Office Press Release 220/94, 3 November 1994.
10 *Liberty* Press Release, 1 November 1994.

---

1 Young offenders

SECURE TRAINING ORDERS

1.1   When Michael Howard, the Home Secretary, opened the debate on the second reading of the Criminal Justice and Public Order Bill ('the Bill') in the House of Commons on 11 January 1994 he spoke of juvenile crime—

> 'The message from police, from magistrates and from local communities throughout the country is clear. There is a small hard core of young tearaways who commit crime after crime, and who cock a snook at our entire criminal justice system. At present the court are unable to deal adequately with persistent juvenile offenders, especially those aged between 12 and 14. The public must be protected from them.'[1]

He went on to set out the proposals for what the Bill described as 'a new secure training order' under which juveniles would serve their sentences in centres that—

> 'will provide high-quality education and training designed to encourage those who benefit to lead law-abiding lives. These young criminals are people in respect of whom other attempts to stop them committing crimes have been tried but have failed. All of them will have been previously convicted and will have offended again. All of them will have received a supervision order and will either have offended during it or will have been in breach of it. All of them will have committed at least one offence that is serious enough to warrant custody.'[2]

---

1   HC 2R, 11 January 1994, col 23.
2   HC 2R, 11 January 1994, col 24.

1.2   It was shortly afterwards that the roof fell in on him. Indeed, with the possible exception of the loss of the right to silence, the proposals must have united more disparate bodies in opposition to them than any others in a very long time. By the time the Bill was debated in Committee, over 25 different bodies including the Law Society, the Justices' Clerks' Society, the National Association of Probation Officers and the Prison Governors Association, as well as numerous organisations such as Barnardos and the Association of Young People in Care, had expressed opposition. The complaints ranged from the cost, to the distance separating the young people in secure units from their families, to the lack of use of other methods to divert young people from crime, such as intensive supervised activities. There were fears that the secure training centres would become prep schools or colleges of crime for the 12 to 15 year olds. During the debate in the House of Commons on the consideration of the Lords amendments[1], Ms Ann Coffey, the Labour member for Stockport, offered some interesting statistics on juvenile crime in her constituency. She pointed out that the total number of juvenile offenders had fallen slightly between 1990 when there were 1600, and 1993 when there were 1400. As is the case in most urban areas, the crimes were mainly shoplifting, car crime and public order offences, although she admitted that there was a small group involved with drug dealing and protection—

'A study by Stockport's Youth Justice team of all juveniles who appeared before Stockport juvenile and Stockport youth courts between 1 January 1990 and 31 March 1994 revealed that from a total of 1,500, four boys legally fitted the terms of the secure training order. At the time of sentencing, the magistrates could have imposed a custodial sentence on three of the boys but did not do so. That leaves only one boy who could have been committed to a secure training centre, which would have made little impact on Stockport's crime statistics and would not have greatly improved its residents' quality of life.'[2]

One of the fears of the myriad of parties and organisations opposing the secure training orders is that whilst at present somewhere between 100 and 200 young people at a time would be the subject of such orders, an expansion policy would creep in and within a short time there would be thousands of young persons the subject of these orders. Parkinson's Law on the availability of places would apply. Even worse, the reason for the increase would be to ensure that the private sector, which would have the opportunity under the Criminal Justice and Public Order Act 1994, s 7 ('the Act') to tender for contracts for the building and running of these centres, would get an adequate return on their money.

---

1   HC Lords amendments, 19 October 1994, col 282.
2   HC Lords amendments, 19 October 1994, col 308.

1.3   The proposals were ravaged in the House of Lords when a series of humiliating defeats was inflicted on the Government. However, as is often the case, the amendments put forward by the House of Lords were rejected when they reached the House of Commons in October 1994. Dealing with the amendments proposed by the House of Lords, Mr Michael Howard reiterated the Government's thinking behind the proposals—

'Throughout the passage of the Bill, the Government have made it clear that the new secure training centres will be different from anything tried before. They will be centres housing a specific category of persistent offender, and the regime will be tailor-made for them so as to provide the right kind of training and care within a secure environment.'[1]

Just when the local authority secure accommodation will be available is not clear. Mr Howard blamed Labour-controlled local authorities for not having presented proposals. During the passage of the Bill Mr Howard made further announcements relating to tougher punishments for young offenders—

'The scales of justice have been tilted too far in favour of the offenders. Victims have had a raw deal. I want to redress that balance. Offenders have to realise that they have an obligation to the victims of their crime and to society. For young offenders this obligation extends to their parents and schools. They have an important part to play in the success of stricter community sentences. The revised national standards make it clear that a sentence served in the community is not a soft option. This will mean that some offenders will have to take part in rigorous physical work in the community, and where possible repair the damage they have done. All pre-sentence reports will include a new section called 'offence analysis' in which the impact of the offence on the victim will be explained to the court. These measures will mean an end to the approach which offers holidays for offenders and the start of a new tougher regime for those on community sentence. Out go holidays and in come tightly controlled community sentences with parents and school playing a key role in the supervision of young offenders. In some cases the aim will be for parental bindover to be imposed on parents who do not accept responsibility for the supervision of their youngsters. Misconduct or failure to comply with the terms of their orders will no longer be met with a string of warnings. Two formal, written warnings will be followed by a penalty, possibly custody.'[2]

---

1   HC Lords amendments, 19 October 1994, col 282.
2   Home Office Press Release, 166/94, 22 September 1994.

1.4   Section 1 of the Act provides that the court may make a secure training order in the case of a young person aged between 12 and 15 years who is convicted of an imprisonable offence (that is one which is punishable by imprisonment for someone aged 21 or over) and

(a)   who was not less than 12 when he committed the offence, and

(b)   has been convicted of three or more imprisonable offences,

and on this or a previous occasion has either been found by a court to be in breach of a supervision order made under the Children and Young Persons Act 1969, or has been convicted of an imprisonable offence committed whilst he was subject to such a supervision order.

1.5   A secure training order is an order for a period of detention in a secure training centre followed by a period of supervision. The order shall not be for less than six months or for longer than two years and the actual detention is to be half the period of the order. The court may specify that the period of detention be in secure accommodation provided by the local authority or by a person or organisation with whom the local authority has made arrangements for the provision of such accommodation. At any time during the currency of the secure training order, the sentencing court, on the application of the local authority, may make a further order regarding the remainder of the period of detention under the order. It may be replaced by a period during which the offender shall be required to live in other local authority accommodation (a period of supervision) or a period of detention in a secure training unit. One problem which has faced the courts in recent years is determining the age of travelling children. The problem is exacerbated as it is by no means easy for them or their relatives to provide hard evidence of their age. Therefore, for the purposes of s 1, the age of a person shall be deemed to be that which it appears to the court to be after considering any available evidence. In fact this provision may not be as harsh as it first appears. Obviously reports will be obtained before such an order is made and this should provide the opportunity for any children under the age of 12 to be eliminated from the system.

1.6   As with hospital orders (made under the Mental Health Act 1983), it is likely that there will often not be a secure training centre place available immediately. If this is the case then under s 2 of the Act the court may commit the offender to such a place and on such conditions as the Secretary of State may direct, or as the Secretary of State may arrange with local authorities, voluntary organisations or persons carrying on a registered children's home (within the meaning of the Children

Act 1989). The period of committal shall not exceed 28 days. If there is still no place available the court may, on application, extend the period of committal. The period of detention in the secure training centre under the order shall then be reduced by the time spent awaiting transfer. The wording of s 2 does not appear to allow the first 28 days to count. Section 2(4) provides the Secretary of State with the power to transfer the offender from a secure training centre to such other place as he may direct, and the period spent outside the secure training centre will count as being part of the custodial period. From Mr Howard's comments, it is clear that the intention of this provision is not to reward good behaviour by the young person with a transfer to a less disciplined regime; instead—

> 'There may be very rare cases in which a juvenile serving the secure part of the secure training order clearly needs to be moved to other accommodation—when he or she develops a mental or physical illness, or when there are grave concerns about his or her ability to cope with the regime.'[1]

It is not to be a power to be used routinely but only to provide an avenue for moving offenders in exceptional cases. Section 2 further provides that the Secretary of State, when satisfied that exceptional circumstances exist, may release the offender on compassionate grounds from the secure training centre. The offender will then be subject to supervision for the remainder of the term of the order. It would appear that the unserved portion of the order will be added to the supervision.

---

1   HC Lords amendments, 19 October 1994, col 286.

1.7   Under s 3(2) of the Act, during the supervision period of a secure training order the offender shall be under the supervision of a probation officer, a social worker of a local authority social services department or such other person as the Secretary of State may designate. The category of supervisor shall be determined by the Secretary of State from time to time. If the supervision is to be provided by a social worker then that person shall be from the local authority within whose area the offender resides for the time being. In the case of a probation officer being the supervisor, then that person shall come from the petty sessions area in which the offender resides for the time being. In each case the probation committee or local authority will be entitled to recover from the Secretary of State expenses reasonably incurred. Before the offender begins the supervision part of his order he must be given a notice specifying the category of person who will be responsible for his supervision and any requirements with which he must comply. If there is to be a change in either the category of his supervisor or in the conditions of the order then he must be given notice before the change comes into effect. The provisions relating to secure training orders that are contained in ss 1–4 of the Act will be brought into force by order as soon as the secure training centre accommodation is available. The implementation will depend on the progress made in awarding contracts and establishing the centres. Under s 1(10) of the 1994 Act, there will be phased implementation of the order, ie progressively downward, beginning with 14 year olds.

1.8   Section 7 of the Act provides that the Secretary of State may enter into a contract with another person for the provision or running by him of any secure training centre. The provision and management of such centres is likely to be the first venture by the private sector into the running of an establishment for young offenders. At present the Wolds in Humberside is run by Group 4 and Blakenhurst is run by United Kingdom Detention Services. The idea of contracting out to the private sector is largely motivated by financial considerations, in particular the desire to ensure that no capital costs will fall on the Government. The cost of running secure training centres is estimated to be £30 million a year and although children's charities and the public sector will have the opportunity to tender, so far they have shown little inclination to do so. Many organisations disapprove of private prisons on ideological grounds but there is no doubt that they are here to stay, at least in the medium term. Those planning to tender for a contract for the provision or running of a secure training centre will do well to note that the Landlord and Tenant Act 1954, Pt II (security of tenure), the Law of Property Act 1925, s 146 (restrictions on and relief against forfeiture), the Landlord and Tenant Act 1927, s 19, and the Landlord and Tenant Act 1988 (covenants not to assign) will not apply.

1.9   Section 8 provides that instead of a governor, every contracted out secure training centre shall have a director who shall be a custody officer appointed by the contractor and approved by the Secretary of State. There shall also be a monitor, who shall be a crown servant appointed by the Secretary of State. All officers employed who perform custodial duties shall be custody officers. Schedule 2 to the Act has effect with respect to the certification of custody officers, and under para 2(2)(b) of that Schedule, a certificate will not be issued until sufficient training as considered appropriate by the Secretary of State has been undertaken. The director shall have such functions as are conferred on him by the Prison Act 1952 so far as it is applicable to secure training units, and as may be conferred on him by secure training centre rules. The function of the monitor is rather different. He is to keep under review, and report to the Secretary of State on, the running of the centre, and investigate allegations made against custody officers performing their duties or officers of directly managed secure training centres temporarily attached to the secure training centre. It is a requirement that the contractor or sub-contractor shall do all that he reasonably can to facilitate the exercise by the monitor of all his functions under s 8(3) of the Act.

1.10   One of the critics' fears of the provisions relating to secure training centres is that staff in children's institutions have become isolated from mainstream childcare developments leading to bad practice or illegal activities. Section 9 sets out the powers and duties of a custody officer and it can be seen that his principal duties are indeed custodial. After setting out the duty to prevent escape, to prevent, detect and report on other unlawful acts, to ensure good order and discipline on the part of the inmates, there is specified the duty to attend to the well-being of the offenders. There is also the power under s 9(4) to use reasonable force where necessary.

1.11   The Strangeways and other jail riots have shown that even the most experienced governors and their staff can temporarily lose control of a prison in the face of determined disruption by inmates. Section 10 provides the Secretary of State with an opportunity to relieve a director who has lost, or appears to be likely to lose, effective control of a centre, or any part of it, and replace him with a Crown servant to act as governor for a specified period of time. During this period the governor will be able to exercise all functions of both the deposed director and the monitor. Once control is restored the appointment shall cease and control be returned to the director. Again, there is an obligation on the contractor or sub-contractor to facilitate the exercise by the governor of the functions of the director and monitor. Under s 11 of the Act custody officers may be contracted to work at directly managed secure training centres.

1.12 Section 12, which deals with escort arrangements, must be read in conjunction with Schs 1 and 2 to the Act. There will be an escort monitor to keep transport arrangements under review and a panel of lay observers whose duty it is to inspect the conditions in which offenders are transported or held. If complaints are made against custody officers acting in this capacity, the escort monitor will be required to investigate and report on them. A custody officer, acting as an escort, has the power to search any offender in accordance with rules made by the Secretary of State. A custody officer may also search any other person who is in, or seeking to enter, any place where any such offender is held or is to be held, and any article in the possession of such a person. However, the power of search is limited. The officer may not require a person to remove any of his clothing other than an outer coat, headgear, jacket or gloves.

1.13 Provision is made under s 13 of the Act for dealing with assaults on custody officers acting in pursuance of escort arrangements, or in the course of their custodial duties at a contracted out secure training centre, or whilst themselves performing contracted out functions at a directly managed secure training unit. An assault in these circumstances will be dealt with summarily and carries a fine not exceeding level 5 on the standard scale and/or six months' imprisonment.

1.14 Section 14 provides sanctions against persons employed as custody officers or otherwise in pursuance of escort arrangements or at a contracted out secure training centre for the wrongful disclosure of any information which is acquired in the course of employment and which relates to a particular offender detained at a secure training establishment. Wrongful disclosure occurs if it is otherwise than in the course of duty or as authorised by the Secretary of State. By virtue of the relatively narrow wording of the section, that is 'and which relates to a particular offender' it would seem not to apply to the blanket disclosure of conditions in a centre to a newspaper. At least there would seem to be an arguable defence. Penalties are a maximum of two years or a fine or both on indictment, and six months or a fine or both if the case is dealt with summarily.

1.15 The definitions of some of the words used in ss 7–14 are set out in s 15 of the Act. Most are self explanatory but it is worth looking at Sch 1, para 1(1) to the Act which empowers the Secretary of State to make arrangements for certain functions to be performed in such cases as may be determined by or under the arrangements by custody officers who are authorised to perform such functions. These functions are: the delivery of offenders from one set of relevant premises (ie court, secure training centre, police station or hospital) to another; the custody of offenders held on the premises of any court (whether or not they would otherwise be in the custody of the court) and their production before the court; the custody of offenders temporarily held in a secure training centre in the course of delivery from one secure training centre to another; and the custody of offenders while they are outside a secure training centre for temporary purposes, eg attending a funeral.

CUSTODIAL SENTENCES FOR YOUNG OFFENDERS

1.16 As part of the policy of toughening sentencing provisions for juveniles, more categories of young persons come within the ambit of long term detention (that is periods over the 24 months provided for in s 17 of the Act). Section 16 amends the

Children and Young Persons Act 1933, s 53, to provide that long term detention may be ordered (where conditions apply) where a person of at least 10 years but not more than 17 years of age is convicted on indictment of an offence (except murder) which is punishable, in the case of an adult, by 14 years' or more imprisonment, or is convicted on indictment of an offence under the Sexual Offences Act 1956, s 14 (an indecent assault on a woman) , or is convicted of causing death by dangerous driving under the Road Traffic Act 1988, s 1(1), or causing death by careless driving whilst under the influence of drink or drugs. It is anticipated that this section will be brought into force by order early in 1995. Under s 17 of the Act the maximum length of detention in a young offenders institution for offenders aged 15, 16 or 17 is doubled to 24 months. Prior to the commencement of the 1994 Act, an 18 year old convicted of criminal damage, or of child abduction, or assault occasioning actual bodily harm, could receive prison terms of ten years, seven years and five years respectively. However, a 17 year old convicted of any of these offences could only receive a maximum of 12 months. When Mr Maclean proposed the clause in the committee stage he pointed out that—

> 'The change that we propose does not remove the disparity: it makes the anomaly not as bad. That, and our desire that youngsters aged between 12 and 14 years of age should not get longer sentences than those in the older category, is the purpose of clause 17.'[1]

It is anticipated that s 18 will be brought into force by order early in 1995. The fallacy, so far as the sentencing disparity between 17 and 18 year old offenders is concerned, is that it is only in rarest of cases that such a sentence would be imposed on an adult let alone an 18 year old. Section 18 provides that young offenders sentenced to custody for life shall now be detained in a young offender institution. It is anticipated that s 18 will be brought into force by order early in 1995.

---

1   HC Standing Committee B, 25 January 1994, col 263.

SECURE ACCOMMODATION FOR CERTAIN YOUNG PERSONS

1.17 The purpose of s 19 is to enable voluntary and private children's homes to provide secure accommodation and so extend its supply. It is anticipated that this section will be brought into force by order early in 1995. Before the passing of this Act, the Children Act 1989 banned such use. One problem with the system for dealing with young persons has been the difficulty for the court to remand the persistent offender to any secure accommodation. A remand in custody has had the practical effect of the young person being taken to a local authority home, and on occasions sent to find his own way back to court if the staff of the home were too busy to bring him. Section 20 now provides for the remand of 15 and 16 year olds to a local authority with a security requirement to be extended to 12 to 14 year olds. The scheme will be phased in with the remand provision being brought into effect initially for 14 year olds. It may be extended at a later date. Its commencement depends on the availability of additional secure accommodation. Section 21 of the Act is not likely to have any relevance for practitioners; it provides that where costs are incurred by local authorities in complying with court-ordered remands to local authority accommodation with a security requirement, these will be defrayed by the Secretary of State on either a case by case basis, or according to a proportion of such costs or a tariff structure determined by the Secretary of State. The commencement of s 21 depends on the availability of additional secure accommodation. By virtue of s 22, the concept of privatisation intrudes into the Act. Local authorities may contract out the management of secure accommodation and, with the consent of the managers, contract out secure accommodation in controlled community homes. Managers will function under an instrument of management.

ARREST OF YOUNG PERSONS IN BREACH OF CONDITIONS OF REMAND

1.18 Section 23 adds the Children and Young Persons Act 1969, s 23A. It is anticipated that this section will be brought into force by order early in 1995. The police now have the power to arrest a child or young person who breaches a condition of his remand to local authority accommodation. Before the section comes into force, the police will still be able to arrest a child or young person who has breached his bail, but not one whom the courts have remanded to the local authority with conditions and who has breached those conditions. On arrest, the young person must be brought before the court for it to reconsider the remand decision. This must happen as soon as is practicable and, in any event, within 24 hours. This is to be before a justice of the peace for the petty sessions area in which he was arrested. If, however, he was due to appear in court within 24 hours of his arrest anyway, then he is to be produced to that court.

POLICE DETENTION OF YOUNG PERSONS

1.19 A problem for custody officers has been what to do with juveniles after charge where there is a risk of serious harm to the public and where no local authority secure accommodation is available. Some custody officers have taken a robust view and kept the juvenile in the cells despite the subsequent outcry. Others, depending upon one's point of view, have been either more pusillanimous or have followed the letter of the law. Now, s 24 gives power to the police to detain juveniles in police cells when both the above conditions apply. It is anticipated that this section will be brought into force by order early in 1995.

2 Bail

GENERAL

2.1   Over the years, there have been a number of relatively isolated but heavily publicised instances of defendants who have been released on bail, particularly in sex cases, who have gone on to be convicted of rape or murder. To combat this, last year in the House of Commons Mr Michael Stephens, the Conservative member for Worthing, proposed a Bill to limit the instances in which bail can be given, and also to provide the prosecution with the opportunity to appeal to the Crown Court against a decision by magistrates. The presumption of the right to bail, of which defending advocates are so fond of telling magistrates, has been further eroded and s 25 of the 1994 Act is an extension of the Criminal Justice Act 1988, s 154, which requires magistrates giving bail in such cases to record their reasons in writing. Now s 25 provides an absolute prohibition against the granting of bail in cases of murder, manslaughter and rape or where the defendant is accused of attempting any of these crimes, if he has a previous conviction for any of them, ie a previous rape conviction will debar a man from obtaining bail in a manslaughter case. In the case of a conviction for manslaughter, this prohibition will only apply if a sentence of imprisonment was passed or, if the defendant was then a child or young person and he was made the subject of long-term detention. One point of interest to practitioners will be the fact that this section applies whether or not there is an appeal pending, where the conviction includes a verdict of not guilty by reason of insanity or that he was unfit to plead, and where the defendant was made the subject of a probation, or an absolute or conditional discharge order. During the debate of the Bill in the Committee stages, an example was cited by Mike O'Brien—

> 'Let us consider the case of a 15 or 16 year old young man who is convicted of attempted rape and sentenced to long-term detention under the Children and Young Persons Act 1969. He serves a period in custody, during which time successful work is done to look at and challenge his offending behaviour. He changes his behaviour and is released. He commits no further offences for some time and becomes a productive, stable, law-abiding member of society with a job, a home and a family. The man's mother becomes ill and remains seriously ill for a long time. She suffers greatly, and subsequently, in completely unconnected and dissimilar circumstances from those in which he was originally sent to prison, the young man is accused of being involved in a so-called mercy killing.'[1]

Mr O'Brien went on to seek a rebuttable presumption against granting bail so that a judge's hands would not be tied. He was unsuccessful and presumably the riposte to him is that hard cases make bad law. It is thought that s 25 will be brought into force in Spring 1995 as part of the simultaneous implementation of the bail provisions contained in Pt II of the 1994 Act.

---

1   HC Standing Committee B, 25 January 1994, col 277.

2.2   The effect of s 26 of the 1994 Act is again a tightening of the screw. It is thought that this section will be brought into force in Spring 1995. Persons who have committed (or who are accused of committing) an offence whilst on bail no longer have a right to bail under the Bail Act 1976. In effect this is Mr O'Brien's rebuttable presumption in application. As cases have taken longer and longer to be heard both at the Crown Court and in the magistrates' courts, some accused have been racking up a string of charges after the initial (and often subsequent) granting of bail. The situation has been particularly prevalent in motor vehicle and burglary cases. Home Office statistics tend to show that 50,000 offences are committed annually by people on bail. Overall studies show that between 10 and 17 per cent of all offences are committed by those on bail. Of course, such figures can be inflated almost by accident. Of 537 suspects arrested in a sting operation 'Operation Bumblebee' in which the police had set up a shop to 'buy' stolen goods, 40 per cent were already on bail. Of course, magistrates have always had the power to refuse to grant bail on the basis that they had reasonable grounds for believing that the accused would commit further offences whilst on bail. But in the late 1980s, given the length of time the man would have served on remand in custody and that very often it would exceed by months the maximum sentence a court could impose, bail was granted on a number of occasions. Although the situation has improved, between 1991 and 1992 there were 6,000 fewer sitting days available to courts with a consequential 11 per cent overall increase in the delay between committal and hearing. In the Midland and Oxford Crown Court, the increase was 37 per cent. Section 26 only applies to offences which are triable on indictment or are either way offences; therefore the routine 'taking without consent' and drink driving offences will still carry the presumption of the right to bail. Many may think that once again the section is merely window-dressing. On the other hand, it does appear that magistrates have been steadily remanding more people in custody. In January 1994 the remand population stood at 12,100, an all-time record. One of the benefits of this section should be that each year up to 40,000 people will no longer be kept overnight in police stations. The Prison Reform Trust believed that the main factor was a response by the courts to the outbreak of 'law and order' rhetoric from politicians of both main parties—

> 'Where marginal decisions between a remand in custody or release on bail are concerned, the courts have been swayed into taking the custodial option.'[1]

---

1 *Whatever Happened to the Bail Act?* Prison Reform Trust, May 1994.

2.3 One of the anomalies of the Bail Act 1976 has been that whilst a custody officer at a police station has had the power to grant bail after charge, he has not been able to impose conditions on the accused. This has resulted in the defendant being remanded in custody over night, or over a weekend, so the magistrates may impose such conditions, often ones that he would have been content to accept from the outset. The alternative has been that the custody officer has bailed the defendant without conditions, not to the next working day of the magistrates' court but, in accordance with current thinking, to a day a week or two in advance. It has then been extremely difficult for the Crown Prosecution Service to argue successfully that the magistrates should impose any conditions at all. Section 27 (which adds the Bail Act 1976, s 3A) now gives the police power to grant conditional bail to persons charged; however, the custody officer cannot impose a condition that the accused resides at a bail hostel. Where an accused decides to chance his arm and apply to the police (before his appearance at the magistrates' court) for a change in the conditions imposed by the custody officer, that officer or any other serving at the same station, may change the conditions and he may impose more onerous ones. Conditions may only be imposed by the custody officer if he believes that, unless such conditions are imposed, the accused will either fail to surrender, or commit an offence whilst on bail, or interfere with witnesses or otherwise obstruct the course of justice whether in relation to himself or any other person. The same applies if and when a defendant seeks to vary the conditions. The magistrates retain the right to impose conditions or remand the defendant in custody when he appears before them. It is thought that s 27 will be brought into force in Spring 1995. Rules of Court governing applications to a court to vary conditions of bail will be made and laid before Parliament before the section comes into force.

2.4   Section 28 of the 1994 Act concerns police detention after charge and amends the Police and Criminal Evidence Act 1984, s 38. It is thought that it will be brought into force in Spring 1995. In practice. however, nothing has changed. A custody officer may detain an individual charged with an imprisonable offence if he has reasonable grounds for believing that the individual would commit an offence if released. Section 29 (which inserts the Police and Criminal Evidence Act 1984, s 46A, and amends ss 34, 37, 41 and 47 thereof) deals with the power to arrest for failure to answer police bail. Where a suspect has been released on police bail (an increasingly common occurrence following the time limits imposed under the Police and Criminal Evidence Act 1984) and has failed to surrender to that bail, the new section provides that he may be arrested by a constable without a warrant and taken to the police station appointed as the place to which he was to surrender to custody, as soon as practicable after the arrest. The section applies whether the person was released on bail before or after the commencement of this section.

2.5   Under s 30 of the 1994 Act, which adds the Bail Act 1976, s 5B, the prosecutor now has the right to apply to the magistrates to reconsider the grant of bail and to vary or impose any conditions, or withdraw bail and remand the defendant in custody. This does not apply to summary only offences. An application may only be made if the information on which it is based was not available to the court, or the constable supplying it, at the time when the decision was taken. An application may be made in the absence of the accused. If bail is now withheld the defendant must surrender himself and, if he fails to do so, may be arrested. If this is the case he must be brought before a justice of the peace for the petty sessions area in which he was arrested as soon as possible and, in any event, within 24 hours. The justice shall then remand him in custody. So far as the period of 24 hours in concerned, the usual rule that Christmas Day, Good Friday and Sundays do not count, again applies here. The Magistrates' Court Rules[1] will be amended so that a notice of application under this section, together with the grounds on which it is based, and including the powers available to the court, shall be given to the accused. It will also say that he shall have the opportunity of making either written or oral representations to be considered by the court before making a decision. It is thought that s 30 will be brought into force in Spring 1995. Rules of Court governing applications to a court to vary conditions of bail will be made and laid before Parliament before the section is brought into force.

---

1   SI 1981/552.

---

3 The course of justice: evidence, pr and related matters

INTRODUCTION

3.1 Of all the sections in this highly unpopular Act, the ones contained in Pt III (ss 31–53 and Schs 4, 5) proved to be the most controversial. In introducing the clauses to the House of Commons during the second reading Mr Howard was at pains to tell the House—

'The provisions will allow a court to draw proper inferences from a suspect's refusal to answer police questions in circumstances which cry out for an innocent explanation, if there is one, or from a defendant's refusal to give evidence in court. That does not mean that a suspect or defendant will be compelled to speak under threat of a criminal penalty. Defendants can still remain silent if they choose. In future, the judge and jury will be able to weigh up why the defendant decided to stay silent and the jury will be able to draw reasonable inferences from that silence; it is about the right to comment on silence.'[1]

He went on to add—

'I do not believe that the innocent have anything to fear from the changes. If there is a good reason for the suspect to remain silent, the jury will be able to consider it. But it is only right that, in a suitable case, the jury should know whether a person has remained silent or whether his story has changed.'[2]

Mr Howard's remarks cut across those of Lord Devlin who had set out in clear terms how the accusatorial system of trial must be accepted. In summing-up in the Bodkin Adams trial he said, in a much quoted passage—

'So great is and always has been our horror that a man might be questioned, forced to speak and perhaps condemn himself out of his own mouth, that we grant to everyone suspected or accused of crime at the beginning, at every stage and until the very end, the right to say 'Ask me no question. I shall answer none. Prove your case'.[3]

---

1 HC 2R, 11 January 1994, col 26.
2 HC 2R, 11 January 1994, col 27.
3 P Devlin *Easing the Passing* (2nd edn, 1985).

3.2 This was not the view taken by the Royal Commission—

'The right of silence is exercised only in a minority of cases. It may tend to be exercised more often in the more serious cases and where legal advice is given. There is no evidence which shows conclusively that silence is used disproportionately by professional criminals. Nor is there evidence to support the belief that silence in the police station leads to improved chances of acquittal. Most of those who are silent in the police station either plead guilty later or are subsequently found guilty. Nevertheless, it is possible that some defendants who are silent and who

rightly or wrongly be convicted if the
were permitted to suggest to the jury that
porting evidence of guilt.'[1]

hree points—

. believe that the possibility of an increase in
is outweighed by the risk that the extra pressure
e police station and the adverse inference invited
result in convictions of the innocent . . . The
nal criminals who wish to remain silent are likely
and will justify their silence by stating at trial that
their so.... advised them to say nothing at least until the
allegations against them have been fully disclosed . . . It is the less
experienced and more vulnerable suspects against whom the threat of
adverse comment would be likely to be more damaging. There are too
many cases of improper pressures being brought to bear on suspects in
police custody, even where the safeguards of PACE and the codes of
practice have been supposedly in force, for the majority to regard this
with equanimity.'[2]

---

1   The Royal Commission on Criminal Justice, pp 53, 54
2   The Royal Commission on Criminal Justice, p 53. For evidence in support of these arguments, see
    M McConville, A Sanders and R Leng *The Case for the Prosecution*, (1991), Ch 4, and K Bottomley
    et al *The Impact of PACE: policing in a northern force* (1991), which found, inter alia, that about three
    quarters of suspects neither ask for nor receive legal advice.

3.3   The argument over the right to silence has been long and drawn out and is
inextricably linked to the questioning and recording techniques of police interviews
over the last half century. It should be remembered that until the 1970s, evidence
given by police to magistrates and juries was, almost invariably, accepted without
question. The concept of the fabrication of evidence by investigating officers was
simply not accepted by the courts. The defendants answered questions and, if they
did not, the police on occasions invented incriminating answers for them. It may well
come as a surprise to the new generation of lawyers that before the Police and
Criminal Evidence Act 1984 ('PACE'), not only were there no such things as video
and tape recorded interviews but that interviews were not even contemporaneously
recorded and, at best, were compiled in the canteen at 'the earliest opportunity' from
the recollections of the officers present. It was only after a number of high profile
cases, in particular, the one regarding the wrongful conviction of three young persons
for the killing of Maxwell Confait[1], that first the Fisher Inquiry[2] and then the Phillips
Commission[3] led to the passing of PACE which provided, for the first time, detailed
codes of conduct offering safeguards to the rights of suspects, including the presence
of a legal representative in a police station when a suspect was to be questioned. It
will be remembered by older practitioners that to obtain details of the whereabouts of
an arrested client was often a day's work in itself, let alone obtaining access to him.[4]

---

1   C Price and J Caplan, *The Confait Confessions* (1977).
2   Sir H Fischer, Report of an Inquiry of the Hon Sir Henry Fischer into the circumstances leading to
    the trial of three on charges arising out of the death of Maxwell Confait and the fire at 27 Doggett
    Road London SE6 (HMSO).
3   Royal Commission on Criminal Procedure, Report (1981) Cmnd 8092.
4   Access to a Solicitor in the Police Station, Crim LR 1972, 342–350.

3.4   In the meantime however, there had been a consolidation of the idea that the rights of suspects should be maintained. A minority of the Royal Commission 1981 had had doubts about the right of silence, believing it to be negotiable if new safeguards were in place to eliminate oppression. In this they followed the minority view of the Criminal Law Revision Committee[1]. In 1989, a Home Office Working Party had come down firmly on the side of a requirement that the defendant answer certain questions. It also recommended that he disclose his defence in advance. More or less parallel research in West Yorkshire and London found that some 23 per cent of suspects in the south east exercised their right of silence in one form or another, with six per cent remaining silent from the outset. In Yorkshire, the figures were about half of those recorded in London. If, however, legal advice had been received by the suspect, then the number who exercised their right to silence effectively doubled. It was not surprising that the police reacted unfavourably to the curtailment of their tried and tested methods of interviewing. They have seen the PACE codes, rightly or wrongly, as a major handicap in their investigation of crime in general and obtaining a confession in particular.

---

1   Criminal Law Revision Committee *Eleventh Report Evidence (General)* (Cmnd 4991).

3.5   There has also been considerable argument about the so-called 'ambush' defence. A simple illustration of this is the defendant charged with dishonestly handling stolen (but untraced) silverware found in his coal shed. He had declined to answer questions at the police station and, for the first time, he says at the trial that he was minding it for his elderly aunt who is then pushed into court in a wheelchair to confirm his story. An acquittal results and the police complain that they have had no time to check out this story, nor have they (as they would have done with an alibi witness) had the opportunity of interviewing the aunt. The police wanted to see all defences put on the same footing as that of the alibi defence, as is the case in Scotland, and their wish has at least been partially granted. It seems that inside the metropolitan area, between 14 and 16 per cent of suspects presently exercise their right of silence at a police station with the percentage outside ranging from six to ten per cent. It is likely that these are the more experienced suspects rather than the weak and vulnerable. It is also likely that these sections will leave the professional criminal (the person at whom it should be aimed) untouched. As was pointed out he is likely to rely on the assistance of his solicitor in saying that he will not answer questions until all the facts against him are disclosed. It may be that the sections will, at least in the short term, prove to be so unpopular that juries will disregard the silence of the accused. Unfortunately, since the Contempt of Court Act 1981, s 8, prevents legitimate research into juries we are unlikely to find out[1].

---

1   There does now seem to have been a softening in attitude by the Court of Appeal in relation to what may be done by solicitors post-trial if they receive information that all has not gone well in the jury room. The latest of the cases is the so-called 'Ouija board case' when it appeared that four of the jurors had a quasi-seance to enquire of the spirit of the deceased whether he had been killed by the defendant. A re-trial was ordered. The conditions under which a solicitor should make inquiries of former jurors are set out in *R v Mickleburgh* (1994), *Times*, 26 July.

IMPUTATIONS ON CHARACTER

3.6   One of the more distressing features of murder and manslaughter cases in recent years has been the wholesale attack on the character of the deceased. The thinking behind the attacks has been that if the deceased's character was made sufficiently black, then the jury would acquit the accused as having really done right by the community in disposing of such an evil and unpleasant person. At present the shield protecting the defendant from having his own character put in issue has not been lost by such an onslaught against the deceased. This shield will now be lost and the Criminal Evidence Act 1898, s 1(f)(ii), is amended so that where this is done, it has the same effect as if the attack had been made on a witness giving evidence. It is thought that s 31 of the 1994 Act will be brought into force by order early in 1995.

CORROBORATION

3.7   Sections 32 and 33 may be of particular importance in criminal proceedings. They relate to the abolition of corroboration rules in the case of accomplice and children's evidence and in sex offence cases. Mr Howard suggested that—

> 'the balance of justice is tipped too far in favour of the guilty and against protesting society in general and especially the victims of crime. Part III of the Bill takes important steps to redress that balance. For example, at the moment, it is compulsory for the judge to give a warning in court about uncorroborated evidence from the victim of a sex attack. That is offensive to the victim and unnecessary. That is why the Bill removes the mandatory requirement for judges to give such warnings in sexual offence and accomplice cases.'[1]

Critics of s 32 might point out, as Roger Evans did at Committee stage, that there is a world of difference between the evidence of the victim of a sexual attack, and that of a partner in crime who is trying to buy his way out of trouble, or at least obtain a lesser sentence by giving evidence against his former friends. It was also pointed out that almost all the evidence against the so-called 'Cardiff Three' was accomplice evidence. Sadly, it is also the case that from time to time, and for a variety of reasons, women (and men) do make false allegations, and children do lie convincingly and outrageously. The effect of s 32 is that it abrogates the rule that a corroboration warning must be given but still allows the judge the discretion of giving it. One danger is that we may see two tier evidence arising. In years to come will juries begin to wonder why, in their particular case, a judge has given the corroboration warning. Does this mean he does not believe that the complainant (or the child or accomplice) is telling the truth? Furthermore, if he doesn't give the corroboration warning should the jury draw an inference from this? Section 33 abrogates the corroboration rule and applies to provisions under the Sexual Offences Act 1956, ss 2(2) (procurement of woman by threats), 2(3) (procurement of woman by false pretences), 4(2) (administering drugs to obtain or facilitate intercourse), 22(2) (causing prostitution of women), and 23(2) (procuration of a girl under the age of 21). It is worth noting that ss 32, 33 will not apply to any trial or committal proceedings which began before their commencement. It is thought that ss 32, 33 will be brought into force by order early in 1995. Furthermore, there is specific provision in s 33(2) that s 33 will not apply in a case where a trial or preliminary proceedings in a magistrates' court have already begun by the time the section is brought into force.

---

1   HC 2R, 11 January 1994, cols 25, 26.

INFERENCES FROM ACCUSED'S SILENCE

3.8 Now follow the sections which, according to *Liberty*, will breach the European Convention on Human Rights, Art 6(2). It should be noted that ss 34–39 will come into force as from a day to be appointed. The Police and Evidence Codes of Practice will first have to be revised, and it is thought that this will be completed by Spring 1995. Section 34 of the Act deals with inferences that may be drawn from the accused's silence prior to him being charged with an offence, or on so being charged. The suspect may still remain silent in the police station but in certain circumstances, when he reaches trial, the court may draw an adverse inference from that silence. However, certain requirements must be fulfilled before this stage can be reached. First, the accused must be being questioned either under caution, or on being charged, and secondly the failure to reply must be to a fact upon which the defendant relies in his defence.

3.9 Section 35 is concerned with the accused's silence at trial. At one time during the debate over the Bill it was suggested that a judge or magistrate might have the right to compel a defendant to step down from the dock and give evidence. It was suggested that he might be guilty of contempt of court if he did not do so. The Act itself has not gone this far, but practitioners of yesterday and the defendants of tomorrow may feel that even the amended provisions are draconian. No longer will the defendant be able to stand silent and let the prosecution attempt to prove their case without any help from him. Lawyers have long known that the highlight of the defence case was the moment the prosecution closed their case. A witness box is not necessarily the place to be seen at one's best, even if one is telling the truth. A prosecutor who cannot make even the most truthful witness look bad is not worth his salt. Section 35 applies where the accused is over 14 years of age and where the issue of his guilt is in question. It does not apply in cases where the court thinks that the defendant's mental or physical condition makes it undesirable for him to give evidence. It is tempting to ask what such a defendant is doing in the dock in the first place. The court must be satisfied that the accused is aware that he knows the stage has been reached when he can, if he wants, give evidence, and that he understands the potential consequences of not doing so. No adverse inference will be drawn if the refusal is 'with good cause'.

3.10 The effect of s 36 of the Act is that on the arrest of a suspect, if a constable sees any object, substance or mark on him, his clothing or footwear or otherwise in his possession, or in any place in which he is in at the time of his arrest and the officer or another reasonably believes that the presence of the object etc may be attributable to the participation of the suspect in the commission of an offence specified by the constable then, if he informs the suspect that it is his belief and requests him to give an explanation and, if the accused fails or refuses to do so, this fact may be used in evidence against him in committal and transfer proceedings, at the case to answer stage and at trial. One problem which may arise is the phrase 'otherwise in his possession'. Section 37 provides similar provisions where an accused fails or refuses to account for his presence at a certain place, at or about the time, the offence for which he was arrested is alleged to have been committed. The effect of this is that in theory, if not always in practice, he will be required to provide an instant alibi.

3.11 None of these sections provide for a person to be convicted solely on the basis of an inference. Silence will not, on its own, prove guilt but allied to other evidence it may be used to do so. During the passage of the Bill, Mr Howard took the opportunity of announcing a new and, presumably, improved caution—

> 'You do not have to say anything. But if you do not mention now something which you later use in your defence, the court may decide that your failure to mention it now strengthens the case against you. A record will be made of anything you say and it may be given in evidence if you are brought to trial.'

The caution takes 20 seconds to deliver, and the 22 words of the old caution nearly trebled to 60 in the new one. John Stalker, the former Deputy Chief Constable of Greater Manchester, writing in the *Daily Express* suggested that it had been drafted in the 'Faculty of Deliberate Ambiguity'. In fact the Law Society has suggested that there will have to be five separate versions of the caution administered depending upon what stage the investigations have reached. Practitioners may well wish to refer to *Changes in the Law Relating to Silence*[1] advice to practitioners from the Criminal Law Committee of the Law Society. The newsletter takes the view that problems will undoubtedly arise. One of the earliest problems will be when a client admits his guilt to a solicitor before police questioning. Should the solicitor (or clerk) then advise his client to make a clean breast of things without waiting to see whether the police decide to press charges and the CPS decide to continue the proceedings? Obviously, an immediate confession will assist in mitigation but the Law Society advises practitioners to be sure that there are significant advantages before advising on this course. Silence may still be golden. The same may also apply where the client is disadvantaged, ie circumstances in which the trial judge may not allow adverse comment. Practitioners may therefore think that if the client is in an emotional state, or is confused and likely to make mistakes (as opposed to telling lies) or indeed a dozen and one other things apply, eg a previous negative experience with a particular police officer, silence may still be the better course. The newsletter also deals with the question of efforts by the police to undermine the suspect's decision to remain silent. This is something which it fears may increase. It recommends that prior to interview clear advice is given to the client, and that the police are told that it is improper to give alternative advice to the client or denigrate the solicitor's role[2].

---

1   Criminal Practitioner Newsletter, No 20.
2   See also J MacKenzie *Silence in Hampshire* 140 (1990) NLJ 696.

3.12   The sections under discussion will provide considerable problems for the solicitor at the police station. Indeed, we may see a tendency for the experienced criminal to change solicitors during the course of a trial and blame the first representative for bad advice at the police station, thus endeavouring to negate adverse comments on his failure to give an explanation under ss 34, 36, and 37. If they do think of blaming their representative they may gain some comfort from the research of Professor McConville who found that the approach of solicitors and their clerks in dealing with interviews with clients to be sadly lacking. The Law Society is doing what it can to improve standards, with training for representatives and an accreditation under the Law Society's Police Station Accreditation Scheme, but there will still be many who will attend a police station in serious cases and will be ground down by the sheer oppression of the situation. As might have been expected, the late Sir David Napley had some robust things to say about the Bill—

'Over many years, legislators and the judiciary have continued to believe that if a jury of ordinary people are told to disregard something that they heard, they are both willing and capable of doing so . . . If a jury are intelligent enough to try a serious crime, they are fully alive to the fact that the accused has failed to reveal at the outset a defence which he has subsequently put forward. Moreover, short of being in a coma, it is impossible for them to fail to notice that the accused had failed to give evidence in his defence at his trial . . . If there is one thing which it is essential a judge should do in the course of a trial, it is to present himself as utterly impartial. Indeed experience also shows that when a judge sides too much with the prosecution, juries revolt and acquit guilty people. The only effect of placing this proposed duty upon the judge will be to give the impression that he has taken sides with the prosecution and is now assisting them in the conduct of their case and, however much the reality may be otherwise, still further damage will have been done with no identifiable gain.'[1]

---

1   *The Times*, 12 April 1994.

3.13 Section 38 provides interpretation and savings for ss 34, 37. Under s 39 of the Act, the Secretary of State may, by order, direct that ss 34–38 shall apply to the armed forces, subject to such modifications as he may specify.

JURIES

3.14 The prohibition of persons on bail in criminal proceedings from serving on a jury is another step down the road to eliminate from jury service anyone who might be thought to be hostile to the prosecution. This prohibition is provided for by s 40 of the Act. The words 'bail in criminal proceedings' have the same meaning as in the Bail Act 1976, and therefore do not include those people who have been summoned. Consequently there is an immediate anomaly between cases where a person may be summoned for an offence triable either way (such as the fraudulent use of a tax disc or a minor theft or even a large fraud) and may still be eligible for jury service, and cases where if he has been charged and bailed he will not be so eligible. No doubt this section will lead to the decline of the use of the summons in cases which the police realise are triable either before a jury or before magistrates. In recent years there has been considerable discussion about potential jurors who suffer from a disability, and in particular whether those with impaired vision or hearing should sit on the panel. A judge has always had the power to discharge a juror to prevent 'scandal or perversion'[1] which probably included a juror who was unwell or deaf. In more recent times Lawton LJ had this to say—

'trial judges, as an aspect of their duty to see that there is a fair trial, have had a right to intervene to ensure that a competent jury is empanelled. The most common form of judicial intervention is when a judge notices that a member of the panel is infirm or has difficulty in reading or hearing; and nowadays jurors for whom taking part in a long trial would be burdensome are often excluded from the jury by the judge.'[2]

Section 41 of the Act inserts the Juries Act 1974, s 9B. If a person is disabled and there is some doubt about his capacity to serve, then the judge should allow him to serve on the jury unless he is of the opinion that the person will not, on account of his disability, be capable of acting effectively as a juror. This does not affect the current position that a disabled person may apply for, and be granted, excusal if there is a good reason. At the end of the Bill's Committee stage in the House of Commons, there were calls for a clause to allow deaf and hard of hearing people to have access of sign language interpreters and computer aided transcription systems in police stations and courts. Mr Maclean, for the Government, pointed out that a person at a police station who appeared to be deaf, or about whom there was doubt relating to his hearing or speaking ability, must be interviewed by an interpreter. He went on to say that the Nuffield Foundation's community interpreter project was producing a national register of qualified sign language interpreters that should be available in 1995. Section 42 of the 1994 Act (which amends the Juries Act 1974, Sch 1) allows for a practising member of a religious society or order, the tenets of which are incompatible with jury service, to be excused.

---

1   *R v Mansell* [1857] 8 E & B 54, p 81.
2   *R v Mason* [1981] QB 881.

3.15   Back in the 18th century once a jury was sworn in it could not separate until after it had delivered its verdict nor, to encourage early unanimity, was it allowed fire, food or drink until it had reached a verdict. Over the years, a more humane attitude was adopted and, whilst jurors may not have had much in the way of comfort, at least they were fed and watered whilst they deliberated. Perhaps because of the kindness shown to them or perhaps because there has been a greater diversity of social, political and racial orientation amongst members, or even perhaps because they have taken their duties more seriously than in the past, there has been an increasing tendency for juries to take longer and longer (as indeed trials have themselves become longer and longer) to reach a verdict. The days are long gone when a jury in the Steinie Morrison case in 1911[1], where the evidence was by no means overwhelming, could reach a verdict in a murder trial in 28 minutes, and reach a verdict even more quickly in the case of the murdering solicitor Herbert Armstrong in 1921[2] where the evidence probably was overwhelming. Gone are the days when the jury used to be told 'There is no need for you retire. If the front row will turn to the back row, perhaps you will be able to reach a verdict'. Now even in the clearest case of theft by shoplifting a lengthy retirement is usually necessary. In the past a jury could be sent out late in the evening or, in the days when no separation was permitted, after being sworn in late at night. However, this practice has been frowned upon by the Court of Appeal. The expensive practice of sending a jury to a hotel for the night has also developed. As a result, there has been a tendency for judges to try to time their summings-up to ensure that a jury is given the better part of a day in which to reach a verdict. In some States in America, in cases where there is little likelihood of jury intimidation or tampering, juries are permitted to separate during the course of their deliberations (eg to visit the coffee machine in the lobby) and to go home at night. Section 43 of the Act allows, but does not compel, a judge to permit a jury to separate during their deliberations. Since jurors can be quite tetchy about having to pack pyjamas and a toothbrush before they go to consider their verdicts and may consequently rush to reach a verdict to avoid an overnight stay, this section may assist them. The warning that they may not discuss the case with anyone outside the jury room is likely to prove specious. It is almost inconceivable that jurors will not discuss the case with their husbands, wives or lovers. The reasoning behind this section is not entirely altruistic; it is estimated the £200,000 will be saved by the provision. However, judges will have to be careful that jurors do not telephone each other at home to discuss how they think things stand. In a recent decision by the Court of Appeal, a conviction was quashed because the judge had not directed the jury before it left for an overnight stay in a hotel that their deliberations should not continue until they returned to court the following morning[3]. Fortunately, since the Contempt of Court Act 1981, s 8, prevents legitimate research into the workings of the jury we shall never know to what extent this happens and so the Court of Appeal (Criminal Division) will not have that albatross around its neck. The section will not apply to cases where a direction has already been given to a jury before the commencement of this section. It is thought that ss 40–43 of the Act will be brought into force, by order, in early 1995.

1   *R v Morrison* (1911) 75 JP 272, 22 Cox CC 214, 6 Cr App Rep 159.
2   *R v Armstrong* [1922] 2 KB 555.
3   *R v Tharakan*, (1994) *Times*, 10 November.

MAGISTRATES' COURTS: PROCEDURE, JURISDICTION AND POWERS

3.16 Over the years, there has been an erosion of the magistrates' powers when sitting as examining justices. Before the Criminal Justice Act 1967, it was necessary for every witness to attend court to give evidence and have his or her deposition taken down. This even would have included the police photographer. The 1967 Act provided for either a s 1 or 2 committal which enabled the defence to accept that there was a *prima facie* case and for the magistrates to rubber stamp the committal to the Crown Court. Occasionally a stipendiary magistrate, with nothing to do at the end of a quiet morning, would actually consider the contents of the statements and ask awkward questions, but in practice the only checks made were as to compliance with the formalities of signature and so forth. By the late 1980s the so called 'old style' committal proceeding may not exactly have fallen into disuse, but a series of cases in the Divisional court had set severe limits on what could be done by the defence. They were no longer entitled to compel the prosecution to call a witness if a *prima facie* case could be established without that witness[1]. Fishing expeditions were curtailed. It was held that magistrates were not to take account of breaches of PACE or the Codes of Conduct under that Act[2]. The thinking behind this being that the matter could be dealt with at the trial. The tougher stipendiary magistrates took to cutting committal proceedings down to a minimum by ruling that a *prima facie* case had been established after hearing one or two witnesses. The end of the committal as a meaningful exercise was inevitable. Now under s 44(1), the committal proceedings are abolished and in their place is a transfer for trial proceeding in cases where either the offence is triable only on indictment, or the magistrates have declined jurisdiction in the case of an offence triable either way, or the accused has not consented to summary trial. If either of these apply then the court is to proceed with a view to transferring the proceedings for the offence to the Crown Court for trial. However, if the prosecutor decides to discontinue the proceedings under the Prosecution of Offences Act 1985, s 23, or the court proceeds to try the information summarily under s 25(3) or (7), or a notice of transfer under the Criminal Justice Act 1987, s 4 (serious fraud) or the Criminal Justice Act 1991, s 53, is served on the court, then there will still be an opportunity to consider a paper submission, supported by oral argument, that there is not a *prima facie* case for the defendant to answer but, sadly, there will no longer be the opportunity to cross-examine prosecution witnesses. Before the new transfer for trial procedure is brought into force, it is thought that there will be extensive consultation about, for example, the revisions to the Rules of Court. Consequently, it is anticipated that the provision will be brought into force by mid-1995.

1   *R v Epping and HarlowJustices, ex p Massaro* [1973] QB 433.
2   *R v Bow Street Stipendiary Magistrates' Courts, ex p DPP* [1992] Crim LR 790.

3.17   The rules relating to the steps to be taken are set out in Sch 4, Pt I to the 1994 Act, which substitutes the Magistrates' Courts Act 1980, ss 4–7. Basically, the prosecution must serve a notice of their case both on the court and the accused. It must specify the charges to be transferred to the Crown Court and the evidence on which those charges are based. Any application for dismissal by the defence, on one or all of the charges, must be in writing and served on the prosecutor, any co-accused and the court. This should include any application to make oral representations. The grounds on which this will be permitted are that the case is difficult or complex. The court must decide if oral representations will be allowed and, if it does so decide, then the prosecutor will be allowed to make oral representations in opposition. The prosecutor may oppose the application for dismissal and if he does, subject to the above provision, this must be in writing. An unrepresented defendant may always make oral representations against a transfer. If no application for dismissal is made, or one is made and rejected, the magistrates will transfer the case and give written notice to all parties. The notice of transfer will specify the place and date of trial and will contain an alibi warning. Witness orders will not be made at this stage. After a transfer the requirement for a person on bail to attend the magistrates' court on a particular day ceases, and the accused is now under a duty to appear before the Crown Court on the day specified in the notice. Sureties will continue as will any conditions imposed. If, however, the court wishes the accused to attend the magistrates' court then it can require him to do so, although this need not be the day of the transfer. The court can then remand the accused on bail on the same or different conditions or remand the accused in custody. Under the arrangement either the defendant or the prosecution may apply for a change in bail conditions, either to the magistrates or to the Crown Court. In the event of a breach of bail or circumstances existing leading the police to believe that a breach is likely to take place, or that the defendant will abscond, he may be arrested and be produced before a single justice who may, as is the case now, remand him in custody or on bail. If a surety wishes to withdraw he must notify the police in writing and the same procedure will apply. Whether all this will work in practice must be open to some doubt. It may work for the white collar criminal but the rather less structured defendant may find the matter confusing, as may both the prosecutor and defence lawyer in relation to post-transfer and pre-arraignment bail applications. Is, for example, the service of the transfer notice on the defending solicitor to be taken as absolute knowledge of the transfer and the alibi warning against the accused? In the past, the practice has been for the surety to produce the defendant if he wishes to withdraw or still take the risk that some of his recognisance will be forfeit. There is likely to be a good deal of case law on the provisions of this section.

3.18 Section 45 of, and Sch 5 to, the 1994 Act, which substitute the Magistrates' Court Act 1980, s 12, now have the practical effect of permitting an accused who is appearing in answer to a summons in a magistrates' court (but not in a youth court) to answer a summary information which carries imprisonment for no more than three months (or, more rarely, an offence specified in an order made by the Secretary of State by statutory instrument) to plead guilty by post. This is, in effect, simply an extension of the practice used in motoring cases. There appears, however, to be no requirement to notify the defendant that the magistrates are intending to commit him to prison. It is to be hoped that in practice the case will be adjourned to enable him to be represented and make submissions. Revised Rules of Court will be required before this section can be brought into force, and it is therefore thought that the provision will take effect as from the Summer of 1995.

3.19 Section 46 amends the Magistrates' Courts Act 1980, s 22, and has the effect of increasing to £5,000 the relevant sum before the defendant may elect trial by jury in the case of criminal damage. This effectively removes the right of trial by jury in criminal damage cases from defendants in all but the most serious of cases. It is estimated that this section may save approximately £3.5 million annually. The trend began in 1967 with a £100 limit and with successive pieces of legislation was by stages increased through £200 and £400 (in 1980) to £2,000 by the Criminal Justice Act 1988. It had been intended that there should have been a further increase in the Criminal Justice Act 1991, but the provisions relating to criminal damage were overlooked which accounts for the 150 per cent increase. By virtue of s 46(2), the increase does not apply to acts done before this section comes into force. There will presumably be a corresponding increase in the guidelines to magistrates of the amount after which they should decline summary trial. At present the guideline is £4,000 or where there is deliberate fire-raising, where the damage is committed by a group, or where there is a clear racial motivation[1]. It is thought that s 46 will be brought into force by order early in 1995. It will not be retrospective. Section 47 provides that a court may apply to deduct fines etc from income support in respect of fines transferred from another court. It is thought that s 47 will be brought into force by order early in 1995.

---

1   Practice Note (Mode of Trial: Guidelines); see *Butterworths Rules of Court: Criminal Court Practice.*

SENTENCING: GUILTY PLEAS

3.20 There is little doubt that the question of what is called plea bargaining (which should strictly be sentence bargaining), has troubled the courts over the years. What, if any, discount should be given for a plea of guilty and when, if ever, should a judge indicate that in return for such a plea he will pass a non-custodial sentence? It has been well established sentencing practice that defendants who plead guilty are usually, but not always, entitled to a discount on the sentence they would have received if they had contested the case to the bitter end and been found guilty. The range of the discount has been from approximately 25–33 per cent. Indeed, it is the duty of counsel and solicitor to advise their clients of the likelihood of this reduction in sentence which may amount to as much as one third. The court is looking for some indication of remorse and a guilty plea is normally deemed to indicate some contrition. Even if it does not, at least it has the merit of saving court time and state money[1]. Last minute pleas of guilty are not always looked on so favourably, as in *R v Hollington and Emmens*[2] where a defendant changed his plea at a late stage so that he could have the benefit of time served on remand. Normally, the court when passing sentence should indicate that a reduction in that sentence has been made. A discount is usually available even if the offender had no possible defence[3] although this must be taken with some caution in view of the decision in *R v Stabler*[4] in which MacPherson said—

> 'We can see no ground for giving any discount in the circumstances of this particular case. This man had no alternative but to plead guilty'.

The court is always likely to give a discount in a case of rape or in cases where a victim has been spared the ordeal of giving evidence and being subjected to cross-examination[5]. In the case of a plea of guilty it is not usual to impose the maximum sentence possible[6]. If the court is being expected to show mercy then often it requires an admission from the defendant[7]. A recent case was that of *Costen*[8] where a woman appealed against a sentence of two years' imprisonment (the maximum) for indecency with a child. The Court of Appeal took the opportunity of reviewing the type of case in which no discount for a plea could be expected. The charge was a specimen and the sentencer had taken the view that in that circumstance there should be no discount. The Court of Appeal thought that there were such cases where no discount need be given but, in this case, reduced the appellant's sentence to one of 21 months' imprisonment.

1 *R v Meade* (1982) 4 Cr App Rep (S) 193: *R v Hercules* (1987) 9 Cr App Rep (S) 291.
2 (1986) 82 Cr App Rep 281.
3 *R v Davis* (1980) 2 Cr App Rep (S) 168, CA.
4 (1984) 6 Cr App Rep (S) 129, CA.
5 *R v Barnes* (1983) 5 Cr App Rep (S) 368, CA.
6 *R v Barnes* (1983) 5 Cr App Rep (S) 368, CA.
7 *R v Harding* (1989) 11 Cr App Rep (S) 190, 191, CA.
8 *R v Costen* (1989) 11 Cr App Rep (S) 182, CA.

3.21 Co-operation with the police is a classic instance when a discount, often a substantial one, can be given by the sentencer[1]. In *R v Azfal*[2] where a defendant concerned with the importation of drugs worth £500,000 had immediately confessed to the police and had given material help over the name of his recruiter, the Court of Appeal thought his co-operation should be marked with a reduction in an otherwise proper sentence.

1 *R v Meade* (1982) 4 Cr App Rep (S) 193.
2 (1989) Times, 14 October.

3.22 In considering a reduction in sentence, it is not proper for the sentencer to take into account the conduct of the defence except in weighing the value of any mitigation[1]. That is to say, the sentencer must not increase a sentence because of an ill founded attack on prosecution witnesses but he is entitled not to give any discount. In *Sharp* it was said—

> 'He put up a wholly lying defence at the trial, which was rebutted at every point. Criminals who do that can hardly expect, when they are finally brought to book, either the trial judge or this Court to extend leniency to them'.[2]

The sentencer must also be particularly careful in picking his words to avoid any expressions which may give the impression that he has increased the penalty. Merely because a defendant has exercised his right to trial by jury the trial judge should not impose a heavier punishment. He may, however, make him pay increased costs[3]. This is a good example of the double thinking which at times pervades the penal system.

---

1   *R v Scott* [1983] Crim LR 568, CA.
2   [1972] CSP C2 2(g).
3   *R v Hayden* (1975) 60 Cr App Rep 304, CA.

3.23 Section 48 has not gone as far as some commentators would have hoped in providing, for example, a sentence bracket for a plea of guilty. It has done nothing more than restate as law the practice which has been prevalent for a number of years. The twin considerations for the sentencer are now at what stage in the proceedings has the offender indicated his intention to plead guilty, and what were the circumstances in which this indication was given. By virtue of s 48(2), if a court imposes a less severe sentence as a result of a plea then it shall state in open court that this is the case. It can be seen that the old case law will apply in most cases. It is thought that s 48 will be brought into force by order early in 1995.

PUBLICATION OF REPORTS IN YOUNG OFFENDER CASES

3.24 Under the Children and Young Persons Act 1933, s 49, the courts have power to ban the publication of information which may lead to the identification of the young person. The same section gives the courts and the Secretary of State the power to dispense with the ban when it is necessary to avoid injustice to the juvenile. In June 1993, the Evening Standard had complained bitterly that in the case of Avie Andrews (a young killer who had escaped from custody) they would have to breach s 49 of the 1933 Act to assist in his recapture—

> 'An alleged killer—believed to be armed and dangerous—is on the loose in London. But he cannot be named and his picture cannot be published. The police are desperate to warn the public—and enlist their help in hunting him down. What prevents them, or the Evening Standard, from identifying the individual involved? The Law. Home Secretary Michael Howard has been told by his officials that he is powerless to act. Today he said that he will review the current law "as a matter of urgency".'[1]

Section 49 of the 1994 Act substitutes the Children and Young Persons Act 1933, s 49. It is thought that it will be brought into force by order early in 1995. The new s 49(5) allows a court to dispense with the restrictions if it is satisfied that it is appropriate to do so for the purpose of avoiding injustice to the child or young person (the present position) or in cases where a child or young person is unlawfully at large and he is charged with, or has been convicted of, a violent offence, a sexual offence, or an offence punishable in a case of a person aged 21 or over with imprisonment for 14 years or more, and it is necessary to dispense with these restrictions for the purpose of catching him. There are further limits to the dispensation. The new s 49(7) provides that the application must be made by the Director of Public Prosecutions, and that notice must be given to the legal representative of the child or young person. Under the new s 49(8), a single magistrate may grant the application. Breaches of the new s 49(1) are punishable on summary conviction with a fine not exceeding level 5 on the standard scale.

1   *Evening Standard* 7 June 1993.

CHILD TESTIMONY

3.25   The purpose of s 50 of the 1994 Act is to give more protection to child witnesses[1]. It is thought that it will be brought into force by order early in 1995. One of the complaints about the law prior to the 1994 Act was that the Criminal Justice Act 1991, s 54, which inserted the Criminal Justice Act 1988, s 32A, did not really help a child witness. Provided that the videotaped evidence was satisfactory there was no 'warm-up' period in which they could be eased into their evidence by the prosecution. Instead, they were left with the defence counsel on the attack from the word go. Mr Kay J, who dealt with the Swansea paedophile ring case, wrote to the Home Secretary expressing his concerns, and suggesting that 'adequately' did not go far enough to protect the child—

> 'I am sure that a number of lessons need to be learned from the Swansea trial. One that seems to me obvious is that the children would have found the giving of evidence far less of an ordeal if before they were subjected to cross-examination they had had the opportunity to answer a few questions from prosecuting counsel who would have appeared to them to be accepting their answers and not challenging them.'[2]

The Opposition endeavoured to move an amendment which would have gone further in protecting children by allowing a judge to permit an examination in chief if he believes it would be in the best interests of the child. It was opposed by the Government on the basis that prosecuting counsel might use the opportunity to cover the same ground as in the video link to try to persuade the jury in a way which the video did not. It is believed that such a 'warm-up' would be of little comfort to the child if it was done on a Monday morning, and on Friday afternoon the boy or girl was still facing a barrage of hostile questions. Since the judge may now allow prosecuting counsel to permit examination in chief on any matter which in the opinion of the court has not been dealt with adequately in the recorded testimony, cynics may wonder whether the temptation to leave out some small piece of evidence from the video will be dismissed. Professor Graham Davies of Leicester University has been commissioned to research into the effectiveness of the children's evidence provisions introduced by the 1991 Act. It is thought his report will be received by the end of 1994. The Government will then consider what, if any, further changes should be introduced.

1   In *R v Rawlings, R v Broadbent* (1994) Times, 19 October, the Court of Appeal considered the replaying of video evidence in two cases of child sex abuse. The Court held that the decision to allow a replay of such evidence is at the discretion of the trial judge but if a replay is to be allowed then three conditions should be fulfilled: first, the replay should be in court in the presence of the judge, counsel and the defendant; second, the judge should warn the jury against giving the video disproportionate weight; third, the trial judge should remind the jury of points raised in the cross-examination and the re-examination of the complainant from his notes.
2   6 July 1994 quoted in HC Lords amendments, 19 October 1994, col 337.

INTIMIDATION, ETC, OF WITNESSES, JURORS AND OTHERS

3.26 One of the problems facing law enforcers over the last half century has been the apparent tampering with witnesses and jurors in efforts to obtain acquittals in criminal trials. It may be that in the past the interference was more feared than perceived, but there is no doubt that it does exist today. In the first six months of 1988 the Metropolitan Police expended 5,500 manpower days in providing jury protection, with the cost per jury per week running at £68,000. Assistant Commissioner John Dellow believed that there were two or three jury nobbling gangs operating in London at the time. One senior officer put it in terms: 'There is a firm in London specialising in jury nobbling and they have got it down to a fine art'.[1] There have been no convictions of major jury nobblers to suggest that the situation has changed. During the committee stage of the debate John Fraser gave this illustration of the anomalies of the criminal justice system—

> 'Within the past year, a constituent, who, I think, was dealing in drugs, was shot at point blank range in the presence of three witnesses, all of whom identified the assailant and gave statements to the police. The witnesses did not turn up at the trial. Indeed, we got the ludicrous situation in which the three witnesses were on the run from charges of contempt of court but, because there was no evidence, the assailant was found not guilty and discharged.'[2]

In Northumbria, for example, it is believed there is a hard core of criminals who are intimidating witnesses. Nationwide, over 20 major trials involving serious violence and some three hundred investigations were abandoned because of witness intimidation during 1992–1993. However, s 51 of the 1994 Act may be nothing more than a cosmetic section reinforcing the Government's commitment to law and order. It is thought that it will be brought into force, by order, early in 1995. Section 51(1) creates a new offence whereby a person is guilty of intimidation if he does to another person an act which intimidates and is intended to intimidate that person, knowing or believing that the other person is assisting in the investigation of an offence or is a witness or potential witness or juror or potential juror in proceedings, and intending thereby to cause the investigation or the course of justice to be obstructed, perverted or interfered with. Under s 51(3), a person does an act 'to' another person not only when he does that thing directly to that person, but also where it is done to a third person. This would obviously include threats against a relative of a juror, witness etc. Under s 51(4), harm may be financial as well as physical. Under s 51(6) a person guilty of an offence under this section shall be liable on conviction on indictment to imprisonment for a term not exceeding five years or to a fine or to both, and on summary conviction to imprisonment for a term not exceeding six months or to a fine or to both. By virtue of s 51(8) if the physical acts or threats are proved then the burden of proof is reversed and the defendant will be presumed, unless the contrary is proved, to have acted with the intent of interfering with the investigation etc. It is this which appeals to the Government, and is just one more step along the road of subtle change in the law over the last 20 years to a destination where, if we are not careful, the burden of proof may one day be changed in all cases. All this is in addition to the common law offences and no doubt, the old conspiracy to pervert charge will continue to be used. After all, it carries the much more substantial penalty of life imprisonment.

---

1   *Daily Telegraph*, 30 September 1988.
2   HC Standing Committee B, 3 February 1994, col 512.

CRIMINAL APPEALS

3.27 Section 52 implements recommendation 329 of the Royal Commission on Criminal Justice and provides that, in certain circumstances, a circuit judge may sit in the Court of Appeal under the Supreme Court Act 1981, s 9. No circuit judge may however, sit on an appeal against sentence or conviction in a case in which a High Court judge sat at first instance. In fact, only about five per cent of Crown court trials are dealt with by High Court judges. In practice the debate is revived whether it is right that judges should sit in judgment of the decisions of their peers. The argument runs that the Court of Appeal should be staffed by superior judges. This has not been the case for many years and the situation is now further weakened. The benefit is that it does allow for senior circuit judges to obtain practice in dealing with appeals before an appointment to the High Court bench.

3.28 Section 53 deals specifically with expenses of both solicitor and counsel in criminal appeals in the Northern Ireland Court of Appeal, and is therefore of limited interest to practitioners in England and Wales. Before the passing of the Act there was no method of appeal against the taxation of costs in the Northern Ireland Court of Appeal. This section provides that an aggrieved barrister or solicitor may now apply to the taxing master for a review and from there to the High Court. The Lord Chancellor will also have a corresponding right of appeal to the High Court whose decision will be final. Is this the backdoor through which the Lord Chancellor may one day be able to make a similar appeal in cases in England and Wales?

4 Police powers

INTRODUCTION

4.1 The Criminal Justice and Public Order Act 1994, Pt IV, is another controversial Part of the Act, as it deals with what many see as vastly extended police powers. An ancillary purpose is the building of a DNA databank specifically to deal with sex offenders. Samples taken simply for the purposes of elimination (ie from non-suspects) may not be used for speculative searches against the database. However, the samples may be retained if they have been processed in a batch with one taken from a person who is then convicted of a recordable offence. This, says the Home Office, is to ensure complete and accurate records, for quality control purposes, and to prevent miscarriages of justice. In general the police welcomed these provisions but raised concerns over just who was going to provide the money for the database and who was going to train officers in its use. David Golding, President of the Superintendents' Association, said—

> 'We're concerned because we were expecting it to be the case that DNA samples were taken in more serious offences like murder, rape and grievous bodily harm . . . But now samples are to be taken for all recordable offences, which may well be an enormous financial burden . . . There's no database to start with, so it isn't clear yet who funds the initial start-up and what the cost will be. It makes it questionable as to whether we can afford to service a database, although we can see it will be very useful . . . We fully support the principle of a database, even if in practice it's not what we expected.'[1]

Predictably, *Liberty* was worried about the provisions which it thought potentially breached the European Convention on Human Rights, Articles 3, 8.

---

1   See *Just the Job*, Claire Casey, *Police Review*, November 11 1994.

POWERS OF POLICE TO TAKE BODY SAMPLES

4.2   Section 54 extends the powers of the police to take intimate samples under the Police and Criminal Evidence Act 1984, s 62. The scope of s 62 has been widened enormously by the insertion of a new sub-s (1A). The effect of the new subsection is that now an intimate sample may be taken from a person who is not in police detention but from whom, in the course of the investigation of an offence, two or more non-intimate samples suitable for the same means of analysis have been taken which have proved insufficient. The authority of a police officer of at least the rank of superintendent must be obtained and the person must give his appropriate consent which must be in writing. The scope of s 62 has been further widened in that it now not only applies to serious arrestable offences as was the case before the Act, but it also applies in the case of recordable offences, of which there are around 15,000 a year. Section 55 amends the Police and Criminal Evidence Act 1984, s 63, and changes the position relating to non-intimate samples. A non-intimate sample may be taken from a person without the appropriate consent if he has been charged with a recordable offence or informed that he will be reported for such an offence.

4.3   Section 56 of the 1994 Act adds the Police and Criminal Evidence Act 1984, s 63A, and is concerned with supplementary provisions for samples and fingerprints. For practitioners, let alone civil libertarians, it is one of the more important sections. Under s 63A(2) of the 1984 Act, where a sample of non-pubic hair is taken this may be done either by cutting hairs or by plucking hairs with their roots, as long as no more are plucked than the person taking the sample considers to be necessary for a sufficient sample. S 63A(3) provides that a sample may be taken in prison or in any institution to which the Prison Act 1952 applies. Under s 63A(4), any constable may require a person (not in police detention or in the custody of the police) to attend a police station to have a sample taken where (a) the person has been charged with a recordable offence or informed that he will be reported for such an offence and either he has not had a sample taken from him in the course of the investigation of the offence by the police or the sample taken was either not suitable or insufficient for analysis; or (b) where he has been convicted of a recordable offence and either has not had a sample taken since the conviction or has had a sample taken (before or after the conviction) which was either not suitable or was insufficient for analysis. The period allowed for requiring a person to attend a police station is one month beginning with the date of the charge or one month beginning with the date the officer was informed of the unsuitability etc of the sample, or one month beginning with the date of the conviction or of learning of the unsuitability etc of the sample. The requirement under s 63A(4) shall give the person at least seven days within which he must so attend and may direct him to attend at a specified time of day or between specified times of day. If the person fails to comply with a requirement be may be arrested without a warrant.

4.4   Under s 57, which amends the Police and Criminal Evidence Act, s 64, fingerprints and samples may be retained if they were taken for the purpose of the same investigation of an offence of which a person from whom one was taken was convicted, but the information derived shall not be used in evidence against the person who is entitled to have the sample destroyed or for the purposes of any investigation of an offence. Section 58 amends the Police and Criminal Evidence Act 1984, s 65. The definition of intimate sample is now—

'(a)   a sample of blood, semen or any other tissue fluid, urine or pubic hair;
(b)   a dental impression;
(c)   a swab taken from a person's body orifice other than the mouth;'.

A non-intimate sample is now—

'(a)   a sample of hair other than pubic hair;
(b)   a sample taken from a nail or from under a nail;
(c)   a swab taken from any part of a person's body including the mouth but not any other body orifice;
(d)   saliva;
(e)   a footprint or a similar impression of any part of a person's body other than a part of his hand;'.

Section 59 aims to combat the concealment of drugs and amends the Police and Criminal Evidence Act, s 65 (treatment of persons by police). Intimate search now means a search which consists of the physical examination of a person's body other than the mouth.

POWERS OF POLICE TO STOP AND SEARCH

4.5 Section 60 is yet another section which has infuriated those involved with civil rights issues. A police officer of the rank of superintendent or above may give authorisation that the powers to stop and search persons and vehicles contained in this section may be exercisable at any place within a locality, for a period not exceeding 24 hours, if he reasonably believes that incidents involving serious violence may take place in any locality in his area, and that it is expedient to do so in order to prevent their occurrence. That authorisation may be exercised by a chief inspector or inspector if he reasonably believes incidents involving serious violence are imminent and no superintendent is available. The period of 24 hours can be extended for a further six hours if it appears to the officer who gave the authorisation that, having regard to the offences committed or which are reasonably suspected to have been committed in connection with any incident falling within the authorisation, it is expedient to do so. The authorisation must be signed in writing by the officer giving it and shall specify the applicable locality and the period of time for which it is operable. The direction to extend the period by six hours must also be signed but, if it is not practicable to do so at the time must be recorded in writing as soon as it is practicable to do so. Under sub-s (4) a uniformed constable may stop and search any pedestrian or anything carried by him for dangerous instruments or offensive weapons. A constable may also stop and search any vehicle, its driver and any passengers for such implements, and for the purposes of this section, 'vehicle' includes a caravan within the meaning of the Caravan Sites and Control of Development Act 1960, s 29(1). This section, with the necessary modifications, applies equally to ships, aircraft and hovercraft.

4.6 It is s 60(5) which has proved to be so controversial. The power under s 60(4) may be exercised whether the constable has any grounds for suspecting that the person or vehicle is carrying weapons. Under s 60(6), any weapons found may be seized. Dangerous instruments are defined as those which have a blade or are sharply pointed; offensive weapons are defined the Police and Criminal Evidence Act 1984, s 1(9). If a pedestrian or the driver of a vehicle (or the passengers) fail to stop when required to do so then he will be liable on summary conviction to imprisonment for a term not exceeding one month or a fine not exceeding level 3 on the standard scale or both. Where a vehicle is stopped the driver is entitled to a written statement that it was stopped under the powers of this section if he applies within a period of 12 months from the day on which the vehicle was stopped. The same applies to a pedestrian who is stopped under this section. At one time in the debate in committee it was argued that there should be a specific power of arrest for failing to comply with the requirement to stop and allow a search. However, the powers under the Police Act 1964, s 51, were thought to be sufficient.

5 Collective trespass or nuisance on land

INTRODUCTION

5.1 Part V of the 1994 Act, which relates to collective trespass or nuisance on land, is another of the more controversial Parts of the Act. Gone are the last vestiges of the old chestnut that trespassers cannot be prosecuted. In one form or another they can if there are a number of them. It is not even a new phenomenon. In 1932, rambling organisations from Sheffield and Manchester held a mass trespass over what was described as 'England's most sacred grouse moor'. Five hundred of them climbed the slopes of Kinder Scour where they encountered the Duke of Devonshire's gamekeepers and watchers armed with heavy sticks. The police were also present. The Sheffield Telegraph reported that the ramblers were unarmed and that 'hooliganism was entirely absent'. Nevertheless, some struggles broke out and five of the ramblers ended in gaol following conviction at the Assizes. The grand jury at the Assizes had, it was noted, contained no less than ten army officers including two major-generals and three colonels.[1] This Part of the Act has been welcomed by supporters of fox hunting and damned by those who wish to demonstrate against it and other activities and policies they see as unacceptable. Indeed on the day the Act received Royal Assent, demonstrators against the widening of the M25 were joined by those demonstrating against the Act in a final gesture of solidarity.

---

1   H Hill, *Freedom to Roam* (1980).

5.2   Section 61 of the Act is aimed at strengthening the position under the Public Order Act 1986, s 39, which will be repealed. Where a police officer (the senior one present at the scene) reasonably believes that two or more people are trespassing and are there for the purpose of residing there for any period, and that reasonable steps have been taken by or on behalf of the occupier to ask them to leave, and that any one of the persons has caused damage to the land or property on the land or used threatening abusive or insulting words or behaviour towards the occupier, a member of his family or an employee or agent of his, or that those persons have between them six or more vehicles on the land, then he may direct all or any of them to leave the land and remove from the land any vehicles or their property. In the event that the officer reasonably believes that people, who were not originally trespassers, have become trespassers on the land then he must ensure that the conditions specified in sub-s (1) are satisfied after those persons became trespassers before he can exercise his powers. The senior officer taking the decision does not have to communicate it directly. This may be done by any constable at the scene. The section works on the same principle as returning to a parking bay although, in this case, the length of absence must be considerably more than the usual one hour.

5.3   If the persons fail to leave the land as soon as reasonably practicable or having left, return within a period of three months beginning on the day on which the direction was given, they commit an offence, and on summary conviction will be liable to a fine not exceeding level 4 on the standard scale or imprisonment for a period not exceeding three months. A constable who reasonably suspects a person of committing an offence under the section may arrest him without warrant. It will be a defence to show that the accused was not trespassing, or that he had reasonable excuse for not leaving as soon as reasonably practicable, or for again entering the land as a trespasser. Under s 62, if a constable reasonably suspects there to have been a contravention, without reasonable excuse, of the directions given under s 61, he may seize and remove from the land any vehicle belonging to, or in the possession or control of, the person to whom the direction was given.

POWERS IN RELATION TO RAVES

5.4   Along with the joke about the judge who asked 'who are the Beatles?' might be added one about judges who ask 'what is a Rave?'. Originally known as an acid house party, it started life informally rather as a blues party did in Harlem to pay the rent. However, it grew quickly into a commercial operation and transmogrified first into a warehouse party and then into a rave. The police also saw raves as places where drugs were readily on sale, where protection was being imposed on organisers and, on occasions, where guns in some quantity could be found. What was once a fairly anarchic affair had become big and dangerous business. Quite apart from the noise that is. One possible answer to the question is—

> 'a large gathering in the open air at which incredibly loud music is played during the night, likely to cause serious distress to local people. In contrast, a licensed rave is a form of entertainment including dance and music that is approved by local authority licensing procedures and which, by definition, is unlikely to cause serious distress to local people.'

15.5 Section 63 in fact applies to a gathering on land in the open air of 100 or more persons (and they do not have to be trespassers) at which amplified music is played during the night (intermissions will not help for the purposes of the section). For the purposes of this section such a gathering continues during the intermissions, and music includes sounds wholly or predominantly characterised by the emission of a succession of repetitive beats. A police officer holding the rank of superintendent or above who reasonably believes that two or more persons are making preparations for holding the gathering, or ten or more persons are waiting for such a gathering to begin, or ten or more persons are attending such a gathering which is in progress, may give a direction that those persons, and any others who come to prepare or wait for or attend the gathering, are to leave the land and remove any vehicles or other property they have with them on the land. The direction to the people may be given by any constable at the scene and the direction shall be treated as being given if reasonable steps are taken to bring it to the attention of the people. The direction does not apply to an exempt person, defined under s 63(10), as the occupier, any member of his family and any employee or agent of his and any person whose home is situated on the land. Land in the open air includes land partly in the open air. Occupier, trespasser and vehicle have the same meaning as in s 61. Section 63(6) provides for a penalty of up to three months' imprisonment and/or a fine not exceeding level 4 on the standard scale, if a person either fails to leave the land as soon as reasonably practicable or returns within a period of seven days beginning on the day on which the direction was given. There is a defence of providing a reasonable excuse for failing to leave the land or for subsequently re-entering. A constable in uniform may arrest without warrant under this section. Section 63 does not apply in England and Wales to a gathering licensed by an entertainment licence, nor does it apply in Scotland to a gathering in premises which, by virtue of the Civic Government (Scotland) Act 1982, s 41, are licensed to be used as a place of public entertainment. Along with s 63, there is inevitably a power of seizure. This is contained in s 64 and includes the power to seize sound equipment, which is defined as equipment designed or adapted for amplifying music and any equipment suitable for use in connection with such equipment. Music has the same meaning as in s 63.

5.6   There is not much point in having the preceding sections unless there is a power to stop people proceeding to raves; s 65 provides just this power. The power is given to a constable in uniform who reasonably believes that a person is on his way to a s 63 gathering and may be exercised only within five miles of the boundary of that gathering. Exempt persons do not count. An arrest may be made by a constable in uniform without warrant. A person who knows that a direction has been given under s 65(1) not to proceed to the gathering and who fails to comply is liable on summary conviction to a fine not exceeding level 3 on the standard scale. Section 66 concerns the court's powers to forfeit sound equipment. Where a person has been convicted of an offence under s 63 the court may order the forfeiture of any equipment seized under s 64(4). The court may do this even if it makes another order. In considering whether to make such an order the court must consider the value of the equipment and the likely financial and other effects on the offender (taken together with any other order that the court contemplates making). There is, after all, not a great deal of point in fining a guitarist and then forfeiting his guitar. Owners of equipment seized and forfeited may make application to the magistrates for its return; and a similar procedure applies in Scotland. Claims must be made within six months. They must show that the claimant did not consent to the offender having the property or that he did not know, and had no reason to suspect, that the property was to be used at an illegal rave. Under s 67 of the Act a financial charge may be made for the retention of seized property. It should be noted that this section applies to vehicles seized under s 62(1), as well as vehicles or sound equipment seized under s 64(4).

DISRUPTIVE TRESPASSERS

5.7   Section 68 was welcomed by Masters of Foxhounds and owners of pheasant shoots. It provides protection for occupiers of private land and their guests against what is to be known as aggravated trespass. The offence is committed by a person who trespasses on land in the open air and who, in relation to any lawful activity which persons are engaging in or are about to engage in on that or adjoining land, does there anything which is intended by him to either intimidate any of those persons so as to deter them from engaging in that activity, or obstruct or disrupt the activity. A constable in uniform may arrest without a warrant and the offence, if proved, carries a penalty of up to three months' imprisonment and/or a fine not exceeding level 4 on the standard scale. For the purposes of this section, land does not include highways and roads excluded from the application of s 61 by sub-s (9)(b) of that section, or a road within the meaning of the Roads (Northern Ireland) Order 1993[1]. It was not long before this section was put into use. On Saturday,

7 November 1994, three days after the Act received the Royal Assent, five hunt saboteurs became the first people to be charged under the Act when they were arrested during the Woodland Pytchley Hunt at Stoke Albany in Northamptonshire. According to various newspaper reports, some 25 hunt saboteurs clashed with 30 riders and foot followers. Two men were arrested after blowing hunting horns and three more after climbing a tree and blowing whistles.

---

1   SI 1993/3160.

5.8   Under s 69 the senior police officer present is given the power to direct a person, whom he believes has committed or intends to commit the offence of aggravated trespass in the open air, to leave the land. He may also so direct when there are two or more persons trespassing on land in the open air with the common purpose of intimidating persons so as to deter them within the meaning of s 68. The most common body of people caught by this section is likely to be anti-hunt saboteurs; but the section will also apply to road protesters and, *Liberty* fears, be used to deter a wide range of more mainstream protests. Failing to leave or returning within three months is an offence carrying a maximum of three months' imprisonment and/or a fine not exceeding level 4 on the standard scale. Again it is a defence for the accused to show that he was not trespassing or that he had a reasonable excuse for failing to leave or for returning. A constable in uniform who reasonably suspects a person is committing an offence under the section does not need a warrant to effect an arrest. 'Lawful activity' and 'land' have the same meaning as in s.68.

TRESPASSORY ASSEMBLIES

5.9   Section 70 and subsequent sections are designed to prevent mass trespass with a view to preventing what is seen as disruption to the life of the community, or to prevent significant damage to land, buildings, or monuments of historic, architectural or archaeological importance. The Public Order Act 1986, Pt II, will be amended to include a new s 14A. If the chief officer of police reasonably believes that an assembly is intended to be held in any district at a place, or on land, to which he public has either no access, or only a limited right of access, and the assembly is likely to be held without the permission of the occupier or is likely to exceed the limits of his permission and that significant damage or disruption to the life of the community will result, then he may apply to the council for the district for an order prohibiting, for a specific period, the holding of all trespassory assemblies in the district or a part of it. In England and Wales the council must obtain the consent of the Secretary of State before making the order, either in the terms of the application or with such modifications as the Secretary of State may approve; and in Scotland the council may make an order in the terms of the application. This does not apply in the City of London or the metropolitan police district. Instead, the Commissioner of either force may apply directly to the Secretary of State. The limits to this section are that the prohibition can be for a maximum of four days, and only for an area represented by a circle with a five mile radius from a specified centre. The order shall be recorded in writing as soon as it is made but there appears to be nothing in the section regarding the advertising of the ban. Organisers and persons who take part in the assembly are guilty of an offence if they know that an order under s 14A is in force and in England

and Wales a person who incites another to commit an offence is himself guilty of an offence. By implication this person must also know of the ban. Section 70 also adds a new s 148 to the 1986 Act. Under this section a constable in uniform may arrest without a warrant anyone he reasonably suspects of committing an offence under the section and once more the penalties for an organiser or inciter on conviction are a maximum of three months' imprisonment and/or a fine not exceeding level 4 on the standard scale. For a participant in the assembly the maximum is a fine not exceeding level three. The offences are triable only in a magistrates' court. As might be expected there are powers for a constable in uniform who reasonably believes a person is on his way to a trespassory assembly to direct him away from the area. These are contained in s 71 of the Act which adds the Public Order Act 1986, s 14C. Failure to comply brings a fine not exceeding level 3 on the standard scale.

SQUATTERS

5.10   The aim of s 72 and the following sections is to provide protection for people who find their homes invaded by squatters. There is already some protection available under the Criminal Law Act 1977, but as Mr Howard said—

> 'We made a commitment in our election manifesto to improve the law in that respect. The Bill provides the teeth behind the new procedures introduced by the Lord Chancellor to give lawful owners and occupiers of property access to a quick and effective remedy against squatting. It will mean that the owner or occupier of a property can go to court immediately and apply for an interim possession order ex parte. If the interim order is granted, the squatters will have 24 hours in which to leave the premises. Failure to do so will be an offence, and the police will have powers to enter property to enforce the order.'[1]

The Home Office is at pains to point out that there are safeguards against abuse of the procedure by unscrupulous landlords. The occupants, if they have complied with the interim order to leave, may ask for a full hearing at which they may be reinstated and obtain damages for their temporary dispossession. It will also be an offence to make a false or misleading statement in order to obtain an interim possession order. The sections under discussion must be read in conjunction with the Criminal Law Act 1977. At present s 6 of that Act penalises violence by a person securing entry into premises where a person on the premises is opposed to, and is known to be opposed, to entry. Section 72 amends s 6 so that it shall not apply to a displaced residential occupier or protected intending occupier (as defined by s 74), or to a person who is acting on behalf of the occupier. If the accused adduces sufficient evidence that he was such an occupier or was acting on behalf of such an occupier, then that shall be presumed to be the case until the contrary is proved by the prosecution. If you think that this is a dog's dinner regarding the burden of proof you would probably be quite right. The Penal Affairs Consortium was particularly critical of this section. 24 hours is a wholly unreasonable period in which to require people to gather together their possessions, leave their homes and find somewhere else to live, making them liable to prosecution and criminal penalties if they do not do so. In the rare case where a residential occupier has been displaced from his or her home by squatters, they can speedily evict the squatters (who are subject to criminal penalties if they do not leave) using procedures provided by the Criminal Law Act 1977. Other cases cannot be said to be so urgent as to justify a procedure which will render people homeless and make them liable to criminal penalties before they have any opportunity to state their case to a court.

---

1   HC 2R, 11 January 1994, cols 29, 30.

5.11 Section 73 substitutes the Criminal law Act 1977, s 7. It is an offence if a trespasser fails to leave residential premises when required to do so by a displaced residential occupier of the premises or an individual who is a protected intending occupier. It is a defence for the trespasser to show that he believed (note the absence of the word reasonably) that the person requiring him to leave the premises was neither a displaced residential occupier nor a person acting on his behalf nor a protected intending occupier. Section 74 (which adds the Criminal Law Act 1977, s 12A) provides supplementary provisions for protected intending occupiers including a lengthy definition of their status. The section also provides that it will be a defence for an accused charged with an offence under the new s 7 of the 1977 Act to prove that although asked to leave the premises by a person claiming to be, or to act on behalf of a protected intending occupier of the premises, that person failed to produce a statement showing him to be such a person. A person who is found guilty of making a false or misleading statement to establish himself as a protected intending occupier shall be liable, on summary conviction, to a fine not exceeding level 5 on the standard scale or six months' imprisonment or both. Under s 75 of the Act the penalties for making a false or misleading statement (which can include making it recklessly) for the purpose of obtaining an interim possession order are on conviction on indictment imprisonment for a maximum of two years or a fine or both, and on summary conviction imprisonment for a term not exceeding six months or a fine not exceeding the statutory maximum or both. The same penalties apply for similar behaviour in resisting the making of an interim possession order. Under s 76 of the Act a person who is present on the premises during the currency of an interim possession order commits an offence unless he leaves within 24 hours of the time of service and does not return, or a copy of the order was not fixed to the premises in accordance with the rules of the court. He also commits an offence if he re-enters as a trespasser or tries to do so after the expiration of the order but within a period of one year beginning on the day on which the order was served. A person guilty of an offence under this section shall be liable on summary conviction to imprisonment for a maximum of six months or fine not exceeding level 5 on the standard scale or both. A constable in uniform may arrest without warrant anyone he reasonably suspects to be guilty of an offence under the section.

POWERS TO REMOVE UNAUTHORISED CAMPERS

5.12 Section 77 provides that local authorities may give a direction to leave land if it appears to them that persons are residing in a vehicle or vehicles on any land forming part of a highway, on any other occupied land, or on any occupied land without the consent of the owner. Notice must be served upon such persons but it is only necessary in the case of multiple occupancy for the direction to specify the land. It may be addressed to the occupants of all vehicles on the land and need not name them. Failure to leave the land as soon as practicable or to remove the vehicle or, having done so, to return within a period of three months beginning on the day the direction was given, is an offence. A person found guilty of an offence under this section shall be liable on summary conviction to imprisonment for a maximum of six months or to a fine not exceeding level 5 on the standard scale or both. It is a defence to show that the accused could not remove the vehicle, or leave the land, or that he subsequently re-entered, because of illness, mechanical breakdown or other immediate emergency. For the purposes of this section a person may be regarded as residing on land even if he has a home elsewhere. Until 1 April 1996 for the purposes of this section 'local authority' means, in Wales, a county or district council.

5.13 Section 78 provides that on a complaint by a local authority a magistrates' court, if it is satisfied that people and vehicles are on land in contravention of a direction under s 77, may make an order requiring the removal of a vehicle or other property on the land and anyone residing in it. Under such an order the local authority may take such steps as are reasonably necessary to ensure that the order is complied with, and may enter upon the land and take such steps as are necessary to make vehicles and other property suitable for removal. This may not be done before a period of at least 24 hours has elapsed from the giving of notice to the owners or occupiers of their intention to take such action unless, after reasonable inquiries, the authority has failed to discover their names and addresses. On a summary conviction for wilfully obstructing anyone in the exercise of the power conferred by an order under this section the penalty is a fine not exceeding level 3 on the standard scale.

5.14 If a summons is issued requiring a person or persons to appear before the magistrates it is to be directed to the occupant of a particular vehicle, or to all the occupants without naming them. If the defendants fail to appear then the question of an arrest warrant under the Magistrates' Courts Act 1980, s 55(2) does not apply to proceedings on a complaint made under this section. Under s 79, if it is impractical to serve a relevant document personally then it will be treated as served if it is fixed in a prominent place to the vehicle or vehicles concerned. The local authority must also take reasonable steps to ensure that any relevant documents are displayed on the land in question in such a way that they can be seen by anyone camping on the land. Notice of any relevant document shall also be given to the owner of the land and any occupier unless, after reasonable inquiries, the authority cannot discover the name and address of the owner and occupier. The owner and occupier may appear and be heard at any proceedings. Some provisions of the Caravan Sites Act 1968 relating to Gipsy caravan sites, and including the local authorities' duty to provide sites, are repealed by s 80, as are provisions of the Local Government, Planning and Land Act 1980 relating to payment of specific grants for sites.

5.15 It is the combination of provisions in Part V, and in particular s 61 and ss 77–80, which civil liberty organisations believe will effectively outlaw a whole way of life and erode the human rights of gypsies and other travellers. The Penal Affairs Consortium, an alliance of 23 reasonably disparate organisations concerned with the penal system, has been quick to condemn this Part of the 1994 Act and has urged the police, prosecutors and the courts to apply the new laws with restraint. The Act could have the potential effect of criminalising a large number of people, including homeless people squatting in empty properties, travellers living in caravans on land other than authorised sites, those organising raves and people participating in a wide range of demonstrations or public protests. It is inappropriate to subject to criminal penalties those involved in the wide range of activities covered by these new offences. *Liberty* has launched a Public Order Monitoring Project to monitor the new public order powers. The organisation fears that the laws which they describe as 'inherently unjust and discriminatory' will be applied in an unjust and less than even handed manner.

6 Prevention of terrorism

GENERAL

6.1   Section 81 of the Act adds the Prevention of Terrorism (Temporary Provisions) Act 1989, s 13A. It allows any police officer of, or above, the rank of commander in the Metropolitan Police or in the City of London Police, or any police officer of, or above, the rank of assistant chief constable in any other area, to authorise that the power to stop and search vehicles and persons conferred by the section shall be exercisable for a period not exceeding 28 days. This period is extendable for a further 28 days. Under s 13A(2), the acts of terrorism to which this section applies are ones connected with the affairs of Northern Ireland or any other acts of terrorism of any description except acts connected solely with the affairs of the United Kingdom (other than Northern Ireland). The work of animal rights activists is intended to be excluded by the Act but it surely can fall within the second part of s 13A(2). However, it would not seem to apply to either extreme Welsh or Scottish Nationalist movements. The powers are almost identical to those designed to prevent violence under s 60, except that failure to stop or wilful obstruction of a constable in the exercise of his powers carries a maximum of six months' imprisonment and/or a fine not exceeding level 5 on the standard scale. As with s 60, a person stopped may obtain a written statement from the constable if he applies within twelve months from the date on which he was stopped. For the purposes of the Prevention of Terrorism (Temporary Provisions) Act 1989, s 27 (temporary provisions), the provision inserted into the Act by this section shall be treated, as from the time when this section comes into force, as having been continued in force by the order under sub-s (6) of that section which has effect at that time.

6.2   Section 82 amends the Prevention of Terrorism (Temporary Provisions) Act 1989 by adding a new Part IVA to that Act (ss 16A, 16B). Two new offences are created. Under the new s 16A, a person who has an article in his possession in circumstances which give rise to a reasonable suspicion that it is for a purpose connected with the commission, preparation or instigation of acts of terrorism to which the section applies (the same as in the new s 13A, ie domestic terrorism is excluded) is guilty of an offence. If a person is charged with an offence under this section and it is proved that at the time of the alleged offence that either, he and the article were both present in any premises, or that the article was in premises of which he was the occupier or which he habitually used other than as a member of the public, then the court may (but need not) accept the fact proved as sufficient evidence of his possessing that article at the time unless it is further proved that he did not know of its presence in the premises in question, or that if he did know, that he had no control over it. It is a defence under s 16A(3) that he was not in possession of the article for the purposes of terrorism. The burden of proof is not reversed if the person is found in possession of an article outside of a premises. Perhaps this is just as well. The number of genuine tourists to be found on any given morning peering at maps circled with prominent London buildings would be enough to cause a further overspill in our already full prisons. A person found guilty of an offence under this section is liable on summary conviction to a maximum of six months' imprisonment and a fine not exceeding level 5 on the standard scale or both, and on conviction on indictment to imprisonment for a term not exceeding ten years or a fine or both. Again, for the purposes of the Prevention of Terrorism (Temporary Provisions) Act 1989, s 27, the provision inserted into the Act by s 82 of the 1994 Act shall be treated, as from the time when that section comes into force, as having been continued in force by the order under s 27(6) which has effect at that time. This section comes into force on 3 January 1995. The new s 16B makes it an offence to, without lawful authority or reasonable excuse, collect or record (whether by photography or any other means) any information which is likely to be of use to terrorists in the planning or carrying out of acts of terrorism to which this section applies (ie the same as in s 13A—domestic terrorism is excluded). The burden of proof is on the defendant to show that he acted with lawful authority or reasonable excuse, and the penalties on conviction are the same as under s 16A. Section 82(5) provides that the court may order the forfeiture of any material to which this section applies.

6.3   Section 83, which amends the Prevention of Terrorism Act (Temporary Provisions) Act 1989, Sch 7, enables the police to apply for a production order which requires a person to produce material in his custody or under his control, and allows the Secretary of State to authorise search warrants and production warrants in connection with the offence, under the Northern Ireland (Emergency Provisions) Act 1991, of directing a terrorist organisation. The 1991 Act is amended to permit investigators appointed under s 57 of that Act to require answers in writing to questionnaires. Again the Prevention of Terrorism (Temporary Provisions) Act 1989, s 27 is deemed to have been continued in force, as is the Northern Ireland (Emergency Provisions) Act 1991, s 69.

7 Obscenity, pornography and videos

OBSCENE PUBLICATIONS AND INDECENT PHOTOGRAPHS OF CHILDREN

7.1   If one Part of the 1994 Act should meet with something approaching universal approval it is Part VII which deals, *inter alia*, with obscene publications and indecent photographs of children. Section 84 of the Act blocks one of the loopholes in the Protection of Children Act 1978. In 1978, the technology now available to the pornographer was neither in place nor, probably, even dreamed about. Now, under s 84(2) the law is extended to cover the taking and distribution of indecent photographs of children by adding the concept of 'pseudo-photographs' (defined as being an image made by computer graphics, or otherwise), that is simulated child pornography manufactured and stored on a computer disc or by electronic means, and capable of being converted into a photograph. Section 85 amends the Police and Criminal Evidence Act 1984, s 24(2), to include as arrestable offences an offence under the Obscene Publications Act 1959, s 2, and an offence under the Protection of Children Act 1978, s 1. The Police and Criminal Evidence Act 1984, Sch 5, Pt II, is also amended to include these two offences as serious arrestable offences. The Police and Criminal Evidence (Northern Ireland) Order 1989[1] is similarly amended. Section 86 increases the penalties on summary conviction under the Criminal Justice Act 1988, s 160(3), which deals with various offences relating to indecent photographs, to allow for a sentence not exceeding six months and/or a fine not exceeding level 5 on the standard scale. There is a similar amendment to the Criminal Justice (Evidence, etc) (Northern Ireland) Order 1988, art 15(3)[2]. Section 87 increases penalties in Scotland under the Civic Government (Scotland) Act 1982, s 51(3), to six months for a summary conviction (from three) and to three years on indictment (from two).

---

1   SI 1989/1341.
2   SI 1988/1847.

VIDEO RECORDINGS

7.2   Before the 1994 Act, supplying, or possessing for supply, unclassified videos under the Video Recordings Act 1984, ss 9, 10, could be dealt with only in the magistrates' court and carried a maximum fine of £20,000 but no possibility of imprisonment. Section 88 of the 1994 Act changes that position. Now both of the offences under ss 9 and 10 are triable either way, and on conviction on indictment carry a term of imprisonment not exceeding two years or a fine or both and on a summary conviction imprisonment for six months or a fine not exceeding £20,000 or both. Other offences under the 1984 Act (including supplying videos in breach of their classification) will still be dealt with summarily, but the maximum fine has been increased to £20,000 and there is now a maximum sentence of six months' imprisonment available to the magistrates. Under the Video Recordings Act 1984, s 2, video games and works which are designed to inform, educate and instruct or which are concerned with sport, religion or music are generally exempt from classification. Section 89 of the 1994 Act amends the said s 2 and provides that in addition to the list of subjects which cannot be depicted to any significant extent in an exempted video are techniques likely to be useful in the commission of criminal offences and the commission of criminal offences themselves in a way likely to encourage imitation. Presumably this means that there will be no more scenes of off-the-ball incidents in England v Wales rugby internationals.

7.3   Section 90 of the Act adds the Video Recordings Act 1984, s 4A, so that the designated authority (the British Board of Film Classification ('BBFC')), in making the determination as to the suitability of a video work, shall have special regard to any harm that may be caused to potential viewers or, through their behaviour to society, by the manner in which the video depicts criminal behaviour, illegal drugs, violent behaviour or incidents, horrific behaviour or incidents, or human sexual activity. For the purposes of s 90, any behaviour of the above kind shall be taken to include any behaviour or activity likely to stimulate or encourage it. The Board must take these matters into account when deciding whether a particular film is suitable for classification and if so in what category. This is, of course, likely to provide all sorts of problems and anomalies. It was pointed out in the House of Lords by Lord Merlyn-Rees that the television detective series *Inspector Morse* could be watched by anyone at home, but as a video, it would receive a 15 classification[1]. Efforts in the House of Lords to change the phrasing to 'to any harm that may be caused to a significant number of potential viewers' came to nothing. Section 90 also adds the Video Recordings Act 1984, s 4B. This provides the Home Secretary with the power to make an order which would establish a system for reviewing works which were classified before the introduction of the new statutory criteria and allow the BBFC to alter a classification in the light of the new criteria. There will be a right of appeal against a classification to the Videos Committee. The purpose of s 91 is to allow local weights and measures authorities to investigate and prosecute offences under the Video Recordings Act 1984 committed outside their area if they are linked to their area. The jurisdiction of magistrates' courts in England and Wales and in Northern Ireland and Sheriff courts in Scotland is similarly extended.

---

1   See HL Committee, 14 June 1994, col 1596.

OBSCENE, OFFENSIVE OR ANNOYING TELEPHONE CALLS

7.4   By virtue of s 92 of the 1994 Act, the penalties which may be imposed on a person convicted of making obscene, offensive or annoying telephone calls in contravention of the Telecommunications Act 1984, s 43(2), are increased to a fine not exceeding level 5 on the standard scale and/or a term of imprisonment not exceeding six months. Before the 1994 Act, the maximum fine was one not exceeding level 3 on the standard scale, and there was no possibility of imprisonment. It will be interesting to see whether the increased penalties available under the section will reverse the trend of prosecutors bringing charges of grievous bodily harm against defendants who have harassed their victims into a state of psychological shock. The section is not retrospective and the new penalties will not apply to an offence committed before the section comes into force.

8 Prison services and the prison service

INTRODUCTION

8.1 Much of the material in the Chapters in Part VIII of the 1994 Act is effectively duplication as the English and Welsh, Scottish and Northern Irish prison services are dealt with in turn. Basically, Part VIII amends and, the Home Office thinks, improves the current provision for the contracting out of prison services and prisoner escort functions in England and Wales. At the same time, it provides for the first time for prisons and prisoner escorts to be contracted out in Scotland and provides for the contracting out of prisoner escort functions in Northern Ireland. One of the aims of the Part is to effect financial savings and, in so far as England and Wales are concerned, significant savings are expected in the long term. The savings in Scotland are also expected to be significant as are the ones in Northern Ireland.

ENGLAND AND WALES

8.2 The Criminal Justice Act 1991, s 80(1), gave the power to the Home Secretary to make prisoner escort arrangements. Transporting prisoners to and from court appearances had long been an expensive game. During the various prisoner officer disputes, prisoners had either been produced hours late or simply had not been produced at all. It was thought that the substantial manpower involved (and there was duplication between the work of the police and prison officers) could have been better employed elsewhere. Separate provision for transporting prisoners had been an idea which had cropped up over the years and gained credence in the Woolf Report following the rioting in Strangeways and other prisons in the Spring of 1990[1]. Section 93 extends the provision of prisoner escort to include transfer from one prison to another as well as to and from courts, police stations or hospitals. By virtue of s 94, the prisoner custody officer is given the duty to effect any order the court has made to search persons before the Crown Court under the Powers Criminal Courts Act 1973, s 34A, as well as the power under the Magistrates' Court Act 1980, s 80, to search for money on a defaulter. Under s 95, if a prisoner, whilst in the charge of a prisoner custody officer breaches the prison discipline rules then he is deemed to have been in the custody of the governor of the prison or the custody of the director of a contracted out prison, as the case may be. Accordingly, he may be the subject of a disciplinary charge brought by the prisoner custody officer. This will be dealt with at the receiving prison. The double jeopardy rule applies. He cannot be punished under prison rules for anything for which he has already been punished by a court. At present, Category B and C prisoners are dealt with by contractors in England and Wales. During the debate on the Bill, it was suggested that to protect prisoners from harassment and bullying by prisoner custody officers there should be a Prisoner Escort Monitoring Board but the proposed amendment foundered.

---

1 Private Sector Involvement in the Remand System, Cm 434; The Practicality of Private Sector Involvement in the Remand System, (1989); Prison Disturbances April 1990: Report of an Enquiry, Cm 1456 (the Woolf Report).

8.3   It is interesting to look back some seven years to the words of the then Home Secretary, Douglas Hurd, who had this to say in the House of Commons—

> 'I do not think that there is a case, and I do not believe that the House would accept that there is a case, for auctioning or privatising prisons, or handing over the business of keeping prisoners safe to anyone other than government servants.'

Now, some seven years later, it is quite apparent from s 96 of the Act that this is both the short and long term aim of the present Government. Section 97 provides for a prison officer who is temporarily attached to a contracted out prison to be a prisoner custody officer. This is most likely to be used in the case where an incident occurs which may euphemistically be described as 'short of what is described as loss of control'. An instance going back nearly a quarter of a century can illustrate this. The authorities at Parkhurst in 1969 believed there was to be at best a demonstration and at worst a riot during the recreation period. Officers were drafted in from neighbouring prisons to assist in handling the incident. Under s 97, if the same or a similar situation occurred in a contracted out prison, officers from directly managed prisons could be drafted in. This section should be read in conjunction with s 99. The Home Office is looking for a policy of co-operation and mutual support between the prison officers and the prisoner custody officers rather than one of rivalry. Section 97 also deals with domestic matters of prison officers in relation to attachment to contracted out prisons. By virtue of s 98, a reference to custodial duties at a contracted out prison refers also to those duties in relation to a prisoner who is outside a prison for temporary purposes. The purpose of this section is to give prisoner custody officers exactly the same jurisdiction as prison officers have outside their prison. Section 98 will be used in instances where a prisoner is attending a hospital or at home on compassionate leave. It is not intended that a prisoner who is in a contracted-out prison but temporarily placed in a directly managed prison should remain in the control of the prisoner custody officer. The Home Secretary envisages at least the possibility of interchange between officers at directly managed prisons and contracted out prisons, and s 99 allows him to enter into contracts for functions at directly managed prisons to be performed by prisoner custody officers.

8.4   Tucked away in s 100 of the 1994 Act is an interesting proposition. It is that there might be a return to a 20th century version of the hulks. Section 100(1) amends the Prison Act 1952, s 33, and empowers the Secretary of State to provide new prisons by declaring (rather in the manner of an Islamic divorce) that any building or part of a building, built for the purpose or vested in him and under his control, will be a prison. It also goes on to add that the same applies to any floating structure or part of such structure constructed for the purpose or vested in him or under his control. An amendment put forward by Dr Norman Godman to ensure that the proposed hulk did not include 'a platform, drilling rig or other structure which is or has been used for or in connection with the getting of gas or oil'[1] was defeated at Committee Stage by three votes. It may be that yet again we are another step down the road to establishing penal colonies in far off places. Section 101 is the usual tidying up section which provides for minor amendments made necessary by the previous sections. For example, in the Criminal Justice Act 1991, s 85(5), the words 'The contractor shall . . .' become 'The contractor and any sub-contractor of his shall each . . .'.

---

1   HC Standing Committee B, 17 February 1994, col 831.

SCOTLAND

8.5   It is perhaps curious that Pt VIII, Ch II, should have been included in the Act which, apart from measures of cross-border support, is largely one dealing with England and Wales. Scottish members found it insensitive. According to Dr Norman Godman—

> 'By showing such insensitivity, the Government have exacerbated the feelings of disaffection that many Scottish people have with the scrutiny of legislation that has a direct impact on our legal system.'[1]

There was some feeling amongst Committee members that the English system should not be grafted onto a Scottish system which 'is a first class service, as good as any, certainly in the European Union and, I should say, in most of the member states of the Council of Europe.'[2]. Dr Godman did not get his way. The Chapter deals with the privatisation of prisons and prisoner services in Scotland.

---

1   HC Standing Committee B, 17 February 1994, col 832.
2   HC Standing Committee B, 17 February 1994, col 833.

8.6   Section 102 echoes s 93 which amended the Criminal Justice Act 1991, s 80. Escort functions may now be performed by authorised prisoner custody officers. The functions are set out in sub-s (2) and relevant premises are defined in sub-s (3)—

> '(a)   the premises of any court, prison, police station or hospital; or
> (b)   the premises of any other place from or to which a prisoner may be required to be taken under the Criminal Procedure (Scotland) Act 1975 or the Mental Health (Scotland) Act 1984'.

Either but not both of the sets of premises may be situated in a part of the British Isles outside Scotland. Under s 103, a single crown servant directly accountable to the Secretary of State shall be a prisoner escort monitor (rather than a Prison Escort Monitoring Board as was suggested for England and Wales) with a duty to keep escort arrangements under review and to report to the Secretary of State. He will also be under a duty to investigate and report to the Secretary of State allegations made against the staff of the contractor and, at the same time, will report on breaches of discipline on the part of the prisoners under escort. One of the fears of the Opposition was that there is no Prison Ombudsman in Scotland and the section would diminish the rights of prisoners. The Government was quick to allay these fears. According to David Maclean, the position of the Crown servant—

> 'provides a high degree of accountability. The Secretary of State can expect a full and immediate report from the prisoner escort monitor, who will be the Secretary of State's full-time employee, of any untoward incident. The Secretary of State will be directly accountable to Parliament and will be able, if necessary, to offer an explanation to Parliament if something goes wrong.'[1]

Section 104 largely mirrors other provisions of the Act, namely s 12 and Sch 1. It should be read in conjunction with these provisions. A search of a prisoner, or any other person, under s 104(1)(b) is intended to include the search of a handbag or briefcase. Section 105, which deals with breaches of discipline by prisoners under escort, mirrors s 95. Again the double jeopardy rule applies.

---

1   HC Standing Committee B, 17 February 1994, col 843.

8.7   Section 106 is similar to s 7 and relates to the provision or running of any prison or part of a prison in Scotland. Whilst a contract under this section is in force, the prison (or part) shall be run in accordance with ss 107 and 108, the Prisons (Scotland) Act 1989 and any prison rules and directions made under or by virtue of the 1989 Act subject to any modification by s 110. In the case of a part, that part and the remaining part shall be treated for the purpose of ss 107–112 as separate prisons. One of the fears of the Labour members at Committee Stage was that a unit, such as the special unit at Barlinnie, which would lend itself to such a move might be contracted out. This would be a 'part' for the purposes of the section. Mr David Maclean, speaking for the Government, assured Committee members that the special unit at Barlinnie was a target. He went on to give the hypothetical example of a separate part of a facility being run by someone with specialist experience, for example, the founding of a specialised psychiatric facility aimed at prisoners who do not require compulsory admission as in-patients. He suggested that it would be entirely appropriate for the Secretary of State to provide such a facility and contract out possibly to the National Health Service. Section 107 of the Act is very similar to s 8. Here, however, a monitor becomes a controller. Sections 108, 109 again effectively mirror earlier sections in the Act, this time ss 9 and 98. Section 110 deals with the necessary modifications to the Prisons (Scotland) Act 1989 and prison rules and directions. In particular, references to 'a governor' are to be construed as references to 'a director'. Once more there are provisions for the Secretary of State to intervene if it appears that a director has lost or is likely to lose control of all or part of a prison, by replacing him for the duration of the trouble. This is s 111 and mirrors the English provisions in s 10. Section 112 closely resembles the provisions of s 11.

8.8   Under s 113, the Secretary of State has similar powers to those under s 100 in relation to the provision of new prisons. Section 114 should be read in conjunction with Sch 6 to the Act, and relates to the certification of prison custody officers in a similar way to the provisions of Sch 1. Section 115 puts prisoner custody officers in the same position, regarding wrongful disclosure of information, as their counterparts at secure training centres under s 14. Sections 116 and 117 contain minor amendments and an interpretation of Chapter II respectively. In particular s 117 provides that 'contracted out prison' and 'the contractor' have the meanings given by s 106(4).

NORTHERN IRELAND

8.9   The Government has made it clear that whilst it is the intention to introduce contract prisoner escorts in Northern Ireland it has, at this stage in its life, no intention of entering into contracts for the provision of prisons and prison management. Section 118 extends to Northern Ireland powers already available in England and Wales under the Criminal Justice Act 1991. However, if at any time in the future there should be a wish to contract out prisons in Northern Ireland or for floating prisons, then all that will be needed is an Order in Council. According to Mr David Maclean, the Government is, of course, well aware that certainly in the immediate past, if not in the present, there have been particular sensitivities in the province—

> 'If someone was taking prisoners from Scotland, England or Wales and delivering them to Northern Ireland, they would need to be very aware of the nature of that country. The normal *modus operandi* in Scotland, England and Wales must be adapted to suit Northern Ireland.'[1]

He went on to say that the Secretary of State had no plans to involve the private sector in escorting high-risk terrorist prisoners. With minor variations ss 118–125 are the same as those provisions relating to England, Wales and Scotland. However, s 123 does provide a specific offence of assaulting a prisoner custody officer in the execution of his duty. There is no similar provision for Scotland, England and Wales. This is because there are already general provisions in Scotland and a power under the Criminal Justice Act 1991 in relation to England and Wales.

---

1   HC Standing Committee B, 17 February 1994, col 868.

THE PRISON SERVICE

8.10 To put it mildly, relations between members of the prison service and the Government have been strained over the last decade or so. It was industrial action which led to the unhealthy practice of putting remand, and later convicted prisoners, in police cells. Industrial action was repeated in 1986. In November 1993, the Prison Officers Association threatened industrial action which would have led to some 1,700 prisoners being locked out of their cells inside three days. This, the Government estimated, would have cost £1 million for the three days alone. An injunction was granted and industrial action was avoided. Prison officers in Scotland, unlike their counterparts in England and Wales, do not have the powers and functions of a constable and so the injunction did not apply to them. They do however, have full legal rights as a trade union. The Government believed that the troubles of November 1993 left 'a lot of unfinished business'. It is this unfinished business to which Pt VIII, Ch IV applies. Speaking on behalf of the Government, Mr David Maclean said—

> 'The starting point must be that it is right for industrial action in the prison service to be deemed unlawful. It cannot be right for that essential law and order service to be disrupted by industrial action, with all the grave and unpredictable consequence that that brings for the operation of the criminal justice system and for public safety.'[1]

There has been another problem. Prison officers and governors do not fall within the definition of workers for the purpose of employment legislation and so they do not benefit from a full range of employment rights. Their associations cannot be trade unions.

---

1   HC Standing Committee B, 22 February 1994, col 882.

8.11 Section 126 goes some way to rectifying the position. The Employment Protection (Consolidation) Act 1978 and the Trade Union and Labour Relations (Consolidation) Act 1992, as well as the Industrial Relations (Northern Ireland) Order 1976[1], the Industrial Relations (No 2) (Northern Ireland) Order 1976[2] and the Industrial Relations (Northern Ireland) Order 1992[3] now have effect as if an individual who is member of the prison service acts in a capacity in which he has the powers and privileges of constable were not, by virtue of his so having those powers or privileges, to be regarded as in police service for the purposes of that legislation. In simple terms, he will be regarded as a member of a trade union. This section enables the various associations to be trade unions. But, where the Government giveth, the Government also taketh away. Under s 127 it becomes an offence to induce a person to withhold his services as such an officer or to induce a person to commit a breach of discipline. This will include prison custody officers but not chaplains, assistant chaplains or medical officers. It is envisaged that peaceful picketing will fall within the ambit of this section. Section 127(1)(b) (inducing a person to commit a breach of discipline) may cause some difficulties. To run a prison successfully a blind eye must be turned from time to time. There have been, as was pointed out, occasions when governors have instructed officers to leave illegally brewed alcohol and drugs in cells. This would clearly fall within this provision. The Secretary of State may bring civil proceedings in respect of actions which lead to a breach of this section. It is doubtful whether prison officers will think that they have necessarily had the best of the bargain. They are now prevented from taking any form of industrial action (in fairness this may always well have been the case but nobody realised it) over either pay and conditions or penal conditions which they feel may have an injurious impact on prisoners and ultimately the public. As to pay and conditions, the Secretary of State may make regulations to provide for the establishment, maintenance and operation of procedures for the determination of pay and allowances for the prison service, and such other terms and conditions of employment in the prison service as may appear to him to fall to be dealt with along with pay and allowances. There is a small crumb of comfort. Before making the regulations the Secretary of State shall consult with such organisations as appear to him to be representative of persons working in the prison service and other people as he thinks fit.

1   SI 1976/1043.
2   SI 1976/2147.
3   SI 1992/807.

8.12 However, at the end of the day the prison service may well think it is not exactly the flavour of the month, nor will it be for some time. Mr Maclean said that the Government had no intention of raking over earlier disputes, or of initiating proceedings in respect of anything which took place before the injunctions of 1993 but it was clear that previous calls to industrial action should not be made lawful in retrospect. On the other hand the Prison Officers Association could not expect the slate to be wiped clean. The Prison Service may want to take warning from the words of Sir John Wheeler, Minister of State, Northern Ireland Office, who wrote to Finlay Spratt, the chairman of the Northern Ireland Prison Officers Association and said 'your Association in England and Wales is not liked in the House of Commons, therefore this Bill is coming in and it will go on the statute book and there will be no amendments.'[1]

1   Quoted by Alun Michael, HC Standing Committee B, 22 February 1994, col 908.

9　Miscellaneous amendments: Scotland

GENERAL

9.1　Part IX of the Act provides a series of miscellaneous amendments relating to Scotland. Sections 130–135 deal with the early release of prisoners. Section 129 deals with the transfer of persons detained by police and customs officers. It amends the Criminal Justice (Scotland) Act 1980, ss 2, 3, and the Criminal Justice Act 1987, ss 48, 49. It allows police and customs officers to move people in custody after arrest from the premises at which they were first detained. It has arisen because of the law peculiar to Scotland that a person may be detained for six hours without the right to see a solicitor. In the late 1980s, a sheriff ruled that s 48 of the 1987 Act did not give the police power to move the prisoner within that six hour period. Therefore, he could not be taken to the scene of the crime to show, for example where stolen property was placed or where he had left a body. It is not envisaged that customs officers will have any greater powers than they had before.

9.2　Section 130 amends provisions in the Prisoners and Criminal Proceedings (Scotland) Act 1993 and brings the provisions relating to the release of children more closely in line with the equivalent provisions for the release of adults. The section does not apply to children detained for murder, but those with a determinate sentence who are later transferred to the penal system. Under s 131 the Parole Board for Scotland is to be consulted not only on the question of the initial conditions of a release licence but also on their subsequent amendment. Section 132 amends the Criminal Procedure (Scotland) Act 1975, s 212A, to enable standard requirements to be included in supervised release orders under that section. One example is that an offender subject to a supervised release should report to the supervising officer on release from prison. Section 133 provides that certain prisoners sentenced by court martial may now be treated in the same way as discretionary life prisoners. The Prisoners and Criminal Proceedings (Scotland) Act 1993, s 10(4), is accordingly amended. At present this situation applies to only one prisoner, but there may well be others in the future. Section 134 amends Sch 6 to the 1993 Act. The effect of this is to allow amendments to certain provisions of the Prisons (Scotland) Act 1989 which continue to apply to prisoners sentenced before 1 October 1993. Section 135 further amends the transitional provisions in the Prisoners and Criminal Proceedings (Scotland) Act 1993, Sch 6, in relation to a discretionary life prisoner.

10 Cross-border enforcement

GENERAL

10.1 Part X of the 1994 Act has been particularly welcomed by the police. One of the most useful provisions, said the ACPO spokesman, is the union between all UK forces which would give officers in England and Wales the power of arrest in Scotland and Northern Ireland and vice versa. This would put an end to the ludicrous situation where an officer, say in Cumbria, could not cross the border to arrest someone in neighbouring Dumfries and Galloway without the bureaucracy of first getting a warrant. 'It will hopefully put an end to an enormous waste of resources,' said the spokesman[1]. Under s 136(1), a warrant issued in England, Wales or Northern Ireland for the arrest of a person charged with an offence may (without any endorsement) be executed in Scotland by any constable of any police force of the country of issue as well as by any other persons within the directions in the warrant. Under s 136(2), the situation is reversed and the provisions apply to warrants issued in Scotland and by virtue of s 136(3) the provisions apply in Northern Ireland to warrants issued in England, Wales and Scotland. This section applies to warrants of commitment and committal and warrants to arrest witnesses. Section 137 gives a similar cross-border power of arrest for any constable who has reasonable grounds for suspecting that an offence has been committed or attempted. For this section to be applicable, the suspected offence must be an arrestable offence, or in the case of any other offence it appears to the constable that the service of a summons is impracticable or inappropriate for any of the reasons specified in s 138. Section 136(7) gives details of the requirement on the constable to take the suspect to a police station as soon as reasonably practicable. The constable in making the arrest may use reasonable force and shall have powers of search conferred under s 139. 'Arrestable offence' and 'designated police station' have the same meanings as in the Police and Criminal Evidence Act 1984 and, in the case of an arrest in Northern Ireland, have the same meaning as in the Police and Criminal Evidence (Northern Ireland) Order 1989[2].

---

1   'Just the Job' Police Review, 11 November 1994.
2   SI 1989/1341.

10.2 Under s 138 of the 1994 Act, to give the officer power of arrest in the case of a non-arrestable offence one or more of the following must apply—

'(a) the name of the suspected person is unknown to, and cannot be readily ascertained by, the constable;
(b) the constable has reasonable grounds for doubting whether a name furnished by the suspected person as his name is his real name;
(c) either—
     (i)   the suspected person has failed to furnish a satisfactory address for service; or
     (ii) the constable has reasonable grounds for doubting whether an address furnished by the suspected person is a satisfactory address for service;

    (d) the constable has reasonable grounds for believing that arrest is necessary
        to prevent the suspected person—
        (i) causing physical injury to himself or any other person;
        (ii) suffering physical injury;
        (iii) causing loss or damage to property;
        (iv) committing an offence against public decency; or
        (v) causing an unlawful obstruction of a highway or road; or
    (e) the constable has reasonable grounds for believing that the arrest is
        necessary to protect a child or other vulnerable person from the
        suspected person.'

In the Criminal Justice (Scotland) Act 1980, ss 2, 3 the reference to a detention being terminated not more than six hours after it begins shall be construed as a reference to its being terminated not more than four hours after the person's arrival at the police station to which he is taken.

10.3 Section 139 provides search powers available when a suspect is arrested under ss 136 and 137. A constable may search a person if he has reasonable grounds for believing that he may be a danger to himself or others, or for anything which may facilitate an escape, or for anything which might be evidence relating to the offence. There is also a power to enter and search premises in which the person was arrested or was in immediately before his arrest. The search is to be for evidence in relation to the offence for which he was arrested. The powers of search do not authorise a constable to require the suspect to remove his clothing in public other than an outer coat, jacket, headgear, gloves or footwear, but they do authorise the search of a person's mouth. The search may only be undertaken if the constable has reasonable grounds for believing that the person has something concealed or that there is evidence to be obtained from the search. There is a limit to the power to search premises. If the premises consists of two or more separate dwellings then the search must be limited to—

    '(a) any dwelling in which the arrest took place or in which the person was
        immediately before his arrest; and
    (b) any parts of the premises which the occupier of any such dwelling uses
        in common with the occupiers of any other dwellings comprised in
        the premises.'

The constable is given a power to retain any item found in the search in relation to which he has reasonable grounds for believing that the person might use to cause physical injury to himself or another. He may also retain items which he has reasonable grounds for believing might be used for an escape or which may be used in evidence or have been obtained as a result of the offence.

10.4 Section 140 deals with reciprocal powers of arrest. Where a constable of a police force in England and Wales would have the power to arrest a person in England and Wales under the Police and Criminal Evidence Act 1984, ss 24(6), (7), 25, then a constable of a police force in Scotland or Northern Ireland shall have the same power of arrest in England and Wales. Reciprocal provision is also made in relation to the powers of arrest of a Scottish or Northern Irish constable. Section 141 of the Act permits chief constables to provide constables or other assistance to enable a force in another United Kingdom jurisdiction to meet any special demand on its resources.

11 Sexual offences

RAPE, MALE RAPE AND BUGGERY

11.1 Section 142 of the Act substitutes the Sexual Offences Act 1956, s 1. The new s 1(2) provides that a man commits rape if—

> '(a) he has sexual intercourse with a person (whether vaginal or anal) who at the time of the intercourse does not consent to it; and
> (b) at the time he knows that the person does not consent to the intercourse or is reckless as to whether that person consents to it.'.

The new s 1(3) provides that a man who induces a married woman to have sexual intercourse with him by impersonating her husband commits rape. This does no more than re-state the law as set out in the old Sexual Offences Act 1956, s 1(2). The law has long been clear that a deception as to the sexual act itself will not allow a defence of consent. The old case of *R v Williams*[1], in which a singing teacher persuaded his pupil to have intercourse on the basis that it would improve her voice, is still good law. The legal definition of rape has been extended but the transsexual or hermaphrodite loophole does not appear to have been closed. Because of the decisions in *Corbett v Corbett*[2] and the European case *Cossey v UK*[3], in which it was established that it was not possible to change one's sex, a male-female transsexual could not be the victim of rape. Now it would seem that, despite the intentions of Parliament, there can still be no vaginal rape of a post-operative transsexual. Critics of the section complain that oral rape is still excluded, as is the penetration of the vagina or anus with objects such as a bottle or knife. Attacks of these kinds will remain to be dealt with under the Sexual Offences Act 1956, ss 14, 15 which carry lower penalties. As a practical consideration, male complainants will face the same attacks which have been made as to the sexual history of women complainants. In particular, if the defence of consent is raised there will no doubt be questions asked of previous homosexual behaviour[4].

---

1 [1923] 1 KB 340.
2 [1971] P 83
3 [1991] 2 FLR 492.
4 See M Morgan-Taylor, *Rape from a Male Perspective*, 144 (1994) NLJ, 1490.

11.2 Section 143 of the 1994 Act amends the Sexual Offences Act 1956, s 12. The anomaly under which it was an offence to commit consensual heterosexual buggery has been removed provided both parties have attained the age of 18.

11.3 Because of the change in the law relating to buggery, there are revised penalties for offences of buggery and indecency between men. The Sexual Offences Act 1956, Sch 2, is accordingly amended and if buggery occurs (subject to s 1(2) of the 1994 Act) with a person under the age of 16 or with an animal, the maximum sentence is life imprisonment. If the accused is aged 21 or over and the other person is under the age of 18, the penalty is a maximum of five years' imprisonment; otherwise, it is two years' imprisonment. There are similar penalties for attempted buggery.

11.4 The penalties for indecency between men are amended. If the indecency is by a man of or over 21 years of age and the other man is under 18 years of age, then the offence carries five years; in other cases, it carries a sentence of two years' imprisonment. The same penalties apply to attempted procurement of commission by a man of an act of gross indecency with another man. In practice, the actual penalties imposed for buggery with an animal are not as draconian as all that. In *R v Higson*[1], a probation order was substituted for a two year sentence on the basis that, as the Court of Appeal said, 'it is the appellant, and indeed his wife, and not the dog, who need help'.

---

1   (1984) 6 Cr App Rep (S) 20

HOMOSEXUALITY

11.5 After considerable lobbying by interested groups, the Sexual Offences Act 1967, s 1, has been amended so that a homosexual act committed in private between persons aged 18 and over is no longer a criminal offence. This amendment, implemented by s 145(1) of the 1994 Act, represents something of a compromise in the face of argument, particularly by gay activists, that the age of consent should be the same for men as for women, ie a reduction to the age of 16. There are similar amendments to the Criminal Justice Act (Scotland) 1980, s 80, and the Homosexual Offences (Northern Ireland) Order 1982, art 3[1].

---

1   SI 1982/1536.

11.6 Homosexual acts in the armed forces and in the merchant navy are no longer to be criminal offences as s 146 of the 1994 Act repeals the Sexual Offences Act 1967, ss 1(5), 2. However, it should be noted that under s 146(6), there is still provision for a competent authority to discharge anyone serving in the forces or on a merchant ship who, but for this section, would have been guilty of a criminal offence. Similar provision is made in relation to Scotland by amending the Criminal Justice (Scotland) Act 1980, s 80. Section 147 provides similar measures for homosexual acts in the armed forces and on merchant ships in relation to Northern Ireland. This section (as indeed did all of Part XI) came into force on the date the Act was passed. The Criminal Justice (Scotland) Act 1980, s 80(6), which defines 'homosexual act', is amended so that after the definition 'gross indecency', there is inserted the definition 'shameless indecency' (the Scottish equivalent of indecent exposure).

12 Miscellaneous and general

THE PAROLE BOARD

12.1 Before the introduction of the Criminal Justice Act 1991, the Parole Board was a purely advisory body offering recommendations to the Home Secretary on the early release of determinate and life sentence prisoners. The 1991 Act gave the Board the power to review, and take the final responsibility on the release of life sentence prisoners serving discretionary life sentences. It was also given the duty to decide whether to release on licence prisoners eligible for parole who are serving between four and seven years. As a result of that Act, the Board has become something of an executive body taking decisions on the early release of certain categories of prisoners. As the local review committees are phased out, the Parole Board now takes the responsibility for some 100 interviews a week of prisoners applying for parole. Its role has shifted from advice to decision making. Section 149 establishes the Board as an executive non-departmental public body. This will mark the independence of the Board. This section should be read in conjunction with Sch 10, para 70, which sets out a new Schedule to be substituted for the Criminal Justice Act 1991, Sch 5, and deals with the status, capacity, membership, and payment to members etc. Section 150 revises the arrangements for the recall of prisoners on licence. By virtue of the Criminal Justice Act 1991, two parallel systems began to operate, one run by the Parole Board and the other by the Home Secretary. This was clearly unsatisfactory and now the decision to recall any person on parole will rest with the Home Secretary.

PRISONS: POWERS IN RELATION TO PRISONERS, VISITORS AND OTHERS

12.2 As has been mentioned earlier, the supply, and use, of drugs in prison has become a major problem. Accordingly, s 151 of the 1994 Act adds the Prison Act 1952, s 16A, as an attempt to alleviate this problem. Under the new s 16A(1), if an authorisation by the governor is in force for the prison, any prison officer at the prison may require any prisoner who is confined to the prison to provide a sample of urine for the purpose of ascertaining whether he has any drug in his body. Section 16A(2) also confers the power to require a prisoner to provide a non-intimate sample either instead of, or in addition to, a sample of urine. Intimate sample has the same meaning as in the Police and Criminal Evidence Act 1984, Pt V. Section 151 also adds the Prisons (Scotland) Act 1989, s 41B. This section is practically identical to s 16A of the 1952 Act, but in this instance 'intimate sample' means a sample of blood, semen or any other tissue fluid, saliva or pubic hair or a swab taken from a person's body orifice. However, there appear to be no provisions as to who will carry out the urine and blood tests or whether a positive result will be the subject of disciplinary proceedings. Section 152 provides for the civilian staff of a directly managed prison to have non-intimate powers of search of a prisoner to discover whether he has any unauthorised property. The term used is 'authorised employee' and the prison governor must take such steps as he considers appropriate to notify to the prisoners descriptions of the persons who are from time to time permitted to exercise the power of search. There are similar provisions for prisons in Scotland.

Here, unauthorised property means property not authorised under the Prisons (Scotland) Act 1989, s 39, or authorised by the governor. The aim of s 152 of the 1994 Act is to allow prison officers to go about their other duties and give the civilian employees, such as those who work in kitchens or workshops, the power to give a 'rub-down search'. A number of problems do arise. Employees are, of course, in a very different position from prison or custody officers and carrying out a search is one of the less pleasant and more difficult tasks to be performed. Training will be provided for the civilians and it will be for the governor of a prison to decide how and when he introduces the provision. But what sanctions may be placed upon an employee who refuses to carry out a search? Section 153 amends the Prisons (Scotland) Act 1989, s 41; the list of articles that it is prohibited to introduce into a prison now comprises—

'(a) any drug;
(b) any firearm or ammunition;
(c) any offensive weapon;
(d) any article to which s 1 of the Carrying of Knives etc (Scotland) Act 1983 applies; or
(e) without prejudice to paragraphs (a) to (d) above, any article which is a prohibited article under s 39 of this Act'.

Where a prison officer has reasonable grounds for suspecting that a person who is in, or seeking to enter, a prison has in his possession any article in paras (a)–(e) above, he has the power to detain and search that person, but may not carry out a physical examination of the person's body orifices. A prison officer may not require a person to remove any of his clothing other than an outer coat, jacket, headgear, gloves and footwear. The officer has the power to use force where reasonably necessary. He also has the power to detain the person in the prison so that a police officer may investigate the offence, but such detention shall be not for longer than six hours. The section provides for the determination of that period of six hours and the procedure to be adopted by the officer on detaining the person, including the sending for the parents of anyone who appears to be under 16 years of age.

OFFENCE OF CAUSING INTENTIONAL HARASSMENT, ALARM OR DISTRESS

12.3 Section 154 of the Act adds the Public Order Act 1986, s 4A. A constable may arrest without warrant anyone who he reasonably suspects is committing an offence under that section; the penalties are a maximum of six months' imprisonment and/or a fine not exceeding level 5 on the standard scale on summary conviction. A person is guilty of an offence if, with intent to cause a person harassment, alarm or distress, he—

'(a) uses threatening, abusive or insulting words or behaviour, or disorderly behaviour, or
(b) displays any writing, sign or other visible representation which is threatening, abusive or insulting,
thereby causing that or another person harassment, alarm or distress.'

A defence is available if the accused proves—

'(a) that he was inside a dwelling and had no reason to believe that the words or behaviour used, or the writing, sign or other visible representation displayed, would be heard or seen by a person outside that or any other dwelling, or
(b) that his conduct was reasonable'.

Clearly, a defendant who lives in a block of flats and who begins to rant and rave every time he hears a family from an ethnic minority who live above him descend the stairs, will not be able to avail himself of the defence. On the other hand, if he rants so they can hear him in their flat upstairs this will possibly not fall foul of s 4A.

OFFENCE OF RACIALLY INFLAMMATORY PUBLICATION TO BE ARRESTABLE

12.4   The offence of publishing material likely to stir up racial hatred (the Public Order Act 1986, s 19) is now an arrestable offence; s 155 of the 1994 Act accordingly amends the Police and Criminal Evidence Act 1984, s 24(2).

PROHIBITION ON THE USE OF CELLS FROM EMBRYOS OR FOETUSES

12.5   Section 156 of the 1994 Act adds the Human Fertilisation and Embryology Act 1990, s 3A. It makes it an offence for a person, for the purpose of providing fertility services to any woman, to use female germ cells (which provide immature foetal eggs) taken or derived from an embryo or foetus, or use embryos created by using such cells.

INCREASE IN CERTAIN PENALTIES

12.6   Section 157 increases the maximum fines and terms of imprisonment for the offences listed in Sch 8 to the 1994 Act. These include certain sea fisheries offences and offences under the Firearms (Northern Ireland) Order 1981[1]. However, practitioners will generally be more interested in the increases of maximum fines under the Misuse of Drugs Act 1971, and increases in terms of imprisonment under the Firearms Act 1982. For example, the maximum term for possessing a shortened shotgun goes up from five to seven years as does the penalty for converting such a gun.

---

1   SI 1981/155.

EXTRADITION

12.7   The purpose of s 158 of the 1994 Act is to cure an anomaly in the Extradition Act 1989. Special provision can now be made for the documentation to be provided in support of extradition requests made by countries in respect of which the requirement to produce prima facie evidence has been removed. Put in simpler language, countries with extradition arrangements under the European Convention on Human Rights may submit 'information' rather than 'evidence' to justify the request for the issue of a warrant of arrest or for a request for a provisional arrest. There are also provisions relating to the move from committal proceedings to transfer proceedings.

12.8 The Backing of Warrants (Republic of Ireland) Act 1965 is amended by s 159 of the 1994 Act to allow for action to be taken against people on their way to the United Kingdom as well as those already here. It also removes the bar on proceedings in respect of tax, duty and exchange offences. The life of provisional arrest warrants is extended from five to seven years, and the maximum period of remand under a provisional warrant is extended from three to seven days. As in the previous section there is a technical change relating to transfer proceedings.

CONSTABULARY POWERS IN UK WATERS

12.9 Section 160 amends the Police Act 1964, s 19, and is similar to the amendment of the Police (Scotland) Act 1967, s 17, relating to the area in which a constable's powers and privileges are exercisable. These powers and privileges now extend to the adjacent UK waters. UK waters means, for the purposes of the section, the sea and other waters within the seaward limits of the territorial sea.

INFORMATION HELD ON COMPUTER

12.10 Under s 161, a new offence of procuring the disclosure of computer-held personal information has been created by amending the Data Protection Act 1984, s 5. The section also provides that a person who sells personal data shall be guilty of an offence if he has procured the disclosure of the data to him. Furthermore, a person who offers to sell personal data procured or to be procured by him is also guilty of an offence. Section 162 amends the Computer Misuse Act 1990, s 10 (the offence of unauthorised access); accordingly that offence shall not apply to law enforcement officers where they are investigating crime such as computer pornography.

CCTV BY LOCAL AUTHORITIES

12.11 Under s 163 of the 1994 Act, local authorities are empowered to use closed-circuit television for the purposes of promoting the prevention of crime or the welfare of victims of crime. Before such arrangements are made the local authority must consult with the chief officer of police for the police area in which the step is to be taken. In Scotland 'chief of police' for the purposes of this section, means the chief constable of a police force maintained for that area.

SERIOUS FRAUD

12.12 The Serious Fraud Office is given extended powers under s 164 of the 1994 Act to investigate serious fraud in Scotland. It may be, however, that unless there is a turn around in the fortune of the office in prosecuting high profile cases, there will soon be no Serious Fraud Office to undertake such an investigation

COPYRIGHT AND ILLICIT RECORDINGS: ENFORCEMENT OF OFFENCES

12.13   Section 165 of the Act adds the Copyright, Designs and Patents Act 1988, ss 107A, 198A. It is now the duty of local weights and measures authorities (in the form of trading standards officers) to enforce the provisions of s 107 (offences relating to copyright and s 198 (offences relating to illicit recordings) within their area.

TICKET TOUTS

12.14   The problem of ticket touts has caused a problem for the police and courts for a long time. In general, touts at football, rugby and, less often, Wimbledon have caused a nuisance and sometimes a danger by attracting around them a crowd who have not got a ticket to enter the ground and wish to buy one. More recently another problem has arisen. There has been a recurrence of violence between rival football supporters and often the clubs and police go to some lengths to try and keep the warring factions apart. Touts can, either by design or error, sell tickets to the wrong people for the wrong end of the ground. It was said that in the past the Glasgow Rangers fans were behind one goal and the Celtic supporters behind the other. At half time they switched ends and woe betide anyone who was left behind. The Hillsborough tragedy increased the feeling that there was a real need for something to be done about the scalpers. During the debate at Committee Stage, wide ranging suggestions were canvassed including the possibility of extending the legislation to opera ticket touts but, when it came down to it, football stood alone. Section 166 makes it an offence for an unauthorised person to sell, or offer or expose for sale, a ticket for a designated football match (ie one designated under the Football (Offences) Act 1991, s 1(1)) in any public place or place to which the public have access or, in the course of a trade or business, in any other place. The offence is an arrestable one, and the power of search under the Police and Criminal Evidence Act 1984, s 32, is available. A person found guilty of this offence is liable to a fine not exceeding level 5 on the standard scale on summary conviction.

12.15   Mini-cab wars have become a feature of the taxi-driving business. First, the licensed black cab drivers took umbrage at what they saw as the erosion of their livelihood by mini-cab drivers and subsequently organised crime moved into certain areas in the form of protection rackets and the hi-jacking of rival vehicles. More recently, with the technology available through mobile phones, trouble has broken out near late night discos as rival concerns fight for business. Section 167 provides that it is an offence, in a public place, to solicit persons to hire vehicles to carry them as passengers. On summary conviction the maximum penalty is a fine not exceeding level 4 on the standard scale, ie £2,500. No offence is committed under this section where the soliciting is for persons to share licensed taxis under a scheme made under the Transport Act 1985, s 10, or where the soliciting is for passengers for a public service vehicle on behalf of the holder of a PSV operator's licence. The offence is an arrestable offence under the Police and Criminal Evidence Act 1984, s 24(2).

GENERAL PROVISIONS

12.16   Section 168 provides for the amendments and repeals set out in Schs 9–11 to have effect. Schedule 9, para 6 amends the Criminal Justice Act 1967, ss 9(8), 11(7), and the Road Traffic Offenders Act 1988, s 1. Written statements, notices of alibi and notices of intended prosecution may be served by first class post. The irrebuttable presumption that notices of intended prosecution have arrived will only apply if sent by registered post or recorded delivery to the person's last known address. Schedule 9, para 8 amends the Firearms Act 1968. This has been necessary because of an ambiguity in the Criminal Justice Act 1991, s 90 (protection of prisoner custody officers). Now the offence of assaulting a prisoner custody officer is aggravated by the possession of a firearm or imitation firearm. There are similar amendments in respect of secure training centre custody officers. Robbery is amongst the offences aggravated by possession of a firearm. Schedule 9, para 11 increases the rehabilitation period for probation orders set out in the Rehabilitation of Offenders Act 1974 to five years. Schedule 9, para 15 amends the Magistrates' Courts Act 1980, s 38, so that those courts can commit offenders aged between 18 and 20 to the Crown Court for sentence where a longer custodial sentence is required to protect the public from serious harm from a sexual or violent offender. Schedule 9, para 34 amends the Criminal Justice Act 1988, s 35, and the Home Secretary will be able to extend the Attorney General's power of referral to a wider range of cases. It is anticipated that this will be used in serious or complex fraud cases and follows the outcry over the sentencing of Roger Levit. Further secondary legislation is required and the extension in serious and complex cases is likely to occur in early 1995. Schedule 9, para 40 is of particular interest to practitioners. The Criminal Justice Act 1991, ss 3, 7, are amended so that there is an increase in the courts' discretion to dispense with the requirement to obtain a pre-sentence report. In the case of a juvenile, the extension of that discretion is subject to a previous report on the offender having already been obtained and the court having regard to that report, or if, as is likely to be the case, there is more than one report, to the latest of them. Schedule 9, para 41 will allow electronically monitored curfew orders. Trials will take place in the City of Manchester, the Borough of Reading and the County of Norfolk. The trials are likely to commence in March or April 1995 and are likely to last for nine months. Schedule 9, para 44 amends s 29 of the 1991 Act (consequences of offending whilst on bail) so that a conditional and absolute discharge become an offence. It should be noted that the confiscation provisions in the Criminal Justice Act 1993, Pts II–IV have not yet been implemented; they will be brought into force in conjunction with the amendments made by Sch 9, paras 28, 53 as part of the Drug Trafficking (Consolidation) Act 1994. That Act received Royal Assent on the same day as the Criminal Justice and Public Order Act 1994 and comes into force three months from that date. Schedule 10, para 63 ensures that the consent of the Director of Private Prosecutions is required before prosecutions can be brought for the three new terrorist offences created by ss 81–83 of the 1994 Act. Under s 169, statutory authority is given for the Secretary of State to, with the consent of the Treasury, make payments or grants to such people as he considers appropriate in connection with measures intended to prevent crime or reduce the fear of it. Whilst it might appear innovatory and laudable to have the intention of making such grants, particularly those which will prevent the use of drugs and the growth of drug addiction, in substance it is a technical measure to avoid reliance on the general provisions of the Appropriation Acts.

12.17   Section 170 provides statutory authority for making grants to the main political parties for security measures at party conferences. Grants will be payable in relation to qualifying political parties, ie those with at least two members elected to the House of

Commons, or which has one member elected and a total of not less than 150,000 votes. The sums of money involved are quite considerable. The total cost paid to the main political parties was £345,000 in 1989-90, rising to £688,000 in 1992-93. In the past, payments were dealt with under the Appropriation Acts. In principle the money will not be used to reimburse the local police force but to deal with situations such as the temporary closure of shops in the vicinity or to compensate a hotel which has had to refuse bookings whilst the conference is in progress. Section 171 deals with expenses under the 1994 Act. It provides for Parliament to pay any sums required by the Secretary of State for making payments under contracts entered into under a number of sections of the Act, and other expenses.

12.18   The final section of the Act is s 172 which deals with its short title, commencement and extent. Subsection (1) provides that the Act shall be cited as the Criminal Justice and Public Order Act 1994. Subsections (2)–(4), (6) provide that the following sections came into force on the passing of the Act (3 November 1994): ie ss 5–15 and Schs 1 and 2 (the provision, management etc of secure training centres); s 61 (the power to remove trespassers on land); s 65 (the power to stop people proceeding to raves); ss 68–71 (the sections dealing with aggravated trespass and trespassory assemblies); ss 77–80 (the powers to remove unauthorised campers); s 81 (power to stop and search vehicles and persons in relation to terrorism); s 83 (investigation into the activities and financial resources of terrorist organisations); s 90 (the criteria for suitability to which special regard is to be had for video recordings); Pt VIII, Chs I, II, ie (ss 93–101 and 126–128) (relating to prison escorts in England and Wales and the prison service in England and Wales and Northern Ireland); ss 142–148 (sexual offences); s 150 (power to recall prisoners on licence); s 158(1), (3), (4) (extradition); s 166 (ticket touts); s 167 (touting for hire car services); s 171 (expenses); Sch 9, para 46 (discretionary life prisoners); some consequential amendments and repeals in Schs 10 and 11; and s 172. Section 82 (offences relating to terrorism) will come force on 3 January 1995, and the remainder of the Act shall come into force on such day or days as the Secretary of State (or in the case of ss 52, 53, the Lord Chancellor) may appoint. Subject to the numerous exceptions set out in s 172(7)–(16), this Act applies to England and Wales only.

Appendix 1

Criminal Justice and Public Order Act 1994

Criminal Justice and Public Order Act 1994

(1994 c 33)

ARRANGEMENT OF SECTIONS

PART I

YOUNG OFFENDERS

Secure training orders

PART II

BAIL

PART III

COURSE OF JUSTICE: EVIDENCE, PROCEDURE, ETC

Imputations on character

Corroboration

Inferences from accused's silence

Juries

Procedure, jurisdiction and powers of magistrates' courts

Sentencing: guilty pleas

Publication of reports in young offender cases

An Act to make further provision in relation to criminal justice (including employment in the prison service); to amend or extend the criminal law and powers for preventing crime and enforcing that law; to amend the Video Recordings Act 1984; and for purposes connected with those purposes.

[3 November 1994]

Parliamentary debates.
House of Commons:
2nd Reading 11 January 1994: 235 HC Official Report (6th series) col 20.
Committee Stage 18 January–15 March 1994: HC Official Report, SC B (Criminal Justice and Public Order Bill); 21 February 1994: 238 HC Official Report (6th series) col 23.
Remaining Stages 28 March 1994: 240 HC Official Report (6th series) col 649; 12 April 1994: 241 HC Official Report (6th series) col 35; 13 April 1994: 241 HC Official Report (6th series) col 214.
Consideration of Lords Amendments 19 October 1994: 248 HC Official Report (6th series) col 282; 20 October 1994: 248 HC Official Report (6th series) col 445.
House of Lords:
2nd Reading 25 April 1994: 554 HL Official Report (5th series) col 380.
Committee Stage 16 May 1994: 555 Official Report (5th series) col 10; 17 May 1994: 555 HL Official Report (5th series) col 134; 23 May 1994: 555 HL Official Report (5th series) col 482; 24 May 1994: 555 HL Official Report (5th series) col 609; 7 June 1994: 555 HL Official Report (5th series) col 1085; 14 June 1994: 555 HL Official Report (5th series) col 1589; 16 June 1994: 555 HL Official Report (5th

series) col 1818; 20 June 1994: 556 HL Official Report (5th series) col 10; 21 June 1994: 556 HL Official Report (5th series) col 179.

Report 5 July 1994: 556 HL Official Report (5th series) col 1141; 7 July 1994: 556 HL Official Report (5th series) col 1386; 11 July 1994: 556 HL Official Report (5th series) col 1516; 12 July 1994: 556 HL Official Report (5th series) col 1643.

3rd Reading 19 July 1994: 557 HL Official Report (5th series) col 141.

Consideration of Commons Amendments and Reasons 25 October 1994: 558 HL Official Report (5th series) col 445.

PART I
YOUNG OFFENDERS

Secure training orders

1   Secure training orders

(1)   Subject to section 8(1) of the Criminal Justice Act 1982 and section 53(1) of the Children and Young Persons Act 1933 (sentences of custody for life and long term detention), where—

(a)   a person of not less than 12 but under 15 years of age is convicted of an imprisonable offence; and

(b)   the court is satisfied of the matters specified in subsection (5) below,

the court may make a secure training order.

(2)   A secure training order is an order that the offender in respect of whom it is made shall be subject to a period of detention in a secure training centre followed by a period of supervision.

(3)   The period of detention and supervision shall be such as the court determines and specifies in the order, being not less than six months nor more than two years.

(4)   The period of detention which the offender is liable to serve under a secure training order shall be one half of the total period specified by the court in making the order.

(5)   The court shall not make a secure training order unless it is satisfied—

(a)   that the offender was not less than 12 years of age when the offence for which he is to be dealt with by the court was committed;

(b)   that the offender has been convicted of three or more imprisonable offences; and

(c)   that the offender, either on this or a previous occasion—

(i)   has been found by a court to be in breach of a supervision order under the Children and Young Persons Act 1969, or

(ii)   has been convicted of an imprisonable offence committed whilst he was subject to such a supervision order.

(6)   A secure training order is a custodial sentence for the purposes of sections 1 to 4 of the Criminal Justice Act 1991 (restrictions etc as to custodial sentences).

(7)   Where a court makes a secure training order, it shall be its duty to state in open court that it is of the opinion that the conditions specified in subsection (5) above are satisfied.

(8)   In this section "imprisonable offence" means an offence (not being one for which the sentence is fixed by law) which is punishable with imprisonment in the case of a person aged 21 or over.

(9)   For the purposes of this section, the age of a person shall be deemed to be that which it appears to the court to be after considering any available evidence.

(10)   This section shall have effect, as from the day appointed for each of the following paragraphs, with the substitution in subsections (1) and (5)—

    (a)   of "14" for "12";

    (b)   of "13" for "14";

    (c)   of "12" for "13";

but no substitution may be brought into force on more than one occasion.

References   See paras 1.4, 1.5.

2   Secure training orders: supplementary provisions as to detention

(1)   The following provisions apply in relation to a person ("the offender") in respect of whom a secure training order ("the order") has been made under section 1.

(2)   Where accommodation for the offender at a secure training centre is not immediately available—

    (a)   the court may commit the offender to such place and on such conditions—

        (i)   as the Secretary of State may direct, or

        (ii)   as the Secretary of State may arrange with a person to whom this sub-paragraph applies,

    and for such period (not exceeding 28 days) as the court may specify or until his transfer to a secure training centre, if earlier;

    (b)   if no such accommodation becomes or will become available before the expiry of the period of the committal the court may, on application, extend the period of committal (subject to the restriction referred to in paragraph (a) above); and

    (c)   the period of detention in the secure training centre under the order shall be reduced by the period spent by the offender in such a place.

(3)   The power conferred by subsection (2)(b) above may, subject to section 1(4), be exercised from time to time and the reference in subsection (2)(b) to the expiry of the period of the committal is, in the case of the initial extension, a reference to the expiry of the period of the committal under subsection (2)(a) above and, in the case of a further extension, a reference to the expiry of the period of the previous committal by virtue of this subsection.

(4)   Where the circumstances of the case require, the Secretary of State may transfer the offender from a secure training centre to such other place and on such conditions—

    (a)   as the Secretary of State may direct, or

    (b)   as the Secretary of State may arrange with a person to whom this paragraph applies;

and the period of detention in the secure training centre under the order shall be reduced by the period spent by the offender in such a place.

(5)   The persons to whom subsections (2)(a)(ii) and (4)(b) apply are local authorities, voluntary organisations and persons carrying on a registered childrens' home.

(6)   Where the Secretary of State is satisfied that exceptional circumstances exist which justify the offender's release on compassionate grounds he may release the

offender from the secure training centre; and the offender shall, on his release, be subject to supervision for the remainder of the term of the order.

(7)   A person detained in pursuance of directions or arrangements made for his detention shall be deemed to be in legal custody.

(8)   In this section "local authority", "voluntary organisation" and "registered childrens' home" have the same meaning as in the Children Act 1989.

Definitions   For "secure training order", see s 1; for "secure training centre", see the Prison Act 1952, s 43(1)(d), as inserted by s 5(1), (2) of this Act; for "the offender" and "the order", see sub-s (1) above; for "local authority", "registered childrens' home" and "voluntary organisation", see sub-s (8) above.
References   See para 1.6.

---

3   Supervision under secure training order

(1)   The following provisions apply as respects the period of supervision of a person ("the offender") subject to a secure training order.

(2)   The offender shall be under the supervision of a probation officer, a social worker of a local authority social services department or such other person as the Secretary of State may designate.

(3)   The category of person to supervise the offender shall be determined from time to time by the Secretary of State.

(4)   Where the supervision is to be provided by a social worker of a local authority social services department, the social worker shall be a social worker of the local authority within whose area the offender resides for the time being.

(5)   Where the supervision is to be provided by a probation officer, the probation officer shall be an officer appointed for or assigned to the petty sessions area within which the offender resides for the time being.

(6)   The probation committee or local authority shall be entitled to recover from the Secretary of State the expenses reasonably incurred by them in discharging their duty under this section.

(7)   The offender shall be given a notice from the Secretary of State specifying—
    (a)   the category of person for the time being responsible for his supervision; and
    (b)   any requirements with which he must for the time being comply.

(8)   A notice under subsection (7) above shall be given to the offender—
    (a)   before the commencement of the period of supervision; and
    (b)   before any alteration in the matters specified in subsection (7)(a) or (b) comes into effect.

(9)   The Secretary of State may by statutory instrument make rules for regulating the supervision of the offender.

(10)   The power to make rules under subsection (9) above includes power to make provision in the rules by the incorporation by reference of provisions contained in other documents.

(11)   A statutory instrument made under subsection (9) above shall be subject to annulment in pursuance of a resolution of either House of Parliament.

(12)   The sums required by the Secretary of State for making payments under subsection (6) shall be defrayed out of money provided by Parliament.

Definitions For "secure training order", see s 1; for "the offender", see sub-s (1) above.
References See para 1.7.

4 Breaches of requirements of supervision of persons subject to secure training orders

(1) Where a secure training order has been made as respects an offender and it appears on information to a justice of the peace acting for a relevant petty sessions area that the offender has failed to comply with requirements under section 3(7)(b) the justice may issue a summons requiring the offender to appear at the place and time specified in the summons before a youth court acting for the area or, if the information is in writing and on oath, may issue a warrant for the offender's arrest requiring him to be brought before such a court.

(2) For the purposes of this section a petty sessions area is a relevant petty sessions area in relation to a secure training order—
    (a) if the secure training centre is situated in it;
    (b) if the order was made by a youth court acting for it; or
    (c) if the offender resides in it for the time being.

(3) If it is proved to the satisfaction of the youth court before which an offender appears or is brought under this section that he has failed to comply with requirements under section 3(7)(b) that court may—
    (a) order the offender to be detained in a secure training centre for such period, not exceeding the shorter of three months or the remainder of the period of the secure training order, as the court may specify, or
    (b) impose on the offender a fine not exceeding level 3 on the standard scale.

(4) Where accommodation for an offender in relation to whom the court decides to exercise their powers under subsection (3)(a) above is not immediately available, paragraphs (a), (b) and (c) of subsection (2) and subsections (5), (7) and (8) of section 2 shall apply in relation to him as they apply in relation to an offender in respect of whom a secure training order is made.

(5) For the purposes of this section references to a failure to comply include references to a contravention.

Definitions For "secure training order", see s 1; for "secure training centre", see the Prison Act 1952, s 43(1)(d), as inserted by s 5(1), (2) of this Act; for "relevant petty sessions area", see sub-s (2) above; for "failure to comply", see sub-s (5) above.

5 Provision etc of secure training centres

(1) Section 43 of the Prison Act 1952 (which enables certain institutions for young offenders to be provided and applies provisions of the Act to them) shall be amended as follows.

(2) In subsection (1), after paragraph (c), there shall be inserted the following paragraph, preceded by the word "and"—

    "(d) secure training centres, that is to say places in which offenders not less than 12 but under 17 years of age in respect of whom secure training orders have been made under section 1 of the Criminal

Justice and Public Order Act 1994 may be detained and given training and education and prepared for their release".

(3) After subsection (4), there shall be inserted the following subsection—

"(4A) Sections 16, 22 and 36 of this Act shall apply to secure training centres and to persons detained in them as they apply to prisons and prisoners.".

(4) In subsection (5), for the words "such centres" there shall be substituted the words "centres of the descriptions specified in subsection (4) above".

(5) After subsection (5), there shall be inserted the following subsection—

"(5A) The other provisions of this Act preceding this section, except sections 5, 5A, 6(2) and (3), 12, 14, 19, 25, 28 and 37(2) and (3) above, shall apply to secure training centres and to persons detained in them as they apply to prisons and prisoners, but subject to such adaptations and modifications as may be specified in rules made by the Secretary of State.".

Definitions   For "prisons", see the Prison Act 1952, s 53(1).

6   Management of secure training centres

(1)   Section 47 of the Prison Act 1952 (rules for the regulation and management of prisons and certain institutions for young offenders) shall be amended as follows.

(2)   In subsection (1), for the words between "remand centres" and "respectively", there shall be substituted the words ", young offender institutions or secure training centres".

(3)   After subsection (4), there shall be inserted the following subsection—

"(4A) Rules made under this section shall provide for the inspection of secure training centres and the appointment of independent persons to visit secure training centres and to whom representations may be made by offenders detained in secure training centres.".

(4)   In subsection (5), for the words between "remand centre" and "not" there shall be substituted the words ", young offender institution or secure training centre".

Definitions   For "secure training centre" and "young offender institution", see the Prison Act 1952, s 43(1), as amended by s 5(1), (2) of this Act.

7   Contracting out of secure training centres

(1)   The Secretary of State may enter into a contract with another person for the provision or running (or the provision and running) by him, or (if the contract so provides) for the running by sub-contractors of his, of any secure training centre or part of a secure training centre.

(2)   While a contract for the running of a secure training centre or part of a secure training centre is in force the centre or part shall be run subject to and in accordance with the Prison Act 1952 and in accordance with secure training centre rules subject to such adaptations and modifications as the Secretary of State may specify in relation to contracted out secure training centres.

(3)   Where the Secretary of State grants a lease or tenancy of land for the purposes of any contract under this section, none of the following enactments shall apply to it, namely—

    (a)   Part II of the Landlord and Tenant Act 1954 (security of tenure);

    (b)   section 146 of the Law of Property Act 1925 (restrictions on and relief against forfeiture); and

    (c)   section 19 of the Landlord and Tenant Act 1927 and the Landlord and Tenant Act 1988 (covenants not to assign etc).

In this subsection "lease or tenancy" includes an underlease or sub-tenancy.

(4)   In this section—

    (a)   the reference to the Prison Act 1952 is a reference to that Act as it applies to secure training centres by virtue of section 43 of that Act; and

    (b)   the reference to secure training centre rules is a reference to rules made under section 47 of that Act for the regulation and management of secure training centres.

Definitions   For "secure training centre", see the Prison Act 1952, s 43(1)(d), as inserted by s 5(1), (2) of this Act; for "contracted out secure training centre" and "sub-contractor", see s 15; for "the Prison Act 1952" and "secure training centre rules", see sub-s (4) above.
References   See para 1.8.

8   Officers of contracted out secure training centres

(1)   Instead of a governor, every contracted out secure training centre shall have—

    (a)   a director, who shall be a custody officer appointed by the contractor and specially approved for the purposes of this section by the Secretary of State; and

    (b)   a monitor, who shall be a Crown servant appointed by the Secretary of State;

and every officer of such a secure training centre who performs custodial duties shall be a custody officer who is authorised to perform such duties or an officer of a directly managed secure training centre who is temporarily attached to the secure training centre.

(2)   The director shall have such functions as are conferred on him by the Prison Act 1952 as it applies to secure training centres and as may be conferred on him by secure training centre rules.

(3)   The monitor shall have such functions as may be conferred on him by secure training centre rules and shall be under a duty—

    (a)   to keep under review, and report to the Secretary of State on, the running of the secure training centre by or on behalf of the director; and

    (b)   to investigate, and report to the Secretary of State on, any allegations made against custody officers performing custodial duties at the secure training centre or officers of directly managed secure training centres who are temporarily attached to the secure training centre.

(4)   The contractor and any sub-contractor of his shall each be under a duty to do all that he reasonably can (whether by giving directions to the officers of the secure training centre or otherwise) to facilitate the exercise by the monitor of all such functions as are mentioned in or imposed by subsection (3) above.

Definitions   For "secure training centre", see the Prison Act 1952, s 43(1)(d), as inserted by s 5(1), (2) of this Act; for "secure training centre rules", see s 7(4)(b); for "custody officer", see s 12(3); for "contracted out secure training centre", "the contractor", "custodial duties", "directly managed secure training centre" and "sub-contractor", see s 15.
References   See para 1.9.

9 Powers and duties of custody officers employed at contracted out secure training centres

(1) A custody officer performing custodial duties at a contracted out secure training centre shall have the following powers, namely—

(a) to search in accordance with secure training centre rules any offender who is detained in the secure training centre; and

(b) to search any other person who is in or who is seeking to enter the secure training centre, and any article in the possession of such a person.

(2) The powers conferred by subsection (1)(b) above to search a person shall not be construed as authorising a custody officer to require a person to remove any of his clothing other than an outer coat, headgear, jacket or gloves.

(3) A custody officer performing custodial duties at a contracted out secure training centre shall have the following duties as respects offenders detained in the secure training centre, namely—

(a) to prevent their escape from lawful custody;

(b) to prevent, or detect and report on, the commission or attempted commission by them of other unlawful acts;

(c) to ensure good order and discipline on their part; and

(d) to attend to their well-being.

(4) The powers conferred by subsection (1) above, and the powers arising by virtue of subsection (3) above, shall include power to use reasonable force where necessary.

Definitions   For "secure training centre", see the Prison Act 1952, s 43(1)(d), as inserted by s 5(1), (2) of this Act; for "secure training centre rules", see s 7(4)(b); for "custody officer", see s 12(3); for "contracted out secure training centre" and "custodial duties", see s 15.
References   See para 1.10.

10 Intervention by Secretary of State in management of contracted out secure training centres

(1) This section applies where, in the case of a contracted out secure training centre, it appears to the Secretary of State—

(a) that the director has lost, or is likely to lose, effective control of the secure training centre or any part of it; and

(b) that the making of an appointment under subsection (2) below is necessary in the interests of preserving the safety of any person, or of preventing serious damage to any property.

(2) The Secretary of State may appoint a Crown servant to act as governor of the secure training centre for the period—

(a) beginning with the time specified in the appointment; and

(b) ending with the time specified in the notice of termination under subsection (4) below.

(3) During that period—

(a) all the functions which would otherwise be exercisable by the director or monitor shall be exercisable by the governor;

(b) the contractor and any sub-contractor of his shall each do all that he reasonably can to facilitate the exercise by the governor of those functions; and

    (c)   the officers of the secure training centre shall comply with any directions given by the governor in the exercise of those functions.

(4)   Where the Secretary of State is satisfied—

    (a)   that the governor has secured effective control of the secure training centre or, as the case may be, the relevant part of it; and

    (b)   that the governor's appointment is no longer necessary for the purpose mentioned in subsection (1)(b) above,

he shall, by a notice to the governor, terminate the appointment at a time specified in the notice.

(5)   As soon as practicable after making or terminating an appointment under this section, the Secretary of State shall give a notice of the appointment, or a copy of the notice of termination, to the contractor, any sub-contractor of his, the director and the monitor.

Definitions   For "secure training centre", see the Prison Act 1952, s 43(1)(d), as inserted by s 5(1), (2) of this Act; for "contracted out secure training centre", "the contractor" and "sub-contractor", see s 15.
References   See para 1.11.

---

11 Contracted out functions at directly managed secure training centres

(1)   The Secretary of State may enter into a contract with another person for any functions at a directly managed secure training centre to be performed by custody officers who are provided by that person and are authorised to perform custodial duties.

(2)   Section 9 shall apply in relation to a custody officer performing contracted out functions at a directly managed secure training centre as it applies in relation to such an officer performing custodial duties at a contracted out secure training centre.

(3)   In relation to a directly managed secure training centre, the reference in section 13(2) of the Prison Act 1952 (legal custody of prisoners) as it applies to secure training centres to an officer of the prison shall be construed as including a reference to a custody officer performing custodial duties at the secure training centre in pursuance of a contract under this section.

(4)   Any reference in subsections (1), (2) and (3) above to the performance of functions or custodial duties at a directly managed secure training centre includes a reference to the performance of functions or such duties for the purposes of, or for purposes connected with, such a secure training centre.

Definitions   For "secure training centre", see the Prison Act 1952, s 43(1)(d), as inserted by s 5(1), (2) of this Act; for "custody officer", see s 12(3); for "contracted out functions", "contracted out secure training centre", "custodial duties" and "directly managed secure training centre", see s 15. Note as to the performance of functions or custodial duties at a directly managed secure training centre, sub-s (4) above.
References   See para 1.11.

---

12 Escort arrangements and officers

(1)   The provisions of Schedule 1 to this Act (which make provision for escort arrangements for offenders detained at a secure training centre) shall have effect.

(2)   The provisions of Schedule 2 to this Act shall have effect with respect to the certification of custody officers.

(3)   In this Part, "custody officer" means a person in respect of whom a certificate is for the time being in force certifying—

    (a)   that he has been approved by the Secretary of State for the purpose of performing escort functions or custodial duties or both in relation to offenders in respect of whom secure training orders have been made; and

    (b)   that he is accordingly authorised to perform them.

Definitions   For "custodial duties", see s 15; for "escort functions", see Sch 1, para 1.
References   See para 1.12.

13 Protection of custody officers at secure training centres

(1)   Any person who assaults a custody officer—

    (a)   acting in pursuance of escort arrangements;

    (b)   performing custodial duties at a contracted out secure training centre; or

    (c)   performing contracted out functions at a directly managed secure training centre,

shall be liable on summary conviction to a fine not exceeding level 5 on the standard scale or to imprisonment for a term not exceeding six months or to both.

(2)   Any person who resists or wilfully obstructs a custody officer—

    (a)   acting in pursuance of escort arrangements;

    (b)   performing custodial duties at a contracted out secure training centre; or

    (c)   performing contracted out functions at a directly managed secure training centre,

shall be liable on summary conviction to a fine not exceeding level 3 on the standard scale.

(3)   For the purposes of this section, a custody officer shall not be regarded as acting in pursuance of escort arrangements at any time when he is not readily identifiable as such an officer (whether by means of a uniform or badge which he is wearing or otherwise).

Definitions   For "custody officer", see s 12(3); for "contracted out functions", "contracted out secure training centre", "custodial duties" and "directly managed secure training centre", see s 15; for "escort arrangements", see Sch 1, para 1; for "acting in pursuance of escort arrangements", see sub-s (3) above.
References   See para 1.13.

14 Wrongful disclosure of information relating to offenders detained at secure training centres

(1)   A person who—

    (a)   is or has been employed (whether as a custody officer or otherwise) in pursuance of escort arrangements or at a contracted out secure training centre; or

    (b)   is or has been employed to perform contracted out functions at a directly managed secure training centre,

commits an offence if he discloses, otherwise than in the course of his duty or as authorised by the Secretary of State, any information which he acquired in the course of his employment and which relates to a particular offender detained at a secure training centre.

(2)   A person guilty of an offence under subsection (1) above shall be liable—

    (a)   on conviction on indictment, to imprisonment for a term not exceeding two years or a fine or both;

(b)   on summary conviction, to imprisonment for a term not exceeding six months or a fine not exceeding the statutory maximum or both.

Definitions   For "custody officer", see s 12(3) of this Act; for "contracted out functions", "contracted out secure training centre" and "directly managed secure training centre", see s 15 of this Act; for "escort arrangements", see Sch 1, para 1.
References   See para 1.14.

15 Interpretation of sections 7 to 14

In sections 7 to 14—

"contracted out functions" means any functions which, by virtue of a contract under section 11, fall to be performed by custody officers;

"contracted out secure training centre" means a secure training centre or part of a secure training centre in respect of which a contract under section 7(1) is for the time being in force;

"the contractor", in relation to a contracted out secure training centre, means the person who has contracted with the Secretary of State for the provision or running (or the provision and running) of it;

"custodial duties" means custodial duties at a secure training centre;

"directly managed secure training centre" means a secure training centre which is not a contracted out secure training centre;

"escort arrangements" means the arrangements specified in paragraph 1 of Schedule 1 to this Act;

"escort functions" means the functions specified in paragraph 1 of Schedule 1 to this Act;

"escort monitor" means a person appointed under paragraph 2(1)(a) of Schedule 1 to this Act;

"secure training centre rules" has the meaning given by section 7(4)(b); and

"sub-contractor", in relation to a contracted out secure training centre, means a person who has contracted with the contractor for the running of it or any part of it.

Definitions   For "custody officers", see s 12(3) of this Act.
References   See para 1.15.

Custodial sentences for young offenders

16 Long term detention of young offenders

(1)   Section 53 of the Children and Young Persons Act 1933 (which provides for the long term detention of children and young persons for certain grave crimes) shall be amended as follows.

(2)   In subsection (1), for the words after "conditions" there shall be substituted—

"—

(a)   as the Secretary of State may direct, or
(b)   as the Secretary of State may arrange with any person.".

(3)   In subsection (2), for the words from the beginning to the words "and the court" there shall be substituted the following—

"(2)   Subsection (3) below applies—

(a)   where a person of at least 10 but not more than 17 years is convicted on indictment of—

      (i) any offence punishable in the case of an adult with imprisonment for fourteen years or more, not being an offence the sentence for which is fixed by law, or

     (ii) an offence under section 14 of the Sexual Offences Act 1956 (indecent assault on a woman);

  (b) where a young person is convicted of—

      (i) an offence under section 1 of the Road Traffic Act 1988 (causing death by dangerous driving), or

     (ii) an offence under section 3A of the Road Traffic Act 1988 (causing death by careless driving while under influence of drink or drugs).

(3)   Where this subsection applies, then, if the court".

(4)   For the words from "as the" in subsection (3) to the end of the section there shall be substituted—

    "—

  (a) as the Secretary of State may direct, or

  (b) as the Secretary of State may arrange with any person.

(4)   A person detained pursuant to the directions or arrangements made by the Secretary of State under this section shall, while so detained, be deemed to be in legal custody.".

Definitions   For "young person", see the Children and Young Persons Act 1933, s 107(1).
References   See para 1.16.

17 Maximum length of detention for young offenders

(1)   Section 1B of the Criminal Justice Act 1982 (maximum length of detention in young offender institution for offenders aged 15, 16 or 17 years) shall be amended as follows.

(2)   In subsection (2)(b), for the words "12 months" there shall be substituted the words "24 months".

(3)   In subsection (4), for the words "12 months" there shall be substituted the words "24 months".

(4)   In subsection (5), for the words "12 months" in both places where they occur there shall be substituted the words "24 months".

References   See para 1.16.

18 Accommodation of young offenders sentenced to custody for life

(1)   In section 1C of the Criminal Justice Act 1982 (young offenders sentenced to detention in a young offender institution to be detained in such an institution unless the Secretary of State otherwise directs)—

  (a) in subsection (1), after the words "young offender institution" there shall be inserted the words "or to custody for life" and for the words "such an institution" there shall be substituted the words "a young offender institution"; and

  (b) in subsection (2), after the words "in a young offender institution" there shall be inserted the words "or to custody for life".

(2)   Subsections (6) and (7) of section 12 of the Criminal Justice Act 1982 (which provide for the detention of young offenders sentenced to custody for life in a prison unless the Secretary of State otherwise directs) are hereby repealed.

(3)   In section 43(1) of the Prison Act 1952 (which relates to the institutions for the detention of young offenders which may be provided by the Secretary of State), in paragraph (aa), at the end, there shall be inserted the words "or to custody for life".

Definitions   For "young offender institution", see the Prison Act 1952, s 43(1), as inserted by the Criminal Justice Act 1982, s 170(1), Sch 15, para 11, and amended by sub-s (3) of this section.
References   See para 1.16.

Secure accommodation for certain young persons

19 Extension of kinds of secure accommodation

(1)   Section 23 of the Children and Young Persons Act 1969 (remands and committals to local authority accommodation) shall be amended by the insertion, in subsection (12), in the definition of "secure accommodation", after the words "community home", of the words ", a voluntary home or a registered children's home", and, at the end of that subsection, of the words "but, for the purposes of the definition of "secure accommodation", "local authority accommodation" includes any accommodation falling within section 61(2) of the Criminal Justice Act 1991.".

(2)   In the Children Act 1989, Schedules 5 and 6 (which provide for the regulation of voluntary homes and registered childrens' homes respectively) shall be amended as follows, that is to say—

    (a)   in Schedule 5, in paragraph 7(2) (regulations as to conduct of voluntary homes)—

        (i)   head (f) (power to prohibit provision of secure accommodation) shall be omitted; and

        (ii)   after that head, there shall be inserted the following—

"(ff)   require the approval of the Secretary of State for the provision and use of accommodation for the purpose of restricting the liberty of children in such homes and impose other requirements (in addition to those imposed by section 25) as to the placing of a child in accommodation provided for that purpose, including a requirement to obtain the permission of any local authority who are looking after the child;"; and

    (b)   in Schedule 6, in paragraph 10(2) (regulations as to conduct, etc of registered childrens' homes)—

        (i)   head (j) (power to prohibit use of accommodation as secure accommodation) shall be omitted; and

        (ii)   after that head, there shall be inserted the following—

"(jj)   require the approval of the Secretary of State for the provision and use of accommodation for the purpose of restricting the liberty of children in such homes and impose other requirements (in addition to those imposed by section 25) as to the placing of a child in accommodation provided for that purpose, including a requirement to obtain the permission of any local authority who are looking after the child.".

(3)   In section 61 of the Criminal Justice Act 1991 (provision by local authorities of secure accommodation)—

    (a)   in subsection (2), at the end, there shall be inserted the words "or by making arrangements with voluntary organisations or persons carrying on a registered childrens' home for the provision or use by them of such accommodation or by making arrangements with the Secretary of State for the use by them of a home provided by him under section 82(5) of the Children Act 1989"; and

(b) in subsection (5), at the end, there shall be inserted the words "and expressions, other than "local authority", used in the Children Act 1989 have the same meanings as in that Act.".

Definitions   In the Children Act 1989, for the meaning of "voluntary home", see s 60 of that Act; for the meaning of "registered children's home", see s 63 thereof; for the meaning of "child" and "local authority", see s 105(1) thereof. For the meaning of "registered childrens' home" and "voluntary organisation" in the Criminal Justice Act 1991, s 61(2), as amended by sub-s (3)(a) above, see, by virtue of sub-s (5) of that section, as amended by sub-s (3)(b) above, the Children Act 1989, ss 63, 105(1) respectively.
References   See para 1.17.

20 Secure remands for young offenders

In section 23(5) of the Children and Young Persons Act 1969 (as substituted by section 60 of the Criminal Justice Act 1991) (conditions for imposing a security requirement in case of young persons remanded to local authority accommodation), for the words "young person who has attained the age of fifteen" there shall be substituted the words—

(a) "person who has attained the age of fourteen";
(b) "person who has attained the age of thirteen"; or
(c) "person who has attained the age of twelve";

but no substitution may be brought into force on more than one occasion.

References   See para 1.17.

21 Cost of secure accommodation

After section 61 of the Criminal Justice Act 1991 there shall be inserted the following section—

"61A Cost of secure accommodation

(1)   The Secretary of State may, in relation to any costs incurred by a local authority in discharging their duty under section 61(1) above—

(a) defray such costs to such extent as he considers appropriate in any particular case;
(b) defray a proportion to be determined by him from time to time of such costs; and
(c) defray or contribute to such costs in accordance with a tariff to be determined by him from time to time.

(2)   The Secretary of State may require any person providing secure accommodation to transmit to him, at such times and in such form as he may direct, such particulars as he may require with respect to any costs to which this section applies.

(3)   Payments under this section shall be made out of money provided by Parliament.".

Definitions   For "local authority", see the Children and Young Persons Act 1969, s 70(1).
References   See para 1.17.

22 Management of secure accommodation

(1)   The Children Act 1989 shall be amended as follows.

(2)   In section 53 (provision and management of community homes)—
    (a)   in subsection (3) (homes which may be community homes)—
        (i)   in paragraph (a), for the words "managed, equipped and maintained" there shall be substituted the words "equipped, maintained and (subject to subsection (3A)) managed"; and
        (ii)   in paragraph (b)(i), for the words "management, equipment and maintenance" there shall be substituted the words "equipment, maintenance and (subject to subsection (3B)) management"; and
    (b)   after subsection (3) there shall be inserted the following subsections—

"(3A) A local authority may make arrangements for the management by another person of accommodation provided by the local authority for the purpose of restricting the liberty of children.

(3B)   Where a local authority are to be responsible for the management of a community home provided by a voluntary organisation, the local authority may, with the consent of the body of managers constituted by the instrument of management for the home, make arrangements for the management by another person of accommodation provided for the purpose of restricting the liberty of children.".

(3)   In Part II of Schedule 4 (management of controlled and assisted community homes)—
    (a)   in paragraph 3(4), after the word "managers" there shall be inserted the words ", except in so far as, under section 53(3B), any of the accommodation is to be managed by another person."; and
    (b)   in paragraph 3(5), after the word "body" there shall be inserted the words "; and similarly, to the extent that a contract so provides, as respects anything done, liability incurred or property acquired by a person by whom, under section 53(3B), any of the accommodation is to be managed".

Definitions   For "community home", see the Children Act 1989, s 53(1); for "child", "local authority" and "voluntary organisation", see s 105(1) of that Act.
References   See para 1.17.

Arrest of young persons in breach of conditions of remand

23 Liability of young persons to arrest for breaking conditions of remand

After section 23 of the Children and Young Persons Act 1969 there shall be inserted the following section—

"23A   Liability to arrest for breaking conditions of remand

(1)   A person who has been remanded or committed to local authority accommodation and in respect of whom conditions under subsection (7) or (10) of section 23 of this Act have been imposed may be arrested without warrant by a constable if the constable has reasonable grounds for suspecting that that person has broken any of those conditions.

(2) A person arrested under subsection (1) above—

(a) shall, except where he was arrested within 24 hours of the time appointed for him to appear before the court in pursuance of the remand or committal, be brought as soon as practicable and in any event within 24 hours after his arrest before a justice of the peace for the petty sessions area in which he was arrested; and

(b) in the said excepted case shall be brought before the court before which he was to have appeared.

In reckoning for the purposes of this subsection any period of 24 hours, no account shall be taken of Christmas Day, Good Friday or any Sunday.

(3) A justice of the peace before whom a person is brought under subsection (2) above—

(a) if of the opinion that that person has broken any condition imposed on him under subsection (7) or (10) of section 23 of this Act shall remand him; and that section shall apply as if he was then charged with or convicted of the offence for which he had been remanded or committed;

(b) if not of that opinion shall remand him to the place to which he had been remanded or committed at the time of his arrest subject to the same conditions as those which had been imposed on him at that time.".

Definitions For "court", see the Children and Young Persons Act 1969, s 23(12); for "local authority accommodation" and "petty sessions area", see s 70(1) of that Act.
References See para 1.18.

Police detention of young persons

24 Detention of arrested juveniles after charge

In section 38(6) of the Police and Criminal Evidence Act 1984 (detention of arrested juveniles after charge), in paragraph (b), for the words "age of 15 years" there shall be substituted the words "age of 12 years".

References See para 1.19.

PART II
BAIL

25 No bail for defendants charged with or convicted of homicide or rape after previous conviction of such offences

(1) A person who in any proceedings has been charged with or convicted of an offence to which this section applies in circumstances to which it applies shall not be granted bail in those proceedings.

(2) This section applies, subject to subsection (3) below, to the following offences, that is to say—

(a) murder;

(b) attempted murder;

(c) manslaughter;

(d) rape; or

(e) attempted rape.

(3)   This section applies to a person charged with or convicted of any such offence only if he has been previously convicted by or before a court in any part of the United Kingdom of any such offence or of culpable homicide and, in the case of a previous conviction of manslaughter or of culpable homicide, if he was then sentenced to imprisonment or, if he was then a child or young person, to long-term detention under any of the relevant enactments.

(4)   This section applies whether or not an appeal is pending against conviction or sentence.

(5)   In this section—

"conviction" includes—

(a) a finding that a person is not guilty by reason of insanity;

(b) a finding under section 4A(3) of the Criminal Procedure (Insanity) Act 1964 (cases of unfitness to plead) that a person did the act or made the omission charged against him; and

(c) a conviction of an offence for which an order is made placing the offender on probation or discharging him absolutely or conditionally;

and "convicted" shall be construed accordingly; and

"the relevant enactments" means—

(a) as respects England and Wales, section 53(2) of the Children and Young Persons Act 1933;

(b) as respects Scotland, sections 205 and 206 of the Criminal Procedure (Scotland) Act 1975;

(c) as respects Northern Ireland, section 73(2) of the Children and Young Persons Act (Northern Ireland) 1968.

(6)   This section does not apply in relation to proceedings instituted before its commencement.

Definitions   For "rape", see the Sexual Offences Act 1956, s 1.
References   See para 2.1.

---

26 No right to bail for persons accused or convicted of committing offence while on bail

In Part I of Schedule 1 to the Bail Act 1976 (exceptions to right to bail for imprisonable offences)—

(a) after paragraph 2, there shall be inserted the following paragraph—

"2A. The defendant need not be granted bail if—

(a) the offence is an indictable offence or an offence triable either way; and

(b) it appears to the court that he was on bail in criminal proceedings on the date of the offence."; and

(b) in paragraph 9, after the words "paragraph 2" there shall be inserted the words "or 2A".

Definitions   For "bail" and "bail in criminal proceedings", see the Bail Act 1976, s 1; for "court" and "offence", see s 2(2) of that Act; for "the defendant", see s 4(6) of that Act.
References   See para 2.2.

---

27 Power for police to grant conditional bail to persons charged

(1)   Part IV of the Police and Criminal Evidence Act 1984 (detention of persons, including powers of police to grant bail) shall have effect with the following amendments, that is to say, in section 47 (bail after arrest)—

    (a)   in subsection (1), for the words after "in accordance with" there shall be substituted the words "sections 3, 3A, 5 and 5A of the Bail Act 1976 as they apply to bail granted by a constable"; and

    (b)   after subsection (1) there shall be inserted the following subsection—

"(1A) The normal powers to impose conditions of bail shall be available to him where a custody officer releases a person on bail under section 38(1) above (including that subsection as applied by section 40(10) above) but not in any other cases.

In this subsection, "the normal powers to impose conditions of bail" has the meaning given in section 3(6) of the Bail Act 1976.".

(2)   Section 3 of the Bail Act 1976 (incidents including conditions of bail in criminal proceedings) shall be amended as follows—

    (a)   in subsection (6), the words "(but only by a court)" shall be omitted;

    (b)   at the end of subsection (6) there shall be inserted—

"and, in any Act, "the normal powers to impose conditions of bail" means the powers to impose conditions under paragraph (a), (b) or (c) above";

    (c)   after subsection (9), there shall be inserted the following subsection—

"(10) This section is subject, in its application to bail granted by a constable, to section 3A of this Act.".

(3)   After section 3 of the Bail Act 1976 there shall be inserted the following section—

"3A   Conditions of bail in case of police bail

(1)   Section 3 of this Act applies, in relation to bail granted by a custody officer under Part IV of the Police and Criminal Evidence Act 1984 in cases where the normal powers to impose conditions of bail are available to him, subject to the following modifications.

(2)   Subsection (6) does not authorise the imposition of a requirement to reside in a bail hostel or any requirement under paragraph (d).

(3)   Subsections (6ZA), (6A) and (6B) shall be omitted.

(4)   For subsection (8), substitute the following—

"(8)   Where a custody officer has granted bail in criminal proceedings he or another custody officer serving at the same police station may, at the request of the person to whom it was granted, vary the conditions of bail; and in doing so he may impose conditions or more onerous conditions.".

(5)   Where a constable grants bail to a person no conditions shall be imposed under subsections (4), (5), (6) or (7) of section 3 of this Act unless it appears to the constable that it is necessary to do so for the purpose of preventing that person from—

    (a)   failing to surrender to custody, or

    (b)   committing an offence while on bail, or

    (c)   interfering with witnesses or otherwise obstructing the course of justice, whether in relation to himself or any other person.

(6) Subsection (5) above also applies on any request to a custody officer under subsection (8) of section 3 of this Act to vary the conditions of bail.".

(4) The further amendments contained in Schedule 3 to this Act shall have effect.

Definitions In the Police and Criminal Evidence Act 1984, for "bail", see s 47(3), (4) of that Act; and for "the normal powers to impose conditions of bail", see s 3(6) of the Bail Act 1976, as amended by sub-s (2)(b) above. In the Bail Act 1976, for "bail" and "bail in criminal proceedings", see s 1 of that Act, as repealed in part by s 168(3), Sch 11 of this Act; for "bail hostel", see s 2(2) of the 1976 Act; for "the normal powers to impose conditions of bail", see s 3(6) thereof, as amended by sub-s (2)(b) above.
References See para 2.3.

28 Police detention after charge

(1) Section 38 of the Police and Criminal Evidence Act 1984 (which requires an arrested person charged with an offence to be released except in specified circumstances) shall be amended as follows.

(2) In subsection (1)(a), for sub-paragraphs (ii) and (iii) there shall be substituted the following sub-paragraphs—

"(ii) the custody officer has reasonable grounds for believing that the person arrested will fail to appear in court to answer to bail;

(iii) in the case of a person arrested for an imprisonable offence, the custody officer has reasonable grounds for believing that the detention of the person arrested is necessary to prevent him from committing an offence;

(iv) in the case of a person arrested for an offence which is not an imprisonable offence, the custody officer has reasonable grounds for believing that the detention of the person arrested is necessary to prevent him from causing physical injury to any other person or from causing loss of or damage to property;

(v) the custody officer has reasonable grounds for believing that the detention of the person arrested is necessary to prevent him from interfering with the administration of justice or with the investigation of offences or of a particular offence; or

(vi) the custody officer has reasonable grounds for believing that the detention of the person arrested is necessary for his own protection;".

(3) After subsection (2), there shall be inserted the following subsection—

"(2A) The custody officer, in taking the decisions required by subsection (1)(a) and (b) above (except (a)(i) and (vi) and (b)(ii)), shall have regard to the same considerations as those which a court is required to have regard to in taking the corresponding decisions under paragraph 2 of Part I of Schedule 1 to the Bail Act 1976.".

(4) After subsection (7), there shall be inserted the following subsection—

"(7A) In this section "imprisonable offence" has the same meaning as in Schedule 1 to the Bail Act 1976.".

Definitions For "bail", see the Police and Criminal Evidence Act 1984, s 47(3), (4); for "imprisonable offence", see s 38(7A) of the 1984 Act, as inserted by sub-s (4) above.
References See para 2.4.

29 Power for police to arrest for failure to answer to police bail

(1)   Part IV of the Police and Criminal Evidence Act 1984 (detention of persons, including powers of police to grant bail) shall be amended as follows.

(2)   After section 46 there shall be inserted the following section—

"46A Power of arrest for failure to answer to police bail

(1)   A constable may arrest without a warrant any person who, having been released on bail under this Part of this Act subject to a duty to attend at a police station, fails to attend at that police station at the time appointed for him to do so.

(2)   A person who is arrested under this section shall be taken to the police station appointed as the place at which he is to surrender to custody as soon as practicable after the arrest.

(3)   For the purposes of—
    (a) section 30 above (subject to the obligation in subsection (2) above), and
    (b) section 31 above,
an arrest under this section shall be treated as an arrest for an offence.".

(3)   In section 34 after subsection (6), there shall be inserted the following subsection—

"(7)   For the purposes of this Part of this Act a person who returns to a police station to answer to bail or is arrested under section 46A below shall be treated as arrested for an offence and the offence in connection with which he was granted bail shall be deemed to be that offence.".

(4)   In consequence of the foregoing amendments—
    (a) in section 37(1), paragraph (b) shall be omitted;
    (b) in sections 41(9), 42(11) and 43(19), at the end, there shall be inserted the words "; but this subsection does not prevent an arrest under section 46A below.";
    (c) in section 47, subsection (5) shall be omitted;
    (d) in section 47(6), for the words "is detained under subsection (5) above" there shall be substituted the words "who has been granted bail and either has attended at the police station in accordance with the grant of bail or has been arrested under section 46A above is detained at a police station"; and
    (e) in section 47(7), at the end, there shall be inserted the words "; but this subsection does not apply to a person who is arrested under section 46A above or has attended a police station in accordance with the grant of bail (and who accordingly is deemed by section 34(7) above to have been arrested for an offence).".

(5)   This section applies whether the person released on bail was granted bail before or after the commencement of this section.

Definitions   In the Police and Criminal Evidence Act 1984, Pt IV, for the meaning of "bail" in that Part, see s 47(3), (4) thereof
References   See para 2.4.

30 Reconsideration of decisions granting bail

After the section 5A of the Bail Act 1976 inserted by Schedule 3 to this Act there shall be inserted the following section—

"5B   Reconsideration of decisions granting bail

(1)   Where a magistrates' court has granted bail in criminal proceedings in connection with an offence, or proceedings for an offence, to which this section applies or a constable has granted bail in criminal proceedings in connection with proceedings for such an offence, that court or the appropriate court in relation to the constable may, on application by the prosecutor for the decision to be reconsidered,—

    (a) vary the conditions of bail,

    (b) impose conditions in respect of bail which has been granted unconditionally, or

    (c) withhold bail.

(2)   The offences to which this section applies are offences triable on indictment and offences triable either way.

(3)   No application for the reconsideration of a decision under this section shall be made unless it is based on information which was not available to the court or constable when the decision was taken.

(4)   Whether or not the person to whom the application relates appears before it, the magistrates' court shall take the decision in accordance with section 4(1) (and Schedule 1) of this Act.

(5)   Where the decision of the court on a reconsideration under this section is to withhold bail from the person to whom it was originally granted the court shall—

    (a) if that person is before the court, remand him in custody, and

    (b) if that person is not before the court, order him to surrender himself forthwith into the custody of the court.

(6)   Where a person surrenders himself into the custody of the court in compliance with an order under subsection (5) above, the court shall remand him in custody.

(7)   A person who has been ordered to surrender to custody under subsection (5) above may be arrested without warrant by a constable if he fails without reasonable cause to surrender to custody in accordance with the order.

(8)   A person arrested in pursuance of subsection (7) above shall be brought as soon as practicable, and in any event within 24 hours after his arrest, before a justice of the peace for the petty sessions area in which he was arrested and the justice shall remand him in custody.

In reckoning for the purposes of this subsection any period of 24 hours, no account shall be taken of Christmas Day, Good Friday or any Sunday.

(9)   Magistrates' court rules shall include provision—

    (a) requiring notice of an application under this section and of the grounds for it to be given to the person affected, including notice of the powers available to the court under it;

    (b) for securing that any representations made by the person affected (whether in writing or orally) are considered by the court before making its decision; and

    (c) designating the court which is the appropriate court in relation to the decision of any constable to grant bail.".

Definitions   For "bail" and "bail in criminal proceedings", see the Bail Act 1976, s 1; for "court", "magistrates' court rules" and "offence", see s 2(2) of that Act.
References   See para 2.5.

PART III
COURSE OF JUSTICE: EVIDENCE, PROCEDURE, ETC

Imputations on character

31 Imputations on character

In section 1 of the Criminal Evidence Act 1898 there shall be inserted at the end of sub-paragraph (ii) of paragraph (f) the words "the deceased victim of the alleged crime; or".

References   See para 3.6.

Corroboration

32 Abolition of corroboration rules

(1)   Any requirement whereby at a trial on indictment it is obligatory for the court to give the jury a warning about convicting the accused on the uncorroborated evidence of a person merely because that person is—
  (a)   an alleged accomplice of the accused, or
  (b)   where the offence charged is a sexual offence, the person in respect of whom it is alleged to have been committed,
is hereby abrogated.

(2)   In section 34(2) of the Criminal Justice Act 1988 (abolition of requirement of corroboration warning in respect of evidence of a child) the words from "in relation to" to the end shall be omitted.

(3)   Any requirement that—
  (a)   is applicable at the summary trial of a person for an offence, and
  (b)   corresponds to the requirement mentioned in subsection (1) above or that mentioned in section 34(2) of the Criminal Justice Act 1988,
is hereby abrogated.

(4)   Nothing in this section applies in relation to—
  (a)   any trial, or
  (b)   any proceedings before a magistrates' court as examining justices,
which began before the commencement of this section.

References   See para 3.7.

33 Abolition of corroboration requirements under Sexual Offences Act 1956

(1)   The following provisions of the Sexual Offences Act 1956 (which provide that a person shall not be convicted of the offence concerned on the evidence of one witness only unless the witness is corroborated) are hereby repealed—
  (a)   section 2(2) (procurement of woman by threats),
  (b)   section 3(2) (procurement of woman by false pretences),

      (c)   section 4(2) (administering drugs to obtain or facilitate intercourse),

      (d)   section 22(2) (causing prostitution of women), and

      (e)   section 23(2) (procuration of girl under twenty-one).

  (2)   Nothing in this section applies in relation to—

      (a)   any trial, or

      (b)   any proceedings before a magistrates' court as examining justices,

which began before the commencement of this section.

References   See para 3.7.

Inferences from accused's silence

34 Effect of accused's failure to mention facts when questioned or charged

  (1)   Where, in any proceedings against a person for an offence, evidence is given that the accused—

      (a)   at any time before he was charged with the offence, on being questioned under caution by a constable trying to discover whether or by whom the offence had been committed, failed to mention any fact relied on in his defence in those proceedings; or

      (b)   on being charged with the offence or officially informed that he might be prosecuted for it, failed to mention any such fact,

being a fact which in the circumstances existing at the time the accused could reasonably have been expected to mention when so questioned, charged or informed, as the case may be, subsection (2) below applies.

  (2)   Where this subsection applies—

      (a)   a magistrates' court, in deciding whether to grant an application for dismissal made by the accused under section 6 of the Magistrates' Courts Act 1980 (application for dismissal of charge in course of proceedings with a view to transfer for trial);

      (b)   a judge, in deciding whether to grant an application made by the accused under—

          (i)   section 6 of the Criminal Justice Act 1987 (application for dismissal of charge of serious fraud in respect of which notice of transfer has been given under section 4 of that Act); or

          (ii)   paragraph 5 of Schedule 6 to the Criminal Justice Act 1991 (application for dismissal of charge of violent or sexual offence involving child in respect of which notice of transfer has been given under section 53 of that Act);

      (c)   the court, in determining whether there is a case to answer; and

      (d)   the court or jury, in determining whether the accused is guilty of the offence charged,

may draw such inferences from the failure as appear proper.

  (3)   Subject to any directions by the court, evidence tending to establish the failure may be given before or after evidence tending to establish the fact which the accused is alleged to have failed to mention.

  (4)   This section applies in relation to questioning by persons (other than constables) charged with the duty of investigating offences or charging offenders as it applies in relation to questioning by constables; and in subsection (1) above "officially informed" means informed by a constable or any such person.

(5)   This section does not—

    (a)   prejudice the admissibility in evidence of the silence or other reaction of the accused in the face of anything said in his presence relating to the conduct in respect of which he is charged, in so far as evidence thereof would be admissible apart from this section; or

    (b)   preclude the drawing of any inference from any such silence or other reaction of the accused which could properly be drawn apart from this section.

(6)   This section does not apply in relation to a failure to mention a fact if the failure occurred before the commencement of this section.

(7)   In relation to any time before the commencement of section 44 of this Act, this section shall have effect as if the reference in subsection (2)(a) to the grant of an application for dismissal was a reference to the committal of the accused for trial.

References   See paras 3.1–3.5, 3.8, 3.11, 3.12.

35   Effect of accused's silence at trial

(1)   At the trial of any person who has attained the age of fourteen years for an offence, subsections (2) and (3) below apply unless—

    (a)   the accused's guilt is not in issue; or

    (b)   it appears to the court that the physical or mental condition of the accused makes it undesirable for him to give evidence;

but subsection (2) below does not apply if, at the conclusion of the evidence for the prosecution, his legal representative informs the court that the accused will give evidence or, where he is unrepresented, the court ascertains from him that he will give evidence.

(2)   Where this subsection applies, the court shall, at the conclusion of the evidence for the prosecution, satisfy itself (in the case of proceedings on indictment, in the presence of the jury) that the accused is aware that the stage has been reached at which evidence can be given for the defence and that he can, if he wishes, give evidence and that, if he chooses not to give evidence, or having been sworn, without good cause refuses to answer any question, it will be permissible for the court or jury to draw such inferences as appear proper from his failure to give evidence or his refusal, without good cause, to answer any question.

(3)   Where this subsection applies, the court or jury, in determining whether the accused is guilty of the offence charged, may draw such inferences as appear proper from the failure of the accused to give evidence or his refusal, without good cause, to answer any question.

(4)   This section does not render the accused compellable to give evidence on his own behalf, and he shall accordingly not be guilty of contempt of court by reason of a failure to do so.

(5)   For the purposes of this section a person who, having been sworn, refuses to answer any question shall be taken to do so without good cause unless—

    (a)   he is entitled to refuse to answer the question by virtue of any enactment, whenever passed or made, or on the ground of privilege; or

    (b)   the court in the exercise of its general discretion excuses him from answering it.

(6)　Where the age of any person is material for the purposes of subsection (1) above, his age shall for those purposes be taken to be that which appears to the court to be his age.

(7)　This section applies—

    (a)　in relation to proceedings on indictment for an offence, only if the person charged with the offence is arraigned on or after the commencement of this section;

    (b)　in relation to proceedings in a magistrates' court, only if the time when the court begins to receive evidence in the proceedings falls after the commencement of this section.

Definitions　For "legal representative", see s 38(1); for "offence charged" in sub-s (3) above, see s 38(2); for "without good cause", see sub-s (5) above.
References　See paras 3.1–3.5, 3.9, 3.11, 3.12.

---

36 Effect of accused's failure or refusal to account for objects, substances or marks

(1)　Where—

    (a)　a person is arrested by a constable, and there is—

        (i)　on his person; or

        (ii)　in or on his clothing or footwear; or

        (iii)　otherwise in his possession; or

        (iv)　in any place in which he is at the time of his arrest,

    any object, substance or mark, or there is any mark on any such object; and

    (b)　that or another constable investigating the case reasonably believes that the presence of the object, substance or mark may be attributable to the participation of the person arrested in the commission of an offence specified by the constable; and

    (c)　the constable informs the person arrested that he so believes, and requests him to account for the presence of the object, substance or mark; and

    (d)　the person fails or refuses to do so,

then if, in any proceedings against the person for the offence so specified, evidence of those matters is given, subsection (2) below applies.

(2)　Where this subsection applies—

    (a)　a magistrates' court, in deciding whether to grant an application for dismissal made by the accused under section 6 of the Magistrates' Courts Act 1980 (application for dismissal of charge in course of proceedings with a view to transfer for trial);

    (b)　a judge, in deciding whether to grant an application made by the accused under—

        (i)　section 6 of the Criminal Justice Act 1987 (application for dismissal of charge of serious fraud in respect of which notice of transfer has been given under section 4 of that Act); or

        (ii)　paragraph 5 of Schedule 6 to the Criminal Justice Act 1991 (application for dismissal of charge of violent or sexual offence involving child in respect of which notice of transfer has been given under section 53 of that Act);

    (c)　the court, in determining whether there is a case to answer; and

(d) the court or jury, in determining whether the accused is guilty of the offence charged,

may draw such inferences from the failure or refusal as appear proper.

(3) Subsections (1) and (2) above apply to the condition of clothing or footwear as they apply to a substance or mark thereon.

(4) Subsections (1) and (2) above do not apply unless the accused was told in ordinary language by the constable when making the request mentioned in subsection (1)(c) above what the effect of this section would be if he failed or refused to comply with the request.

(5) This section applies in relation to officers of customs and excise as it applies in relation to constables.

(6) This section does not preclude the drawing of any inference from a failure or refusal of the accused to account for the presence of an object, substance or mark or from the condition of clothing or footwear which could properly be drawn apart from this section.

(7) This section does not apply in relation to a failure or refusal which occurred before the commencement of this section.

(8) In relation to any time before the commencement of section 44 of this Act, this section shall have effect as if the reference in subsection (2)(a) to the grant of an application for dismissal was a reference to the committal of the accused for trial.

References See paras 3.1–3.5, 3.10–3.12.

37 Effect of accused's failure or refusal to account for presence at a particular place

(1) Where—
(a) a person arrested by a constable was found by him at a place at or about the time the offence for which he was arrested is alleged to have been committed; and
(b) that or another constable investigating the offence reasonably believes that the presence of the person at that place and at that time may be attributable to his participation in the commission of the offence; and
(c) the constable informs the person that he so believes, and requests him to account for that presence; and
(d) the person fails or refuses to do so,

then if, in any proceedings against the person for the offence, evidence of those matters is given, subsection (2) below applies.

(2) Where this subsection applies—
(a) a magistrates' court, in deciding whether to grant an application for dismissal made by the accused under section 6 of the Magistrates' Courts Act 1980 (application for dismissal of charge in course of proceedings with a view to transfer for trial);
(b) a judge, in deciding whether to grant an application made by the accused under—
(i) section 6 of the Criminal Justice Act 1987 (application for dismissal of charge of serious fraud in respect of which notice of transfer has been given under section 4 of that Act); or

> (ii) paragraph 5 of Schedule 6 to the Criminal Justice Act 1991 (application for dismissal of charge of violent or sexual offence involving child in respect of which notice of transfer has been given under section 53 of that Act);
>
> (c) the court, in determining whether there is a case to answer; and
>
> (d) the court or jury, in determining whether the accused is guilty of the offence charged,

may draw such inferences from the failure or refusal as appear proper.

(3) Subsections (1) and (2) do not apply unless the accused was told in ordinary language by the constable when making the request mentioned in subsection (1)(c) above what the effect of this section would be if he failed or refused to comply with the request.

(4) This section applies in relation to officers of customs and excise as it applies in relation to constables.

(5) This section does not preclude the drawing of any inference from a failure or refusal of the accused to account for his presence at a place which could properly be drawn apart from this section.

(6) This section does not apply in relation to a failure or refusal which occurred before the commencement of this section.

(7) In relation to any time before the commencement of section 44 of this Act, this section shall have effect as if the reference in subsection (2)(a) to the grant of an application for dismissal was a reference to the committal of the accused for trial.

Definitions   For "place", see s 38(1); as to "offence charged" in sub-s (2) above, see s 38(2).
References   See paras 3.1–3.5, 3.10–3.12.

---

38 Interpretation and savings for sections 34, 35, 36 and 37

(1) In sections 34, 35, 36 and 37 of this Act—

"legal representative" means an authorised advocate or authorised litigator, as defined by section 119(1) of the Courts and Legal Services Act 1990; and

"place" includes any building or part of a building, any vehicle, vessel, aircraft or hovercraft and any other place whatsoever.

(2) In sections 34(2), 35(3), 36(2) and 37(2), references to an offence charged include references to any other offence of which the accused could lawfully be convicted on that charge.

(3) A person shall not have the proceedings against him transferred to the Crown Court for trial, have a case to answer or be convicted of an offence solely on an inference drawn from such a failure or refusal as is mentioned in section 34(2), 35(3), 36(2) or 37(2).

(4) A judge shall not refuse to grant such an application as is mentioned in section 34(2)(b), 36(2)(b) and 37(2)(b) solely on an inference drawn from such a failure as is mentioned in section 34(2), 36(2) or 37(2).

(5) Nothing in sections 34, 35, 36 or 37 prejudices the operation of a provision of any enactment which provides (in whatever words) that any answer or evidence given by a person in specified circumstances shall not be admissible in evidence

against him or some other person in any proceedings or class of proceedings (however described, and whether civil or criminal).

In this subsection, the reference to giving evidence is a reference to giving evidence in any manner, whether by furnishing information, making discovery, producing documents or otherwise.

(6)   Nothing in sections 34, 35, 36 or 37 prejudices any power of a court, in any proceedings, to exclude evidence (whether by preventing questions being put or otherwise) at its discretion.

References   See para 3.13.

39 Power to apply sections 34 to 38 to armed forces

(1)   The Secretary of State may by order direct that any provision of sections 34 to 38 of this Act shall apply, subject to such modifications as he may specify, to any proceedings to which this section applies.

(2)   This section applies—
  (a)   to proceedings whereby a charge is dealt with summarily under Part II of the Army Act 1955;
  (b)   to proceedings whereby a charge is dealt with summarily under Part II of the Air Force Act 1955;
  (c)   to proceedings whereby a charge is summarily tried under Part II of the Naval Discipline Act 1957;
  (d)   to proceedings before a court martial constituted under the Army Act 1955;
  (e)   to proceedings before a court martial constituted under the Air Force Act 1955;
  (f)   to proceedings before a court martial constituted under the Naval Discipline Act 1957;
  (g)   to proceedings before a disciplinary court constituted under section 50 of the Naval Discipline Act 1957;
  (h)   to proceedings before the Courts-Martial Appeal Court;
  (i)   to proceedings before a Standing Civilian Court;
and it applies wherever the proceedings take place.

(3)   An order under this section shall be made by statutory instrument and shall be subject to annulment in pursuance of a resolution of either House of Parliament.

References   See para 3.13.

Juries

40 Disqualification for jury service of persons on bail in criminal proceedings

(1)   A person who is on bail in criminal proceedings shall not be qualified to serve as a juror in the Crown Court.

(2)   In this section "bail in criminal proceedings" has the same meaning as in the Bail Act 1976.

References   See para 3.14.

41 Jury service: disabled persons

After section 9A of the Juries Act 1974 there shall be inserted the following section—

"9B Discharge of summonses to disabled persons only if incapable of acting effectively as a juror

(1)   Where it appears to the appropriate officer, in the case of a person attending in pursuance of a summons under this Act, that on account of physical disability there is doubt as to his capacity to act effectively as a juror, the person may be brought before the judge.

(2)   The judge shall determine whether or not the person should act as a juror; but he shall affirm the summons unless he is of the opinion that the person will not, on account of his disability, be capable of acting effectively as a juror, in which case he shall discharge the summons.

(3)   In this section "the judge" means any judge of the High Court or any Circuit judge or Recorder.".

Definitions   For "appropriate officer", see the Juries Act 1974, s 23(2).
References   See para 3.14.

42 Jury service: excusal on religious grounds

In Schedule 1 to the Juries Act 1974, in Part III (Persons excusable as of right), after the entry entitled *Medical and other similar professions*, there shall be inserted the following—

"Members of certain religious bodies

A practising member of a religious society or order the tenets or beliefs of which are incompatible with jury service.".

References   See para 3.14.

43 Separation of jury during consideration of verdict

(1)   For section 13 of the Juries Act 1974 (under which a jury may be allowed to separate at any time before they consider their verdict) there shall be substituted—

"13   Separation

If, on the trial of any person for an offence on indictment, the court thinks fit, it may at any time (whether before or after the jury have been directed to consider their verdict) permit the jury to separate.".

(2)   The amendment made by subsection (1) above shall not have effect in relation to a trial where a direction to the jury to consider their verdict has been given before the commencement of this section.

References   See para 3.15.

Procedure, jurisdiction and powers of magistrates' courts

44 Transfer for trial instead of committal proceedings

(1)   The functions of a magistrates' court as examining justices are hereby abolished.

(2)   The provisions set out in Part I of Schedule 4 to this Act as sections 4 to 8C of the Magistrates' Courts Act 1980 shall be substituted for sections 4 to 8 of that Act (which provide for the functions of magistrates' courts as examining justices).

(3)   The amendments specified in Part II of that Schedule shall also have effect.

(4)   Subsections (1) and (2) above do not apply in relation to proceedings in which a magistrates' court has begun to inquire into a case as examining justices before the commencement of this section.

References   See para 3.16.

45 Extension of procedures enabling magistrates' courts to deal with cases in which accused pleads guilty

The amendments to the Magistrates' Courts Act 1980 specified in Schedule 5 (being amendments designed principally to extend the procedures applicable in magistrates' courts when the accused pleads guilty) shall have effect.

References   See para 3.18.

46 Criminal damage, etc as summary offence: relevant sum

(1)   In subsection (1) of section 22 of the Magistrates' Courts Act 1980 (under which, where an offence of or related to criminal damage or, in certain circumstances, an offence of aggravated vehicle-taking, is charged and it appears clear to the magistrates' court that the value involved does not exceed the relevant sum, the court is to proceed as if the offence were triable only summarily) in the second paragraph (which states the relevant sum), for "£2,000" there shall be substituted "£5,000".

(2)   Subsection (1) above does not apply to an offence charged in respect of an act done before this section comes into force.

References   See para 3.19.

47 Recovery of fines, etc by deduction from income support

(1)   In section 89 of the Magistrates' Courts Act 1980 (which gives a magistrates' court power to make a transfer of fine order), after subsection (2) there shall be inserted the following subsection—

> "(2A) The functions of the court to which subsection (2) above relates shall be deemed to include the court's power to apply to the Secretary of State under any regulations made by him under section 24(1)(a) of the Criminal Justice Act (power to deduct fines etc from income support).".

(2)   In section 90 of the Magistrates' Courts Act 1980 (which gives a magistrates' court power to transfer a fine to Scotland), after subsection (3) there shall be inserted the following subsection—

> "(3A) The functions of the court which shall cease to be exercisable by virtue of subsection (3) above shall be deemed to include the court's power to apply to the Secretary of State under regulations made by him under section 24(1)(a) of the Criminal Justice Act 1991 (power to deduct fines from income support).".

(3)   In section 24(3) of the Criminal Justice Act 1991 (which relates to the Secretary of State's power to authorise deduction of fines etc from income support), after paragraph (b) there shall be inserted the following paragraph—

> "(c)   the reference in paragraph (a) to "the court" includes a reference to a court to which the function in that paragraph has been transferred by virtue of a transfer of fine order under section 89(1) or (3) or 90(1)(a) of the 1980 Act (power of magistrates' court to make transfer of fine order) or under section 403(1)(a) or (b) of the Criminal Procedure (Scotland) Act 1975 (analogous provision as respects Scotland) and a reference to a court to which that function has been remitted by virtue of section 196(2) of the said Act of 1975 (enforcement of fine imposed by High Court of Justiciary).".

(4)   In section 403 of the Criminal Procedure (Scotland) Act 1975 (which gives a court of summary jurisdiction in Scotland power to make a transfer of fine order), after subsection (4) there shall be inserted the following subsection—

> "(4A) The functions of the court to which subsection (4) above relates shall be deemed to include the court's power to apply to the Secretary of State under any regulations made by him under section 24(1)(a) of the Criminal Justice Act 1991 (power to deduct fines etc from income support).".

References   See para 3.19.

Sentencing: guilty pleas

48 Reduction in sentences for guilty pleas

(1)   In determining what sentence to pass on an offender who has pleaded guilty to an offence in proceedings before that or another court a court shall take into account—

(a)   the stage in the proceedings for the offence at which the offender indicated his intention to plead guilty, and

(b)   the circumstances in which this indication was given.

(2)   If, as a result of taking into account any matter referred to in subsection (1) above, the court imposes a punishment on the offender which is less severe than the punishment it would otherwise have imposed, it shall state in open court that it has done so.

References   See paras 3.20–3.23.

Publication of reports in young offender cases

49 Restrictions on reports of proceedings in which children or young persons are concerned

For section 49 of the Children and Young Persons Act 1933 (restrictions on reports of proceedings in which children or young persons are concerned) there shall be substituted—

"49 Restrictions on reports of proceedings in which children or young persons are concerned

(1)   The following prohibitions apply (subject to subsection (5) below) in relation to any proceedings to which this section applies, that is to say—

  (a) no report shall be published which reveals the name, address or school of any child or young person concerned in the proceedings or includes any particulars likely to lead to the identification of any child or young person concerned in the proceedings; and

  (b) no picture shall be published or included in a programme service as being or including a picture of any child or young person concerned in the proceedings.

(2)   The proceedings to which this section applies are—

  (a) proceedings in a youth court;

  (b) proceedings on appeal from a youth court (including proceedings by way of case stated);

  (c) proceedings under section 15 or 16 of the Children and Young Persons Act 1969 (proceedings for varying or revoking supervision orders); and

  (d) proceedings on appeal from a magistrates' court arising out of proceedings under section 15 or 16 of that Act (including proceedings by way of case stated).

(3)   The reports to which this section applies are reports in a newspaper and reports included in a programme service; and similarly as respects pictures.

(4)   For the purposes of this section a child or young person is "concerned" in any proceedings whether as being the person against or in respect of whom the proceedings are taken or as being a witness in the proceedings.

(5)   Subject to subsection (7) below, a court may, in relation to proceedings before it to which this section applies, by order dispense to any specified extent with the requirements of this section in relation to a child or young person who is concerned in the proceedings if it is satisfied—

  (a) that it is appropriate to do so for the purpose of avoiding injustice to the child or young person; or

  (b) that, as respects a child or young person to whom this paragraph applies who is unlawfully at large, it is necessary to dispense with those requirements for the purpose of apprehending him and bringing him before a court or returning him to the place in which he was in custody.

(6)   Paragraph (b) of subsection (5) above applies to any child or young person who is charged with or has been convicted of—

  (a) a violent offence,

  (b) a sexual offence, or

  (c) an offence punishable in the case of a person aged 21 or over with imprisonment for fourteen years or more.

(7)   The court shall not exercise its power under subsection (5)(b) above—

  (a) except in pursuance of an application by or on behalf of the Director of Public Prosecutions; and

  (b) unless notice of the application has been given by the Director of Public Prosecutions to any legal representative of the child or young person.

(8)   The court's power under subsection (5) above may be exercised by a single justice.

(9)   If a report or picture is published or included in a programme service in contravention of subsection (1) above, the following persons, that is to say—

    (a) in the case of publication of a written report or a picture as part of a newspaper, any proprietor, editor or publisher of the newspaper;

    (b) in the case of the inclusion of a report or picture in a programme service, any body corporate which provides the service and any person having functions in relation to the programme corresponding to those of an editor of a newspaper,

shall be liable on summary conviction to a fine not exceeding level 5 on the standard scale.

(10)   In any proceedings under section 15 or 16 of the Children and Young Persons Act 1969 (proceedings for varying or revoking supervision orders) before a magistrates' court other than a youth court or on appeal from such a court it shall be the duty of the magistrates' court or the appellate court to announce in the course of the proceedings that this section applies to the proceedings; and if the court fails to do so this section shall not apply to the proceedings.

(11)   In this section—

    "legal representative" means an authorised advocate or authorised litigator, as defined by section 119(1) of the Courts and Legal Services Act 1990;

    "programme" and "programme service" have the same meaning as in the Broadcasting Act 1990;

    "sexual offence" has the same meaning as in section 31(1) of the Criminal Justice Act 1991;

    "specified" means specified in an order under this section;

    "violent offence" has the same meaning as in section 31(1) of the Criminal Justice Act 1991;

and a person who, having been granted bail, is liable to arrest (whether with or without a warrant) shall be treated as unlawfully at large.".

Definitions   For "child" and "young person", see the Children and Young Person's Act 1933, s 107(1); for ""concerned" in any proceedings", see s 49(4) of the 1933 Act, as substituted above; for "legal representative", "programme", "programme service", "sexual offence", "specified", "unlawfully at large" and "violent offence", see s 49(11) thereof, as so substituted.
References   See para 3.24.

Child testimony

50 Video recordings of testimony from child witnesses

In section 32A of the Criminal Justice Act 1988, in subsection (5)(b), the word "adequately" shall be inserted after the words "dealt with".

References   See para 3.25.

Intimidation, etc, of witnesses, jurors and others

51 Intimidation, etc, of witnesses, jurors and others

(1)   A person who does to another person—

    (a) an act which intimidates, and is intended to intimidate, that other person;

    (b) knowing or believing that the other person is assisting in the investigation of an offence or is a witness or potential witness or a juror or potential juror in proceedings for an offence; and

    (c)   intending thereby to cause the investigation or the course of justice to be obstructed, perverted or interfered with,

commits an offence.

  (2)   A person who does or threatens to do to another person—
    (a)   an act which harms or would harm, and is intended to harm, that other person;
    (b)   knowing or believing that the other person, or some other person, has assisted in an investigation into an offence or has given evidence or particular evidence in proceedings for an offence, or has acted as a juror or concurred in a particular verdict in proceedings for an offence; and
    (c)   does or threatens to do the act because of what (within paragraph (b)) he knows or believes,

commits an offence.

  (3)   A person does an act "to" another person with the intention of intimidating, or (as the case may be) harming, that other person not only where the act is done in the presence of that other and directed at him directly but also where the act is done to a third person and is intended, in the circumstances, to intimidate or (as the case may be) harm the person at whom the act is directed.

  (4)   The harm that may be done or threatened may be financial as well as physical (whether to the person or a person's property) and similarly as respects an intimidatory act which consists of threats.

  (5)   The intention required by subsection (1)(c) and the motive required by subsection (2)(c) above need not be the only or the predominating intention or motive with which the act is done or, in the case of subsection (2), threatened.

  (6)   A person guilty of an offence under this section shall be liable—
    (a)   on conviction on indictment, to imprisonment for a term not exceeding five years or a fine or both;
    (b)   on summary conviction, to imprisonment for a term not exceeding six months or a fine not exceeding the statutory maximum or both.

  (7)   If, in proceedings against a person for an offence under subsection (1) above, it is proved that he did an act falling within paragraph (a) with the knowledge or belief required by paragraph (b), he shall be presumed, unless the contrary is proved, to have done the act with the intention required by paragraph (c) of that subsection.

  (8)   If, in proceedings against a person for an offence under subsection (2) above, it is proved that he did or threatened to do an act falling within paragraph (a) within the relevant period with the knowledge or belief required by paragraph (b), he shall be presumed, unless the contrary is proved, to have done the act with the motive required by paragraph (c) of that subsection.

  (9)   In this section—
    "investigation into an offence" means such an investigation by the police or other person charged with the duty of investigating offences or charging offenders;
    "offence" includes an alleged or suspected offence;
    "potential", in relation to a juror, means a person who has been summoned for jury service at the court at which proceedings for the offence are pending; and

"the relevant period"—

    (a) in relation to a witness or juror in any proceedings for an offence, means the period beginning with the institution of the proceedings and ending with the first anniversary of the conclusion of the trial or, if there is an appeal or reference under section 17 of the Criminal Appeal Act 1968, of the conclusion of the appeal;

    (b) in relation to a person who has, or is believed by the accused to have, assisted in an investigation into an offence, but was not also a witness in proceedings for an offence, means the period of one year beginning with any act of his, or any act believed by the accused to be an act of his, assisting in the investigation; and

    (c) in relation to a person who both has, or is believed by the accused to have, assisted in the investigation into an offence and was a witness in proceedings for the offence, means the period beginning with any act of his, or any act believed by the accused to be an act of his, assisting in the investigation and ending with the anniversary mentioned in paragraph (a) above.

(10) For the purposes of the definition of the relevant period in subsection (9) above—

    (a) proceedings for an offence are instituted at the earliest of the following times—

        (i) when a justice of the peace issues a summons or warrant under section 1 of the Magistrates' Courts Act 1980 in respect of the offence;

        (ii) when a person is charged with the offence after being taken into custody without a warrant;

        (iii) when a bill of indictment is preferred by virtue of section 2(2)(b) of the Administration of Justice (Miscellaneous Provisions) Act 1933;

    (b) proceedings at a trial of an offence are concluded with the occurrence of any of the following, the discontinuance of the prosecution, the discharge of the jury without a finding, the acquittal of the accused or the sentencing of or other dealing with the accused for the offence of which he was convicted; and

    (c) proceedings on an appeal are concluded on the determination of the appeal or the abandonment of the appeal.

(11) This section is in addition to, and not in derogation of, any offence subsisting at common law.

References   See para 3.26.

Criminal appeals

52 Circuit judges to act as judges of criminal division of Court of Appeal

(1) Section 9 of the Supreme Court Act 1981 (which provides for certain judges to act on request in courts other than that to which they were appointed) shall have effect with the amendments specified in subsections (2) to (5) below.

(2) In subsection (1)—

    (a) after the words "Table may", there shall be inserted the words ", subject to the proviso at the end of that Table,";

    (b)   in the Table, in column 2, in the entry specifying the court relating to entry 5 in column 1 (Circuit judges), after the words "High Court" there shall be inserted the words "and the Court of Appeal"; and

    (c)   at the end of the Table there shall be inserted the following—

"The entry in column 2 specifying the Court of Appeal in relation to a Circuit judge only authorises such a judge to act as a judge of a court in the criminal division of the Court of Appeal.".

(3)   In subsection (2)—

    (a)   in the definition of "the appropriate authority" after the words "High Court" there shall be inserted the words "or a Circuit judge"; and

    (b)   at the end, there shall be inserted the following—

"but no request shall be made to a Circuit judge to act as a judge of a court in the criminal division of the Court of Appeal unless he is approved for the time being by the Lord Chancellor for the purpose of acting as a judge of that division.".

(4)   In subsection (5), for the words "subsection (6)" there shall be substituted the words "subsections (6) and (6A)".

(5)   After subsection (6) there shall be inserted the following subsection—

"(6A) A Circuit judge or Recorder shall not by virtue of subsection (5) exercise any of the powers conferred on a single judge by sections 31 and 44 of the Criminal Appeal Act 1968 (powers of single judge in connection with appeals to the Court of Appeal and appeals from the Court of Appeal to the House of Lords).".

(6)   The further amendments specified in subsections (7) to (9) below (which supplement the foregoing amendments) shall have effect.

(7)   In section 55 of the Supreme Court Act 1981 (composition of criminal division of Court of Appeal)—

    (a)   in subsections (2) and (4), at the beginning, there shall be inserted the words "Subject to subsection (6),"; and

    (b)   after subsection (5), there shall be inserted the following subsection—

"(6) A court shall not be duly constituted if it includes more than one Circuit judge acting as a judge of the court under section 9.".

(8)   After section 56 of the Supreme Court Act 1981 there shall be inserted the following section—

"56A Circuit judges not to sit on certain appeals

No Circuit judge shall act in the criminal division of the Court of Appeal as a judge of that court under section 9 on the hearing of, or shall determine any application in proceedings incidental or preliminary to, an appeal against—

    (a)   a conviction before a judge of the High Court; or

    (b)   a sentence passed by a judge of the High Court.".

(9)   After the section 56A of the Supreme Court Act 1981 inserted by subsection (8) above there shall be inserted the following section—

"56B Allocation of cases in criminal division

(1)   The appeals or classes of appeals suitable for allocation to a court of the criminal division of the Court of Appeal in which a Circuit judge is acting

under section 9 shall be determined in accordance with directions given by or on behalf of the Lord Chief Justice with the concurrence of the Lord Chancellor.

(2)   In subsection (1) "appeal" includes the hearing of, or any application in proceedings incidental or preliminary to, an appeal.".

References   See para 3.27.

53 Expenses in criminal appeals in Northern Ireland Court of Appeal

(1)   After section 28(2) of the Criminal Appeal (Northern Ireland) Act 1980 (certain expenses to be defrayed up to amount allowed by the Master (Taxing Office)) there shall be inserted the following subsections—

"(2A) Where a solicitor or counsel is dissatisfied with the amount of any expenses allowed by the Master (Taxing Office) under subsection (2)(a) above, he may apply to that Master to review his decision.

(2B)   On a review under subsection (2A) the Master (Taxing Office) may confirm or vary the amount of expenses allowed by him.

(2C)   An application under subsection (2A) shall be made, and a review under that subsection shall be conducted, in accordance with rules of court.

(2D)   Where a solicitor or counsel is dissatisfied with the decision of the Master (Taxing Office) on a review under subsection (2A) above, he may appeal against that decision to the High Court and the Lord Chancellor may appear and be represented on any such appeal.

(2E)   Where the Lord Chancellor is dissatisfied with the decision of the Master (Taxing Office) on a review under subsection (2A) above in relation to the expenses of a solicitor or counsel, he may appeal against that decision to the High Court and the solicitor or barrister may appear or be represented on any such appeal.

(2F)   On any appeal under subsection (2D) or (2E) above the High Court may confirm or vary the amount of expenses allowed by the Master (Taxing Office) and the decision of the High Court shall be final.

(2G)   The power of the Master (Taxing Office) or the High Court to vary the amount of expenses allowed under subsection (2)(a) above includes power to increase or reduce that amount to such extent as the Master or (as the case may be) the High Court thinks fit; and the reference in subsection (2) above to the amount allowed by the Master (Taxing Office) shall, in a case where that amount has been so varied, be construed as a reference to that amount as so varied.".

(2)   Subsection (1) above does not have effect in relation to expenses allowed by the Master (Taxing Office) under section 28(2)(a) of the Criminal Appeal (Northern Ireland) Act 1980 before the date on which that subsection comes into force.

References   See para 3.28.

PART IV
POLICE POWERS

Powers of police to take body samples

54 Powers of police to take intimate body samples

(1)   Section 62 of the Police and Criminal Evidence Act 1984 (regulation of taking of intimate samples) shall be amended as follows.

(2)   After subsection (1) there shall be inserted the following subsection—

"(1A) An intimate sample may be taken from a person who is not in police detention but from whom, in the course of the investigation of an offence, two or more non-intimate samples suitable for the same means of analysis have been taken which have proved insufficient—

    (a) if a police officer of at least the rank of superintendent authorises it to be taken; and

    (b) if the appropriate consent is given.".

(3)   In subsection (2)—

    (a) after the word "authorisation" there shall be inserted the words "under subsection (1) or (1A) above"; and

    (b) in paragraph (a), for the words "serious arrestable offence" there shall be substituted the words "recordable offence".

(4)   In subsection (3), after the words "subsection (1)" there shall be inserted the words "or (1A)".

(5)   In subsection (9)—

    (a) for the words "or saliva" there shall be substituted the words "or a dental impression"; and

    (b) at the end there shall be inserted the words "and a dental impression may only be taken by a registered dentist".

Definitions   For "appropriate consent", see the Police and Criminal Evidence Act 1984, s 65; for "intimate sample", see s 65 of the 1984 Act as amended by s 58(1), (2) of this Act; for "non-intimate sample", see s 65 of the 1984 Act as amended by s 58(1), (3) of this Act; for "insufficient" and "registered dentist", see s 65 of the 1984 Act as amended by s 58(1), (4) of this Act; for "recordable offence", see s 118(1) of the 1984 Act; as to when a person is and is not in police detention, see s 118(2) of the 1984 Act.
References   See paras 4.1, 4.2.

---

55 Powers of police to take non-intimate body samples

(1)   Section 63 of the Police and Criminal Evidence Act 1984 (regulation of taking of non-intimate samples) shall be amended as follows.

(2)   After subsection (3), there shall be inserted the following subsections—

"(3A) A non-intimate sample may be taken from a person (whether or not he falls within subsection (3)(a) above) without the appropriate consent if—

    (a) he has been charged with a recordable offence or informed that he will be reported for such an offence; and

    (b) either he has not had a non-intimate sample taken from him in the course of the investigation of the offence by the police or he has had a non-intimate sample taken from him but either it was not suitable for the same means of analysis or, though so suitable, the sample proved insufficient.

(3B) A non-intimate sample may be taken from a person without the appropriate consent if he has been convicted of a recordable offence.".

(3) In subsection (4), in paragraph (a), for the words "serious arrestable offence" there shall be substituted the words "recordable offence".

(4) After subsection (8), there shall be inserted the following subsection—

"(8A) In a case where by virtue of subsection (3A) or (3B) a sample is taken from a person without the appropriate consent—
    (a) he shall be told the reason before the sample is taken; and
    (b) the reason shall be recorded as soon as practicable after the sample is taken.".

(5) In subsection (9), after the words "subsection (8)" there shall be inserted the words "or (8A)".

(6) After subsection (9) there shall be inserted the following subsection—

"(10) Subsection (3B) above shall not apply to persons convicted before the date on which that subsection comes into force.".

Definitions   For "appropriate consent", see the Police and Criminal Evidence Act 1984, s 65; for "non-intimate sample", see s 65 of the 1984 Act as amended by s 58(1), (3) of this Act; for "insufficient", see s 65 of the 1984 Act as amended by s 58(1), (4) of this Act; for "recordable offence", see s 118(1) of the 1984 Act.
References   See paras 4.1, 4.2.

---

56 Fingerprints and samples: supplementary provisions

The following section shall be inserted after section 63 of the Police and Criminal Evidence Act 1984—

"63A Fingerprints and samples: supplementary provisions

(1) Fingerprints or samples or the information derived from samples taken under any power conferred by this Part of this Act from a person who has been arrested on suspicion of being involved in a recordable offence may be checked against other fingerprints or samples or the information derived from other samples contained in records held by or on behalf of the police or held in connection with or as a result of an investigation of an offence.

(2) Where a sample of hair other than pubic hair is to be taken the sample may be taken either by cutting hairs or by plucking hairs with their roots so long as no more are plucked than the person taking the sample reasonably considers to be necessary for a sufficient sample.

(3) Where any power to take a sample is exercisable in relation to a person the sample may be taken in a prison or other institution to which the Prison Act 1952 applies.

(4) Any constable may, within the allowed period, require a person who is neither in police detention nor held in custody by the police on the authority of a court to attend a police station in order to have a sample taken where—
    (a) the person has been charged with a recordable offence or informed that he will be reported for such an offence and either he has not had

a sample taken from him in the course of the investigation of the offence by the police or he has had a sample so taken from him but either it was not suitable for the same means of analysis or, though so suitable, the sample proved insufficient; or

(b) the person has been convicted of a recordable offence and either he has not had a sample taken from him since the conviction or he has had a sample taken from him (before or after his conviction) but either it was not suitable for the same means of analysis or, though so suitable, the sample proved insufficient.

(5)   The period allowed for requiring a person to attend a police station for the purpose specified in subsection (4) above is—

(a) in the case of a person falling within paragraph (a), one month beginning with the date of the charge or one month beginning with the date on which the appropriate officer is informed of the fact that the sample is not suitable for the same means of analysis or has proved insufficient, as the case may be;

(b) in the case of a person falling within paragraph (b), one month beginning with the date of the conviction or one month beginning with the date on which the appropriate officer is informed of the fact that the sample is not suitable for the same means of analysis or has proved insufficient, as the case may be.

(6)   A requirement under subsection (4) above—

(a) shall give the person at least 7 days within which he must so attend; and

(b) may direct him to attend at a specified time of day or between specified times of day.

(7)   Any constable may arrest without a warrant a person who has failed to comply with a requirement under subsection (4) above.

(8)   In this section "the appropriate officer" is—

(a) in the case of a person falling within subsection (4)(a), the officer investigating the offence with which that person has been charged or as to which he was informed that he would be reported;

(b) in the case of a person falling within subsection (4)(b), the officer in charge of the police station from which the investigation of the offence of which he was convicted was conducted.".

Definitions   For "fingerprints", see the Police and Criminal Evidence Act 1984, s 65; for "insufficient", see s 65 of that Act as amended by s 58(1), (4) of this Act; for "recordable offence", see s 118(1) of that Act; as to when a person is in or is not in police detention, see s 118(2) of that Act; for "the appropriate officer", see s 63A(8) of the 1984 Act, as inserted above.
References   See paras 4.1, 4.3.

---

57 Retention of samples in certain cases

(1)   Section 64 of the Police and Criminal Evidence Act 1984 (which prescribes the situations in which fingerprints and samples must be destroyed) shall be amended as follows.

(2)   In subsections (1), (2) and (3), after the words "they must" there shall be inserted the words ", except as provided in subsection (3A) below,".

(3)   After subsection (3), there shall be inserted the following subsections—

"(3A) Samples which are required to be destroyed under subsection (1), (2) or (3) above need not be destroyed if they were taken for the purpose of the same investigation of an offence of which a person from whom one was taken has been convicted, but the information derived from the sample of any person entitled (apart from this subsection) to its destruction under subsection (1), (2) or (3) above shall not be used—

(a) in evidence against the person so entitled; or

(b) for the purposes of any investigation of an offence.

(3B) Where samples are required to be destroyed under subsections (1), (2) or (3) above, and subsection (3A) above does not apply, information derived from the sample of any person entitled to its destruction under subsection (1), (2) or (3) above shall not be used—

(a) in evidence against the person so entitled; or

(b) for the purposes of any investigation of an offence.".

References   See paras 4.1, 4.4.

---

58 Samples: intimate and non-intimate etc

(1)   Section 65 of the Police and Criminal Evidence Act 1984 (which contains definitions of intimate and non-intimate samples and other relevant definitions) shall be amended as follows.

(2)   For the definition of "intimate sample" there shall be substituted—

""intimate sample" means—

(a) a sample of blood, semen or any other tissue fluid, urine or pubic hair;

(b) a dental impression;

(c) a swab taken from a person's body orifice other than the mouth;".

(3)   For the definition of "non-intimate sample" there shall be substituted—

""non-intimate sample" means—

(a) a sample of hair other than pubic hair;

(b) a sample taken from a nail or from under a nail;

(c) a swab taken from any part of a person's body including the mouth but not any other body orifice;

(d) saliva;

(e) a footprint or a similar impression of any part of a person's body other than a part of his hand;".

(4)   After the definition of "non-intimate sample" there shall be inserted the following definitions—

""registered dentist" has the same meaning as in the Dentists Act 1984;

"speculative search", in relation to a person's fingerprints or samples, means such a check against other fingerprints or samples or against information derived from other samples as is referred to in section 63A(1) above;

"sufficient" and "insufficient", in relation to a sample, means sufficient or insufficient (in point of quantity or quality) for the purpose of enabling information to be produced by the means of analysis used or to be used in relation to the sample.".

Definitions   For "fingerprints", see the Police and Criminal Evidence Act 1984, s 65; for "registered dentist" in the Dentists Act 1984, see s 58(1) of that Act.
References   See paras 4.1, 4.4.

59 Extension of powers to search persons' mouths

(1)   In section 65 of the Police and Criminal Evidence Act 1984 (definitions for purposes of Part V: treatment of persons by police), after the definition of "intimate sample" there shall be inserted the following definition—

> ""intimate search" means a search which consists of the physical examination of a person's body orifices other than the mouth;".

(2)   In section 32 of that Act (powers of search upon arrest), in subsection (4), at the end, there shall be inserted "but they do authorise a search of a person's mouth".

References   See paras 4.1, 4.4.

Powers of police to stop and search

60 Powers to stop and search in anticipation of violence

(1)   Where a police officer of or above the rank of superintendent reasonably believes that—
   (a)   incidents involving serious violence may take place in any locality in his area, and
   (b)   it is expedient to do so to prevent their occurrence,
he may give an authorisation that the powers to stop and search persons and vehicles conferred by this section shall be exercisable at any place within that locality for a period not exceeding twenty four hours.

(2)   The power conferred by subsection (1) above may be exercised by a chief inspector or an inspector if he reasonably believes that incidents involving serious violence are imminent and no superintendent is available.

(3)   If it appears to the officer who gave the authorisation or to a superintendent that it is expedient to do so, having regard to offences which have, or are reasonably suspected to have, been committed in connection with any incident falling within the authorisation, he may direct that the authorisation shall continue in being for a further six hours.

(4)   This section confers on any constable in uniform power—
   (a)   to stop any pedestrian and search him or anything carried by him for offensive weapons or dangerous instruments;
   (b)   to stop any vehicle and search the vehicle, its driver and any passenger for offensive weapons or dangerous instruments.

(5)   A constable may, in the exercise of those powers, stop any person or vehicle and make any search he thinks fit whether or not he has any grounds for suspecting that the person or vehicle is carrying weapons or articles of that kind.

(6)   If in the course of a search under this section a constable discovers a dangerous instrument or an article which he has reasonable grounds for suspecting to be an offensive weapon, he may seize it.

(7)   This section applies (with the necessary modifications) to ships, aircraft and hovercraft as it applies to vehicles.

(8)   A person who fails to stop or (as the case may be) to stop the vehicle when required to do so by a constable in the exercise of his powers under this section shall be liable on summary conviction to imprisonment for a term not exceeding one month or to a fine not exceeding level 3 on the standard scale or both.

(9)   Any authorisation under this section shall be in writing signed by the officer giving it and shall specify the locality in which and the period during which the powers conferred by this section are exercisable and a direction under subsection (3) above shall also be given in writing or, where that is not practicable, recorded in writing as soon as it is practicable to do so.

(10)   Where a vehicle is stopped by a constable under this section, the driver shall be entitled to obtain a written statement that the vehicle was stopped under the powers conferred by this section if he applies for such a statement not later than the end of the period of twelve months from the day on which the vehicle was stopped and similarly as respects a pedestrian who is stopped and searched under this section.

(11)   In this section—
> "dangerous instruments" means instruments which have a blade or are sharply pointed;
> "offensive weapon" has the meaning given by section 1(9) of the Police and Criminal Evidence Act 1984; and
> "vehicle" includes a caravan as defined in section 29(1) of the Caravan Sites and Control of Development Act 1960.

(12)   The powers conferred by this section are in addition to and not in derogation of, any power otherwise conferred.

References   See paras 4.1, 4.5.

PART V
PUBLIC ORDER: COLLECTIVE TRESPASS OR NUISANCE ON LAND

Powers to remove trespassers on land

61 Power to remove trespassers on land

(1)   If the senior police officer present at the scene reasonably believes that two or more persons are trespassing on land and are present there with the common purpose of residing there for any period, that reasonable steps have been taken by or on behalf of the occupier to ask them to leave and—
> (a)   that any of those persons has caused damage to the land or to property on the land or used threatening, abusive or insulting words or behaviour towards the occupier, a member of his family or an employee or agent of his, or
> (b)   that those persons have between them six or more vehicles on the land,
he may direct those persons, or any of them, to leave the land and to remove any vehicles or other property they have with them on the land.

(2)   Where the persons in question are reasonably believed by the senior police officer to be persons who were not originally trespassers but have become trespassers on the land, the officer must reasonably believe that the other conditions specified in subsection (1) are satisfied after those persons became trespassers before he can exercise the power conferred by that subsection.

(3)   A direction under subsection (1) above, if not communicated to the persons referred to in subsection (1) by the police officer giving the direction, may be communicated to them by any constable at the scene.

(4)   If a person knowing that a direction under subsection (1) above has been given which applies to him—
  (a)   fails to leave the land as soon as reasonably practicable, or
  (b)   having left again enters the land as a trespasser within the period of three months beginning with the day on which the direction was given,
he commits an offence and is liable on summary conviction to imprisonment for a term not exceeding three months or a fine not exceeding level 4 on the standard scale, or both.

(5)   A constable in uniform who reasonably suspects that a person is committing an offence under this section may arrest him without a warrant.

(6)   In proceedings for an offence under this section it is a defence for the accused to show—
  (a)   that he was not trespassing on the land, or
  (b)   that he had a reasonable excuse for failing to leave the land as soon as reasonably practicable or, as the case may be, for again entering the land as a trespasser.

(7)   In its application in England and Wales to common land this section has effect as if in the preceding subsections of it—
  (a)   references to trespassing or trespassers were references to acts and persons doing acts which constitute either a trespass as against the occupier or an infringement of the commoners' rights; and
  (b)   references to "the occupier" included the commoners or any of them or, in the case of common land to which the public has access, the local authority as well as any commoner.

(8)   Subsection (7) above does not—
  (a)   require action by more than one occupier; or
  (b)   constitute persons trespassers as against any commoner or the local authority if they are permitted to be there by the other occupier.

(9)   In this section—
  "common land" means common land as defined in section 22 of the Commons Registration Act 1965;
  "commoner" means a person with rights of common as defined in section 22 of the Commons Registration Act 1965;
  "land" does not include—
    (a) buildings other than—
      (i)   agricultural buildings within the meaning of, in England and Wales, paragraphs 3 to 8 of Schedule 5 to the Local Government Finance Act 1988 or, in Scotland, section 7(2) of the Valuation and Rating (Scotland) Act 1956, or
      (ii) scheduled monuments within the meaning of the Ancient Monuments and Archaeological Areas Act 1979;
    (b) land forming part of—
      (i)   a highway unless it falls within the classifications in section 54 of the Wildlife and Countryside Act 1981 (footpath, bridleway or byway open to all traffic or road used as a

public path) or is a cycle track under the Highways Act 1980 or the Cycle Tracks Act 1984; or

(ii) a road within the meaning of the Roads (Scotland) Act 1984 unless it falls within the definitions in section 151(2)(a)(ii) or (b) (footpaths and cycle tracks) of that Act or is a bridleway within the meaning of section 47 of the Countryside (Scotland) Act 1967;

"the local authority", in relation to common land, means any local authority which has powers in relation to the land under section 9 of the Commons Registration Act 1965;

"occupier" (and in subsection (8) "the other occupier") means—

(a) in England and Wales, the person entitled to possession of the land by virtue of an estate or interest held by him; and

(b) in Scotland, the person lawfully entitled to natural possession of the land;

"property", in relation to damage to property on land, means—

(a) in England and Wales, property within the meaning of section 10(1) of the Criminal Damage Act 1971; and

(b) in Scotland, either—

(i) heritable property other than land; or

(ii) corporeal moveable property,

and "damage" includes the deposit of any substance capable of polluting the land;

"trespass" means, in the application of this section—

(a) in England and Wales, subject to the extensions effected by subsection (7) above, trespass as against the occupier of the land;

(b) in Scotland, entering, or as the case may be remaining on, land without lawful authority and without the occupier's consent; and

"trespassing" and "trespasser" shall be construed accordingly;

"vehicle" includes—

(a) any vehicle, whether or not it is in a fit state for use on roads, and includes any chassis or body, with or without wheels, appearing to have formed part of such a vehicle, and any load carried by, and anything attached to, such a vehicle; and

(b) a caravan as defined in section 29(1) of the Caravan Sites and Control of Development Act 1960;

and a person may be regarded for the purposes of this section as having a purpose of residing in a place notwithstanding that he has a home elsewhere.

References   See para 5.2.

62 Supplementary powers of seizure

(1)   If a direction has been given under section 61 and a constable reasonably suspects that any person to whom the direction applies has, without reasonable excuse—

(a) failed to remove any vehicle on the land which appears to the constable to belong to him or to be in his possession or under his control; or

(b) entered the land as a trespasser with a vehicle within the period of three months beginning with the day on which the direction was given,

the constable may seize and remove that vehicle.

(2)   In this section, "trespasser" and "vehicle" have the same meaning as in section 61.

References   See para 5.3.

Powers in relation to raves

63 Powers to remove persons attending or preparing for a rave

(1)   This section applies to a gathering on land in the open air of 100 or more persons (whether or not trespassers) at which amplified music is played during the night (with or without intermissions) and is such as, by reason of its loudness and duration and the time at which it is played, is likely to cause serious distress to the inhabitants of the locality; and for this purpose—

    (a)   such a gathering continues during intermissions in the music and, where the gathering extends over several days, throughout the period during which amplified music is played at night (with or without intermissions); and

    (b)   "music" includes sounds wholly or predominantly characterised by the emission of a succession of repetitive beats.

(2)   If, as respects any land in the open air, a police officer of at least the rank of superintendent reasonably believes that—

    (a)   two or more persons are making preparations for the holding there of a gathering to which this section applies,

    (b)   ten or more persons are waiting for such a gathering to begin there, or

    (c)   ten or more persons are attending such a gathering which is in progress,

he may give a direction that those persons and any other persons who come to prepare or wait for or to attend the gathering are to leave the land and remove any vehicles or other property which they have with them on the land.

(3)   A direction under subsection (2) above, if not communicated to the persons referred to in subsection (2) by the police officer giving the direction, may be communicated to them by any constable at the scene.

(4)   Persons shall be treated as having had a direction under subsection (2) above communicated to them if reasonable steps have been taken to bring it to their attention.

(5)   A direction under subsection (2) above does not apply to an exempt person.

(6)   If a person knowing that a direction has been given which applies to him—

    (a)   fails to leave the land as soon as reasonably practicable, or

    (b)   having left again enters the land within the period of 7 days beginning with the day on which the direction was given,

he commits an offence and is liable on summary conviction to imprisonment for a term not exceeding three months or a fine not exceeding level 4 on the standard scale, or both.

(7)   In proceedings for an offence under this section it is a defence for the accused to show that he had a reasonable excuse for failing to leave the land as soon as reasonably practicable or, as the case may be, for again entering the land.

(8)   A constable in uniform who reasonably suspects that a person is committing an offence under this section may arrest him without a warrant.

(9)   This section does not apply—
   (a)   in England and Wales, to a gathering licensed by an entertainment licence; or
   (b)   in Scotland, to a gathering in premises which, by virtue of section 41 of the Civic Government (Scotland) Act 1982, are licensed to be used as a place of public entertainment.

(10)   In this section—
   "entertainment licence" means a licence granted by a local authority under—
      (a)   Schedule 12 to the London Government Act 1963;
      (b)   section 3 of the Private Places of Entertainment (Licensing) Act 1967; or
      (c)   Schedule 1 to the Local Government (Miscellaneous Provisions) Act 1982;
   "exempt person", in relation to land (or any gathering on land), means the occupier, any member of his family and any employee or agent of his and any person whose home is situated on the land;
   "land in the open air" includes a place partly open to the air;
   "local authority" means—
      (a)   in Greater London, a London borough council or the Common Council of the City of London;
      (b)   in England outside Greater London, a district council or the council of the Isles of Scilly;
      (c)   in Wales, a county council or county borough council;
   and "occupier", "trespasser" and "vehicle" have the same meaning as in section 61.

(11)   Until 1st April 1996, in this section "local authority" means, in Wales, a district council.

References   See para 5.5.

---

64 Supplementary powers of entry and seizure

(1)   If a police officer of at least the rank of superintendent reasonably believes that circumstances exist in relation to any land which would justify the giving of a direction under section 63 in relation to a gathering to which that section applies he may authorise any constable to enter the land for any of the purposes specified in subsection (2) below.

(2)   Those purposes are—
   (a)   to ascertain whether such circumstances exist; and
   (b)   to exercise any power conferred on a constable by section 63 or subsection (4) below.

(3)   A constable who is so authorised to enter land for any purpose may enter the land without a warrant.

(4)   If a direction has been given under section 63 and a constable reasonably suspects that any person to whom the direction applies has, without reasonable excuse—
   (a)   failed to remove any vehicle or sound equipment on the land which appears to the constable to belong to him or to be in his possession or under his control; or

(b)   entered the land as a trespasser with a vehicle or sound equipment within the period of 7 days beginning with the day on which the direction was given,

the constable may seize and remove that vehicle or sound equipment.

(5)   Subsection (4) above does not authorise the seizure of any vehicle or sound equipment of an exempt person.

(6)   In this section—

"exempt person" has the same meaning as in section 63;

"sound equipment" means equipment designed or adapted for amplifying music and any equipment suitable for use in connection with such equipment, and "music" has the same meaning as in section 63; and

"vehicle" has the same meaning as in section 61.

References   See para 5.5.

65 Raves: power to stop persons from proceeding

(1)   If a constable in uniform reasonably believes that a person is on his way to a gathering to which section 63 applies in relation to which a direction under section 63(2) is in force, he may, subject to subsections (2) and (3) below—

(a)   stop that person, and

(b)   direct him not to proceed in the direction of the gathering.

(2)   The power conferred by subsection (1) above may only be exercised at a place within 5 miles of the boundary of the site of the gathering.

(3)   No direction may be given under subsection (1) above to an exempt person.

(4)   If a person knowing that a direction under subsection (1) above has been given to him fails to comply with that direction, he commits an offence and is liable on summary conviction to a fine not exceeding level 3 on the standard scale.

(5)   A constable in uniform who reasonably suspects that a person is committing an offence under this section may arrest him without a warrant.

(6)   In this section, "exempt person" has the same meaning as in section 63.

References   See para 5.6.

66 Power of court to forfeit sound equipment

(1)   Where a person is convicted of an offence under section 63 in relation to a gathering to which that section applies and the court is satisfied that any sound equipment which has been seized from him under section 64(4), or which was in his possession or under his control at the relevant time, has been used at the gathering the court may make an order for forfeiture under this subsection in respect of that property.

(2)   The court may make an order under subsection (1) above whether or not it also deals with the offender in respect of the offence in any other way and without regard to any restrictions on forfeiture in any enactment.

(3)   In considering whether to make an order under subsection (1) above in respect of any property a court shall have regard—

(a)   to the value of the property; and

(b) to the likely financial and other effects on the offender of the making of the order (taken together with any other order that the court contemplates making).

(4) An order under subsection (1) above shall operate to deprive the offender of his rights, if any, in the property to which it relates, and the property shall (if not already in their possession) be taken into the possession of the police.

(5) Except in a case to which subsection (6) below applies, where any property has been forfeited under subsection (1) above, a magistrates' court may, on application by a claimant of the property, other than the offender from whom it was forfeited under subsection (1) above, make an order for delivery of the property to the applicant if it appears to the court that he is the owner of the property.

(6) In a case where forfeiture under subsection (1) above has been by order of a Scottish court, a claimant such as is mentioned in subsection (5) above may, in such manner as may be prescribed by act of adjournal, apply to that court for an order for the return of the property in question.

(7) No application shall be made under subsection (5), or by virtue of subsection (6), above by any claimant of the property after the expiration of 6 months from the date on which an order under subsection (1) above was made in respect of the property.

(8) No such application shall succeed unless the claimant satisfies the court either that he had not consented to the offender having possession of the property or that he did not know, and had no reason to suspect, that the property was likely to be used at a gathering to which section 63 applies.

(9) An order under subsection (5), or by virtue of subsection (6), above shall not affect the right of any person to take, within the period of 6 months from the date of an order under subsection (5), or as the case may be by virtue of subsection (6), above, proceedings for the recovery of the property from the person in possession of it in pursuance of the order, but on the expiration of that period the right shall cease.

(10) The Secretary of State may make regulations for the disposal of property, and for the application of the proceeds of sale of property, forfeited under subsection (1) above where no application by a claimant of the property under subsection (5), or by virtue of subsection (6), above has been made within the period specified in subsection (7) above or no such application has succeeded.

(11) The regulations may also provide for the investment of money and for the audit of accounts.

(12) The power to make regulations under subsection (10) above shall be exercisable by statutory instrument which shall be subject to annulment in pursuance of a resolution of either House of Parliament.

(13) In this section—
> "relevant time", in relation to a person—
>> (a) convicted in England and Wales of an offence under section 63, means the time of his arrest for the offence or of the issue of a summons in respect of it;
>> (b) so convicted in Scotland, means the time of his arrest for, or of his being cited as an accused in respect of, the offence;
> "sound equipment" has the same meaning as in section 64.

References See para 5.6.

Retention and charges for seized property

67 Retention and charges for seized property

(1)   Any vehicles which have been seized and removed by a constable under section 62(1) or 64(4) may be retained in accordance with regulations made by the Secretary of State under subsection (3) below.

(2)   Any sound equipment which has been seized and removed by a constable under section 64(4) may be retained until the conclusion of proceedings against the person from whom it was seized for an offence under section 63.

(3)   The Secretary of State may make regulations—
   (a)   regulating the retention and safe keeping and the disposal and the destruction in prescribed circumstances of vehicles; and
   (b)   prescribing charges in respect of the removal, retention, disposal and destruction of vehicles.

(4)   Any authority shall be entitled to recover from a person from whom a vehicle has been seized such charges as may be prescribed in respect of the removal, retention, disposal and destruction of the vehicle by the authority.

(5)   Regulations under subsection (3) above may make different provisions for different classes of vehicles or for different circumstances.

(6)   Any charges under subsection (4) above shall be recoverable as a simple contract debt.

(7)   Any authority having custody of vehicles under regulations under subsection (3) above shall be entitled to retain custody until any charges under subsection (4) are paid.

(8)   The power to make regulations under subsection (3) above shall be exercisable by statutory instrument which shall be subject to annulment in pursuance of a resolution of either House of Parliament.

(9)   In this section—
   "conclusion of proceedings" against a person means—
      (a)   his being sentenced or otherwise dealt with for the offence or his acquittal;
      (b)   the discontinuance of the proceedings; or
      (c)   the decision not to prosecute him,
   whichever is the earlier;
   "sound equipment" has the same meaning as in section 64; and
   "vehicle" has the same meaning as in section 61.

References See para 5.6.

Disruptive trespassers

68 Offence of aggravated trespass

(1)   A person commits the offence of aggravated trespass if he trespasses on land in the open air and, in relation to any lawful activity which persons are engaging in or

are about to engage in on that or adjoining land in the open air, does there anything which is intended by him to have the effect—

    (a) of intimidating those persons or any of them so as to deter them or any of them from engaging in that activity,

    (b) of obstructing that activity, or

    (c) of disrupting that activity.

(2)   Activity on any occasion on the part of a person or persons on land is "lawful" for the purposes of this section if he or they may engage in the activity on the land on that occasion without committing an offence or trespassing on the land.

(3)   A person guilty of an offence under this section is liable on summary conviction to imprisonment for a term not exceeding three months or a fine not exceeding level 4 on the standard scale, or both.

(4)   A constable in uniform who reasonably suspects that a person is committing an offence under this section may arrest him without a warrant.

(5)   In this section "land" does not include—

    (a) the highways and roads excluded from the application of section 61 by paragraph (b) of the definition of "land" in subsection (9) of that section; or

    (b) a road within the meaning of the Roads (Northern Ireland) Order 1993.

References   See para 5.7.

69 Powers to remove persons committing or participating in aggravated trespass

(1)   If the senior police officer present at the scene reasonably believes—

    (a) that a person is committing, has committed or intends to commit the offence of aggravated trespass on land in the open air; or

    (b) that two or more persons are trespassing on land in the open air and are present there with the common purpose of intimidating persons so as to deter them from engaging in a lawful activity or of obstructing or disrupting a lawful activity,

he may direct that person or (as the case may be) those persons (or any of them) to leave the land.

(2)   A direction under subsection (1) above, if not communicated to the persons referred to in subsection (1) by the police officer giving the direction, may be communicated to them by any constable at the scene.

(3)   If a person knowing that a direction under subsection (1) above has been given which applies to him—

    (a) fails to leave the land as soon as practicable, or

    (b) having left again enters the land as a trespasser within the period of three months beginning with the day on which the direction was given,

he commits an offence and is liable on summary conviction to imprisonment for a term not exceeding three months or a fine not exceeding level 4 on the standard scale, or both.

(4)   In proceedings for an offence under subsection (3) it is a defence for the accused to show—

    (a)   that he was not trespassing on the land, or

    (b)   that he had a reasonable excuse for failing to leave the land as soon as practicable or, as the case may be, for again entering the land as a trespasser.

(5)   A constable in uniform who reasonably suspects that a person is committing an offence under this section may arrest him without a warrant.

(6)   In this section "lawful activity" and "land" have the same meaning as in section 68.

References   See para 5.8.

Trespassory assemblies

70 Trespassory assemblies

In Part II of the Public Order Act 1986 (processions and assemblies), after section 14, there shall be inserted the following sections—

"14A Prohibiting trespassory assemblies

(1)   If at any time the chief officer of police reasonably believes that an assembly is intended to be held in any district at a place on land to which the public has no right of access or only a limited right of access and that the assembly—

    (a)   is likely to be held without the permission of the occupier of the land or to conduct itself in such a way as to exceed the limits of any permission of his or the limits of the public's right of access, and

    (b)   may result—

        (i)   in serious disruption to the life of the community, or

        (ii)   where the land, or a building or monument on it, is of historical, architectural, archaeological or scientific importance, in significant damage to the land, building or monument,

he may apply to the council of the district for an order prohibiting for a specified period the holding of all trespassory assemblies in the district or a part of it, as specified.

(2)   On receiving such an application, a council may—

    (a)   in England and Wales, with the consent of the Secretary of State make an order either in the terms of the application or with such modifications as may be approved by the Secretary of State; or

    (b)   in Scotland, make an order in the terms of the application.

(3)   Subsection (1) does not apply in the City of London or the metropolitan police district.

(4)   If at any time the Commissioner of Police for the City of London or the Commissioner of Police of the Metropolis reasonably believes that an assembly is intended to be held at a place on land to which the public has no right of access or only a limited right of access in his police area and that the assembly—

    (a)   is likely to be held without the permission of the occupier of the land or to conduct itself in such a way as to exceed the limits of any permission of his or the limits of the public's right of access, and

    (b) may result—
        (i) in serious disruption to the life of the community, or
        (ii) where the land, or a building or monument on it, is of historical, architectural, archaeological or scientific importance, in significant damage to the land, building or monument,

he may with the consent of the Secretary of State make an order prohibiting for a specified period the holding of all trespassory assemblies in the area or a part of it, as specified.

(5)   An order prohibiting the holding of trespassory assemblies operates to prohibit any assembly which—

    (a) is held on land to which the public has no right of access or only a limited right of access, and
    (b) takes place in the prohibited circumstances, that is to say, without the permission of the occupier of the land or so as to exceed the limits of any permission of his or the limits of the public's right of access.

(6)   No order under this section shall prohibit the holding of assemblies for a period exceeding 4 days or in an area exceeding an area represented by a circle with a radius of 5 miles from a specified centre.

(7)   An order made under this section may be revoked or varied by a subsequent order made in the same way, that is, in accordance with subsection (1) and (2) or subsection (4), as the case may be.

(8)   Any order under this section shall, if not made in writing, be recorded in writing as soon as practicable after being made.

(9)   In this section and sections 14B and 14C—
    "assembly" means an assembly of 20 or more persons;
    "land" means land in the open air;
    "limited", in relation to a right of access by the public to land, means that their use of it is restricted to use for a particular purpose (as in the case of a highway or road) or is subject to other restrictions;
    "occupier" means—
        (a) in England and Wales, the person entitled to possession of the land by virtue of an estate or interest held by him; or
        (b) in Scotland, the person lawfully entitled to natural possession of the land,
    and in subsections (1) and (4) includes the person reasonably believed
    by the authority applying for or making the order to be the occupier;
    "public" includes a section of the public; and
    "specified" means specified in an order under this section.

(10)   In relation to Scotland, the references in subsection (1) above to a district and to the council of the district shall be construed—

    (a) as respects applications before 1st April 1996, as references to the area of a regional or islands authority and to the authority in question; and
    (b) as respects applications on and after that date, as references to a local government area and to the council for that area.

(11)   In relation to Wales, the references in subsection (1) above to a district and to the council of the district shall be construed, as respects applications on and after 1st April 1996, as references to a county or county borough and to the council for that county or county borough.

14B Offences in connection with trespassory assemblies and arrest therefor

(1)   A person who organises an assembly the holding of which he knows is prohibited by an order under section 14A is guilty of an offence.

(2)   A person who takes part in an assembly which he knows is prohibited by an order under section 14A is guilty of an offence.

(3)   In England and Wales, a person who incites another to commit an offence under subsection (2) is guilty of an offence.

(4)   A constable in uniform may arrest without a warrant anyone he reasonably suspects to be committing an offence under this section.

(5)   A person guilty of an offence under subsection (1) is liable on summary conviction to imprisonment for a term not exceeding 3 months or a fine not exceeding level 4 on the standard scale or both.

(6)   A person guilty of an offence under subsection (2) is liable on summary conviction to a fine not exceeding level 3 on the standard scale.

(7)   A person guilty of an offence under subsection (3) is liable on summary conviction to imprisonment for a term not exceeding 3 months or a fine not exceeding level 4 on the standard scale or both, notwithstanding section 45(3) of the Magistrates' Courts Act 1980.

(8)   Subsection (3) above is without prejudice to the application of any principle of Scots Law as respects art and part guilt to such incitement as is mentioned in that subsection.".

Definitions   For "the City of London" and "the metropolitan police district", see the Public Order Act 1986, s 16; for "assembly", "land", "limited", "occupier", "public" and "specified", see s 14A(9) of the 1986 Act, as inserted above.
References   See para 5.9.

---

71 Trespassory assemblies: power to stop persons from proceeding

After the section 14B inserted by section 70 in the Public Order Act 1986 there shall be inserted the following section—

"14C Stopping persons from proceeding to trespassory assemblies

(1)   If a constable in uniform reasonably believes .that a person is on his way to an assembly within the area to which an order under section 14A applies which the constable reasonably believes is likely to be an assembly which is prohibited by that order, he may, subject to subsection (2) below—
    (a) stop that person, and
    (b) direct him not to proceed in the direction of the assembly.

(2)   The power conferred by subsection (1) may only be exercised within the area to which the order applies.

(3)   A person who fails to comply with a direction under subsection (1) which he knows has been given to him is guilty of an offence.

(4)   A constable in uniform may arrest without a warrant anyone he reasonably suspects to be committing an offence under this section.

(5)   A person guilty of an offence under subsection (3) is liable on summary conviction to a fine not exceeding level 3 on the standard scale.".

References   See para 5.9.

Squatters

72   Violent entry to premises: special position of displaced residential occupiers and intending occupiers

(1)   Section 6 of the Criminal Law Act 1977 (which penalises violence by a person for securing entry into premises where a person on the premises is opposed and is known to be opposed to entry) shall be amended as follows.

(2)   After subsection (1), there shall be inserted the following subsection—

"(1A) Subsection (1) above does not apply to a person who is a displaced residential occupier or a protected intending occupier of the premises in question or who is acting on behalf of such an occupier; and if the accused adduces sufficient evidence that he was, or was acting on behalf of, such an occupier he shall be presumed to be, or to be acting on behalf of, such an occupier unless the contrary is proved by the prosecution.".

(3)   In subsection (2), at the beginning, there shall be inserted the words "Subject to subsection (1A) above,".

(4)   Subsection (3) (which is superseded by the provision made by subsection (2) above) shall be omitted.

(5)   In subsection (7), at the end, there shall be inserted the words "and section 12A below contains provisions which apply for determining when any person is to be regarded for the purposes of this Part of this Act as a protected intending occupier of any premises or of any access to any premises.".

Definitions   For "access" and "premises", see the Criminal Law Act 1977, s 12(1), as read with s 12(2); for "displaced residential occupier", see s 12(3)–(7) of that Act; for "protected intending occupier", see s 12A(1)–(7) of that Act, as inserted by s 74 of this Act.
References   See para 5.10.

73   Adverse occupation of residential premises

For section 7 of the Criminal Law Act 1977 (trespassers failing to leave premises after being requested to do so by specified persons to be guilty of an offence) there shall be substituted the following section—

"7   Adverse occupation of residential premises

(1)   Subject to the following provisions of this section and to section 12A(9) below, any person who is on any premises as a trespasser after having entered as such is guilty of an offence if he fails to leave those premises on being required to do so by or on behalf of—

(a)   a displaced residential occupier of the premises; or
(b)   an individual who is a protected intending occupier of the premises.

(2)   In any proceedings for an offence under this section it shall be a defence for the accused to prove that he believed that the person requiring him to leave the premises was not a displaced residential occupier or protected intending occupier of the premises or a person acting on behalf of a displaced residential occupier or protected intending occupier.

(3)   In any proceedings for an offence under this section it shall be a defence for the accused to prove—

    (a) that the premises in question are or form part of premises used mainly for non-residential purposes; and

    (b) that he was not on any part of the premises used wholly or mainly for residential purposes.

(4)   Any reference in the preceding provisions of this section to any premises includes a reference to any access to them, whether or not any such access itself constitutes premises, within the meaning of this Part of this Act.

(5)   A person guilty of an offence under this section shall be liable on summary conviction to imprisonment for a term not exceeding six months or to a fine not exceeding level 5 on the standard scale or to both.

(6)   A constable in uniform may arrest without warrant anyone who is, or whom he, with reasonable cause, suspects to be, guilty of an offence under this section.

(7)   Section 12 below contains provisions which apply for determining when any person is to be regarded for the purposes of this Part of this Act as a displaced residential occupier of any premises or of any access to any premises and section 12A below contains provisions which apply for determining when any person is to be regarded for the purposes of this Part of this Act as a protected intending occupier of any premises or of any access to any premises.".

Definitions   For "access" and "premises", see the Criminal Law Act 1977, s 12(1), as read with s 12(2); for "displaced residential occupier", see s 12(3)–(7) of that Act; for "protected intending occupier", see s 12A(1)–(7) of that Act, as inserted by s 69 of this Act.
References   See para 5.11.

---

74 Protected intending occupiers: supplementary provisions

After section 12 of the Criminal Law Act 1977 there shall be inserted the following section—

"12A Protected intending occupiers: supplementary provisions

(1)   For the purposes of this Part of this Act an individual is a protected intending occupier of any premises at any time if at that time he falls within subsection (2), (4) or (6) below.

(2)   An individual is a protected intending occupier of any premises if—

    (a) he has in those premises a freehold interest or a leasehold interest with not less than two years still to run;

    (b) he requires the premises for his own occupation as a residence;

    (c) he is excluded from occupation of the premises by a person who entered them, or any access to them, as a trespasser; and

    (d) he or a person acting on his behalf holds a written statement—

        (i)   which specifies his interest in the premises;

        (ii) which states that he requires the premises for occupation as a residence for himself; and

        (iii) with respect to which the requirements in subsection (3) below are fulfilled.

(3)   The requirements referred to in subsection (2)(d)(iii) above are—

(a) that the statement is signed by the person whose interest is specified in it in the presence of a justice of the peace or commissioner for oaths; and

(b) that the justice of the peace or commissioner for oaths has subscribed his name as a witness to the signature.

(4)   An individual is also a protected intending occupier of any premises if—

(a) he has a tenancy of those premises (other than a tenancy falling within subsection (2)(a) above or (6)(a) below) or a licence to occupy those premises granted by a person with a freehold interest or a leasehold interest with not less than two years still to run in the premises;

(b) he requires the premises for his own occupation as a residence;

(c) he is excluded from occupation of the premises by a person who entered them, or any access to them, as a trespasser; and

(d) he or a person acting on his behalf holds a written statement—

(i)   which states that he has been granted a tenancy of those premises or a licence to occupy those premises;

(ii)   which specifies the interest in the premises of the person who granted that tenancy or licence to occupy ("the landlord");

(iii) which states that he requires the premises for occupation as a residence for himself; and

(iv)   with respect to which the requirements in subsection (5) below are fulfilled.

(5)   The requirements referred to in subsection (4)(d)(iv) above are—

(a) that the statement is signed by the landlord and by the tenant or licensee in the presence of a justice of the peace or commissioner for oaths;

(b) that the justice of the peace or commissioner for oaths has subscribed his name as a witness to the signatures.

(6)   An individual is also a protected intending occupier of any premises if—

(a) he has a tenancy of those premises (other than a tenancy falling within subsection (2)(a) or (4)(a) above) or a licence to occupy those premises granted by an authority to which this subsection applies;

(b) he requires the premises for his own occupation as a residence;

(c) he is excluded from occupation of the premises by a person who entered the premises, or any access to them, as a trespasser; and

(d) there has been issued to him by or on behalf of the authority referred to in paragraph (a) above a certificate stating that—

(i)   he has been granted a tenancy of those premises or a licence to occupy those premises as a residence by the authority; and

(ii)   the authority which granted that tenancy or licence to occupy is one to which this subsection applies, being of a description specified in the certificate.

(7)   Subsection (6) above applies to the following authorities—

(a) any body mentioned in section 14 of the Rent Act 1977 (landlord's interest belonging to local authority etc);

(b) the Housing Corporation;

(c) Housing for Wales; and

(d) a registered housing association within the meaning of the Housing Associations Act 1985.

(8)   A person is guilty of an offence if he makes a statement for the purposes of subsection (2)(d) or (4)(d) above which he knows to be false in a material particular or if he recklessly makes such a statement which is false in a material particular.

(9)   In any proceedings for an offence under section 7 of this Act where the accused was requested to leave the premises by a person claiming to be or to act on behalf of a protected intending occupier of the premises—

    (a)   it shall be a defence for the accused to prove that, although asked to do so by the accused at the time the accused was requested to leave, that person failed at that time to produce to the accused such a statement as is referred to in subsection (2)(d) or (4)(d) above or such a certificate as is referred to in subsection (6)(d) above; and

    (b)   any document purporting to be a certificate under subsection (6)(d) above shall be received in evidence and, unless the contrary is proved, shall be deemed to have been issued by or on behalf of the authority stated in the certificate.

(10)   A person guilty of an offence under subsection (8) above shall be liable on summary conviction to imprisonment for a term not exceeding six months or to a fine not exceeding level 5 on the standard scale or to both.

(11)   A person who is a protected intending occupier of any premises shall be regarded for the purposes of this Part of this Act as a protected intending occupier also of any access to those premises.".

Definitions   For "access" and "premises", see the Criminal Law Act 1977, s 12(1), as read with s 12(2); for "the landlord", see s 12A(4)(d)(ii) of that Act, as inserted above.
References   See para 5.11.

75 Interim possession orders: false or misleading statements

(1)   A person commits an offence if, for the purpose of obtaining an interim possession order, he—

    (a)   makes a statement which he knows to be false or misleading in a material particular; or

    (b)   recklessly makes a statement which is false or misleading in a material particular.

(2)   A person commits an offence if, for the purpose of resisting the making of an interim possession order, he—

    (a)   makes a statement which he knows to be false or misleading in a material particular; or

    (b)   recklessly makes a statement which is false or misleading in a material particular.

(3)   A person guilty of an offence under this section shall be liable—

    (a)   on conviction on indictment, to imprisonment for a term not exceeding two years or a fine or both;

    (b)   on summary conviction, to imprisonment for a term not exceeding six months or a fine not exceeding the statutory maximum or both.

(4)   In this section—

    "interim possession order" means an interim possession order (so entitled) made under rules of court for the bringing of summary proceedings for possession of premises which are occupied by trespassers;

"premises" has the same meaning as in Part II of the Criminal Law Act 1977 (offences relating to entering and remaining on property); and

"statement", in relation to an interim possession order, means any statement, in writing or oral and whether as to fact or belief, made in or for the purposes of the proceedings.

References   See para 5.11,

76 Interim possession orders: trespassing during currency of order

(1)   This section applies where an interim possession order has been made in respect of any premises and served in accordance with rules of court; and references to "the order" and "the premises" shall be construed accordingly.

(2)   Subject to subsection (3), a person who is present on the premises as a trespasser at any time during the currency of the order commits an offence.

(3)   No offence under subsection (2) is committed by a person if—
    (a)   he leaves the premises within 24 hours of the time of service of the order and does not return; or
    (b)   a copy of the order was not fixed to the premises in accordance with rules of court.

(4)   A person who was in occupation of the premises at the time of service of the order but leaves them commits an offence if he re-enters the premises as a trespasser or attempts to do so after the expiry of the order but within the period of one year beginning with the day on which it was served.

(5)   A person guilty of an offence under this section shall be liable on summary conviction to imprisonment for a term not exceeding six months or a fine not exceeding level 5 on the standard scale or both.

(6)   A person who is in occupation of the premises at the time of service of the order shall be treated for the purposes of this section as being present as a trespasser.

(7)   A constable in uniform may arrest without a warrant anyone who is, or whom he reasonably suspects to be, guilty of an offence under this section.

(8)   In this section—
    "interim possession order" has the same meaning as in section 75 above and "rules of court" is to be construed accordingly; and
    "premises" has the same meaning as in that section, that is to say, the same meaning as in Part II of the Criminal Law Act 1977 (offences relating to entering and remaining on property).

References   See para 5.11.

Powers to remove unauthorised campers

77 Power of local authority to direct unauthorised campers to leave land

(1)   If it appears to a local authority that persons are for the time being residing in a vehicle or vehicles within that authority's area—
    (a)   on any land forming part of a highway;
    (b)   on any other unoccupied land; or
    (c)   on any occupied land without the consent of the occupier,

the authority may give a direction that those persons and any others with them are to leave the land and remove the vehicle or vehicles and any other property they have with them on the land.

(2) Notice of a direction under subsection (1) must be served on the persons to whom the direction applies, but it shall be sufficient for this purpose for the direction to specify the land and (except where the direction applies to only one person) to be addressed to all occupants of the vehicles on the land, without naming them.

(3) If a person knowing that a direction under subsection (1) above has been given which applies to him—

(a) fails, as soon as practicable, to leave the land or remove from the land any vehicle or other property which is the subject of the direction, or

(b) having removed any such vehicle or property again enters the land with a vehicle within the period of three months beginning with the day on which the direction was given,

he commits an offence and is liable on summary conviction to a fine not exceeding level 3 on the standard scale.

(4) A direction under subsection (1) operates to require persons who re-enter the land within the said period with vehicles or other property to leave and remove the vehicles or other property as it operates in relation to the persons and vehicles or other property on the land when the direction was given.

(5) In proceedings for an offence under this section it is a defence for the accused to show that his failure to leave or to remove the vehicle or other property as soon as practicable or his re-entry with a vehicle was due to illness, mechanical breakdown or other immediate emergency.

(6) In this section—

"land" means land in the open air;

"local authority" means—

(a) in Greater London, a London borough or the Common Council of the City of London;

(b) in England outside Greater London, a county council, a district council or the Council of the Isles of Scilly;

(c) in Wales, a county council or a county borough council;

"occupier" means the person entitled to possession of the land by virtue of an estate or interest held by him;

"vehicle" includes—

(a) any vehicle, whether or not it is in a fit state for use on roads, and includes any body, with or without wheels, appearing to have formed part of such a vehicle, and any load carried by, and anything attached to, such a vehicle; and

(b) a caravan as defined in section 29(1) of the Caravan Sites and Control of Development Act 1960;

and a person may be regarded for the purposes of this section as residing on any land notwithstanding that he has a home elsewhere.

(7) Until 1st April 1996, in this section "local authority" means, in Wales, a county council or a district council.

References See para 5.12.

78 Orders for removal of persons and their vehicles unlawfully on land

(1)　A magistrates' court may, on a complaint made by a local authority, if satisfied that persons and vehicles in which they are residing are present on land within that authority's area in contravention of a direction given under section 77, make an order requiring the removal of any vehicle or other property which is so present on the land and any person residing in it.

(2)　An order under this section may authorise the local authority to take such steps as are reasonably necessary to ensure that the order is complied with and, in particular, may authorise the authority, by its officers and servants—

(a)　to enter upon the land specified in the order; and

(b)　to take, in relation to any vehicle or property to be removed in pursuance of the order, such steps for securing entry and rendering it suitable for removal as may be so specified.

(3)　The local authority shall not enter upon any occupied land unless they have given to the owner and occupier at least 24 hours notice of their intention to do so, or unless after reasonable inquiries they are unable to ascertain their names and addresses.

(4)　A person who wilfully obstructs any person in the exercise of any power conferred on him by an order under this section commits an offence and is liable on summary conviction to a fine not exceeding level 3 on the standard scale.

(5)　Where a complaint is made under this section, a summons issued by the court requiring the person or persons to whom it is directed to appear before the court to answer to the complaint may be directed—

(a)　to the occupant of a particular vehicle on the land in question; or

(b)　to all occupants of vehicles on the land in question, without naming him or them.

(6)　Section 55(2) of the Magistrates' Courts Act 1980 (warrant for arrest of defendant failing to appear) does not apply to proceedings on a complaint made under this section.

(7)　Section 77(6) of this Act applies also for the interpretation of this section.

Definitions　For "land", "local authority", "occupier", "vehicle" and "residing", see, by virtue of sub-s (7) above, s 77(6), (7) of this Act.
References　See para 5.13.

79 Provisions as to directions under s 77 and orders under s 78

(1)　The following provisions apply in relation to the service of notice of a direction under section 77 and of a summons under section 78, referred to in those provisions as a "relevant document".

(2)　Where it is impracticable to serve a relevant document on a person named in it, the document shall be treated as duly served on him if a copy of it is fixed in a prominent place to the vehicle concerned; and where a relevant document is directed to the unnamed occupants of vehicles, it shall be treated as duly served on those occupants if a copy of it is fixed in a prominent place to every vehicle on the land in question at the time when service is thus effected.

(3)　A local authority shall take such steps as may be reasonably practicable to secure that a copy of any relevant document is displayed on the land in question (otherwise than by being fixed to a vehicle) in a manner designed to ensure that it is likely to be seen by any person camping on the land.

(4)   Notice of any relevant document shall be given by the local authority to the owner of the land in question and to any occupier of that land unless, after reasonable inquiries, the authority is unable to ascertain the name and address of the owner or occupier; and the owner of any such land and any occupier of such land shall be entitled to appear and to be heard in the proceedings.

(5)   Section 77(6) applies also for the interpretation of this section.

Definitions   For "land", "local authority", "occupier", and "vehicle" see, by virtue of sub-s (7) above, s 77(6), (7) of this Act.
References   See para 5.14.

80 Repeal of certain provisions relating to gipsy sites

(1)   Part II of the Caravan Sites Act 1968 (duty of local authorities to provide sites for gipsies and control of unauthorised encampments) together with the definition in section 16 of that Act of "gipsies" is hereby repealed.

(2)   In section 24 of the Caravan Sites and Control of Development Act 1960 (power to provide sites for caravans)—

(a)   in subsection (2), after paragraph (b) there shall be inserted the following—

", or

(c)   to provide, in or in connection with sites for the accommodation of gipsies, working space and facilities for the carrying on of such activities as are normally carried on by them," ; and

(b)   in subsection (8), at the end, there shall be inserted the words "and "gipsies" means persons of nomadic habit of life, whatever their race or origin, but does not include members of an organised group of travelling showmen, or persons engaged in travelling circuses, travelling together as such.".

(3)   The repeal by subsection (1) above of section 8 of the said Act of 1968 shall not affect the validity of directions given under subsection (3)(a) of that section; and in the case of directions under subsection (3)(c), the council may elect either to withdraw the application or request the Secretary of State to determine the application and if they so request the application shall be treated as referred to him under section 77 of the Town and Country Planning Act 1990.

(4)   The repeal by subsection (1) above of the definition of "gipsies" in section 16 of the said Act of 1968 shall not affect the interpretation of that word in the definition of "protected site" in section 5(1) of the Mobile Homes Act 1983 or in any document embodying the terms of any planning permission granted under the Town and Country Planning Act 1990 before the commencement of this section.

(5)   Section 70 of the Local Government, Planning and Land Act 1980 (power to pay grant to local authorities in respect of capital expenditure in providing gipsy caravan sites) is hereby repealed so far as it extends to England and Wales except for the purposes of applications for grant received by the Secretary of State before the commencement of this section.

References   See para 5.14.

PART VI
PREVENTION OF TERRORISM

81 Powers to stop and search vehicles, etc and persons

(1)   In Part IV of the Prevention of Terrorism (Temporary Provisions) Act 1989 (powers of arrest, detention and control of entry) there shall be inserted, before section 14, the following section—

"13A Powers to stop and search vehicles etc and persons

(1)   Where it appears to—
(a) any officer of police of or above the rank of commander of the metropolitan police, as respects the metropolitan police area;
(b) any officer of police of or above the rank of commander of the City of London police, as respects the City of London; or
(c) any officer of police of or above the rank of assistant chief constable for any other police area,

that it is expedient to do so in order to prevent acts of terrorism to which this section applies he may give an authorisation that the powers to stop and search vehicles and persons conferred by this section shall be exercisable at any place within his area or a specified locality in his area for a specified period not exceeding twenty eight days.

(2)   The acts of terrorism to which this section applies are—
(a) acts of terrorism connected with the affairs of Northern Ireland; and
(b) acts of terrorism of any other description except acts connected solely with the affairs of the United Kingdom or any part of the United Kingdom other than Northern Ireland.

(3)   This section confers on any constable in uniform power—
(a) to stop any vehicle;
(b) to search any vehicle, its driver or any passenger for articles of a kind which could be used for a purpose connected with the commission, preparation or instigation of acts of terrorism to which this section applies;
(c) to stop any pedestrian and search any thing carried by him for articles of a kind which could be used for a purpose connected with the commission, preparation or instigation of acts of terrorism to which this section applies.

(4)   A constable may, in the exercise of those powers, stop any vehicle or person and make any search he thinks fit whether or not he has any grounds for suspecting that the vehicle or person is carrying articles of that kind.

(5)   This section applies (with the necessary modifications) to ships and aircraft as it applies to vehicles.

(6)   A person is guilty of an offence if he—
(a) fails to stop or (as the case may be) to stop the vehicle when required to do so by a constable in the exercise of his powers under this section; or
(b) wilfully obstructs a constable in the exercise of those powers.

(7)   A person guilty of an offence under subsection (6) above shall be liable on summary conviction to imprisonment for a term not exceeding six months or a fine not exceeding level 5 on the standard scale or both.

(8)   If it appears to a police officer of the rank specified in subsection (1)(a), (b) or (c) (as the case may be) that the exercise of the powers conferred by this section ought to continue beyond the period for which their exercise has been authorised under this section he may, from time to time, authorise the exercise of those powers for a further period, not exceeding twenty eight days.

(9)   Where a vehicle is stopped by a constable under this section, the driver shall be entitled to obtain a written statement that the vehicle was stopped under the powers conferred by this section if he applies for such a statement not later than the end of the period of twelve months from the day on which the vehicle was stopped; and similarly as respects a pedestrian who is stopped under this section for a search of anything carried by him.

(10)   In this section—
"authorise" and "authorisation" mean authorise or an authorisation in writing signed by the officer giving it; and
"specified" means specified in an authorisation under this section.

(11)   Nothing in this section affects the exercise by constables of any power to stop vehicles for purposes other than those specified in subsection (1) above.".

(2)   In consequence of the insertion in Part IV of the Prevention of Terrorism (Temporary Provisions) Act 1989 of section 13A, for the title to that Part, there shall be substituted the following title—

"POWERS OF ARREST, STOP AND SEARCH, DETENTION AND CONTROL OF ENTRY".

(3)   For the purposes of section 27 of the Prevention of Terrorism (Temporary Provisions) Act 1989 (temporary provisions), the provisions inserted in that Act by this section shall be treated, as from the time when this section comes into force, as having been continued in force by the order under subsection (6) of that section which has effect at that time.

Definitions   For "aircraft", "ship", "terrorism" and "vehicle", see the Prevention of Terrorism (Temporary Provisions) Act 1989, s 20(1), (and note also as to "vehicle", s 13A(5) of that Act, as inserted above). Note as to the acts of terrorism to which s 13A of the 1989 Act applies, sub-s (2) thereof, as inserted by sub-s (1) above, and as to "authorise", "authorisation" and "specified" in that section, sub-s (10) thereof, as so inserted.
References   See para 6.1.

---

82 Offences relating to terrorism

(1)   The Prevention of Terrorism (Temporary Provisions) Act 1989 shall be amended by the insertion, as Part IVA of that Act, of the following provisions—

"PART IVA
OFFENCES AGAINST PUBLIC SECURITY

16A Possession of articles for suspected terrorist purposes

(1)   A person is guilty of an offence if he has any article in his possession in circumstances giving rise to a reasonable suspicion that the article is in his possession for a purpose connected with the commission, preparation or instigation of acts of terrorism to which this section applies.

(2) The acts of terrorism to which this section applies are—
  (a) acts of terrorism connected with the affairs of Northern Ireland; and
  (b) acts of terrorism of any other description except acts connected solely with the affairs of the United Kingdom or any part of the United Kingdom other than Northern Ireland.

(3) It is a defence for a person charged with an offence under this section to prove that at the time of the alleged offence the article in question was not in his possession for such a purpose as is mentioned in subsection (1) above.

(4) Where a person is charged with an offence under this section and it is proved that at the time of the alleged offence—
  (a) he and that article were both present in any premises; or
  (b) the article was in premises of which he was the occupier or which he habitually used otherwise than as a member of the public,
the court may accept the fact proved as sufficient evidence of his possessing that article at that time unless it is further proved that he did not at that time know of its presence in the premises in question, or, if he did know, that he had no control over it.

(5) A person guilty of an offence under this section is liable—
  (a) on conviction on indictment, to imprisonment for a term not exceeding ten years or a fine or both;
  (b) on summary conviction, to imprisonment for a term not exceeding six months or a fine not exceeding the statutory maximum or both.

(6) This section applies to vessels, aircraft and vehicles as it applies to premises.

16B Unlawful collection, etc of information

(1) No person shall, without lawful authority or reasonable excuse (the proof of which lies on him)—
  (a) collect or record any information which is of such a nature as is likely to be useful to terrorists in planning or carrying out any act of terrorism to which this section applies; or
  (b) have in his possession any record or document containing any such information as is mentioned in paragraph (a) above.

(2) The acts of terrorism to which this section applies are—
  (a) acts of terrorism connected with the affairs of Northern Ireland; and
  (b) acts of terrorism of any other description except acts connected solely with the affairs of the United Kingdom or any part of the United Kingdom other than Northern Ireland.

(3) In subsection (1) above the reference to recording information includes a reference to recording it by means of photography or by any other means.

(4) Any person who contravenes this section is guilty of an offence and liable—
  (a) on conviction on indictment, to imprisonment for a term not exceeding ten years or a fine or both;
  (b) on summary conviction, to imprisonment for a term not exceeding six months or a fine not exceeding the statutory maximum or both.

(5) The court by or before which a person is convicted of an offence under this section may order the forfeiture of any record or document mentioned in subsection (1) above which is found in his possession.".

(2)   For the purposes of section 27 of the Prevention of Terrorism (Temporary Provisions) Act 1989 (temporary provisions), the provisions constituting Part IVA of that Act inserted by this section shall be treated, as from the time when those provisions come into force, as having been continued in force by the order under subsection (6) of that section which has effect at that time.

(3)   This section shall come into force at the end of the period of two months beginning with the date on which this Act is passed.

Definitions   For "aircraft", "premises", "terrorism" and "vehicle", see the Prevention of Terrorism (Temporary Provisions) Act 1989, s 20(1), (and note also as to "premises", s 16A(6) of that Act, as inserted by sub-s (1) above). Note as to the acts of terrorism to which s 16A of the 1989 Act applies, sub-s (2) thereof, as so inserted, and as to the acts of terrorism to which s 16B of the 1989 Act apples, sub-s (2) thereof, as so inserted.
References   See para 6.2.

83 Investigations into activities and financial resources of terrorist organisations

(1)   In Schedule 7 to the Prevention of Terrorism (Temporary Provisions) Act 1989, in Part I (England, Wales and Northern Ireland)—
- (a)   in paragraph 3 (orders for production of excluded or special procedure material)—
  - (i)   in sub-paragraph (2) for the words from "he may make" to "shall" there shall be substituted the words "he may order a person who appears to him to have in his possession, custody or power any of the material to which the application relates, to—" and after the word "possession" where it subsequently appears in that sub-paragraph there shall be inserted in both places the words ", custody or power"; and
  - (ii)   in sub-paragraph (5)(b)(ii), for the words from "in possession" to the end there shall be substituted the words "has the material in his possession, custody or power";
- (b)   in paragraph 4(6) (order for production made to government department)—
  - (i)   after the word "possession" where it first appears there shall be inserted the words ", custody or power"; and
  - (ii)   for the words "be in possession of" there shall be substituted the words "have in his possession, custody or power"; and
- (c)   in paragraph 8(1) (orders of Secretary of State authorising searches for certain investigations), at the end, there shall be inserted the words "or an offence under section 27 of the Northern Ireland (Emergency Provisions) Act 1991".

(2)   In Schedule 7 to the Prevention of Terrorism (Temporary Provisions) Act 1989, in Part II (Scotland)—
- (a)   in paragraph 12 (order for production of material)—
  - (i)   in sub-paragraph (2) for the words from "he may make" to "shall" there shall be substituted the words "he may order a person who appears to him to have in his possession, custody or power any of the material to which the application relates, to—" and after the word "possession" where it subsequently appears in that sub-paragraph there shall be inserted in both places the words ", custody or power";

>>> (ii) in sub-paragraph (5)(b)(ii), for the words from "in possession" to the end there shall be substituted the words "has the material in his possession, custody or power"; and

>> (b) in paragraph 13(5) (order for production made to government department)—

>>> (i) after the word "possession" where it first appears there shall be inserted the words ", custody or power"; and

>>> (ii) for the words "be in possession of" there shall be substituted the words "have in his possession, custody or power".

> (3) In Schedule 5 to the Northern Ireland (Emergency Provisions) Act 1991, in paragraph 2 (investigative powers of authorised investigators), after sub-paragraph (1), there shall be inserted the following sub-paragraph—

>> "(1A) An authorised investigator may by notice in writing require any such person to furnish specified information relevant to the investigation within a specified time or such further time as the investigator may allow and in a specified manner or in such other manner as the investigator may allow.".

> (4) For the purposes of section 27 of the Prevention of Terrorism (Temporary Provisions) Act 1989 (temporary provisions) the amendments made in that Act by subsections (1) and (2) above shall be treated, as from the time when those subsections come into force, as having been continued in force by the order under subsection (6) of that section which has effect at that time.

> (5) For the purposes of section 69 of the Northern Ireland (Emergency Provisions) Act 1991 (temporary provisions) the amendments made in that Act by subsection (3) above shall be treated, as from the time when that subsection comes into force, as having been continued in force by the order under subsection (3) of that section which has effect at that time.

References   See para 6.3.

PART VII
OBSCENITY AND PORNOGRAPHY AND VIDEOS

Obscene publications and indecent photographs of children

84 Indecent pseudo-photographs of children

(1) The Protection of Children Act 1978 shall be amended as provided in subsections (2) and (3) below.

(2) In section 1 (which penalises the taking and distribution of indecent photographs of children and related acts)—

> (a) in paragraph (a) of subsection (1)—

>> (i) after the word "taken" there shall be inserted the words "or to make", and the words following "child" shall be omitted;

>> (ii) after the word "photograph" there shall be inserted the words "or pseudo-photograph";

> (b) in paragraphs (b), (c) and (d) of subsection (1), after the word "photographs" there shall be inserted the words "or pseudo-photographs";

> (c) in subsection (2), after the word "photograph" there shall be inserted the words "or pseudo-photograph"; and

    (d)   in paragraphs (a) and (b) of subsection (4), after the word "photographs" there shall be inserted the words "or pseudo-photographs".

  (3)   In section 7 (interpretation)—
    (a)   in subsection (3), at the end, there shall be inserted the words "and so as respects pseudo-photographs"; and
    (b)   for subsection (4) there shall be substituted the following subsection—

  "(4)   References to a photograph include—
    (a)   the negative as well as the positive version; and
    (b)   data stored on a computer disc or by other electronic means which is capable of conversion into a photograph.".

    (c)   after subsection (5) there shall be inserted the following subsections—

  "(6)   "Child", subject to subsection (8), means a person under the age of 16.

  (7)   "Pseudo-photograph" means an image, whether made by computer-graphics or otherwise howsoever, which appears to be a photograph.

  (8)   If the impression conveyed by a pseudo-photograph is that the person shown is a child, the pseudo-photograph shall be treated for all purposes of this Act as showing a child and so shall a pseudo-photograph where the predominant impression conveyed is that the person shown is a child notwithstanding that some of the physical characteristics shown are those of an adult.

  (9)   References to an indecent pseudo-photograph include—
    (a)   a copy of an indecent pseudo-photograph; and
    (b)   data stored on a computer disc or by other electronic means which is capable of conversion into a pseudo-photograph.".

  (4)   Section 160 of the Criminal Justice Act 1988 (which penalises the possession of indecent photographs of children) shall be amended as follows—
    (a)   in subsection (1), after the word "photograph" there shall be inserted the words "or pseudo-photograph" and the words from "(meaning" to "16)" shall be omitted; and
    (b)   in paragraphs (a), (b) and (c) of subsection (2), after the word "photograph" there shall be inserted the words "or pseudo-photograph"; and
    (c)   in subsection (5), the reference to the coming into force of that section shall be construed, for the purposes of the amendments made by this subsection, as a reference to the coming into force of this subsection.

  (5)   The Civic Government (Scotland) Act 1982 shall be amended as provided in subsections (6) and (7) below.

  (6)   In section 52 (which, for Scotland, penalises the taking and distribution of indecent photographs of children and related acts)—
    (a)   in paragraph (a) of subsection (1)—
      (i)   after the word "taken" there shall be inserted the words "or makes"; and
      (ii)   for the words from "of a" to the end there shall be substituted the words "or pseudo-photograph of a child";
    (b)   in paragraphs (b), (c) and (d) of subsection (1), after the word "photograph" there shall be inserted the words "or pseudo-photograph"; and

    (c) in subsection (2), at the beginning there shall be inserted "In subsection (1) above "child" means, subject to subsection (2B) below, a person under the age of 16; and";

    (d) after subsection (2), there shall be added—

"(2A) In this section, "pseudo-photograph" means an image, whether produced by computer-graphics or otherwise howsoever, which appears to be a photograph.

(2B) If the impression conveyed by a pseudo-photograph is that the person shown is a child, the pseudo-photograph shall be treated for all purposes of this Act as showing a child and so shall a pseudo- photograph where the predominant impression conveyed is that the person shown is a child notwithstanding that some of the physical characteristics shown are those of an adult.

(2C) In this section, references to an indecent pseudo-photograph include—

    (a) a copy of an indecent pseudo-photograph;

    (b) data stored on a computer disc or by other electronic means which is capable of conversion into a pseudo-photograph.".

    (e) in subsection (3)—

        (i) in paragraph (a), for the words "3 months" there shall be substituted the words "6 months"; and

        (ii) in paragraph (b), for the words "two years" there shall be substituted the words "3 years";

    (f) in subsection (4), and in paragraphs (a) and (b) of subsection (5), after the word "photograph" there shall be inserted the words "or pseudo-photograph"; and

    (g) for subsection (8)(c) there shall be substituted—

"(c) references to a photograph include—

        (i) the negative as well as the positive version; and

        (ii) data stored on a computer disc or by other electronic means which is capable of conversion into a photograph.".

(7) In section 52A (which, for Scotland, penalises the possession of indecent photographs of children)—

    (a) in subsection (1), for the words from "of a" to "16)" there shall be substituted the words "or pseudo-photograph of a child";

    (b) in subsection (2), in each of paragraphs (a) to (c), after the word "photograph" there shall be inserted the words "or pseudo-photograph";

    (c) in subsection (3)—

        (i) after the word "to" there shall be inserted the words "imprisonment for a period not exceeding 6 months or to"; and

        (ii) at the end there shall be added the words "or to both.";

    (d) in subsection (4), after the word "(2)" there shall be inserted the words "to (2C)".

(8) The Protection of Children (Northern Ireland) Order 1978 shall be amended as provided in subsections (9) and (10) below.

(9) In Article 2 (interpretation)—

    (a) in paragraph (2)—

        (i) in the definition of "child", after "child" there shall be inserted the words "subject to paragraph (3)(c)";

        (ii) for the definition of "photograph" there shall be substituted the following definitions—

""indecent pseudo-photograph" includes—
  (a)   a copy of an indecent pseudo-photograph; and
  (b)   data stored on a computer disc or by other electronic means which is capable of conversion into a pseudo-photograph;
"photograph" includes—
  (a)   the negative as well as the positive version; and
  (b)   data stored on a computer disc or by other electronic means which is capable of conversion into a photograph;
"pseudo-photograph" means an image, whether made by computer-graphics or otherwise howsoever, which appears to be a photograph;";

  (b)   in paragraph (3)—
    (i)   in sub-paragraph (a), after the word "photograph" there shall be inserted the words "or pseudo-photograph";
    (ii)   in sub-paragraph (b), at the end, there shall be inserted the words "and so as respects pseudo-photographs; and";
    (iii) after sub-paragraph (b) there shall be inserted the following sub-paragraph—

  "(c)   if the impression conveyed by a pseudo-photograph is that the person shown is a child, the pseudo-photograph shall be treated as showing a child and so shall a pseudo-photograph where the predominant impression conveyed is that the person shown is a child notwithstanding that some of the physical characteristics shown are those of an adult.".

(10) In Article 3 (which, for Northern Ireland, penalises the taking and distribution of indecent photographs of children and related acts)—
  (a)   in sub-paragraph (a) of paragraph (1)—
    (i)   after the word "taken" there shall be inserted the words "or to make";
    (ii)   after the word "photograph" there shall be inserted the words "or pseudo-photograph";
  (b)   in sub-paragraphs (b), (c) and (d) of paragraph (1), after the word "photographs" there shall be inserted the words "or pseudo-photographs";
  (c)   in sub-paragraphs (a) and (b) of paragraph (3), after the word "photographs" there shall be inserted the words "or pseudo-photographs".

(11) Article 15 of the Criminal Justice (Evidence, etc) (Northern Ireland) Order 1988 (which, for Northern Ireland, penalises the possession of indecent photographs of children) shall be amended as follows—
  (a)   in paragraph (1), after the word "photograph" there shall be inserted the words "or pseudo-photograph" and the words from "(meaning" to "16)" shall be omitted;
  (b)   in sub-paragraphs (a), (b) and (c) of paragraph (2), after the word "photograph" there shall be inserted the words "or pseudo-photograph"; and
  (c)   in paragraph (6), the reference to the coming into operation of that Article shall be construed, for the purposes of the amendments made by this subsection, as a reference to the coming into force of this subsection.

References   See para 7.1.

85 Arrestable offences to include certain offences relating to obscenity or indecency

(1)   The Police and Criminal Evidence Act 1984 shall be amended as follows.

(2)   In section 24(2) (arrestable offences), after paragraph (e), there shall be inserted the following paragraphs—

> "(f) an offence under section 2 of the Obscene Publications Act 1959 (publication of obscene matter);
> (g) an offence under section 1 of the Protection of Children Act 1978 (indecent photographs and pseudo-photographs of children);".

(3)   At the end of Part II of Schedule 5 (serious arrestable offences mentioned in section 116(2)(b)) there shall be inserted the following paragraphs—

> *"Protection of Children Act 1978 (c 37)*

14.   Section 1 (indecent photographs and pseudo-photographs of children).

> *Obscene Publications Act 1959 (c 66)*

15.   Section 2 (publication of obscene matter).".

(4)   The Police and Criminal Evidence (Northern Ireland) Order 1989 shall be amended as provided in subsections (5) and (6) below.

(5)   In Article 26(2) (arrestable offences), after sub-paragraph (e), there shall be inserted the following sub-paragraph—

> "(f) an offence under Article 3 of the Protection of Children (Northern Ireland) Order 1978 (indecent photographs and pseudo-photographs of children).".

(6)   At the end of Part II of Schedule 5 (serious arrestable offences mentioned in Article 87(2)(b)) there shall be inserted the following paragraph—

> *"Protection of Children (Northern Ireland) Order 1978 (1978 NI 17)*

13.   Article 3 (indecent photographs and pseudo-photographs of children).".

References   See para 7.1.

86 Indecent photographs of children: sentence of imprisonment

(1)   In section 160(3) of the Criminal Justice Act 1988 (which makes a person convicted of certain offences relating to indecent photographs of children liable to a fine not exceeding level 5 on the standard scale) there shall be inserted after the word "to" the words "imprisonment for a term not exceeding six months or" and at the end the words ", or both".

(2)   In Article 15(3) of the Criminal Justice (Evidence, etc) (Northern Ireland) Order 1988 (which makes a person convicted in Northern Ireland of certain offences relating to indecent photographs of children liable to a fine not exceeding level 5 on

the standard scale) there shall be inserted after the word "to" the words "imprisonment for a term not exceeding 6 months or" and at the end the words ", or both".

References   See para 7.1.

---

87 Publishing, displaying, selling or distributing etc obscene material in Scotland: sentence of imprisonment

In section 51(3) of the Civic Government (Scotland) Act 1982 (which makes persons convicted in summary proceedings in Scotland of certain offences relating to obscene material liable, among other penalties, for imprisonment for a period not exceeding 3 months and persons convicted there on indictment of such offences liable, among other penalties, to imprisonment for a period not exceeding 2 years), for the words "3 months" there shall be substituted the words "6 months" and for the words "two years" there shall be substituted the words "3 years".

References   See para 7.1.

Video recordings

88 Video recordings: increase in penalties

(1)   The following provisions of the Video Recordings Act 1984 (which create offences for which section 15(1) and (3) prescribe maximum fines of, in the case of sections 9 and 10, £20,000 and, in the case of other offences, level 5) shall be amended as follows.

(2)   In section 9 (supplying videos of unclassified work), after subsection (2), there shall be inserted the following subsection—

"(3)   A person guilty of an offence under this section shall be liable—
  (a) on conviction on indictment, to imprisonment for a term not exceeding two years or a fine or both,
  (b) on summary conviction, to imprisonment for a term not exceeding six months or a fine not exceeding £20,000 or both.".

(3)   In section 10 (possessing videos of unclassified work for supply), after subsection (2), there shall be inserted the following subsection—

"(3)   A person guilty of an offence under this section shall be liable—
  (a) on conviction on indictment, to imprisonment for a term not exceeding two years or a fine or both,
  (b) on summary conviction, to imprisonment for a term not exceeding six months or a fine not exceeding £20,000 or both.".

(4)   In section 11 (supplying videos in breach of classification), after subsection (2), there shall be inserted the following subsection—

"(3)   A person guilty of an offence under this section shall be liable, on summary conviction, to imprisonment for a term not exceeding six months or a fine not exceeding level 5 on the standard scale or both.".

(5)   In section 12 (supplying videos in places other than licensed sex shops), after subsection (4), there shall be inserted the following subsection—

"(4A) A person guilty of an offence under subsection (1) or (3) above shall be liable, on summary conviction, to imprisonment for a term not exceeding six months or a fine not exceeding level 5 on the standard scale or both.".

(6) In section 14 (supplying videos with false indication as to classification), after subsection (4), there shall be inserted the following subsection—

"(5) A person guilty of an offence under subsection (1) or (3) above shall be liable, on summary conviction, to imprisonment for a term not exceeding six months or a fine not exceeding level 5 on the standard scale or both.".

(7) The amendments made by this section shall not apply to offences committed before this section comes into force.

References   See para 7.2.

89 Video recordings: restriction of exemptions

(1) Section 2 of the Video Recordings Act 1984 (exempted works) shall be amended as follows.

(2) In subsection (1), after the words "subsection (2)" there shall be inserted the words "or (3)".

(3) In subsection (2)—
(a) after paragraph (c), there shall be inserted the following paragraph—

"(d) techniques likely to be useful in the commission of offences;"; and

(b) for the word "designed" (in both places) there shall be substituted the word "likely".

(4) After subsection (2), there shall be inserted the following subsection—

"(3) A video work is not an exempted work for those purposes if, to any significant extent, it depicts criminal activity which is likely to any significant extent to stimulate or encourage the commission of offences.".

References   See para 7.2.

90 Video recordings: suitability

(1) After section 4 of the Video Recordings Act 1984 there shall be inserted the following sections—

"4A   Criteria for suitability to which special regard to be had

(1) The designated authority shall, in making any determination as to the suitability of a video work, have special regard (among the other relevant factors) to any harm that may be caused to potential viewers or, through their behaviour, to society by the manner in which the work deals with—
(a) criminal behaviour;
(b) illegal drugs;
(c) violent behaviour or incidents;
(d) horrific behaviour or incidents; or
(e) human sexual activity.

(2) For the purposes of this section—

"potential viewer" means any person (including a child or young person) who is likely to view the video work in question if a classification certificate or a classification certificate of a particular description were issued;

"suitability" means suitability for the issue of a classification certificate or suitability for the issue of a certificate of a particular description;

"violent behaviour" includes any act inflicting or likely to result in the infliction of injury;

and any behaviour or activity referred to in subsection (1)(a) to (e) above shall be taken to include behaviour or activity likely to stimulate or encourage it.

4B   Review of determinations as to suitability

(1)   The Secretary of State may by order make provision enabling the designated authority to review any determination made by them, before the coming into force of section 4A of this Act, as to the suitability of a video work.

(2)   The order may in particular provide—
(a) for the authority's power of review to be exercisable in relation to such determinations as the authority think fit;
(b) for the authority to determine, on any review, whether, if they were then determining the suitability of the video work to which the determination under review relates, they—
   (i)   would issue a classification certificate, or
   (ii) would issue a different classification certificate;
(c) for the cancellation of a classification certificate, where they determine that they would not issue a classification certificate;
(d) for the cancellation of a classification certificate and issue of a new classification certificate, where they determine that they would issue a different classification certificate;
(e) for any such cancellation or issue not to take effect until the end of such period as may be determined in accordance with the order;
(f) for such persons as may appear to the authority to fall within a specified category of person to be notified of any such cancellation or issue in such manner as may be specified;
(g) for treating a classification certificate, in relation to any act or omission occurring after its cancellation, as if it had not been issued;
(h) for specified provisions of this Act to apply to determinations made on a review subject to such modifications (if any) as may be specified;
(i) for specified regulations made under section 8 of this Act to apply to a video work in respect of which a new classification certificate has been issued subject to such modifications (if any) as may be specified.

(3)   In subsection (2) above "specified" means specified by an order made under this section.

(4)   The Secretary of State shall not make any order under this section unless he is satisfied that adequate arrangements will be made for an appeal against determinations made by the designated authority on a review.

(5)   The power to make an order under this section shall be exercisable by statutory instrument which shall be subject to annulment in pursuance of a resolution of either House of Parliament.

(6)   In this section "suitability" has the same meaning as in section 4A of this Act.".

(2)   In section 7(2) of the Video Recordings Act 1984 (contents of classification certificates), in paragraph (a), after the words "viewing by children", there shall be inserted the words "or young children".

Definitions   For "video work", see the Video Recordings Act 1984, s 1(2), as amended by s 168(1) of, Sch 9, para 22(a) to, this Act; for "designated authority", see s 4(8) of that Act; for "classification certificate", see s 7(1) of the 1984 Act; for "potential viewer", "suitability" and "violent behaviour", see s 4A(2) of the 1984 Act, as inserted by sub-s (1) above; for "suitability" in s 4B of the 1984 Act, as so inserted, by virtue of sub-s (6) thereof , see s 4A(2) of the 1984 Act, as so inserted; for "specified" in s 4B(2) of the 1984 Act, as so inserted, see sub-s (3) thereof, as so inserted.
References   See para 7.3.

---

91 Enforcement by enforcing authorities outside their areas

(1)   The Video Recordings Act 1984 shall have effect with the following amendments.

(2)   In section 16A (enforcement)—

(a)   after subsection (1) there shall be inserted the following subsections—

"(1A) Subject to subsection (1B) below, the functions of a local weights and measures authority shall also include the investigation and prosecution outside their area of offences under this Act suspected to be linked to their area as well as the investigation outside their area of offences suspected to have been committed within it.

(1B)   The functions available to an authority under subsection (1A) above shall not be exercisable in relation to any circumstances suspected to have arisen within the area of another local weights and measures authority without the consent of that authority.";

(b)   in subsection (4), for the words "Subsection (1)" there shall be substituted the words "Subsections (1) and (1A)";

(c)   after subsection (4), there shall be inserted the following subsection—

"(4A) For the purposes of subsections (1A), (1B) and (2) above—

(a)   offences in another area are "linked" to the area of a local weights and measures authority if—

(i)   the supply or possession of video recordings in contravention of this Act within their area is likely to be or to have been the result of the supply or possession of those recordings in the other area; or

(ii)   the supply or possession of video recordings in contravention of this Act in the other area is likely to be or to have been the result of the supply or possession of those recordings in their area; and

(b)   "investigation" includes the exercise of the powers conferred by sections 27 and 28 of the Trade Descriptions Act 1968 as applied by subsection (2) above;

and sections 29 and 33 of that Act shall apply accordingly.".

(3)   After section 16A there shall be inserted the following sections—

"16B Extension of jurisdiction of magistrates' courts in linked cases

(1)   A justice of the peace for an area to which section 1 of the Magistrates' Courts Act 1980 applies may issue a summons or warrant under and in accordance with that section as respects an offence under this Act committed or suspected of having been committed outside the area for which he acts if it appears to the justice that the offence is linked to the supply or possession of video recordings within the area for which he acts.

(2)   Where a person charged with an offence under this Act appears or is brought before a magistrates' court in answer to a summons issued by virtue of subsection (1) above, or under a warrant issued under subsection (1) above, the court shall have jurisdiction to try the offence.

(3)   For the purposes of this section an offence is "linked" to the supply or possession of video recordings within the area for which a justice acts if—

    (a)   the supply or possession of video recordings within his area is likely to be or to have been the result of the offence; or

    (b)   the offence is likely to be or to have been the result of the supply or possession of video recordings in his area.

16C Extension of jurisdiction of sheriff in linked cases

(1)   Subsection (4) of section 287 of the Criminal Procedure (Scotland) Act 1975 (jurisdiction of sheriff as respects offences committed in more than one district) shall apply in respect of linked offences, whether or not alleged to have been committed by one and the same person, as that subsection applies in respect of offences alleged to have been committed by one person in more than one sheriff court district which, if committed in one of those districts, could be tried under one complaint.

(2)   For the purposes of subsection (1) above, offences are linked if, being offences under this Act, they comprise the supply or possession of video recordings each within a different sheriff court district but such supply or possession within the one district is likely to be, or to have been, the result of such supply or possession within the other.

16D Extension of jurisdiction of magistrates' courts in Northern Ireland in linked cases

(1)   Paragraph (2) of Article 16 of the Magistrates' Courts (Northern Ireland) Order 1981 (jurisdiction of magistrates' court as respects offences committed in another division) shall apply in respect of linked offences as that paragraph applies in respect of summary offences committed in other county court divisions.

(2)   For the purposes of subsection (1) above, an offence is a linked offence if the supply or possession of video recordings within one county court division is likely to be or to have been the result of the supply or possession of those recordings in another such division.".

Definitions   For "video recording", see the Video Recordings Act 1984, s 1(3), as amended by s 167(1) of, Sch 9, para 22(b) to, this Act; for "supply", see s 1(4) of the 1984 Act; for "investigation" and "linked" in s 16A(1A), (1B) of the 1984 Act, as inserted by sub-s (2) above, see s 16A(4A) of that Act, as so inserted; for "linked" in s 16B of the 1984 Act, as inserted by sub-s (3) above, see sub-s (3) thereof, as so inserted.
References   See para 7.3.

Obscene, offensive or annoying telephone calls

92 Obscene, offensive or annoying telephone calls: increase in penalty

(1)   In section 43(1) of the Telecommunications Act 1984 (which makes a person convicted of certain offences relating to improper use of public telecommunication systems liable to a fine not exceeding level 3 on the standard scale), for the words "a fine not exceeding level 3 on the standard scale" there shall be substituted the words "imprisonment for a term not exceeding six months or a fine not exceeding level 5 on the standard scale or both".

(2)   Subsection (1) above does not apply to an offence committed before this section comes into force.

References   See para 7.4.

PART VIII
PRISON SERVICES AND THE PRISON SERVICE

CHAPTER I
ENGLAND AND WALES

Prisoner escorts

93 Arrangements for the provision of prisoner escorts

(1)   In subsection (1) of section 80 (arrangements for the provision of prisoner escorts) of the Criminal Justice Act 1991 ("the 1991 Act")—

    (a)   for paragraph (a) there shall be substituted the following paragraph—

        "(a) the delivery of prisoners from one set of relevant premises to another;";

    (b)   in paragraph (b), for the words "such premises" there shall be substituted the words "the premises of any court"; and

    (c)   for paragraphs (c) and (d) there shall be substituted the following paragraph—

        "(c) the custody of prisoners temporarily held in a prison in the course of delivery from one prison to another; and".

(2)   After that subsection there shall be inserted the following subsection—

    "(1A) In paragraph (a) of subsection (1) above "relevant premises" means a court, prison, police station or hospital; and either (but not both) of the sets of premises mentioned in that paragraph may be situated in a part of the British Islands outside England and Wales.".

(3)   In subsection (3) of that section, for the words "a warrant of commitment" there shall be substituted the words "a warrant or a hospital order or remand" and for the words "that warrant" there shall be substituted the words "the warrant, order or remand".

(4)   After that subsection there shall be inserted the following subsection—

    "(4) In this section—

        "hospital" has the same meaning as in the Mental Health Act 1983;

"hospital order" means an order for a person's admission to hospital made under section 37, 38 or 44 of that Act, section 5 of the Criminal Procedure (Insanity) Act 1964 or section 6, 14 or 14A of the Criminal Appeal Act 1968;

"hospital remand" means a remand of a person to hospital under section 35 or 36 of the Mental Health Act 1983;

"warrant" means a warrant of commitment, a warrant of arrest or a warrant under section 46, 47, 48, 50 or 74 of that Act.".

(5) In subsection (1) of section 92 of that Act (interpretation of Part IV), for the definition of "prisoner" there shall be substituted the following definition—

""prisoner, means any person for the time being detained in legal custody as a result of a requirement imposed by a court or otherwise that he be so detained;".

(6) In subsection (3) of that section—

(a) for the words from "kept" to "accommodation)" there shall be substituted the words "remanded or committed to local authority accommodation under section 23 of the 1969 Act"; and

(b) for the words "section 80(1)(c) to (e)" there shall be substituted the words "section 80(1)(c) or (e) or (1A)".

(7) After that subsection there shall be inserted the following subsection—

"(4) In sections 80, 82 and 83 above, "prison'—

(a) so far as relating to the delivery of prisoners to or from a prison situated in Scotland, includes a remand centre or young offenders institution within the meaning of section 19 of the Prisons (Scotland) Act 1989; and

(b) so far as relating to the delivery of prisoners to or from a prison situated in Northern Ireland, includes a remand centre or young offenders centre.".

Definitions For "prison" and "prisoner", see the Criminal Justice Act 1991, s 92(1), (3), as amended, in the case of s 92(1), by sub-s (5) above and s 101(7) of this Act, and in the case of s 92(3), by sub-s (6) above (and note also as to "prison", s 92(4) of the 1991 Act, as added by sub-s (7) above); for "the 1991 Act", see sub-s (1) above; for "relevant premises", see s 80(1A) of the 1991 Act, as inserted by sub-s (2) above; for "hospital", "hospital order", "hospital remand", and "warrant", see s 80(4) of the 1991 Act, as added by sub-s (4) above.

References See para 8.2.

---

94 Powers and duties of prisoner custody officers acting in pursuance of such arrangements

(1) For subsection (4) of section 82 of the 1991 Act (powers and duties of prisoner custody officers acting in pursuance of such arrangements) there shall be substituted the following subsection—

"(4) Where a prisoner custody officer acting in pursuance of prisoner escort arrangements is on any premises in which the Crown Court or a magistrates' court is sitting, it shall be his duty to give effect to any order of that court made—

(a) in the case of the Crown Court, under section 34A of the 1973 Act (power of Court to order search of persons before it); or

(b) in the case of a magistrates' court, under section 80 of the 1980 Act (application of money found on defaulter).".

(2)   After subsection (2) of section 6 of the Imprisonment (Temporary Provisions) Act 1980 (detention in the custody of a police constable) there shall be inserted the following subsection—

"(3)   Any reference in this section to a constable includes a reference to a prisoner custody officer (within the meaning of Part IV of the Criminal Justice Act 1991) acting in pursuance of prisoner escort arrangements (within the meaning of that Part).".

Definitions   For "prisoner escort arrangements", see the Criminal Justice Act 1991, s 80(2); for "prisoner custody officer", see s 89(1) of that Act.
References   See para 8.2.

95 Breaches of discipline by prisoners under escort

For section 83 of the 1991 Act there shall be substituted the following section—

"83   Breaches of discipline by prisoners under escort

(1)   This section applies where a prisoner for whose delivery or custody a prisoner custody officer has been responsible in pursuance of prisoner escort arrangements is delivered to a prison.

(2)   For the purposes of such prison rules as relate to disciplinary offences, the prisoner shall be deemed to have been—

(a) in the custody of the governor of the prison; or

(b) in the case of a contracted out prison, in the custody of its director,

at all times during the period for which the prisoner custody officer was so responsible.

(3)   In the case of any breach by the prisoner at any time during that period of such prison rules as so relate, a disciplinary charge may be laid against him by the prisoner custody officer.

(4)   Nothing in this section shall enable a prisoner to be punished under prison rules for any act or omission of his for which he has already been punished by a court.

(5)   In this section "prison rules", in relation to a prison situated in a part of the British Islands outside England and Wales, means rules made under any provision of the law of that part which corresponds to section 47 of the 1952 Act.".

Definitions   For "prisoner escort arrangements", see the Criminal Justice Act 1991, s 80(2); for "contracted out prison", see s 84(4) of that Act, as substituted by s 96 of this Act; for "prisoner custody officer", see s 89(1) of that Act; for "prison rules", see s 92(1) of that Act, as amended by s 101(7)(d) of this Act, and see also s 83(5) of that Act, as substituted above; for "prison" and "prisoner", see s 92(1) of that Act, as amended by s 93(5) of this Act (and note also as to "prison", s 92(4) of the 1991 Act, as added by s 93(7) of this Act).
References   See para 8.2.

Contracted out prisons etc

96 Contracted out parts of prisons, etc

For section 84 of the 1991 Act there shall be substituted the following section—

"84 Contracting out prisons etc

(1)   The Secretary of State may enter into a contract with another person for the provision or running (or the provision and running) by him, or (if the contract so provides) for the running by sub-contractors of his, of any prison or part of a prison.

(2)   While a contract under this section for the running of a prison or part of a prison is in force—

>   (a) the prison or part shall be run subject to and in accordance with sections 85 and 86 below, the 1952 Act (as modified by section 87 below) and prison rules; and

>   (b) in the case of a part, that part and the remaining part shall each be treated for the purposes of sections 85 to 88A below as if they were separate prisons.

(3)   Where the Secretary of State grants a lease or tenancy of land for the purposes of any contract under this section, none of the following enactments shall apply to it, namely—

>   (a) Part II of the Landlord and Tenant Act 1954 (security of tenure);

>   (b) section 146 of the Law of Property Act 1925 (restrictions on and relief against forfeiture);

>   (c) section 19(1), (2) and (3) of the Landlord and Tenant Act 1927 and the Landlord and Tenant Act 1988 (covenants not to assign etc); and

>   (d) the Agricultural Holdings Act 1986.

In this subsection "lease or tenancy" includes an underlease or sub-tenancy.

(4)   In this Part—

>   "contracted out prison" means a prison or part of a prison for the running of which a contract under this section is for the time being in force;

>   "the contractor", in relation to a contracted out prison, means the person who has contracted with the Secretary of State for the running of it; and

>   "sub-contractor", in relation to a contracted out prison, means a person who has contracted with the contractor for the running of it or any part of it.".

Definitions   For "prison" and "prison rules", see the Criminal Justice Act 1991, s 92(1), as amended by s 101(7)(d); for "contracted out prison", "the contractor" and "sub-contractor", see s 84(4) of the 1991 Act, as substituted above.
References   See para 8.3.

97 Temporary attachment of prison officers

(1)   At the end of subsection (1) of section 85 of the 1991 Act (officers of contracted out prisons) there shall be inserted the words "or a prison officer who is temporarily attached to the prison".

(2)   At the end of paragraph (b) of subsection (4) of that section there shall be inserted the words "or prison officers who are temporarily attached to the prison".

(3)   For subsection (3) of section 87 of that Act (consequential modifications of 1952 Act) there shall be substituted the following subsection—

>   "(3)   Section 8 (powers of prison officers) shall not apply in relation to a prisoner custody officer performing custodial duties at the prison.".

(4)   After subsection (4) of that section there shall be inserted the following subsection—

"(4A) Section 11 (ejectment of prison officers and their families refusing to quit) shall not apply.".

(5)   At the end of subsections (6) and (7) of that section there shall be inserted the words "or a prison officer who is temporarily attached to the prison".

Definitions   For "prisoner custody officer", see the Criminal Justice Act 1991, s 89(1); for "prison officer", see s 92(1) of that Act, as amended by s 101(7)(d) of this Act; as to custodial duties at a contracted out prison, see s 92(1A) of the 1991 Act, as inserted by s 98 of this Act.
References   See para 8.3.

98 Prisoners temporarily out of prison

After subsection (1) of section 92 of the 1991 Act (interpretation of Part IV) there shall be inserted the following subsection—

"(1A) Any reference in this Part to custodial duties at a contracted out prison includes a reference to custodial duties in relation to a prisoner who is outside such a prison for temporary purposes.".

Definitions   For "contracted out prison", see the Criminal Justice Act 1991, s 84(4), as substituted by s 96 of this Act; for "prison" and "prisoner", see s 92(1) of the 1991 Act, as amended by s 93(5) of this Act.
References   See para 8.3.

Miscellaneous

99 Contracted out functions at directly managed prisons

After section 88 of the 1991 Act there shall be inserted the following section—

"Contracted out functions

88A Contracted out functions at directly managed prisons

(1)   The Secretary of State may enter into a contract with another person for any functions at a directly managed prison to be performed by prisoner custody officers who are provided by that person and are authorised to perform custodial duties.

(2)   Section 86 above shall apply in relation to a prisoner custody officer performing contracted out functions at a directly managed prison as it applies in relation to such an officer performing custodial duties at a contracted out prison.

(3)   In relation to a directly managed prison—
(a) the reference in section 13(2) of the 1952 Act (legal custody of prisoners) to an officer of the prison; and
(b) the reference in section 14(2) of that Act (cells) to a prison officer,
shall each be construed as including a reference to a prisoner custody officer performing custodial duties at the prison in pursuance of a contract under this section.

(4)   Any reference in subsections (1) to (3) above to the performance of functions or custodial duties at a directly managed prison includes a reference

to the performance of functions or such duties for the purposes of, or for purposes connected with, such a prison.

(5)   In this Part—

"contracted out functions" means any functions which, by virtue of a contract under this section, fall to be performed by prisoner custody officers;

"directly managed prison" means a prison which is not a contracted out prison.".

Definitions   For "prisoner custody officer", see the Criminal Justice Act 1991, s 89(1); for "prison" and "prison officer", see s 92(1) of that Act, as amended by s 101(7)(d) of this Act. Note as to the performance of functions or custodial duties at a contracted out prison, s 88A(4) of the 1991 Act, as inserted above, and as to "contracted out functions" and "directly managed prison", s 88A(5) of that Act, as so inserted.
References   See para 8.3.

100 Provision of prisons by contractors

(1)   For subsection (2) of section 33 of the Prison Act 1952 (power to declare buildings etc to be prisons) there shall be substituted the following subsection—

"(2)   The Secretary of State may provide new prisons by declaring to be a prison—

(a)   any building or part of a building built for the purpose or vested in him or under his control; or

(b)   any floating structure or part of such a structure constructed for the purpose or vested in him or under his control.".

(2)   Subsections (3) and (4) below apply where the Secretary of State enters into a contract with another person ("the contractor") for the provision by him of a prison.

(3)   Section 33(2) of the Prison Act 1952 shall have effect as if it also included references to—

(a)   any building or part of a building built by the contractor for the purpose or vested in him or under his control; and

(b)   any floating structure or part of such a structure constructed by the contractor for the purpose or vested in him or under his control.

(4)   Nothing in section 35(1) of that Act (prison property to be vested in the Secretary of State) shall require the prison or any real or personal property belonging to the prison to be vested in the Secretary of State.

References   See para 8.4.

Supplemental

101 Minor and consequential amendments

(1)   In subsection (5) of section 85 of the 1991 Act (officers of contracted out prisons), for the words "The contractor shall" there shall be substituted the words "The contractor and any sub-contractor of his shall each".

(2)   In subsection (3)(b) of section 88 of that Act (intervention by the Secretary of State), for the words "the contractor shall" there shall be substituted the words "the contractor and any sub-contractor of his shall each".

(3)   In subsection (5) of that section, after the words "the contractor," there shall be inserted the words "any sub-contractor of his,".

(4)   In subsection (3) of section 89 of that Act (certification of prisoner custody officers), for the words "contracted out prison" there shall be substituted the words "contracted out or directly managed prison".

(5)   In subsections (1) and (3) of section 90 of that Act (protection of prisoner custody officers), for the words from "acting" to "prison" there shall be substituted the words—

> "(a) acting in pursuance of prisoner escort arrangements;
> (b) performing custodial duties at a contracted out prison; or
> (c) performing contracted out functions at a directly managed prison,".

(6)   In subsection (1) of section 91 of that Act (wrongful disclosure of information), for the words from "is or has been" to "prison" there shall be substituted the words—

> "(a) is or has been employed (whether as a prisoner custody officer or otherwise) in pursuance of prisoner escort arrangements, or at a contracted out prison; or
> (b) is or has been employed to perform contracted out functions at a directly managed prison,".

(7)   In subsection (1) of section 92 of that Act (interpretation of Part IV)—
> (a) after the words "In this Part" there shall be inserted the words "unless the context otherwise requires";
> (b) in the definitions of "contracted out prison" and "contractor", for the words "section 84(2)" there shall be substituted the words "section 84(4)";
> (c) after those definitions there shall be inserted the following definitions—

> > ""contracted out functions" and "directly managed prison" have the meanings given by section 88A(5) above;";

> (d) after the definition of "prison" there shall be inserted the following definitions—

> > ""prison officer" means an officer of a directly managed prison;
> > "prison rules" means rules made under section 47 of the 1952 Act;"; and

> (e) after the definition of "prisoner escort arrangements" there shall be inserted the following definition—

> > ""sub-contractor" has the meaning given by section 84(4) above.".

(8)   After subsection (7) of section 102 of the 1991 Act (short title, commencement and extent) there shall be inserted the following subsection—

> "(7A) Sections 80, 82 and 83 above, so far as relating to the delivery of prisoners to or from premises situated in a part of the British Islands outside England and Wales, extend to that part of those Islands.".

(9)   For sub-paragraph (1) of paragraph 3 of Schedule 10 to that Act (certification of prisoner custody officers) there shall be substituted the following sub-paragraph—

> "(1)   This paragraph applies where at any time—
> > (a) in the case of a prisoner custody officer acting in pursuance of prisoner escort arrangements, it appears to the prisoner escort

monitor for the area concerned that the officer is not a fit and proper person to perform escort functions;

(b) in the case of a prisoner custody officer performing custodial duties at a contracted out prison, it appears to the controller of that prison that the officer is not a fit and proper person to perform custodial duties; or

(c) in the case of a prisoner custody officer performing contracted out functions at a directly managed prison, it appears to the governor of that prison that the officer is not a fit and proper person to perform custodial duties.".

(10) In sub-paragraph (2) of that paragraph, for the words "or controller" there shall be substituted the words "controller or governor".

Definitions   For "prisoner escort arrangements", see the Criminal Justice Act 1991, s 80(2); for "prisoner escort monitor", see s 81(1)(a) of that Act; for "contracted out prison", "the contractor" and "sub-contractor", see s 84(4) of that Act, as substituted by s 96 of this Act; for "contracted out functions" and "directly managed prison", see s 88A(5) of the 1991 Act, as inserted by s 99 of this Act; for "prisoner custody officer", see s 89(1) of that Act; for "custodial duties", see s 89(3) of that Act, as amended by sub-s (4) above; for "prisoner" see s 92(1) of the 1991 Act, this title, as amended by s 93(5) of this Act.
References   See para 8.4.

CHAPTER II
SCOTLAND

Prisoner escorts

102 Arrangements for the provision of prisoner escorts

(1)   The Secretary of State may make arrangements for any of the functions specified in subsection (2) below ("escort functions") to be performed in such cases as may be determined by or under the arrangements by prisoner custody officers who are authorised to perform such functions.

(2)   Those functions are—
   (a) the transfer of prisoners from one set of relevant premises to another;
   (b) the custody of prisoners held on court premises (whether or not they would otherwise be in the custody of the court) and their production before the court;
   (c) the custody of prisoners temporarily held in a prison in the course of transfer from one prison to another; and
   (d) the custody of prisoners while they are outside a prison for temporary purposes.

(3)   In paragraph (a) of subsection (2) above, "relevant premises" means—
   (a) the premises of any court, prison, police station or hospital; or
   (b) the premises of any other place from or to which a prisoner may be required to be taken under the Criminal Procedure (Scotland) Act 1975 or the Mental Health (Scotland) Act 1984;

and either (but not both) of the sets of premises mentioned in that paragraph may be situated in a part of the British Islands outside Scotland.

(4)   Arrangements made by the Secretary of State under this section ("prisoner escort arrangements") may include entering into contracts with other persons for the provision by them of prisoner custody officers.

(5)   Any person who, under a warrant or hospital order, is responsible for the performance of any such function as is mentioned in subsection (2) above shall be deemed to have complied with that warrant or order if he does all that he reasonably can to secure that the function is performed by a prisoner custody officer acting in pursuance of prisoner escort arrangements.

(6)   In this section—

"hospital" has the same meaning as in the Mental Health (Scotland) Act 1984;

"hospital order" means an order for a person's detention in, or admission to and detention in, a hospital under section 174, 174A, 175, 375A or 376 of the Act of 1975 or section 70 of the Act of 1984; and

"warrant" means a warrant for committal, a warrant for arrest, a warrant under section 69, 73, 74 or 75 of the Act of 1984, a transfer direction under section 71 of that Act or any other warrant, order or direction under the Act of 1975 or the Act of 1984 requiring a person to be taken to a particular place.

Definitions: For "prison" see s 117(1),(3); for "prisoner", see s 117(1); for "prisoner custody officer", see s 114(1); for "escort functions", see sub-s(2) above, for "prisoner escort arrangements", see sub-s(4) above and for "hospital", "hospital order" and "warrant", see sub-s(6) above.
References   See para 8.6.

103 Monitoring of prisoner escort arrangements

(1)   Prisoner escort arrangements shall include the appointment of a prisoner escort monitor, that is to say, a Crown servant whose duty it shall be—

(a) to keep the arrangements under review and to report on them to the Secretary of State;

(b) to investigate and report to the Secretary of State on any allegations made against prisoner custody officers acting in pursuance of the arrangements; and

(c) to report to the Secretary of State on any alleged breaches of discipline on the part of prisoners for whose transfer or custody such officers so acting are responsible.

(2)   In section 7(2) (functions of Her Majesty's Chief Inspector of Prisons for Scotland) of the 1989 Act—

(a) after "Inspector" there shall be inserted "—(a)"; and

(b) at the end there shall be inserted—

"; and

(b) to inspect the conditions in which prisoners are transported or held in pursuance of prisoner escort arrangements (within the meaning of section 102 of the Criminal Justice and Public Order Act 1994) and to report to the Secretary of State on them.".

Definitions: For "prisoner" and "the 1989 Act" see s117(1), for "prisoner custody officer", see s 114(1); for "prisoner escort arrangements", see s 102(4).
References   See para 8.6.

104 Powers and duties of prisoner custody officers performing escort functions

(1)   A prisoner custody officer acting in pursuance of prisoner escort arrangements shall have power to search—

(a) any prisoner for whose transfer or custody he is responsible in accordance with the arrangements; and

(b) any other person who is in or is seeking to enter any place where any such prisoner is or is to be held and any article in the possession of such a person.

(2) The power conferred by subsection (1)(b) above to search a person shall not be construed as authorising a prisoner custody officer to require a person to remove any of his clothing other than an outer coat, jacket, headgear and gloves.

(3) A prisoner custody officer shall, as respects prisoners for whose transfer or custody he is responsible in pursuance of prisoner escort arrangements, have the duty—

(a) to prevent their escape from legal custody;

(b) to prevent, or detect and report on, the commission or attempted commission by them of other unlawful acts;

(c) to ensure good order and discipline on their part;

(d) to attend to their wellbeing; and

(e) to give effect to any directions as to their treatment which are given by a court.

(4) Where a prisoner custody officer acting in pursuance of prisoner escort arrangements is on any premises in which a court of summary jurisdiction is sitting he shall have the duty to give effect to any order of the court under section 395(2) of the Criminal Procedure (Scotland) Act 1975 requiring an offender to be searched.

(5) The powers conferred by subsection (1) above and the powers arising by virtue of subsections (3) and (4) above shall include power to use reasonable force where necessary.

(6) Prison rules may make provision in relation to—

(a) the power conferred by subsection (1) above; and

(b) the duty imposed by subsection (3)(d) above.

Definitions For "prisoner escort arrangements", see s 102(4); for "prisoner custody officer", see s 114(1); for "prisoner" and "prison rules", see s 117(1); for "prison", see s 117(1), (3).
References See para 8.6.

105 Breaches of discipline by prisoners under escort

(1) Where a prisoner for whose transfer or custody a prisoner custody officer has been responsible in pursuance of prisoner escort arrangements is delivered to a prison, he shall be deemed, for the purposes of such prison rules as relate to breaches of discipline, to have been—

(a) in the custody of the governor of the prison; or

(b) in the case of a contracted out prison, in the custody of its director,

at all times during the period for which that officer was so responsible, and that officer may bring a charge of breach of such rules as so relate against the prisoner in respect of any such time.

(2) Nothing in subsection (1) above shall render a prisoner liable to be punished under prison rules for any act or omission of his for which he has already been punished by a court.

(3) In this section "prison rules", in relation to a prison situated in a part of the British Islands outside Scotland, means rules made under any provision of the law of that part which corresponds to section 39 of the 1989 Act.

Contracted out prisons

106 Contracting out of prisons

(1)   The Secretary of State may enter into a contract with another person for the provision or running (or the provision and running) by him, or (if the contract so provides) for the running by sub-contractors of his, of any prison or part of a prison in Scotland.

(2)   While a contract under this section for the running of a prison or part of a prison is in force—
    (a) the prison or part shall be run subject to and in accordance with—
        (i) sections 107 and 108 below; and
        (ii) the 1989 Act and prison rules and directions made under or by virtue of that Act (all as modified by section 110 below); and
    (b) in the case of a part, that part and the remaining part shall each be treated for the purposes of sections 107 to 112 below as if they were separate prisons.

(3)   Where the Secretary of State grants a lease for the purpose of any contract under this section, none of the following enactments shall apply to it—
    (a) sections 4 to 7 of the Law Reform (Miscellaneous Provisions) (Scotland) Act 1985 (irritancy clauses); and
    (b) the Agricultural Holdings (Scotland) Act 1991.

In this subsection "lease" includes a sub-lease.

(4)   In this Chapter—
"contracted out prison" means a prison or part of a prison for the running of which a contract under this section is for the time being in force;
"the contractor", in relation to a contracted out prison, means the person who has contracted with the Secretary of State for the running of it; and
"sub-contractor", in relation to a contracted out prison, means a person who has contracted with the contractor for the running of it or any part of it.

107 Officers of contracted out prisons

(1)   Instead of a governor, every contracted out prison shall have—
    (a) a director, who shall be a prisoner custody officer appointed by the contractor and specially approved for the purposes of this section by the Secretary of State; and
    (b) a controller, who shall be a Crown servant appointed by the Secretary of State,
and every officer of such a prison who performs custodial duties shall be a prisoner custody officer who is authorised to perform such duties or a prison officer who is temporarily attached to the prison.

(2)   Subject to subsection (3) below, the director shall have the same functions as are conferred on a governor by the 1989 Act and by prison rules.

(3)   The director shall not—
- (a)   have any function which is conferred on a controller by virtue of subsection (4) below;
- (b)   inquire into a disciplinary charge brought against a prisoner, conduct the hearing of such a charge or make, remit or mitigate an award in respect of such a charge; or
- (c)   except in cases of urgency, order the removal of a prisoner from association with other prisoners, the temporary confinement of a prisoner in a special cell or the application to a prisoner of any other special control or restraint.

(4)   The controller shall have such functions as may be conferred on him by prison rules and shall be under a duty—
- (a)   to keep under review, and report to the Secretary of State on, the running of the prison by or on behalf of the director; and
- (b)   to investigate, and report to the Secretary of State on, any allegations made against prisoner custody officers performing custodial duties at the prison or prison officers who are temporarily attached to the prison.

(5)   The contractor and any sub-contractor of his shall each be under a duty to do all that he reasonably can (whether by giving directions to the officers of the prison or otherwise) to facilitate the exercise by the controller of all such functions as are mentioned in or conferred by subsection (4) above.

(6)   Every contracted out prison shall have a medical officer, who shall be a registered medical practitioner appointed by the contractor or, if the contract provides for the running of the prison by a sub-contractor, by the sub-contractor.

Definitions   For "contracted out prison" and " the contractor" see s 106(4); for "prison", "prison officer" , "prison rules", "prisoner" and "the 1989 Act" see s 117(1); for "prisoner custody officer", see s 114(1); for "sub-contractor", see s 106(4); for custodial duties at a contracted out prison, see s 117(2).
References   See para 8.7.

108 Powers and duties of prisoner custody officers employed at contracted out prisons

(1)   A prisoner custody officer performing custodial duties at a contracted out prison shall have power to search—
- (a)   any prisoner who is confined in the prison or for whose custody he is responsible; and
- (b)   any other person who is in or is seeking to enter the prison and any article in the possession of such a person.

(2)   The power conferred by subsection (1)(b) above to search a person shall not be construed as authorising a prisoner custody officer to require a person to remove any of his clothing other than an outer coat, jacket, headgear and gloves.

(3)   A prisoner custody officer performing custodial duties at a contracted out prison shall, as respects the prisoners for whose custody he is responsible, have the duty—
- (a)   to prevent their escape from legal custody;
- (b)   to prevent, or detect and report on, the commission or attempted commission by them of other unlawful acts;

(c) to ensure good order and discipline on their part; and

(d) to attend to their wellbeing.

(4)   The powers conferred by subsection (1) above and the powers arising by virtue of subsection (3) above shall include power to use reasonable force where necessary.

Definitions   For "contracted out prison", see s 106(4); for "custodial duties", "prison" and "prisoner", see s 117(1); for "prisoner custody officer", see s 114(1); for custodial duties at a contracted out prison, see s 117(2).
References   See para 8.7.

109 Breaches of discipline by prisoners temporarily out of contracted out prison

(1)   This section applies where a prisoner custody officer who performs custodial duties at a contracted out prison is responsible for the custody of a prisoner who is outside the prison for temporary purposes.

(2)   For the purposes of such prison rules as relate to breaches of discipline the prisoner shall be deemed to have been in the custody of the director of the prison at all times during the period for which the prisoner custody officer was so responsible, and that officer may bring a charge of breach of such rules as so relate against the prisoner in respect of any such time.

(3)   Nothing in subsection (1) above shall render a prisoner liable to be punished under prison rules for any act or omission of his for which he has already been punished by a court.

Definitions   For "contracted out prison", see s 106(4); for "custodial duties", "prison", "prison rules" and "prisoner", see s 117(1); for "prisoner custody officer", see s 114(1); for custodial duties at a contracted out prison, see s 117(2).
References   See para 8.7.

110 Consequential modifications of 1989 Act, prison rules and directions

(1)   In relation to a contracted out prison, the provisions specified in subsections (2) to (7) below shall have effect subject to the modifications so specified.

(2)   In section 3 of the 1989 Act (general superintendence of prisons)—
(a) in subsection (1), the words from "who shall appoint" to the end shall be omitted; and
(b) subsection (3) shall not apply.

(3)   In sections 9(5), 11(4), 15(1) and (3) (various functions of the governor of a prison), 33A (power of governor to delegate functions), 34 (duty of governor where prisoner dies), 39(8) and (12) (prison rules), 41(4) (detention of person suspected of bringing prohibited article into prison) and 41B(3) (testing prisoners for drugs) of that Act, in prison rules and in directions made by virtue of section 39(8) of that Act the reference to the governor shall be construed as a reference to the director.

(4)   In sections 11(4) (execution of certain warrants by prison officers etc), 13(b) (legal custody of prisoners), 33A (power of governor to delegate functions), 40(1) (persons unlawfully at large), 41(3), (4), (6) and (8) (detention of person suspected of bringing prohibited article into prison) and 41B(1) (testing prisoners for drugs) of that Act, the reference to an officer of a prison (or, as the case may be, a prison officer) shall be construed as a reference to a prisoner custody officer performing custodial duties at the prison or a prison officer temporarily attached to the prison.

(5)   Section 36 of that Act (vesting of prison property in Secretary of State) shall have effect subject to the provisions of the contract entered into under section 106 above.

(6)   Sections 37 (discontinuance of prison), 41(2A) and (2B) (power to search for prohibited articles) and 41A (powers of search by authorised employees) of that Act shall not apply.

(7)   In prison rules, in subsection (8) of section 39 of that Act (directions supplementing prison rules) and in any direction made by virtue of that subsection, the reference to an officer of a prison (or, as the case may be, a prison officer) shall be construed as including a reference to a prisoner custody officer performing custodial duties at the prison.

Definitions   For "contracted out prison" , see s 106(4); for "custodial duties", "prison", "prison rules" and "prisoner", see s 117(1); for "prisoner custody officer", see s 114(1); for custodial duties at a contracted out prison, see s 117(2).
References   See para 8.7.

111 Intervention by the Secretary of State

(1)   This section applies where, in the case of a contracted out prison, it appears to the Secretary of State—
   (a)   that the director has lost or is likely to lose effective control of the prison or any part of it; and
   (b)   that the making of an appointment under subsection (2) below is necessary in the interests of preserving the safety of any person or preventing serious damage to any property.

(2)   The Secretary of State may appoint a Crown servant to act as governor of the prison for the period—
   (a)   beginning with the time specified in the appointment; and
   (b)   ending with the time specified in the notice of termination under subsection (4) below.

(3)   During that period—
   (a)   all the functions which would otherwise be exercisable by the director or the controller shall be exercisable by the governor;
   (b)   the contractor and any sub-contractor of his shall each do all that he reasonably can to facilitate the exercise by the governor of those functions; and
   (c)   the officers of the prison shall comply with any directions given by the governor in the exercise of those functions.

(4)   Where the Secretary of State is satisfied—
   (a)   that the governor has secured effective control of the prison or, as the case may be, the relevant part of it; and
   (b)   that the governor's appointment is no longer necessary as mentioned in subsection (1)(b) above,
he shall, by a notice to the governor, terminate the appointment at a time specified in the notice.

(5)   As soon as practicable after making or terminating an appointment under this section, the Secretary of State shall give a notice of the appointment, or a copy of the notice of termination, to the contractor, any sub-contractor of his, the director and the controller.

Definitions   For "contracted out prison", "sub-contractor", "the contractor", see s 106(4); for "prison" and "prison officer", see s 117(1).
References   See para 8.7.

Contracted out functions

112 Contracted out functions at directly managed prisons

(1)   The Secretary of State may enter into a contract with another person for any functions at a directly managed prison to be performed by prisoner custody officers who are provided by that person and are authorised to perform custodial duties.

(2)   Sections 108 and 109 above shall apply in relation to a prisoner custody officer performing contracted out functions at a directly managed prison as they apply in relation to such an officer performing custodial duties at a contracted out prison, but as if the reference in section 109(2) to the director of the contracted out prison were a reference to the governor of the directly managed prison.

(3)   In relation to a directly managed prison, the references to an officer of a prison (or, as the case may be, a prison officer) in the provisions specified in subsection (4) below shall each be construed as including a reference to a prisoner custody officer performing custodial duties at the prison in pursuance of a contract under this section.

(4)   Those provisions are—
　　(a)   section 11(4) of the 1989 Act (execution of certain warrants by prison officers etc);
　　(b)   section 13(b) of that Act (legal custody of prisoners);
　　(c)   section 33A of that Act (power of governor to delegate functions);
　　(d)   subsection (8) of section 39 of that Act (directions supplementing prison rules) and directions made by virtue of that subsection;
　　(e)   section 40(1) of that Act (persons unlawfully at large);
　　(f)   section 41(3), (4), (6) and (8) of that Act (prohibited articles); and
　　(g)   prison rules.

(5)   Section 41(2A) and (2B) of the 1989 Act (search of person suspected of bringing prohibited article into prison) shall not apply in relation to a prisoner custody officer performing contracted out functions at a directly managed prison.

(6)   Any reference in the foregoing provisions of this section to the performance of functions or custodial duties at a directly managed prison includes a reference to the performance of functions or such duties for the purposes of, or for purposes connected with, such a prison.

(7)   In this Chapter—
　　"contracted out functions" means any functions which, by virtue of a contract under this section, fall to be performed by prisoner custody officers; and
　　"directly managed prison" means a prison which is not a contracted out prison.

Definitions   For "contracted out prison", see s 106(4); for "custodial duties", "prison officer", "prison rules" and "the 1989 Act", see s 117(1); for "prison custody officer" see s 114(1); for custodial duties at a directly managed prison, see s 117(2) and as to "contracted out functions" and "directly managed prison" sub-s (7) above.
References   See para 8.7.

Provision of new prisons

113 Provision of new prisons

(1)   The Secretary of State may declare to be a prison—
   (a)   any building or part of a building built or adapted for the purpose; and
   (b)   any floating structure or part of such a structure constructed or adapted for the purpose,
whether vested in, or under the control of, the Secretary of State or any other person.

(2)   Section 106(1) and subsection (1) above are without prejudice to the Secretary of State's powers under the 1989 Act with respect to the provision of prisons.

(3)   A declaration under subsection (1) above—
   (a)   shall have effect for the purposes of the 1989 Act and any other enactment (including an enactment contained in subordinate legislation);
   (b)   shall not be sufficient to vest the legal estate in any building or structure in the Secretary of State; and
   (c)   may be revoked by the Secretary of State at any time other than a time when the prison to which it relates is a contracted out prison.

(4)   Nothing in section 36 of the 1989 Act (prison property to be vested in the Secretary of State) shall require the legal estate in—
   (a)   any prison provided under a contract entered into under section 106(1) above;
   (b)   any prison declared to be such under subsection (1) above and not vested in the Secretary of State; or
   (c)   any heritable or moveable property belonging to any prison mentioned in paragraph (a) or (b) above,
to be vested in the Secretary of State.

Definitions   For "contracted out prison", see s 106(4); for "prison" and "the 1989 Act", see s 117(1).
References   See para 8.8.

Supplemental

114 Prisoner custody officers: general provisions

(1)   In this Chapter "prisoner custody officer" means a person in respect of whom a certificate is for the time being in force certifying—
   (a)   that he has been approved by the Secretary of State for the purpose of performing escort functions or custodial duties or both; and
   (b)   that he is accordingly authorised to perform them.

(2)   Schedule 6 to this Act shall have effect with respect to the certification of prisoner custody officers.

(3)   Prison rules may make provision regarding the powers and duties of prisoner custody officers performing custodial duties.

Definitions   For "custodial duties", see s 117(1); for "escort functions", see s 102(1); for "prisoner custody officer", see sub-s (1) above.
References   See para 8.8.

115 Wrongful disclosure of information

(1) A person who—

    (a) is or has been employed (whether as a prisoner custody officer or otherwise) in pursuance of prisoner escort arrangements, or at a contracted out prison; or

    (b) is or has been employed to perform contracted out functions at a directly managed prison,

shall be guilty of an offence if he discloses, otherwise than in the course of his duty or as authorised by the Secretary of State, any information which he acquired in the course of his employment and which relates to a particular prisoner.

(2) A person guilty of an offence under subsection (1) above shall be liable—

    (a) on conviction on indictment, to imprisonment for a term not exceeding two years or a fine or both;

    (b) on summary conviction, to imprisonment for a term not exceeding six months or a fine not exceeding the statutory maximum or both.

Definitions   For "contracted out functions" and "directly managed prison" see s 112(7); for "contracted out prison", see s 106(4); for "prisoner", see s 117(1); for "prisoner custody officer", see s 114(1); for "prisoner escort arrangements", see s 102(4).
References   See para 8.8.

116 Minor and consequential amendments

(1) In section 19(4)(b) of the 1989 Act (remand centres and young offenders institutions), for "33" there shall be substituted "33A".

(2) Section 33 of that Act (miscellaneous duties of prison governor) shall cease to have effect.

(3) After section 33 of that Act there shall be inserted the following section—

"33A Power of governor to delegate functions

Rules made under section 39 of this Act may permit the governor of a prison to authorise an officer of the prison, or a class of such officers, to exercise on his behalf such of the governor's functions as the rules may specify.".

(4) In section 39 of that Act (prison rules)—

    (a) in subsection (1), after "Act" there shall be inserted "or any other enactment";

    (b) in subsection (8), for "the purpose so specified" there shall be substituted "any purpose specified in the rules"; and

    (c) after subsection (11), there shall be inserted the following subsection—

"(12) Rules made under this section may (without prejudice to the generality of subsection (1) above) confer functions on a governor.".

Definitions   For "the 1989 Act", see s 117(1).
References   See para 8.8.

117 Interpretation of Chapter II

(1) In this Chapter, except where otherwise expressly provided—

    "the 1989 Act" means the Prisons (Scotland) Act 1989;

        "contracted out prison" and "the contractor" have the meanings given by section 106(4) above;

"contracted out functions" and "directly managed prison" have the meanings given by section 112(7) above;

"custodial duties" means custodial duties at a contracted out or a directly managed prison;

"escort functions" has the meaning given by section 102(1) above;

"prison" includes—

(a) any prison other than a naval, military or air force prison; and

(b) a remand centre or young offenders institution within the meaning of section 19 of the 1989 Act;

"prison officer" means an officer of a directly managed prison;

"prison rules" means rules made under section 39 of the 1989 Act;

"prisoner" means any person who is in legal custody or is deemed to be in legal custody under section 215 or 426 of the Criminal Procedure (Scotland) Act 1975;

"prisoner custody officer" has the meaning given by section 114(1) above;

"prisoner escort arrangements" has the meaning given by section 102(4) above; and

"sub-contractor" has the meaning given by section 106(4) above.

(2) Any reference in this Chapter to custodial duties at a contracted out or directly managed prison includes a reference to custodial duties in relation to a prisoner who is outside such a prison for temporary purposes.

(3) In sections 102(1) to (3), 104 and 105 above, "prison"—

(a) so far as relating to the transfer of prisoners to or from a prison situated in England and Wales, includes a young offender institution and a remand centre; and

(b) so far as relating to the transfer of prisoners to or from a prison situated in Northern Ireland, includes a young offenders centre and a remand centre.

References   See para 8.8.

CHAPTER III
NORTHERN IRELAND

Prisoner escorts

118 Arrangements for the provision of prisoner escorts

(1) The Secretary of State may make arrangements for any of the following functions, namely—

(a) the delivery of prisoners from one set of relevant premises to another;

(b) the custody of prisoners held on the premises of any court (whether or not they would otherwise be in the custody of the court) and their production before the court;

(c) the custody of prisoners temporarily held in a prison in the course of delivery from one prison to another; and

(d) the custody of prisoners while they are outside a prison for temporary purposes;

to be performed in such cases as may be determined by or under the arrangements by prisoner custody officers who are authorised to perform such functions.

(2) In paragraph (a) of subsection (1) above, "relevant premises" means a court, prison, police station or hospital; and either (but not both) of the sets of premises

mentioned in that paragraph may be situated in a part of the British Islands outside Northern Ireland.

(3) Arrangements made by the Secretary of State under this section ("prisoner escort arrangements") may include entering into contracts with other persons for the provision by them of prisoner custody officers.

(4) Any person who, under a warrant or a hospital order or remand, is responsible for the performance of any such function as is mentioned in subsection (1) above shall be deemed to have complied with that warrant, order or remand if he does all that he reasonably can to secure that the function is performed by a prisoner custody officer acting in pursuance of prisoner escort arrangements.

(5) In this section—
> "hospital" has the same meaning as in the Mental Health (Northern Ireland) Order 1986;
> "hospital order" means an order for a person's admission to hospital under Article 44, 45, 49 or 50 of that Order, or section 11 or 13 of the Criminal Appeal (Northern Ireland) Act 1980;
> "hospital remand" means a remand of a person to hospital under Article 42 or 43 of the Mental Health (Northern Ireland) Order 1986;
> "warrant" means a warrant of commitment, a warrant of arrest or a warrant under Article 52, 53, 54, 56 or 79 of that Order.

Definitions   For "prisoner custody officer", see s 122(1); for "prisoner", see s 125(1), (2)(a); for "prison", see s 125(1), (2)(b), (3); for "prisoner escort arrangements", see sub-s (3) above; for "hospital", "hospital order", "hospital remand" and "warrant", see sub-s (5) above.
References   See para 8.9.

119 Monitoring etc of prisoner escort arrangements

(1) Prisoner escort arrangements shall include the appointment of a prisoner escort monitor, that is to say, a Crown servant whose duty it shall be to keep the arrangements under review and to report on them to the Secretary of State.

(2) It shall also be the duty of a prisoner escort monitor to investigate and report to the Secretary of State on—
> (a) any allegations made against prisoner custody officers acting in pursuance of the arrangements; and
> (b) any alleged breaches of discipline on the part of prisoners for whose delivery or custody such officers so acting are responsible.

Definitions   For "prisoner escort arrangements", see s 118(3); for "prisoner custody officer", see s 122(1); for "prisoner", see s 125(1), (2)(a); for "prisoner escort monitor", see sub-s (1) above.
References   See para 8.9.

120 Powers and duties of prisoner custody officers acting in pursuance of such arrangements

(1) A prisoner custody officer acting in pursuance of prisoner escort arrangements shall have the following powers, namely—
> (a) to search in accordance with rules made by the Secretary of State any prisoner for whose delivery or custody he is responsible in accordance with the arrangements; and
> (b) to search any other person who is in or is seeking to enter any place where any such prisoner is or is to be held and any article in the possession of such a person.

(2) The powers conferred by subsection (1)(b) above to search a person shall not be construed as authorising a prisoner custody officer to require a person to remove any of his clothing other than an outer coat, hat, jacket or gloves.

(3) A prisoner custody officer shall have the following duties as respects prisoners for whose delivery or custody he is responsible in pursuance of prisoner escort arrangements, namely—

    (a) to prevent their escape from lawful custody;

    (b) to prevent, or detect and report on, the commission or attempted commission by them of other unlawful acts;

    (c) to ensure good order and discipline on their part;

    (d) to attend to their wellbeing; and

    (e) to give effect to any directions as to their treatment which are given by a court,

and the Secretary of State may make rules with respect to the performance by prisoner custody officers of their duty under paragraph (d) above.

(4) Where a prisoner custody officer acting in pursuance of prisoner escort arrangements is on any premises in which a magistrates' court is sitting, it shall be his duty to give effect to any order of that court made under Article 110 of the Magistrates' Courts (Northern Ireland) Order 1981 (application of funds found upon defaulter).

(5) The powers conferred by subsection (1) above and the powers arising by virtue of subsections (3) and (4) above shall include power to use reasonable force where necessary.

(6) The power to make rules under this section shall be exercisable by statutory instrument which shall be subject to annulment in pursuance of a resolution of either House of Parliament.

Definitions   For "prisoner escort arrangements", see s 118(3) of this Act; for "prisoner custody officer", see s 122(1) thereof; for "prisoner", see s 125(1), (2)(a) thereof; for "prison", see s 125(1), (3) thereof.
References   See para 8.9.

---

121 Breaches of discipline by prisoners under escort

(1) This section applies where a prisoner for whose delivery or custody a prisoner custody officer has been responsible in pursuance of prisoner escort arrangements is delivered to a prison.

(2) For the purpose of such prison rules as relate to disciplinary offences, the prisoner shall be deemed to have been in the custody of the governor of the prison at all times during the period for which the prisoner custody officer was so responsible.

(3) In the case of any breach by the prisoner at any time during the period of such prison rules as so relate, a disciplinary charge may be laid against him by the prisoner custody officer.

(4) Nothing in this section shall enable a prisoner to be punished under prison rules for any act or omission of his for which he has already been punished by a court.

(5) In this section "prison rules", in relation to a prison situated in a part of the British Islands outside Northern Ireland, means rules made under any provision of the law of that part which corresponds to section 13 of the Prison Act (Northern Ireland) 1953.

Definitions For "prisoner escort arrangements", see s 118(3); for "prisoner custody officer", see s 122(1); for "prison rules" and "prisoner", see s 125(1) (and note also as to "prison rules", sub-s (5) above); for "prison", see s 125(1), (3).
References See para 8.9.

Supplemental

122 Certification of custody officers

(1)   In this Chapter "prisoner custody officer" means a person in respect of whom a certificate is for the time being in force certifying—

> (a)   that he has been approved by the Secretary of State for the purpose of performing escort functions; and
>
> (b)   that he is accordingly authorised to perform them.

(2)   Schedule 7 to this Act shall have effect with respect to the certification of prisoner custody officers.

(3)   In this section and Schedule 7 to this Act "escort functions" means the functions specified in section 118(1) above.

References See para 8.9.

123 Protection of prisoner custody officers

(1)   Any person who assaults a prisoner custody officer acting in pursuance of prisoner escort arrangements shall be liable on summary conviction to a fine not exceeding level 5 on the standard scale or to imprisonment for a term not exceeding six months or to both.

(2)   Article 18(2) of the Firearms (Northern Ireland) Order 1981 (additional penalty for possession of firearms when committing certain offences) shall apply to offences under subsection (1) above.

(3)   Any person who resists or wilfully obstructs a prisoner custody officer acting in pursuance of prisoner escort arrangements shall be liable on summary conviction to a fine not exceeding level 3 on the standard scale.

(4)   For the purposes of this section, a prisoner custody officer shall not be regarded as acting in pursuance of prisoner escort arrangements at any time when he is not readily identifiable as such an officer (whether by means of a uniform or badge which he is wearing or otherwise).

Definitions For "prisoner escort arrangements", see s 118(3); for "prisoner custody officer", see s 122(1). Note as to when a prisoner custody officer is and is not acting in pursuance of prisoner escort arrangements, sub-s (4) above.
References See para 8.9.

124 Wrongful disclosure of information

(1)   A person who is or has been employed (whether as a prisoner custody officer or otherwise) in pursuance of prisoner escort arrangements shall be guilty of an offence if he discloses, otherwise than in the course of his duty or as authorised by the Secretary of State, any information which he acquired in the course of his employment and which relates to a particular prisoner.

(2) A person guilty of an offence under subsection (1) above shall be liable—

    (a) on conviction on indictment, to imprisonment for a term not exceeding two years or a fine or both;

    (b) on summary conviction, to imprisonment for a term not exceeding six months or a fine not exceeding the statutory maximum or both.

Definitions   For "prisoner escort arrangements", see s 118(3); for "prisoner", see s 125(1), (2)(a).
References   See para 8.9.

125 Interpretation of Chapter III

(1) In this Chapter—

"prison" includes a young offenders centre or remand centre;

"prisoner custody officer" has the meaning given by section 122(1) above;

"prison rules" means rules made under section 13 of the Prison Act (Northern Ireland) 1953;

"prisoner" means any person for the time being detained in lawful custody as the result of a requirement imposed by a court or otherwise that he be so detained;

"prisoner escort arrangements" has the meaning given by section 118(3) above.

(2) Sections 118, 119(1) and (2)(a), 120 and 122 to 124 above, subsection (1) above and Schedule 7 to this Act shall have effect as if—

    (a) any reference in section 118(1), 119(1), 120 or 124 above to prisoners included a reference to persons remanded or committed to custody in certain premises under section 51, 74 or 75 of the Children and Young Persons Act (Northern Ireland) 1968 or ordered to be sent to a training school under section 74 or 78 of that Act; and

    (b) any reference in section 118(1)(c) or (d) or (2) above to a prison included a reference to such premises or training school.

(3) In sections 118, 120 and 121 above, "prison"—

    (a) so far as relating to the delivery of prisoners to or from a prison situated in England and Wales, includes a remand centre or young offender institution; and

    (b) so far as relating to the delivery of prisoners to or from a prison situated in Scotland, includes a remand centre or young offenders institution within the meaning of section 19 of the Prisons (Scotland) Act 1989.

References   See para 8.9.

CHAPTER IV
THE PRISON SERVICE

126 Service in England and Wales and Northern Ireland

(1) The relevant employment legislation shall have effect as if an individual who as a member of the prison service acts in a capacity in which he has the powers or privileges of a constable were not, by virtue of his so having those powers or privileges, to be regarded as in police service for the purposes of any provision of that legislation.

(2)   In this section "the relevant employment legislation" means—
   (a) the Employment Protection (Consolidation) Act 1978 and the Trade Union and Labour Relations (Consolidation) Act 1992; and
   (b) the Industrial Relations (Northern Ireland) Order 1976, the Industrial Relations (No 2) (Northern Ireland) Order 1976 and the Industrial Relations (Northern Ireland) Order 1992.

(3)   For the purposes of this section a person is a member of the prison service if he is an individual holding a post to which he has been appointed for the purposes of section 7 of the Prison Act 1952 or under section 2(2) of the Prison Act (Northern Ireland) 1953 (appointment of prison staff).

(4)   Except for the purpose of validating anything that would have been a contravention of section 127(1) below if it had been in force, subsection (1) above, so far as it relates to the question whether an organisation consisting wholly or mainly of members of the prison service is a trade union, shall be deemed always to have had effect and to have applied, in relation to times when provisions of the relevant employment legislation were not in force, to the corresponding legislation then in force.

(5)   Subsection (6) below shall apply where—
   (a) the certificate of independence of any organisation has been cancelled, at any time before the passing of this Act, in consequence of the removal of the name of that organisation from a list of trade unions kept under provisions of the relevant employment legislation; but
   (b) it appears to the Certification Officer that the organisation would have remained on the list, and that the certificate would have remained in force, had that legislation had effect at and after that time in accordance with subsection (1) above.

(6)   Where this subsection applies—
   (a) the Certification Officer shall restore the name to the list and delete from his records any entry relating to the cancellation of the certificate;
   (b) the removal of the name from the list, the making of the deleted entry and the cancellation of the certificate shall be deemed never to have occurred; and
   (c) the organisation shall accordingly be deemed, for the purposes for which it is treated by virtue of subsection (4) above as having been a trade union, to have been independent throughout the period between the cancellation of the certificate and the deletion of the entry relating to that cancellation.

References   See paras 8.10, 8.11.

---

127 Inducements to withhold services or to indiscipline

(1)   A person contravenes this subsection if he induces a prison officer—
   (a) to withhold his services as such an officer; or
   (b) to commit a breach of discipline.

(2)   The obligation not to contravene subsection (1) above shall be a duty owed to the Secretary of State.

(3)   Without prejudice to the right of the Secretary of State, by virtue of the preceding provisions of this section, to bring civil proceedings in respect of any

apprehended contravention of subsection (1) above, any breach of the duty mentioned in subsection (2) above which causes the Secretary of State to sustain loss or damage shall be actionable, at his suit or instance, against the person in breach.

(4)   In this section "prison officer" means any individual who—

(a)   holds any post, otherwise than as a chaplain or assistant chaplain or as a medical officer, to which he has been appointed for the purposes of section 7 of the Prison Act 1952 or under section 2(2) of the Prison Act (Northern Ireland) 1953 (appointment of prison staff),

(b)   holds any post, otherwise than as a medical officer, to which he has been appointed under section 3(1) of the Prisons (Scotland) Act 1989, or

(c)   is a custody officer within the meaning of Part I of this Act or a prisoner custody officer, within the meaning of Part IV of the Criminal Justice Act 1991 or Chapter II or III of this Part.

(5)   The reference in subsection (1) above to a breach of discipline by a prison officer is a reference to a failure by a prison officer to perform any duty imposed on him by the prison rules or any code of discipline having effect under those rules or any other contravention by a prison officer of those rules or any such code.

(6)   In subsection (5) above "the prison rules" means any rules for the time being in force under section 47 of the Prison Act 1952, section 39 of the Prisons (Scotland) Act 1989 or section 13 of the Prison Act (Northern Ireland) 1953 (prison rules).

(7)   This section shall be disregarded in determining for the purposes of any of the relevant employment legislation whether any trade union is an independent trade union.

(8)   Nothing in the relevant employment legislation shall affect the rights of the Secretary of State by virtue of this section.

(9)   In this section "the relevant employment legislation" has the same meaning as in section 126 above.

Definitions   For "custody officer", in Pt I and Schs 1, 2 of this Act, see s 12(3) of this Act, for "prisoner custody officer" in Chs II, III of this Part, see ss 114(1), 122(1) respectively; for "prisoner custody officer" in Pt IV of the Criminal Justice Act 1991, see s 89(1) thereof.
References   See paras 8.10, 8.11.

---

128 Pay and related conditions

(1)   The Secretary of State may by regulations provide for the establishment, maintenance and operation of procedures for the determination from time to time of—

(a)   the rates of pay and allowances to be applied to the prison service; and

(b)   such other terms and conditions of employment in that service as may appear to him to fall to be determined in association with the determination of rates of pay and allowances.

(2)   Before making any regulations under this section the Secretary of State shall consult with such organisations appearing to him to be representative of persons working in the prison service and with such other persons as he thinks fit.

(3)   The power to make regulations under this section shall be exercisable by statutory instrument subject to annulment in pursuance of a resolution of either House of Parliament.

(4)   Regulations under this section may—

(a) provide for determinations with respect to matters to which the regulations relate to be made wholly or partly by reference to such factors, and the opinion or recommendations of such persons, as may be specified or described in the regulations;

(b) authorise the matters considered and determined in pursuance of the regulations to include matters applicable to times and periods before they are considered or determined;

(c) make such incidental, supplemental, consequential and transitional provision as the Secretary of State thinks fit; and

(d) make different provision for different cases.

(5) For the purposes of this section the prison service comprises all the individuals who are prison officers within the meaning of section 127 above, apart from those who are custody officers within the meaning of Part I of this Act or prisoner custody officers within the meaning of Part IV of the Criminal Justice Act 1991 or Chapter II or III of this Part.

Definitions For "custody officer", in Pt I and Schs 1, 2 of this Act, see s 12(3) of this Act, for "prisoner custody officer" in Chs II, III of this Part, see ss 114(1), 122(1) respectively; for "prisoner custody officer" in Pt IV of the Criminal Justice Act 1991, see s 89(1) thereof.
References See paras 8.10, 8.11.

PART IX

MISCELLANEOUS AMENDMENTS: SCOTLAND

129 Transfer of persons detained by police and customs officers

(1) In subsection (1) of section 2 of the Criminal Justice (Scotland) Act 1980 (detention of suspect at police station or other premises)—

(a) after the word "premises" there shall be inserted the words "and may thereafter for that purpose take him to any other place"; and

(b) for the word "there" there shall be substituted the words "at the police station, or as the case may be the other premises or place".

(2) In subsection (4) of that section—

(a) after paragraph (a) there shall be inserted the following paragraph—

"(aa) any other place to which the person is, during the detention, thereafter taken;"; and

(b) in paragraph (f), for the words "departure from the police station or other premises" there shall be substituted the words "release from detention".

(3) In section 3(1)(b) of that Act (intimation to solicitor and other person of detention under section 2)—

(a) for the words "in a police station or other premises" there shall be substituted the words "and has been taken to a police station or other premises or place"; and

(b) for the words "place where he is being detained" there shall be substituted the words "police station or other premises or place".

(4) In subsection (1) of section 48 of the Criminal Justice (Scotland) Act 1987 (detention of suspect by customs officer)—

(a) after the word "premises" there shall be inserted the words "and may thereafter for that purpose take him to any other place"; and

(b) for the word "there" there shall be substituted the words "at the customs office, or as the case may be the other premises or place.".

(5)   In subsection (5) of that section—
  (a)   after paragraph (a) there shall be inserted the following paragraph—

"(aa) any other place to which the person is, during the detention, thereafter taken;"; and

  (b)   in paragraph (f), for the words "departure from the customs office or other premises" there shall be substituted the words "release from detention".

(6)   In section 49(1) of that Act (intimation to solicitor and other person of detention under section 48)—
  (a)   for the words "at a customs office or other premises" there shall be substituted the words "and has been taken to a customs office or other premises or place"; and
  (b)   for the words "place where he is being detained" there shall be substituted the words "customs office or other premises or place".

References   See para 9.1.

130 Detention and release of children: Scotland

(1)   In section 7 of the Prisoners and Criminal Proceedings (Scotland) Act 1993 (children detained in solemn proceedings), after subsection (1) there shall be inserted—

"(1A) The Secretary of State may by order provide—
  (a)   that the reference to—
      (i)   four years, in paragraph (a) of subsection (1) above; or
      (ii)   four or more years, in paragraph (b) of that subsection,
    shall be construed as a reference to such other period as may be specified in the order;
  (b)   that the reference to—
      (i)   half, in the said paragraph (a); or
      (ii)   two thirds, in the said paragraph (b),
    shall be construed as a reference to such other proportion of the period specified in the sentence as may be specified in the order.

(1B)   An order under subsection (1A) above may make such transitional provision as appears to the Secretary of State necessary or expedient in connection with any provision made by the order.".

(2)   In section 45(3) of that Act (procedure in respect of certain orders), for the words "7(6)" there shall be substituted "7(1A) or (6)".

(3)   In Schedule 6 to that Act (transitional provisions and savings)—
  (a)   in paragraph 8, after the word "revoked" there shall be inserted "by virtue of paragraph 10 of this Schedule"; and
  (b)   after paragraph 9 there shall be added—

"10. Section 17 of this Act shall apply in respect of a release on licence under paragraph 4 of this Schedule as that section applies in respect of the release on licence, under Part I of this Act, of a long-term prisoner.".

(4)   In section 39(7) of the Prisons (Scotland) Act 1989 (award of additional days), at the end there shall be added—

"; and the foregoing provisions of this subsection (except paragraph (b)) shall apply in respect of a person sentenced to be detained under section 206 of the 1975 Act, the detention not being without limit of time, as those provisions apply in respect of any such short-term or long-term prisoner.".

References   See paras 9.1, 9.2.

131 Conditions in licence of released prisoner: requirement for Parole Board recommendations

In section 12(3)(a) of the Prisoners and Criminal Proceedings (Scotland) Act 1993 (requirement of Parole Board recommendations for inclusion of conditions in licences of certain released prisoners), after the word "inclusion" there shall be inserted the words "or subsequent insertion, variation or cancellation".

References   See paras 9.1, 9.2.

132 Provision for standard requirements in supervised release orders in Scotland

In section 212A of the Criminal Procedure (Scotland) Act 1975 (which makes provision for the supervised release of short-term prisoners)—
 (a) in subsection (2)—
   (i) for the words from "and", where it occurs immediately after paragraph (a), to the end of sub-paragraph (i) of paragraph (b), there shall be substituted—

"(b) comply with—
   (i) such requirements as may be imposed by the court in the order;"; and

   (ii) at the end there shall be added—

"; and
   (c) comply with the standard requirements imposed by virtue of subsection (3)(a)(i) below"; and

 (b) in subsection (3), for paragraph (a) there shall be substituted—

"(a) shall—
   (i) without prejudice to subsection (2)(b) above, contain such requirements (in this section referred to as the "standard requirements"); and
   (ii) be as nearly as possible in such form,

as may be prescribed by Act of Adjournal;".

References   See paras 9.1, 9.2.

133 Extension of categories of prisoner to whom Part I of Prisoners and Criminal Proceedings (Scotland) Act 1993 applies

In section 10(4) of the Prisoners and Criminal Proceedings (Scotland) Act 1993 (interpretation of expression "transferred life prisoner")—
 (a) in paragraph (a), after the word "Scotland" there shall be inserted the words "or a court-martial"; and
 (b) in paragraph (b)—

(i)   for the word "(whether" there shall be substituted—

", or in the case of a sentence imposed by a court martial in Scotland to a prison in Scotland (in either case whether";

(ii)   after sub-paragraph (ii) there shall be inserted—

"; or
(iii)   rules made under section 122(1)(a) of the Army Act 1955 (imprisonment and detention rules); or
(iv)   rules made under section 122(1)(a) of the Air Force Act 1955 (imprisonment and detention rules); or
(v)   a determination made under section 81(3) of the Naval Discipline Act 1957 (place of imprisonment or detention),"; and

(iii)   at the end there shall be added—

"; and in this subsection "prison" has the same meaning as in the 1989 Act.".

References   See paras 9.1, 9.2.

---

134 Amendment of provisions continued in effect for certain prisoners by Prisoners and Criminal Proceedings (Scotland) Act 1993

(1)   In Schedule 6 to the Prisoners and Criminal Proceedings (Scotland) Act 1993 (transitional provisions and savings)—
(a)   in paragraph 1—
(i)   in the definition of "existing provisions", at the end there shall be added "except that an amendment or repeal effected by any enactment shall apply for the purposes of the existing provisions if expressly stated to do so"; and
(ii)   in the definition of "new provisions", after the word "amended" there shall be added "by this Act"; and
(b)   in paragraph 2(1), for the words from "and to" to "Schedule" there shall be substituted—

", to the following provisions of this Schedule and to the exception in the definition of "existing provisions" in paragraph 1 above,".

(2)   Sections 18 (constitution and functions of Parole Board etc), 22 (release on licence of persons serving determinate sentences), 28 (revocation of licences and conviction of prisoners on licence) and 42(3) (exercise of power to make rules etc) of the Prisons (Scotland) Act 1989, being provisions which, notwithstanding their repeal by the Prisoners and Criminal Proceedings (Scotland) Act 1993, are "existing provisions" for the purposes of that Act of 1993, shall for those purposes be amended in accordance with the following subsections.

(3)   In the said section 18, for subsections (3) and (4) there shall be substituted—

"(3A)   The Secretary of State may by rules make provision with respect to the proceedings of the Board, including provision—
(a)   authorising cases to be dealt with in whole or in part by a prescribed number of members of the Board in accordance with such procedure as may be prescribed;
(b)   requiring cases to be dealt with at prescribed times; and
(c)   as to what matters may be taken into account by the Board (or by such number) in dealing with a case.

(3B)   The Secretary of State may give the Board directions as to the matters to be taken into account by it in discharging its functions under this Part of this Act; and in giving any such directions the Secretary of State shall in particular have regard to—

(a) the need to protect the public from serious harm from offenders; and
(b) the desirability of preventing the commission by offenders of further offences and of securing their rehabilitation.".

(4)   In each of the said sections 22 and 28, after subsection (1) there shall be inserted—

"(1A) The Secretary of State may by order provide that, in relation to such class of case as may be specified in the order, subsection (1) above shall have effect subject to the modification that for the word "may" there shall be substituted the word "shall".".

(5)   In the said section 22, at the beginning of subsection (7) there shall be inserted the words "In a case where the Parole Board has recommended that a person be released on licence, and by virtue of subsection (1A) above such release is then mandatory, no licence conditions shall be included in the licence, or subsequently inserted, varied or cancelled in it, except in accordance with recommendations of the Board; and in any other case".

(6)   In the said section 42—

(a) in each of subsections (1) and (4), for the words "22(2)" there shall be substituted "22(1A) or (2), 28(1A),"; and
(b) in subsection (3), for the word "(3)" there shall be substituted "(3A)".

References   See paras 9.1, 9.2.

---

135 Further amendment of Schedule 6 to the Prisoners and Criminal Proceedings (Scotland) Act 1993: application of "new provisions"

In Schedule 6 to the Prisoners and Criminal Proceedings (Scotland) Act 1993 (transitional provisions and savings), after paragraph 6 there shall be inserted the following paragraphs—

"6A.—(1)This paragraph applies where a prisoner sentenced before the relevant date to a sentence of imprisonment for life for an offence the sentence for which is not fixed by law has been (whether before, on or after that date) released on licence under the 1989 Act.

(2)   Without prejudice to section 22(6) of the 1989 Act, in a case to which this paragraph applies, the new provisions shall apply as if the prisoner were a discretionary life prisoner, within the meaning of section 2 of this Act, whose licence has been granted under subsection (4) of that section of this Act on his having served the relevant part of his sentence.

6B.—(1)This paragraph applies where—

(a) a prisoner was, at the relevant date, serving a sentence or sentences of imprisonment, on conviction of an offence, passed before that date and that sentence was for a term of, or as the case may be those sentences fall to be treated as for a single term of, two or more years; and
(b) on or after that date he is, or has been, sentenced to a further term or terms of imprisonment, on conviction of an offence, to be served

consecutively to, or concurrently with, the sentence or sentences mentioned in head (a) above.

(2)   In a case to which this paragraph applies—

(a)   the sentence or sentences mentioned in head (b) of sub-paragraph (1) above shall be treated as a single term with the sentences mentioned in head (a) of that sub-paragraph and that single term as imposed on or after the relevant date (so however that nothing in the foregoing provisions of this head shall affect the application of sections 39(7) (which makes provision as respects the award of additional days for breaches of discipline) and 24 (which makes provision as respects remission for good conduct) of the 1989 Act); and

(b)   the new provisions shall apply accordingly, except that—

(i)   where the prisoner is a long-term prisoner by virtue only of the aggregation provided for in head (a) of this sub-paragraph, he shall be released unconditionally on the same day as he would have been but for that aggregation;

(ii)   where, notwithstanding the aggregation so provided for, the prisoner remains a short-term prisoner, subsection (1) of section 1 of this Act shall in its application be construed as subject to the qualification that the prisoner shall be released no earlier than he would have been but for that aggregation;

(iii) that section shall in its application be construed as if for subsection (3) there were substituted—

"(3)   Without prejudice to subsection (1) above and to sub-paragraph (2)(b)(i) of paragraph 6B of Schedule 6 to this Act, after a prisoner to whom that paragraph applies has either served one-third of the sentence, or as the case may be sentences, mentioned in sub-paragraph (1)(a) of that paragraph, or (if it results in a later date of release) has served twelve months of that sentence or those sentences, the Secretary of State may, if recommended to do so by the Parole Board under this section, release him on licence; and where such a prisoner has been released on licence under section 22 of the 1989 Act, that licence shall be deemed to have been granted by virtue of this subsection.";

(iv) section 11(1) shall in its application be construed as if the sentence referred to were the further term or terms mentioned in head (b) of sub-paragraph (1) above; and

(v)   section 16 shall in its application be construed as if the original sentence (within the meaning of that section) were the further term or terms so mentioned.".

References   See paras 9.1, 9.2.

PART X
CROSS-BORDER ENFORCEMENT

136 Execution of warrants

(1)   A warrant issued in England, Wales or Northern Ireland for the arrest of a person charged with an offence may (without any endorsement) be executed in Scotland by any constable of any police force of the country of issue or of the country of execution as well as by any other persons within the directions in the warrant.

(2)   A warrant issued in—
    (a)   Scotland; or
    (b)   Northern Ireland,
for the arrest of a person charged with an offence may (without any endorsement) be executed in England or Wales by any constable of any police force of the country of issue or of the country of execution as well as by any other persons within the directions in the warrant.

(3)   A warrant issued in—
    (a)   England or Wales; or
    (b)   Scotland,
for the arrest of a person charged with an offence may (without any endorsement) be executed in Northern Ireland by any constable of any police force of the country of issue or of the country of execution as well as by any other persons within the directions in the warrant.

(4)   A person arrested in pursuance of a warrant shall be taken, as soon as reasonably practicable, to any place to which he is committed by, or may be conveyed under, the warrant.

(5)   A constable executing a warrant—
    (a)   under subsection (1), (2)(b) or (3)(a) of this section may use reasonable force and shall have the powers of search conferred by section 139;
    (b)   under subsection (2)(a) or (3)(b) of this section shall have the same powers and duties, and the person arrested the same rights, as they would have had if execution had been in Scotland by a constable of a police force in Scotland.

(6)   Any other person within the directions in a warrant executing that warrant under this section shall have the same powers and duties, and the person arrested the same rights, as they would have had if execution had been in the country of issue by the person within those directions.

(7)   This section applies as respects—
    (a)   a warrant of commitment and a warrant to arrest a witness issued by a judicial authority in England, Wales or Northern Ireland as it applies to a warrant for arrest; and
    (b)   a warrant for committal, a warrant to imprison (or to apprehend and imprison) and a warrant to arrest a witness issued by a judicial authority in Scotland as it applies to a warrant for arrest.

(8)   In this section "judicial authority" means any justice of the peace or the judge of any court exercising jurisdiction in criminal proceedings; and any reference to a part of the United Kingdom in which a warrant may be executed includes a reference to the adjacent sea and other waters within the seaward limits of the territorial sea.

References   See para 10.1.

137 Cross-border powers of arrest etc

(1)   If the conditions applicable to this subsection are satisfied, any constable of a police force in England and Wales who has reasonable grounds for suspecting that an offence has been committed or attempted in England or Wales and that the suspected person is in Scotland or in Northern Ireland may arrest without a warrant the suspected person wherever he is in Scotland or in Northern Ireland.

(2)   If the condition applicable to this subsection is satisfied, any constable of a police force in Scotland who has reasonable grounds for suspecting that an offence has been committed or attempted in Scotland and that the suspected person is in England or Wales or in Northern Ireland may, as respects the suspected person, wherever he is in England or Wales or in Northern Ireland, exercise the same powers of arrest or detention as it would be competent for him to exercise were the person in Scotland.

(3)   If the conditions applicable to this subsection are satisfied, any constable of a police force in Northern Ireland who has reasonable grounds for suspecting that an offence has been committed or attempted in Northern Ireland and that the suspected person is in England or Wales or in Scotland may arrest without a warrant the suspected person wherever he is in England or Wales or in Scotland.

(4)   The conditions applicable to subsection (1) above are—
    (a)   that the suspected offence is an arrestable offence; or
    (b)   that, in the case of any other offence, it appears to the constable that service of a summons is impracticable or inappropriate for any of the reasons specified in subsection (3) of section 138.

(5)   The condition applicable to subsection (2) above is that it appears to the constable that it would have been lawful for him to have exercised the powers had the suspected person been in Scotland.

(6)   The conditions applicable to subsection (3) above are—
    (a)   that the suspected offence is an arrestable offence; or
    (b)   that, in the case of any other offence, it appears to the constable that service of a summons is impracticable or inappropriate for any of the reasons specified in subsection (3) of section 138.

(7)   It shall be the duty of a constable who has arrested or, as the case may be detained, a person under this section—
    (a)   if he arrested him in Scotland, to take the person arrested either to the nearest convenient designated police station in England or in Northern Ireland or to a designated police station in a police area in England and Wales or in Northern Ireland in which the offence is being investigated;
    (b)   if he arrested him in England or Wales, to take the person arrested to the nearest convenient police station in Scotland or to a police station within a sheriffdom in which the offence is being investigated or to the nearest convenient designated police station in Northern Ireland or to a designated police station in Northern Ireland in which the offence is being investigated;
    (c)   if he detained him in England or Wales, to take the person detained to either such police station in Scotland as is mentioned in paragraph (b) above, or to the nearest convenient designated police station in England or Wales;
    (d)   if he arrested him in Northern Ireland, to take the person arrested either to the nearest convenient designated police station in England or Wales or to a designated police station in a police area in England and Wales in which the offence is being investigated or to the nearest convenient police station in Scotland or to a police station within a sheriffdom in which the offence is being investigated;
    (e)   if he detained him in Northern Ireland, to take the person detained to either such police station in Scotland as is mentioned in paragraph (b)

above, or to the nearest convenient designated police station in Northern Ireland;

and to do so as soon as reasonably practicable.

(8) A constable—

    (a) arresting a person under subsection (1) or (3) above, may use reasonable force and shall have the powers of search conferred by section 139;

    (b) arresting a person under subsection (2) above shall have the same powers and duties, and the person arrested the same rights, as they would have had if the arrest had been in Scotland; and

    (c) detaining a person under subsection (2) above shall act in accordance with the provisions applied by subsection (2) (as modified by subsection (6)) of section 138.

(9) In this section—

    "arrestable offence" and "designated police station" have the same meaning as in the Police and Criminal Evidence Act 1984 and, in relation to Northern Ireland, have the same meaning as in the Police and Criminal Evidence (Northern Ireland) Order 1989; and

    "constable of a police force", in relation to Northern Ireland, means a member of the Royal Ulster Constabulary or the Royal Ulster Constabulary Reserve.

(10) This section shall not prejudice any power of arrest conferred apart from this section.

Definitions   In the Police and Criminal Evidence Act 1984, for "arrestable offence" and "designated police station", see ss 24, 35 respectively thereof. Section 24 is amended by ss 85(1), (2), 155, 166(4), 167(7) of this Act.
References   See para 10.1.

138 Powers of arrest etc: supplementary provisions

(1) The following provisions have effect to supplement section 137 ("the principal section").

(2) Where a person is detained under subsection (2) of the principal section, subsections (2) to (7) of section 2 (detention and questioning at police station) and subsections (1) and (3) to (5) of section 3 (right to have someone informed when arrested or detained) of the Criminal Justice (Scotland) Act 1980 and section 28 (prints, samples etc in criminal investigations) of the Prisoners and Criminal Proceedings (Scotland) Act 1993 shall apply to detention under that subsection of the principal section as they apply to detention under subsection (1) of the said section 2, but with the modifications mentioned in subsection (6) below.

(3) The reasons referred to in subsections (4)(b) and (6)(b) of the principal section are that—

    (a) the name of the suspected person is unknown to, and cannot readily be ascertained by, the constable;

    (b) the constable has reasonable grounds for doubting whether a name furnished by the suspected person as his name is his real name;

    (c) either—

        (i) the suspected person has failed to furnish a satisfactory address for service; or

        (ii) the constable has reasonable grounds for doubting whether an address furnished by the suspected person is a satisfactory address for service;

    (d) the constable has reasonable grounds for believing that arrest is necessary to prevent the suspected person—
        (i) causing physical injury to himself or any other person;
        (ii) suffering physical injury;
        (iii) causing loss of or damage to property;
        (iv) committing an offence against public decency; or
        (v) causing an unlawful obstruction of a highway or road; or
    (e) the constable has reasonable grounds for believing that arrest is necessary to protect a child or other vulnerable person from the suspected person.

(4)   For the purposes of subsection (3) above an address is a satisfactory address for service if it appears to the constable—
    (a) that the suspected person will be at it for a sufficiently long period for it to be possible to serve him with process; or
    (b) that some other person specified by the suspected person will accept service of process for the suspected person at it.

(5)   Nothing in subsection (3)(d) above authorises the arrest of a person under sub-paragraph (iv) of that paragraph except where members of the public going about their normal business cannot reasonably be expected to avoid the person to be arrested.

(6)   The following are the modifications of sections 2 and 3 of the Criminal Justice (Scotland) Act 1980 which are referred to in subsection (2) above—
    (a) in section 2—
        (i) in subsection (2), the reference to detention being terminated not more than six hours after it begins shall be construed as a reference to its being terminated not more than four hours after the person's arrival at the police station to which he is taken under subsection (7)(c) of the principal section; and
        (ii) in subsections (4) and (7), references to "other premises" shall be disregarded; and
    (b) in section 3(1), references to "other premises" shall be disregarded.

References   See para 10.2.

139 Search powers available on arrests under sections 136 and 137

(1)   The following powers are available to a constable in relation to a person arrested under section 136(1), (2)(b) or (3)(a) or 137(1) or (3).

(2)   A constable to whom this section applies may search the person if the constable has reasonable grounds for believing that the person may present a danger to himself or others.

(3)   Subject to subsections (4) to (6) below, a constable to whom this section applies may—
    (a) search the person for anything—
        (i) which he might use to assist him to escape from lawful custody; or
        (ii) which might be evidence relating to an offence; and
    (b) enter and search any premises in which the person was when, or was immediately before, he was arrested for evidence relating to the offence for which he was arrested.

(4)   The power to search conferred by subsection (3) above is only a power to search to the extent that is reasonably required for the purpose of discovering any such thing or any such evidence.

(5)   The powers conferred by this section to search a person are not to be construed as authorising a constable to require a person to remove any of his clothing in public other than an outer coat, jacket, headgear, gloves or footwear but they do authorise a search of a person's mouth.

(6)   A constable may not search a person in the exercise of the power conferred by subsection (3)(a) above unless he has reasonable grounds for believing that the person to be searched may have concealed on him anything for which a search is permitted under that paragraph.

(7)   A constable may not search premises in the exercise of the power conferred by subsection (3)(b) above unless he has reasonable grounds for believing that there is evidence for which a search is permitted under that paragraph.

(8)   In so far as the power of search conferred by subsection (3)(b) above relates to premises consisting of two or more separate dwellings, it is limited to a power to search—
  (a)   any dwelling in which the arrest took place or in which the person arrested was immediately before his arrest; and
  (b)   any parts of the premises which the occupier of any such dwelling uses in common with the occupiers of any other dwellings comprised in the premises.

(9)   A constable searching a person in the exercise of the power conferred by subsection (2) above may seize and retain anything he finds, if he has reasonable grounds for believing that the person searched might use it to cause physical injury to himself or to any other person.

(10)   A constable searching a person in the exercise of the power conferred by subsection (3)(a) above may seize and retain anything he finds, other than an item subject to legal privilege, if he has reasonable grounds for believing—
  (a)   that he might use it to assist him to escape from lawful custody; or
  (b)   that it is evidence of an offence, or has been obtained in consequence of the commission of an offence.

(11)   Nothing in this section shall be taken to affect the power conferred by section 15(3), (4) and (5) of the Prevention of Terrorism (Temporary Provisions) Act 1989.

(12)   In this section—
    "item subject to legal privilege" has the meaning given to it—
      (a)   as respects anything in the possession of a person searched in England and Wales, by section 10 of the Police and Criminal Evidence Act 1984;
      (b)   as respects anything in the possession of a person searched in Scotland, by section 40 of the Criminal Justice (Scotland) Act 1987;
      (c)   as respects anything in the possession of a person searched in Northern Ireland, by Article 12 of the Police and Criminal Evidence (Northern Ireland) Order 1989;
    "premises" includes any place and, in particular, includes—
      (a)   any vehicle, vessel, aircraft or hovercraft;
      (b)   any offshore installation; and
      (c)   any tent or movable structure; and
    "offshore installation" has the meaning given to it by section 1 of the Mineral Workings (Offshore Installations) Act 1971.

References See para 10.3.

140 Reciprocal powers of arrest

(1)   Where a constable of a police force in England and Wales would, in relation to an offence, have power to arrest a person in England or Wales under section 24(6) or (7) or 25 of the Police and Criminal Evidence Act 1984 (arrestable offences and non-arrestable offences in certain circumstances) a constable of a police force in Scotland or in Northern Ireland shall have the like power of arrest in England and Wales.

(2)   Where a constable of a police force in Scotland or in Northern Ireland arrests a person in England or Wales by virtue of subsection (1) above—

(a)   the constable shall be subject to requirements to inform the arrested person that he is under arrest and of the grounds for it corresponding to the requirements imposed by section 28 of that Act;

(b)   the constable shall be subject to a requirement to take the arrested person to a police station corresponding to the requirement imposed by section 30 of that Act and so also as respects the other related requirements of that section; and

(c)   the constable shall have powers to search the arrested person corresponding to the powers conferred by section 32 of that Act.

(3)   Where a constable of a police force in Scotland would, in relation to an offence, have power to arrest a person in Scotland, a constable of a police force in England and Wales or in Northern Ireland shall have the like power of arrest in Scotland.

(4)   Where a constable of a police force in England or Wales or in Northern Ireland arrests a person in Scotland by virtue of subsection (3) above, the arrested person shall have the same rights and the constable the same powers and duties as they would have were the constable a constable of a police force in Scotland.

(5)   Where a constable of a police force in Northern Ireland would, in relation to an offence, have power to arrest a person in Northern Ireland under Article 26(6) or (7) or 27 of the Police and Criminal Evidence (Northern Ireland) Order 1989 (arrestable offences and non-arrestable offences in certain circumstances) a constable of a police force in England and Wales or Scotland shall have the like power of arrest in Northern Ireland.

(6)   Where a constable of a police force in England and Wales or in Scotland arrests a person in Northern Ireland by virtue of subsection (5) above—

(a)   the constable shall be subject to requirements to inform the arrested person that he is under arrest and of the grounds for it corresponding to the requirements imposed by Article 30 of that Order;

(b)   the constable shall be subject to a requirement to take the arrested person to a police station corresponding to the requirement imposed by Article 32 of that Order and so as respects the other related requirements of that Article; and

(c)   the constable shall have powers to search the arrested person corresponding to the powers conferred by Article 34 of that Order.

(7)   In this section "constable of a police force", in relation to Northern Ireland, means a member of the Royal Ulster Constabulary or the Royal Ulster Constabulary Reserve.

References   See para 10.4.

141 Aid of one police force by another

(1)   The chief officer of police of a police force in England and Wales may, on the application of the chief officer of a police force in Scotland or the chief constable of the Royal Ulster Constabulary in Northern Ireland, provide constables or other assistance for the purpose of enabling the Scottish force or the Royal Ulster Constabulary to meet any special demand on its resources.

(2)   The chief officer of a police force in Scotland may, on the application of the chief officer of police of a police force in England and Wales or the chief constable of the Royal Ulster Constabulary in Northern Ireland, provide constables or other assistance for the purpose of enabling the English or Welsh force or the Royal Ulster Constabulary to meet any special demand on its resources.

(3)   The chief constable of the Royal Ulster Constabulary in Northern Ireland may, on the application of the chief officer of police of a police force in England and Wales or the chief officer of a police force in Scotland, provide constables or other assistance for the purpose of enabling the English or Welsh force or the Scottish force to meet any special demand on its resources.

(4)   If it appears to the Secretary of State to be expedient in the interests of public safety or order that any police force should be reinforced or should receive other assistance for the purpose of enabling it to meet any special demand on its resources, and that satisfactory arrangements under subsection (1), (2) or (3) above cannot be made, or cannot be made in time, he may direct the chief officer of police of any police force in England and Wales, the chief officer of any police force in Scotland or the chief constable of the Royal Ulster Constabulary, as the case may be, to provide such constables or other assistance for that purpose as may be specified in the direction.

(5)   While a constable is provided under this section for the assistance of another police force he shall, notwithstanding any enactment,—

    (a)   be under the direction and control of the chief officer of police of that other force (or, where that other force is a police force in Scotland or the Royal Ulster Constabulary in Northern Ireland, of its chief officer or the chief constable of the Royal Ulster Constabulary respectively); and

    (b)   have in any place the like powers and privileges as a member of that other force therein as a constable.

(6)   The police authority maintaining a police force for which assistance is provided under this section shall pay to the police authority maintaining the force from which that assistance is provided such contribution as may be agreed upon between those authorities or, in default of any such agreement, as may be provided by any agreement subsisting at the time between all police authorities generally, or, in default of such general agreement, as may be determined by the Secretary of State.

(7)   Any expression used in the Police Act 1964, the Police (Scotland) Act 1967 or the Police Act (Northern Ireland) 1970 and this section in its application to England and Wales, Scotland and Northern Ireland respectively has the same meaning in this section as in that Act.

(8)   In this section "constable of a police force", in relation to Northern Ireland, means a member of the Royal Ulster Constabulary or the Royal Ulster Constabulary Reserve.

Definitions By virtue of sub-s (7) above, for "chief officer of police", "police authority", and "police force", see the Police Act 1962, s 62; for "police authority" and "police force", see the Police (Scotland) Act 1967, s 50(b), (c); for "chief officer of a police force", see s 50(d)(i) of the 1967 Act; for "constable", see s 51(1) of the 1967 Act; for "enactment", see s 64(2) of the 1964 Act, and s 51(1) of the 1967 Act; for "constable of a police force", in relation to Northern Ireland, see sub-s (8) above.

References See para 10.4.

PART XI
SEXUAL OFFENCES

Rape

142 Rape of women and men

For section 1 of the Sexual Offences Act 1956 (rape of a woman) there shall be substituted the following section—

"1 Rape of woman or man

(1) It is an offence for a man to rape a woman or another man.

(2) A man commits rape if—

(a) he has sexual intercourse with a person (whether vaginal or anal) who at the time of the intercourse does not consent to it; and

(b) at the time he knows that the person does not consent to the intercourse or is reckless as to whether that person consents to it.

(3) A man also commits rape if he induces a married woman to have sexual intercourse with him by impersonating her husband.

(4) Subsection (2) applies for the purpose of any enactment.".

Definitions For "sexual intercourse", see the Sexual Offences Act 1956, s 44; for "man" and "woman", see s 46 of that Act.

References See para 11.1.

Male rape and buggery

143 Male rape and buggery

(1) Section 12 of the Sexual Offences Act 1956 (offence of buggery) shall be amended as follows.

(2) In subsection (1), after the words "another person" there shall be inserted the words "otherwise than in the circumstances described in subsection (1A) below".

(3) After subsection (1), there shall be inserted the following subsections—

"(1A) The circumstances referred to in subsection (1) are that the act of buggery takes place in private and both parties have attained the age of eighteen.

(1B) An act of buggery by one man with another shall not be treated as taking place in private if it takes place—

(a) when more than two persons take part or are present; or

(b) in a lavatory to which the public have or are permitted to have access, whether on payment or otherwise.

(1C) In any proceedings against a person for buggery with another person it shall be for the prosecutor to prove that the act of buggery took place otherwise than in private or that one of the parties to it had not attained the age of eighteen.".

References   See para 11.2.

Revised penalties for certain sexual offences

144 Revised penalties for buggery and indecency between men

(1)   The following paragraphs of the Second Schedule to the Sexual Offences Act 1956 (which prescribe the punishments for offences of buggery and of indecency between men) shall be amended as follows.

(2)   In paragraph 3—
> (a)   in sub-paragraph (a) (buggery), for the entry in the third column there shall be substituted "If with a person under the age of sixteen or with an animal, life; if the accused is of or over the age of twenty-one and the other person is under the age of eighteen, five years, but otherwise two years."; and
> (b)   in sub-paragraph (a) (attempted buggery), for the entry in the third column there shall be substituted "If with a person under the age of sixteen or with an animal, life; if the accused is of or over the age of twenty-one and the other person is under the age of eighteen, five years, but otherwise two years.".

(3)   In paragraph 16—
> (a)   in sub-paragraph (a) (indecency between men), for the entry in the third column there shall be substituted "If by a man of or over the age of twenty-one with a man under the age of eighteen, five years; otherwise two years."; and
> (b)   in sub-paragraph (b) (attempted procurement of commission by a man of an act of gross indecency with another man), for the entry in the third column there shall be substituted "If the attempt is by a man of or over the age of twenty-one to procure a man under the age of eighteen to commit an act of gross indecency with another man, five years; otherwise two years.".

References   See paras 11.3, 11.4.

Homosexuality

145 Age at which homosexual acts are lawful

(1)   In section 1 of the Sexual Offences Act 1967 (amendment of law relating to homosexual acts in private), for "twenty-one" in both places where it occurs there is substituted "eighteen".

(2)   In section 80 of the Criminal Justice (Scotland) Act 1980 (homosexual offences), for "twenty-one" in each place where it occurs there is substituted "eighteen".

(3)   In Article 3 of the Homosexual Offences (Northern Ireland) Order 1982 (homosexual acts in private), for "21" in both places where it occurs there is substituted "18".

References See para 11.5.

146 Extension of Sexual Offences Act 1967 to the armed forces and merchant navy

(1)   Section 1(5) of the Sexual Offences Act 1967 (homosexual acts in the armed forces) is repealed.

(2)   In section 80 of the Criminal Justice (Scotland) Act 1980—
    (a)   subsection (5) (homosexual acts in the armed forces) shall cease to have effect;
    (b)   in subsection (7)—
        (i)   after paragraph (b) there shall be inserted the word ""or"; and
        (ii)   paragraph (d) (homosexual acts on merchant ships) and the word "; or" immediately preceding that paragraph shall cease to have effect; and
    (c)   subsection (8) (interpretation) shall cease to have effect.

(3)   Section 2 of the Sexual Offences Act 1967 (homosexual acts on merchant ships) is repealed.

(4)   Nothing contained in this section shall prevent a homosexual act (with or without other acts or circumstances) from constituting a ground for discharging a member of Her Majesty's armed forces from the service or dismissing a member of the crew of a United Kingdom merchant ship from his ship or, in the case of a member of Her Majesty's armed forces, where the act occurs in conjunction with other acts or circumstances, from constituting an offence under the Army Act 1955, the Air Force Act 1955 or the Naval Discipline Act 1957.

Expressions used in this subsection and any enactment repealed by this section have the same meaning in this subsection as in that enactment.

References See para 11.6.

147 Homosexuality on merchant ships and in the armed forces: Northern Ireland

(1)   In the Homosexual Offences (Northern Ireland) Order 1982, the following are revoked—
    (a)   in article 3(1) (homosexual acts in private), the words "and Article 5 (merchant seamen)"; and
    (b)   article 5 (homosexual acts on merchant ships).

(2)   Article 3(4) of the Homosexual Offences (Northern Ireland) Order 1982 (homosexual acts in the armed forces) is revoked.

(3)   Nothing in this section shall prevent a homosexual act (with or without other acts or circumstances) from constituting a ground for discharging a member of Her Majesty's armed forces from the service or dismissing a member of the crew of a United Kingdom merchant ship from his ship or, in the case of a member of Her Majesty's armed forces, where the act occurs in conjunction with other acts or circumstances, from constituting an offence under the Army Act 1955, the Air Force Act 1955 or the Naval Discipline Act 1957.

Expressions used in this subsection and any enactment repealed by this section have the same meaning in this subsection as in that enactment.

References   See para 11.6.

148 Amendment of law relating to homosexual acts in Scotland

In section 80(6) of the Criminal Justice (Scotland) Act 1980 (which defines "homosexual act" for the purpose of section 80), after "gross indecency" there is inserted "or shameless indecency".

References   See para 11.6.

PART XII
MISCELLANEOUS AND GENERAL

The Parole Board

149 Incorporation of the Parole Board

In section 32 of the Criminal Justice Act 1991 (which provides the constitution and basic functions of the Parole Board), for subsection (1), there shall be substituted the following subsection—

"(1)   The Parole Board shall be, by that name, a body corporate and as such shall be constituted in accordance with, and have the functions conferred by, this Part.".

References   See para 12.1.

150 Powers to recall prisoners released on licence

In section 50 of the Criminal Justice Act 1991 (power by order to transfer certain functions to the Parole Board) subsection (4) shall cease to have effect and, in subsection (1), for the words "(2) to (4)" there shall be substituted the words "(2) or (3)".

References   See para 12.1.

Prisons: powers in relation to prisoners, visitors and others

151 Power to test prisoners for drugs

(1)   After section 16 of the Prison Act 1952 there shall be inserted the following section—

"16A Testing prisoners for drugs

(1)   If an authorisation is in force for the prison, any prison officer may, at the prison, in accordance with prison rules, require any prisoner who is confined in the prison to provide a sample of urine for the purpose of ascertaining whether he has any drug in his body.

(2)   If the authorisation so provides, the power conferred by subsection (1) above shall include power to require a prisoner to provide a sample of any

other description specified in the authorisation, not being an intimate sample, whether instead of or in addition to a sample of urine.

(3)   In this section—

"authorisation" means an authorisation by the governor;

"drug" means any drug which is a controlled drug for the purposes of the Misuse of Drugs Act 1971;

"intimate sample" has the same meaning as in Part V of the Police and Criminal Evidence Act 1984;

"prison officer" includes a prisoner custody officer within the meaning of Part IV of the Criminal Justice Act 1991; and

"prison rules" means rules under section 47 of this Act.".

(2)   After section 41A of the Prisons (Scotland) Act 1989 there shall be inserted the following section—

"41B   Testing prisoners for drugs

(1)   If an authorisation is in force for the prison, any officer of the prison may, at the prison, in accordance with rules under section 39 of this Act, require any prisoner who is confined in the prison to provide a sample of urine for the purpose of ascertaining whether he has any drug in his body.

(2)   If the authorisation so provides, the power conferred by subsection (1) above shall include power to require a prisoner to provide a sample of any other description specified in the authorisation, not being an intimate sample, whether instead of or in addition to a sample of urine.

(3)   In this section—

"authorisation" means an authorisation by the governor;

"drug" means any drug which is a controlled drug for the purposes of the Misuse of Drugs Act 1971; and

"intimate sample" means a sample of blood, semen or any other tissue fluid, saliva or pubic hair, or a swab taken from a person's body orifice.".

Definitions   For "prison", see the Prison Act 1952, s 53(1); for "authorisation", "drug", "intimate sample", "prison officer" and "prison rules", see s 16A(3) of the 1952 Act, as inserted by sub-s (1) above.
References   See para 12.2.

152 Powers of search by authorised employees in prisons

(1)   In the Prison Act 1952, after section 8, there shall be inserted the following section—

"8A   Powers of search by authorised employees

(1)   An authorised employee at a prison shall have the power to search any prisoner for the purpose of ascertaining whether he has any unauthorised property on his person.

(2)   An authorised employee searching a prisoner by virtue of this section—

(a)   shall not be entitled to require a prisoner to remove any of his clothing other than an outer coat, jacket, headgear, gloves and footwear;

(b)   may use reasonable force where necessary; and

(c)   may seize and detain any unauthorised property found on the prisoner in the course of the search.

(3)   In this section "authorised employee" means an employee of a description for the time being authorised by the governor to exercise the powers conferred by this section.

(4)   The governor of a prison shall take such steps as he considers appropriate to notify to prisoners the descriptions of persons who are for the time being authorised to exercise the powers conferred by this section.

(5)   In this section "unauthorised property", in relation to a prisoner, means property which the prisoner is not authorised by prison rules or by the governor to have in his possession or, as the case may be, in his possession in a particular part of the prison.".

(2)   In the Prisons (Scotland) Act 1989, after section 41, there shall be inserted the following section—

"41A Powers of search by authorised employees

(1)   An authorised employee at a prison shall have the power to search any prisoner for the purpose of ascertaining whether he has any unauthorised property on his person.

(2)   An authorised employee searching a prisoner by virtue of this section—
  (a) shall not be entitled to require a prisoner to remove any of his clothing other than an outer coat, jacket, headgear, gloves and footwear;
  (b) may use reasonable force where necessary; and
  (c) may seize and detain any unauthorised property found on the prisoner in the course of the search.

(3)   In this section "authorised employee" means an employee of a description for the time being authorised by the governor to exercise the powers conferred by this section.

(4)   The governor of a prison shall take such steps as he considers appropriate to notify to prisoners the descriptions of employees who are for the time being authorised employees.

(5)   In this section—
  "employee" means an employee (not being an officer of a prison) appointed under section 2(1) of this Act; and
  "unauthorised property", in relation to a prisoner, means property which the prisoner is not authorised by rules under section 39 of this Act or by the governor to have in his possession or, as the case may be, in his possession in a particular part of the prison.".

Definitions   For "prison", see the Prison Act 1952, s 53(1); for "authorised employee", see s 8A(3) of the 1952 Act, as inserted by sub-s (1) above; for "unauthorised property", see s 8A(5) of that Act, as so inserted.
References   See para 12.2.

153 Prohibited articles in Scottish prisons

(1)   Section 41 of the Prisons (Scotland) Act 1989 (unlawful introduction of tobacco, etc into prison) shall be amended as follows.

(2)   In subsection (1), for the words from the beginning to "shall be guilty" there shall be substituted—

"(1)   Any person who without reasonable excuse brings or introduces, or attempts by any means to bring or introduce, into a prison—

(a) any drug;

(b) any firearm or ammunition;

(c) any offensive weapon;

(d) any article to which section 1 of the Carrying of Knives etc (Scotland) Act 1993 applies; or

(e) without prejudice to paragraphs (a) to (d) above, any article which is a prohibited article within the meaning of rules under section 39 of this Act,

shall be guilty".

(3)   After subsection (2) there shall be inserted the following subsections—

"(2A) Where an officer of a prison has reasonable grounds for suspecting that a person who is in or is seeking to enter a prison has in his possession any article mentioned in paragraphs (a) to (e) of subsection (1) above he shall, without prejudice to any other power of search under this Act, have power to search that person and any article in his possession and to seize and detain any article mentioned in those paragraphs found in the course of the search.

(2B)   The power conferred by subsection (2A) above—

(a) shall be exercised in accordance with rules under section 39 of this Act;

(b) shall not be construed as authorising the physical examination of a person's body orifices;

(c) so far as relating to any article mentioned in paragraph (c), (d) or (e) of subsection (1) above (and not falling within paragraph (a) or (b) of that subsection), shall not be construed as authorising an officer of a prison to require a person to remove any of his clothing other than an outer coat, jacket, headgear, gloves and footwear; and

(d) shall include power to use reasonable force where necessary.".

(4)   For subsection (3) there shall be substituted the following subsections—

"(3)   Where an officer of a prison has reasonable grounds for suspecting that any person has committed or is committing an offence under subsection (1) above he may, for the purpose of facilitating investigation by a constable into the offence, detain that person in any place in the prison in question and may, where necessary, use reasonable force in doing so.

(4)   Detention under subsection (3) above shall be terminated not more than six hours after it begins or (if earlier)—

(a) when the person is detained in pursuance of any other enactment or subordinate instrument;

(b) when the person is arrested by a constable; or

(c) where the governor of the prison or a constable investigating the offence concludes that there are no such grounds as are mentioned in subsection (3) above or the officer of the prison concludes that there are no longer such grounds,

and the person detained shall be informed immediately upon the termination of his detention that his detention has been terminated.

(5)   Where a person has been released at the termination of a period of detention under subsection (3) above he shall not thereafter be detained under

that subsection on the same grounds or on any grounds arising out of the same circumstances.

(6)   At the time when an officer of a prison detains a person under subsection (3) above he shall inform the person of his suspicion, of the suspected offence and of the reason for the detention; and there shall be recorded—

(a) the place where and the time when the detention begins;

(b) the suspected offence;

(c) the time when a constable or an officer of the police authority is informed of the suspected offence and the detention;

(d) the time when the person is informed of his rights in terms of subsection (7) below and the identity of the officer of the prison so informing him;

(e) where the person requests such intimation as is specified in subsection (7) below to be sent, the time when such request is—

(i)   made; and

(ii)   complied with; and

(f) the time when, in accordance with subsection (4) above, the person's detention terminates.

(7)   A person who is being detained under subsection (3) above, other than a person in respect of whose detention subsection (8) below applies, shall be entitled to have intimation of his detention and of the place where he is being detained sent without delay to a solicitor and to one other person reasonably named by him and shall be informed of that entitlement when his detention begins.

(8)   Where a person who is being detained under subsection (3) above appears to the officer of the prison to be under 16 years of age, the officer of the prison shall send without delay to the person's parent, if known, intimation of the person's detention and of the place where he is being detained; and the parent—

(a) in a case where there is reasonable cause to suspect that he has been involved in the alleged offence in respect of which the person has been detained, may; and

(b) in any other case, shall,

be permitted access to the person.

(9)   The nature and extent of any access permitted under subsection (8) above shall be subject to any restriction essential for the furtherance of the investigation or the well-being of the person.

(10)   In this section—

"drug" means any drug which is a controlled drug for the purposes of the Misuse of Drugs Act 1971;

"firearm" and "ammunition" have the same meanings as in the Firearms Act 1968;

"offensive weapon" has the same meaning as in the Prevention of Crime Act 1953; and

"parent" includes a guardian and any person who has actual custody of a person under 16 years of age.".

References   See para 12.2.

Harassment, alarm or distress

154 Offence of causing intentional harassment, alarm or distress

In Part I of the Public Order Act 1986 (offences relating to public order), after section 4, there shall be inserted the following section—

"4A   Intentional harassment, alarm or distress

(1)   A person is guilty of an offence if, with intent to cause a person harassment, alarm or distress, he—

(a)   uses threatening, abusive or insulting words or behaviour, or disorderly behaviour, or

(b)   displays any writing, sign or other visible representation which is threatening, abusive or insulting,

thereby causing that or another person harassment, alarm or distress.

(2)   An offence under this section may be committed in a public or a private place, except that no offence is committed where the words or behaviour are used, or the writing, sign or other visible representation is displayed, by a person inside a dwelling and the person who is harassed, alarmed or distressed is also inside that or another dwelling.

(3)   It is a defence for the accused to prove—

(a)   that he was inside a dwelling and had no reason to believe that the words or behaviour used, or the writing, sign or other visible representation displayed, would be heard or seen by a person outside that or any other dwelling, or

(b)   that his conduct was reasonable.

(4)   A constable may arrest without warrant anyone he reasonably suspects is committing an offence under this section.

(5)   A person guilty of an offence under this section is liable on summary conviction to imprisonment for a term not exceeding 6 months or a fine not exceeding level 5 on the standard scale or both.".

References   See para 12.3.

Offence of racially inflammatory publication etc to be arrestable

155 Offence of racially inflammatory publication etc to be arrestable

In section 24(2) of the Police and Criminal Evidence Act 1984 (arrestable offences), after the paragraph (h) inserted by section 166(4) of this Act, there shall be inserted the following paragraph—

"(i) an offence under section 19 of the Public Order Act 1986 (publishing, etc material intended or likely to stir up racial hatred);".

References   See para 12.4.

Prohibition on use of cells from embryos or foetuses

156 Prohibition on use of cells from embryos or foetuses

(1)   The Human Fertilisation and Embryology Act 1990 shall be amended as follows.

(2)   After section 3 there shall be inserted the following section—

"3A Prohibition in connection with germ cells

(1)   No person shall, for the purpose of providing fertility services for any woman, use female germ cells taken or derived from an embryo or a foetus or use embryos created by using such cells.

(2)   In this section—

"female germ cells" means cells of the female germ line and includes such cells at any stage of maturity and accordingly includes eggs; and

"fertility services" means medical, surgical or obstetric services provided for the purpose of assisting women to carry children.".

(3)   In section 41(1)(a) (offences under the Act) after the words "section 3(2)" there shall be inserted ", 3A".

Definitions   For "embryo", see the Human Fertilisation and Embryology Act 1990, s 1(1); for "eggs", see s 1(3) of that Act; for "female germ cells" and "fertility services", see s 3A(2) of that Act, as inserted by sub-ss (1), (2) above.
References   See para 12.5.

Increase in certain penalties

157 Increase in penalties for certain offences

(1)   The enactments specified in column 2 of Part I of Schedule 8 to this Act which relate to the maximum fines for the offences mentioned (and broadly described) in column 1 of that Part of that Schedule shall have effect as if the maximum fine that may be imposed on summary conviction of any offence so mentioned were a fine not exceeding the amount specified in column 4 of that Part of that Schedule instead of a fine of an amount specified in column 3 of that Part of that Schedule.

(2)   For the amount of the maximum fine specified in column 3 of Part II of Schedule 8 to this Act that may be imposed under the enactments specified in column 2 of that Part of that Schedule on summary conviction of the offences mentioned (and broadly described) in column 1 of that Part of that Schedule there shall be substituted the amount specified in column 4 of that Part of that Schedule.

(3)   For the maximum term of imprisonment specified in column 3 of Part III of Schedule 8 to this Act that may be imposed under the enactments specified in column 2 of that Part of that Schedule on conviction on indictment, or on conviction on indictment or summary conviction, of the offences mentioned (and broadly described) in column 1 of that Part of that Schedule there shall be substituted the maximum term of imprisonment specified in column 4 of that Part of that Schedule.

(4)   Any reference in column 2 of Part II of Schedule 8 to this Act to a numbered column of Schedule 4 to the Misuse of Drugs Act 1971 is a reference to the column of that number construed with section 25(2)(b) of that Act.

(5)   Any reference in column 2 of Part III of Schedule 8 to this Act—

    (a)   to a numbered column of Schedule 6 to the Firearms Act 1968 is a reference to the column of that number construed with section 51(2)(b) of that Act; or

    (b)   to a numbered column of Schedule 2 to the Firearms (Northern Ireland) Order 1981 is a reference to the column of that number construed with Article 52(2)(b) of that Order.

(6)   Section 143 of the Magistrates' Courts Act 1980 (power of Secretary of State by order to alter sums specified in certain provisions) shall have effect with the insertion, in subsection (2), after paragraph (p), of the following paragraph—

    "(q) column 5 or 6 of Schedule 4 to the Misuse of Drugs Act 1971 so far as the column in question relates to the offences under provisions of that Act specified in column 1 of that Schedule in respect of which the maximum fines were increased by Part II of Schedule 8 to the Criminal Justice and Public Order Act 1994.".

(7)   Section 289D of the Criminal Procedure (Scotland) Act 1975 (power of Secretary of State by order to alter sums specified in certain provisions of Scots law) shall have effect with the insertion, in subsection (1A), after paragraph (e), of the following paragraph—

    "(ee) column 5 or 6 of Schedule 4 to the Misuse of Drugs Act 1971 so far as the column in question relates to the offences under provisions of that Act specified in column 1 of that Schedule in respect of which the maximum fines were increased by Part II of Schedule 8 to the Criminal Justice and Public Order Act 1994.".

(8)   Article 17 of the Fines and Penalties (Northern Ireland) Order 1984 (power of Secretary of State by order to alter sums specified in certain provisions of the law of Northern Ireland) shall have effect with the insertion, in paragraph (2), after sub-paragraph (j) of the following sub-paragraph—

    "(k) column 5 or 6 of Schedule 4 to the Misuse of Drugs Act 1971 so far as the column in question relates to the offences under provisions of that Act specified in column 1 of that Schedule in respect of which the maximum fines were increased by Part II of Schedule 8 to the Criminal Justice and Public Order Act 1994.".

(9)   Subsections (1), (2) and (3) above do not apply to an offence committed before this section comes into force.

References   See para 12.6.

Extradition procedures

158 Extradition procedures

(1)   The Extradition Act 1989 shall be amended as follows.

(2)   In section 4 (extradition Orders), in subsection (5), for the words "warrant his trial if" there shall be substituted the words "make a case requiring an answer by that person if the proceedings were a summary trial of an information against him and".

(3) In section 7 (extradition request and authority to proceed)—
　(a) in subsection (2), in paragraph (b), after the word "evidence" there shall be inserted the words "or, in a case falling within subsection (2A) below, information"; and
　(b) after subsection (2), there shall be inserted the following subsection—

"(2A) Where—
　(a) the extradition request is made by a foreign state; and
　(b) an Order in Council falling within section 4(5) above is in force in relation to that state,
it shall be a sufficient compliance with subsection (2)(b) above to furnish information sufficient to justify the issue of a warrant for his arrest under this Act.".

(4) In section 8 (arrest for purposes of committal)—
　(a) in subsection (3) after the word "evidence" there shall be inserted the words "or, in a case falling within subsection (3A) below, information"; and
　(b) after subsection (3) there shall be inserted the following subsection—

"(3A) Where—
　(a) the extradition request or, where a provisional warrant is applied for, the request for the person's arrest is made by a foreign state; and
　(b) an Order in Council falling within section 4(5) above is in force in relation to that state,
it shall be sufficient for the purposes of subsection (3) above to supply such information as would, in the opinion of the person so empowered, justify the issue of a warrant of arrest.".

(5) In section 9 (committal proceedings)—
　(a) in subsection (2), for the words from "jurisdiction" to the end there shall be substituted the words "powers, as nearly as may be, including powers to adjourn the case and meanwhile to remand the person arrested under the warrant either in custody or on bail, as if the proceedings were the summary trial of an information against him; and section 16(1)(c) of the Prosecution of Offences Act 1985 (costs on dismissal) shall apply accordingly reading the reference to the dismissal of the information as a reference to the discharge of the person arrested.";
　(b) after subsection (2) there shall be inserted the following subsection—

"(2A) If a court of committal in England and Wales exercises its power to adjourn the case it shall on so doing remand the person arrested in custody or on bail.";

　(c) in subsection (4), for the words from "warrant the trial" to the end there shall be substituted the words "make a case requiring an answer by the arrested person if the proceedings were the summary trial of an information against him."; and
　(d) in subsection (8)(a), for the words from "warrant his trial" to the end, there shall be substituted the words "make a case requiring an answer by that person if the proceedings were the summary trial of an information against him.".

(6) In section 22 (International Convention cases), in subsection (5), for the words from "warrant his trial" to the end, there shall be substituted the words "make a case requiring an answer by that person if the proceedings were the summary trial of an information against him".

(7)   In section 35 (interpretation), after subsection (2), there shall be inserted the following subsection—

"(3)   For the purposes of the application of this Act by virtue of any Order in Council in force under it or section 2 of the Extradition Act 1870, any reference in this Act to evidence making a case requiring an answer by an accused person shall be taken to indicate a determination of the same question as is indicated by a reference (however expressed) in any such Order (or arrangements embodied or recited in it) to evidence warranting or justifying the committal for trial of an accused person.".

(8)   In Schedule 1 (provisions applying to foreign states in respect of which an Order in Council under section 2 of the Extradition Act 1870 is in force)—

(a)   in paragraph 6(1) (hearing of case), for the words from "hear the case" to the end there shall be substituted the words "have the same powers, as near as may be, including power to adjourn the case and meanwhile to remand the prisoner either in custody or on bail, as if the proceedings were the summary trial of an information against him for an offence committed in England and Wales; and section 16(1)(c) of the Prosecution of Offences Act 1985 (costs on dismissal) shall apply accordingly reading the reference to the dismissal of the information as a reference to the discharge of the prisoner.";

(b)   after paragraph 6(1) there shall be inserted the following sub-paragraph—

"(1A) If the metropolitan magistrate exercises his power to adjourn the case he shall on so doing remand the prisoner either in custody or on bail."; and

(c)   in paragraph 7(1) (committal or discharge of prisoner), for the words from "justify the committal" to "England or Wales" there shall be substituted the words "make a case requiring an answer by the prisoner if the proceedings were for the trial in England and Wales of an information for the crime,".

Definitions   For "foreign state", see the Extradition Act 1989, s 3(2); for "extradition request", see s 7(1) of that Act; for "warrant", see s 7(6) of that Act; for "provisional warrant", see s 8(1) of that Act; for "court of committal", see s 9(1) of that Act; for "metropolitan magistrate", see s 35(1) of that Act; as to "evidence making a case requiring an answer by an accused person", see s 35(3) of the 1989 Act as inserted by sub-ss (1), (7) above.
References   See para 12.7.

159 Backing of warrants: Republic of Ireland

(1)   The Backing of Warrants (Republic of Ireland) Act 1965 shall be amended as follows.

(2)   In section 1 (conditions for endorsement of warrants issued in Republic of Ireland), in subsection (1)(b), after the word "acts" there shall be inserted the words "or on his way to the United Kingdom".

(3)   In section 2 (proceedings for delivery of person arrested under endorsed warrant), in subsection (2)(a) (excluded offences) the words from ", or an offence under an enactment" to "control" shall be omitted.

(4)   In section 4 (procedure for provisional warrants)—

(a)   in subsection (1)(c), after the word "acts" there shall be inserted the words "or on his way to the United Kingdom";

(b)   in subsection (2), for the words "five days" there shall be substituted the words "seven days"; and

    (c) in subsection (3)(b), for the words "three days" there shall be substituted the words "seven days".

(5)   In the Schedule (proceedings before magistrates' court), in paragraph 3, for the words from "and the proceedings" to the end, there shall be substituted the words "as if the proceedings were the summary trial of an information against that person.".

References   See para 12.8.

Constabulary powers in United Kingdom waters

160 Extension of powers, etc, of constables to United Kingdom waters

(1)   Section 19 of the Police Act 1964 (area within which a constable's powers and privileges are exercisable) shall be amended as follows—
    (a) in subsection (1), after the words "England and Wales" there shall be inserted the words "and the adjacent United Kingdom waters.";
    (b) in subsection (2), after the words "area for which he is appointed" there shall be inserted the words "and, where the boundary of that area includes the coast, in the adjacent United Kingdom waters"; and
    (c) after subsection (5), there shall be inserted the following subsection—

"(5A) In this section—
    "powers" includes powers under any enactment, whenever passed or made;
    "United Kingdom waters" means the sea and other waters within the seaward limits of the territorial sea;
and this section, so far as it relates to powers under any enactment, makes them exercisable throughout those waters whether or not the enactment applies to those waters apart from this provision.".

(2)   Section 17 of the Police (Scotland) Act 1967 (general functions and jurisdiction of constables) shall be amended as follows—
    (a) in subsection (4), after the word "Scotland" there shall be inserted the words "and (without prejudice to section 1(2) of this Act) the adjacent United Kingdom waters"; and
    (b) after subsection (7) there shall be inserted the following subsection—

"(7A) In this section—
    "powers" includes powers under any enactment, whenever passed or made;
    "United Kingdom waters" means the sea and other waters within the seaward limits of the territorial sea;
and this section, so far as it relates to powers under any enactment, makes them exercisable throughout those waters whether or not the enactment applies to those waters apart from this provision.".

Definitions   For "enactment", see the Police Act 1964, s 64(2).
References   See para 12.9.

Obtaining computer-held information

161 Procuring disclosure of, and selling, computer-held personal information

(1)   In section 5 of the Data Protection Act 1984 (prohibitions in relation to personal data, including disclosure), after subsection (5), there shall be inserted the following subsections—

"(6)   A person who procures the disclosure to him of personal data the disclosure of which to him is in contravention of subsection (2) or (3) above, knowing or having reason to believe that the disclosure constitutes such a contravention, shall be guilty of an offence.

(7)   A person who sells personal data shall be guilty of an offence if (in contravention of subsection (6) above) he has procured the disclosure of the data to him.

(8)   A person who offers to sell personal data shall be guilty of an offence if (in contravention of subsection (6) above) he has procured or subsequently procures the disclosure of the data to him.

(9)   For the purposes of subsection (8) above, an advertisement indicating that personal data are or may be for sale is an offer to sell the data.

(10)   For the purposes of subsections (7) and (8) above, "selling", or "offering to sell", in relation to personal data, includes selling, or offering to sell, information extracted from the data.

(11)   In determining, for the purposes of subsection (6), (7) or (8) above, whether a disclosure is in contravention of subsection (2) or (3) above, section 34(6)(d) below shall be disregarded.".

(2)   In consequence of the amendment made by subsection (1) above—
   (a)   in subsection (5) of that section, after the word "other" there shall be inserted the word "foregoing"; and
   (b)   in section 28 (exemptions: crime and taxation), in subsection (3)—
       (i)   after the words "section 26(3)(a) above" there shall be inserted the words "or for an offence under section 5(6) above"; and
       (ii) after the words "to make" there shall be inserted the words "or (in the case of section 5(6)) to procure".

Definitions   For "personal data", see the Data Protection Act 1984, ss 1(3), 26(1); as to disclosure, see s 1(9) of that Act.
References   See para 12.10.

162 Access to computer material by constables and other enforcement officers

(1)   In section 10 of the Computer Misuse Act 1990 (offence of unauthorised access not to apply to exercise of law enforcement powers), after paragraph (b), there shall be inserted the following words—
   "and nothing designed to indicate a withholding of consent to access to any program or data from persons as enforcement officers shall have effect to make access unauthorised for the purposes of the said section 1(1).

   In this section "enforcement officer" means a constable or other person charged with the duty of investigating offences; and withholding consent from a person "as" an enforcement officer of any description includes the operation, by the person entitled to control access, of rules whereby enforcement officers of that description are, as such, disqualified from membership of a class of persons who are authorised to have access.".

(2)   In section 17(5) of that Act (when access is unauthorised), after paragraph (b), there shall be inserted the following words—
   "but this subsection is subject to section 10.".

Definitions   For "access to any program or data", see the Computer Misuse Act 1990, s 17(2); as to when access is "unauthorised", see s 17(5) of that Act, as amended by sub-s (2) above; for "program", see s 17(10) of that Act.
References   See para 12.10.

Closed-circuit television by local authorities

163 Local authority powers to provide closed-circuit television

(1)   Without prejudice to any power which they may exercise for those purposes under any other enactment, a local authority may take such of the following steps as they consider will, in relation to their area, promote the prevention of crime or the welfare of the victims of crime—

(a)   providing apparatus for recording visual images of events occurring on any land in their area;

(b)   providing within their area a telecommunications system which, under Part II of the Telecommunications Act 1984, may be run without a licence;

(c)   arranging   for   the   provision   of   any   other   description   of telecommunications system within their area or between any land in their area and any building occupied by a public authority.

(2)   Any power to provide, or to arrange for the provision of, any apparatus includes power to maintain, or operate, or, as the case may be, to arrange for the maintenance or operation of, that apparatus.

(3)   Before taking such a step under this section, a local authority shall consult the chief officer of police for the police area in which the step is to be taken.

(4)   In this section—

"chief officer of police", in relation to a police area in Scotland, means the chief constable of a police force maintained for that area;

"local authority"—

(a)   in England, means a county council or district council;

(b)   in Wales, means a county council or county borough council; and

(c)   in Scotland, has the meaning given by section 235(1) of the Local Government (Scotland) Act 1973; and

"telecommunications system" has the meaning given in section 4 of the Telecommunications Act 1984 and "licence" means a licence under section 7 of that Act.

(5)   Until 1st April 1996, in this section "local authority" means, in Wales, a county council or district council.

References   See para 12.11.

Serious fraud

164 Extension of powers of Serious Fraud Office and of powers to investigate serious fraud in Scotland

(1)   Section 4 of the Criminal Justice (International Co-operation) Act 1990 (obtaining evidence in the United Kingdom for use overseas) shall be amended as follows—

(a)   after subsection (2), there shall be inserted the following subsections—

"(2A) Except where the evidence is to be obtained as is mentioned in subsection (2B) below, if the Secretary of State is satisfied—

    (a) that an offence under the law of the country or territory in question has been committed or that there are reasonable grounds for suspecting that such an offence has been committed; and

    (b) that proceedings in respect of that offence have been instituted in that country or territory or that an investigation into that offence is being carried on there,

and it appears to him that the request relates to an offence involving serious or complex fraud, he may, if he thinks fit, refer the request or any part of the request to the Director of the Serious Fraud Office for him to obtain such of the evidence to which the request or part referred relates as may appear to the Director to be appropriate for giving effect to the request or part referred.

(2B) Where the evidence is to be obtained in Scotland, if the Lord Advocate is satisfied as to the matters mentioned in paragraphs (a) and (b) of subsection (2A) above and it appears to him that the request relates to an offence involving serious or complex fraud, he may, if he thinks fit, give a direction under section 51 of the Criminal Justice (Scotland) Act 1987.";

    (b) in subsection (3), after the words "subsection (2)" there shall be inserted the words "(2A) or (2B)"; and

    (c) in subsection (4), after the words "subsection (2)(a) and (b)" there shall be inserted the words "or (2A)(a) and (b)".

(2)   Section 2 of the Criminal Justice Act 1987 (investigative powers of Director of Serious Fraud Office) shall be amended as follows—

    (a) in subsection (1), for the words from "the Attorney-General" to "the request" there shall be substituted "an authority entitled to make such a request";

    (b) after subsection (1), there shall be inserted the following subsections—

"(1A) The authorities entitled to request the Director to exercise his powers under this section are—

    (a) the Attorney-General of the Isle of Man, Jersey or Guernsey, acting under legislation corresponding to section 1 of this Act and having effect in the Island whose Attorney-General makes the request; and

    (b) the Secretary of State acting under section 4(2A) of the Criminal Justice (International Co-operation) Act 1990, in response to a request received by him from an overseas court, tribunal or authority (an "overseas authority").

(1B) The Director shall not exercise his powers on a request from the Secretary of State acting in response to a request received from an overseas authority within subsection (1A)(b) above unless it appears to the Director on reasonable grounds that the offence in respect of which he has been requested to obtain evidence involves serious or complex fraud.";

    (c) after subsection (8), there shall be inserted the following subsections—

"(8A) Any evidence obtained by the Director for use by an overseas authority shall be furnished by him to the Secretary of State for transmission to the overseas authority which requested it.

(8B) If in order to comply with the request of the overseas authority it is necessary for any evidence obtained by the Director to be accompanied by any certificate, affidavit or other verifying document, the Director shall also furnish for transmission such document of that nature as may be specified by the Secretary of State when asking the Director to obtain the evidence.

(8C) Where any evidence obtained by the Director for use by an overseas authority consists of a document the original or a copy shall be transmitted, and where it consists of any other article the article itself or a description, photograph or other representation of it shall be transmitted, as may be necessary in order to comply with the request of the overseas authority."; and

(d) in subsection (18), at the end, there shall be inserted the words "; and "evidence" (in relation to subsections (1A)(b), (8A), (8B) and (8C) above) includes documents and other articles.".

(3) In section 51(1) of the Criminal Justice (Scotland) Act 1987 (investigative powers of Lord Advocate as respects serious or complex fraud), at the end there shall be added "; and he may also give such a direction by virtue of section 4(2B) of the Criminal Justice (International Co-operation) Act 1990 or on a request being made to him by the Attorney-General of the Isle of Man, Jersey or Guernsey acting under legislation corresponding to this section and sections 52 to 54 of this Act.".

(4) In section 52 of the Criminal Justice (Scotland) Act 1987 (investigation by nominated officer)—

(a) after subsection (7) there shall be inserted—

"(7A) Any evidence obtained by the Lord Advocate by virtue of section 4(2B) of the Criminal Justice (International Co-operation) Act 1990 shall be furnished by him to the Secretary of State for transmission to the overseas authority in compliance with whose request (in the following subsections referred to as the "relevant request") it was so obtained.

(7B) If, in order to comply with the relevant request it is necessary for that evidence to be accompanied by any certificate, affidavit or other verifying document, the Lord Advocate shall also furnish for transmission such document of that nature as appears to him to be appropriate.

(7C) Where any evidence obtained by virtue of the said section 4(2B) consists of a document, the original or a copy shall be transmitted and where it consists of any other article the article itself or a description, photograph or other representation of it shall be transmitted, as may be necessary in order to comply with the relevant request."; and

(b) in subsection (8), after the definition of "documents" there shall be inserted—

""evidence", in relation to a relevant request, includes documents and other articles;".

Copyright and illicit recordings: enforcement of offences

165 Enforcement of certain offences relating to copyright and illicit recordings

(1) The Copyright, Designs and Patents Act 1988 shall be amended as follows.

(2) After section 107 (offences relating to copyright) there shall be inserted the following section—

"107A Enforcement by local weights and measures authority

(1)   It is the duty of every local weights and measures authority to enforce within their area the provisions of section 107.

(2)   The following provisions of the Trade Descriptions Act 1968 apply in relation to the enforcement of that section by such an authority as in relation to the enforcement of that Act—

section 27 (power to make test purchases),

section 28 (power to enter premises and inspect and seize goods and documents),

section 29 (obstruction of authorised officers), and

section 33 (compensation for loss, &c of goods seized).

(3)   Subsection (1) above does not apply in relation to the enforcement of section 107 in Northern Ireland, but it is the duty of the Department of Economic Development to enforce that section in Northern Ireland.

For that purpose the provisions of the Trade Descriptions Act 1968 specified in subsection (2) apply as if for the references to a local weights and measures authority and any officer of such an authority there were substituted references to that Department and any of its officers.

(4)   Any enactment which authorises the disclosure of information for the purpose of facilitating the enforcement of the Trade Descriptions Act 1968 shall apply as if section 107 were contained in that Act and as if the functions of any person in relation to the enforcement of that section were functions under that Act.

(5)   Nothing in this section shall be construed as authorising a local weights and measures authority to bring proceedings in Scotland for an offence.".

(3)   After section 198 (offences relating to illicit recordings) there shall be inserted the following section—

"198A Enforcement by local weights and measures authority

(1)   It is the duty of every local weights and measures authority to enforce within their area the provisions of section 198.

(2)   The following provisions of the Trade Descriptions Act 1968 apply in relation to the enforcement of that section by such an authority as in relation to the enforcement of that Act—

section 27 (power to make test purchases),

section 28 (power to enter premises and inspect and seize goods and documents),

section 29 (obstruction of authorised officers), and

section 33 (compensation for loss, &c of goods seized).

(3)   Subsection (1) above does not apply in relation to the enforcement of section 198 in Northern Ireland, but it is the duty of the Department of Economic Development to enforce that section in Northern Ireland.

For that purpose the provisions of the Trade Descriptions Act 1968 specified in subsection (2) apply as if for the references to a local weights and measures authority and any officer of such an authority there were substituted references to that Department and any of its officers.

(4)   Any enactment which authorises the disclosure of information for the purpose of facilitating the enforcement of the Trade Descriptions Act 1968

shall apply as if section 198 were contained in that Act and as if the functions of any person in relation to the enforcement of that section were functions under that Act.

(5)   Nothing in this section shall be construed as authorising a local weights and measures authority to bring proceedings in Scotland for an offence.".

References   See para 12.13.

Ticket touts

166 Sale of tickets by unauthorised persons

(1)   It is an offence for an unauthorised person to sell, or offer or expose for sale, a ticket for a designated football match in any public place or place to which the public has access or, in the course of a trade or business, in any other place.

(2)   For this purpose—
   (a)   a person is "unauthorised" unless he is authorised in writing to sell tickets for the match by the home club or by the organisers of the match;
   (b)   a "ticket" means anything which purports to be a ticket; and
   (c)   a "designated football match" means a football match, or football match of a description, for the time being designated under section 1(1) of the Football (Offences) Act 1991.

(3)   A person guilty of an offence under this section is liable on summary conviction to a fine not exceeding level 5 on the standard scale.

(4)   In section 24(2) of the Police and Criminal Evidence Act 1984 (arrestable offences), after the paragraph (g) inserted by section 85(2) of this Act there shall be inserted the following paragraph—

   "(h)   an offence under section 166 of the Criminal Justice and Public Order Act 1994 (sale of tickets by unauthorised persons);".

(5)   Section 32 of the Police and Criminal Evidence Act 1984 (search of persons and premises (including vehicles) upon arrest) shall have effect, in its application in relation to an offence under this section, as if the power conferred on a constable to enter and search any vehicle extended to any vehicle which the constable has reasonable grounds for believing was being used for any purpose connected with the offence.

(6)   The Secretary of State may by order made by statutory instrument apply this section, with such modifications as he thinks fit, to such sporting event or category of sporting event for which 6,000 or more tickets are issued for sale as he thinks fit.

(7)   An order under subsection (6) above may provide that—
   (a)   a certificate (a "ticket sale certificate") signed by a duly authorised officer certifying that 6,000 or more tickets were issued for sale for a sporting event is conclusive evidence of that fact;
   (b)   an officer is duly authorised if he is authorised in writing to sign a ticket sale certificate by the home club or the organisers of the sporting event; and
   (c)   a document purporting to be a ticket sale certificate shall be received in evidence and deemed to be such a certificate unless the contrary is proved.

(8)   Where an order has been made under subsection (6) above, this section also applies, with any modifications made by the order, to any part of the sporting event specified or described in the order, provided that 6,000 or more tickets are issued for sale for the day on which that part of the event takes place.

References   See para 12.14.

Taxi touts

167 Touting for hire car services

(1)   Subject to the following provisions, it is an offence, in a public place, to solicit persons to hire vehicles to carry them as passengers.

(2)   Subsection (1) above does not imply that the soliciting must refer to any particular vehicle nor is the mere display of a sign on a vehicle that the vehicle is for hire soliciting within that subsection.

(3)   No offence is committed under this section where soliciting persons to hire licensed taxis is permitted by a scheme under section 10 of the Transport Act 1985 (schemes for shared taxis) whether or not supplemented by provision made under section 13 of that Act (modifications of the taxi code).

(4)   It is a defence for the accused to show that he was soliciting for passengers for public service vehicles on behalf of the holder of a PSV operator's licence for those vehicles whose authority he had at the time of the alleged offence.

(5)   A person guilty of an offence under this section shall be liable on summary conviction to a fine not exceeding level 4 on the standard scale.

(6)   In this section—
> "public place" includes any highway and any other premises or place to which at the material time the public have or are permitted to have access (whether on payment or otherwise); and
> "public service vehicle" and "PSV operator's licence" have the same meaning as in Part II of the Public Passenger Vehicles Act 1981.

(7)   In section 24(2) of the Police and Criminal Evidence Act 1984 (arrestable offences), after the paragraph (i) inserted by section 155 of this Act there shall be inserted the following paragraph—
> "(j) an offence under section 167 of the Criminal Justice and Public Order Act 1994 (touting for hire car services).".

Definitions   In the Public Passenger Vehicles Act 1981, Pt II, for "public service vehicle", see s 1, for "PSV operator's licence in that Part, see s 82(1) of that Act.
References   See para 12.15.

General

168 Minor and consequential amendments and repeals

(1)   The enactments mentioned in Schedule 9 to this Act shall have effect with the amendments there specified (being minor amendments).

(2)   The enactments mentioned in Schedule 10 to this Act shall have effect with the amendments there specified (amendments consequential on the foregoing provisions of this Act).

(3)   The enactments mentioned in Schedule 11 to this Act (which include enactments which are spent) are repealed or revoked to the extent specified in the third column of that Schedule.

References   See para 12.16.

169 Power of Secretary of State to make payments or grants in relation to crime prevention, etc

(1)   The Secretary of State may, with the consent of the Treasury—
(a)   make such payments, or
(b)   pay such grants, to such persons,
as he considers appropriate in connection with measures intended to prevent crime or reduce the fear of crime.

(2)   Any grant under subsection (1)(b) above may be made subject to such conditions as the Secretary of State may, with the agreement of the Treasury, see fit to impose.

(3)   Payments under this section shall be made out of money provided by Parliament.

References   See para 12.16.

170 Security costs at party conferences

(1)   The Secretary of State may, with the consent of the Treasury, pay grants towards expenditure incurred by a qualifying political party, or by a person acting for a qualifying political party, on measures to which this section applies.

(2)   This section applies to measures which are—
(a)   taken for the protection of persons or property in connection with a conference held in Great Britain for the purposes of the party, and
(b)   certified by a chief officer of police as having been appropriate.

(3)   A political party is a "qualifying political party" for the purposes of this section if, at the last general election before the expenditure was incurred,—
(a)   at least two members of the party were elected to the House of Commons, or
(b)   one member of the party was elected to the House of Commons and not less than 150,000 votes were given to candidates who were members of the party.

(4)   Payments under this section shall be made out of money provided by Parliament.

References   See para 12.17.

171 Expenses etc under Act

There shall be paid out of money provided by Parliament—
(a)   any sums required by the Secretary of State for making payments under contracts entered into under or by virtue of sections 2, 3, 7, 11, 96, 99, 100, 102(4), 106(1), 112(1) or 118(3) or paragraph 1 of Schedule 1;

(b)   any administrative expenses incurred by the Secretary of State; and

(c)   any increase attributable to this Act in the sums payable out of money so provided under any other Act.

References   See para 12.17.

.

172 Short title, commencement and extent

(1)   This Act may be cited as the Criminal Justice and Public Order Act 1994.

(2)   With the exception of section 82 and subject to subsection (4) below, this Act shall come into force on such day as the Secretary of State or, in the case of sections 52 and 53, the Lord Chancellor may appoint by order made by statutory instrument, and different days may be appointed for different provisions or different purposes.

(3)   Any order under subsection (2) above may make such transitional provisions and savings as appear to the authority making the order necessary or expedient in connection with any provision brought into force by the order.

(4)   The following provisions and their related amendments, repeals and revocations shall come into force on the passing of this Act, namely sections 5 to 15 (and Schedules 1 and 2), 61, 63, 65, 68 to 71, 77 to 80, 81, 83, 90, Chapters I and IV of Part VIII, sections 142 to 148, 150, 158(1), (3) and (4), 166, 167, 171, paragraph 46 of Schedule 9 and this section.

(5)   No order shall be made under subsection (6) of section 166 above unless a draft of the order has been laid before, and approved by a resolution of, each House of Parliament.

(6)   For the purposes of subsection (4) above—

(a)   the following are the amendments related to the provisions specified in that subsection, namely, in Schedule 10, paragraphs 26, 35, 36, 59, 60 and 63(1), (3), (4) and (5);

(b)   the repeals and revocations related to the provisions specified in that subsection are those specified in the Note at the end of Schedule 11.

(7)   Except as regards any provisions applied under section 39 and subject to the following provisions, this Act extends to England and Wales only.

(8)   Sections 47(3), 49, 61 to 67, 70, 71, 81, 82, 146(4), 157(1), 163, 169 and 170 also extend to Scotland.

(9)   Section 83(1) extends to England and Wales and Northern Ireland.

(10)   This section, sections 68, 69, 83(3) to (5), 88 to 92, 136 to 141, 156, 157(2), (3), (4), (5) and (9), 158, 159, 161, 162, 164, 165, 168, 171 and Chapter IV of Part VIII extend to the United Kingdom and sections 158 and 159 also extend to the Channel Islands and the Isle of Man.

(11)   Sections 93, 95 and 101(8), so far as relating to the delivery of prisoners to or from premises situated in a part of the British Islands outside England and Wales, extend to that part of those Islands.

(12)   Sections 102(1) to (3), 104, 105 and 117, so far as relating to the transfer of prisoners to or from premises situated in a part of the British Islands outside Scotland, extend to that part of those Islands, but otherwise Chapter II of Part VIII extends to Scotland only.

(13) Sections 47(4), 83(2), 84(5) to (7), 87, Part IX, sections 145(2), 146(2), 148, 151(2), 152(2), 153, 157(7) and 160(2) extend to Scotland only.

(14) Sections 118, 120, 121 and 125, so far as relating to the delivery of prisoners to or from premises situated in a part of the British Islands outside Northern Ireland, extend to that part of those islands, but otherwise Chapter III of Part VIII extends to Northern Ireland only.

(15) Sections 53, 84(8) to (11), 85(4) to (6), 86(2), 145(3), 147 and 157(8) extend to Northern Ireland only.

(16) Where any enactment is amended, repealed or revoked by Schedule 9, 10 or 11 to this Act the amendment, repeal or revocation has the same extent as that enactment; except that Schedules 9 and 11 do not extend to Scotland in so far as they relate to section 17(1) of the Video Recordings Act 1984.

References   See para 12.18.

SCHEDULES

SCHEDULE 1

Section 12

ESCORT ARRANGEMENTS: ENGLAND AND WALES

Arrangements for the escort of offenders detained at secure training centres

1.—(1) The Secretary of State may make arrangements for any of the following functions namely—

    (a)   the delivery of offenders from one set of relevant premises to another;

    (b)   the custody of offenders held on the premises of any court (whether or not they would otherwise be in the custody of the court) and their production before the court;

    (c)   the custody of offenders temporarily held in a secure training centre in the course of delivery from one secure training centre to another; and

    (d)   the custody of offenders while they are outside a secure training centre for temporary purposes,

to be performed in such cases as may be determined by or under the arrangements by custody officers who are authorised to perform such functions.

(2) In sub-paragraph (1)(a) above, "relevant premises" means a court, secure training centre, police station or hospital.

(3) Arrangements made by the Secretary of State under sub-paragraph (1) above ("escort arrangements") may include entering into contracts with other persons for the provision by them of custody officers.

(4) Any person who, under a warrant or a hospital order or hospital remand is responsible for the performance of any such function as is mentioned in sub-paragraph (1) above shall be deemed to have complied with the warrant, order or remand if he does all that he reasonably can to secure that the function is performed by a custody officer acting in pursuance of escort arrangements.

(5) In this paragraph—

    "hospital" has the same meaning as in the Mental Health Act 1983;

    "hospital order" means an order for a person's admission to hospital made under section 37, 38 or 44 of that Act, section 5 of the Criminal Procedure (Insanity) Act 1964 or section 6, 14 or 14A of the Criminal Appeal Act 1968;

"hospital remand" means a remand of a person to hospital under section 35 or 36 of the Mental Health Act 1983;

"warrant" means a warrant of commitment, a warrant of arrest or a warrant under section 46, 47, 48, 50 or 74 of that Act.

Monitoring etc of escort arrangements

2.—(1) Escort arrangements shall include the appointment of—

 (a) an escort monitor, that is to say, a Crown servant whose duty it shall be to keep the arrangements under review and to report on them to the Secretary of State; and

 (b) a panel of lay observers whose duty it shall be to inspect the conditions in which offenders are transported or held in pursuance of the arrangements and to make recommendations to the Secretary of State.

(2) It shall also be the duty of an escort monitor to investigate and report to the Secretary of State on any allegations made against custody officers acting in pursuance of escort arrangements.

(3) Any expenses incurred by members of lay panels may be defrayed by the Secretary of State to such extent as he may with the approval of the Treasury determine.

Powers and duties of custody officers acting in pursuance of escort arrangements

3.—(1) A custody officer acting in pursuance of escort arrangements shall have the following powers, namely—

 (a) to search in accordance with rules made by the Secretary of State any offender for whose delivery or custody he is responsible in pursuance of the arrangements; and

 (b) to search any other person who is in or is seeking to enter any place where any such offender is or is to be held, and any article in the possession of such a person.

(2) The powers conferred by sub-paragraph (1)(b) above to search a person shall not be construed as authorising a custody officer to require a person to remove any of his clothing other than an outer coat, headgear, jacket or gloves.

(3) A custody officer shall have the following duties as respects offenders for whose delivery or custody he is responsible in pursuance of escort arrangements, namely—

 (a) to prevent their escape from lawful custody;

 (b) to prevent, or detect and report on, the commission or attempted commission by them of other unlawful acts;

 (c) to ensure good order and discipline on their part;

 (d) to attend to their wellbeing; and

 (e) to give effect to any directions as to their treatment which are given by a court,

and the Secretary of State may make rules with respect to the performance by custody officers of their duty under (d) above.

(4) The powers conferred by sub-paragraph (1) above, and the powers arising by virtue of sub-paragraph (3) above, shall include power to use reasonable force where necessary.

(5) The power to make rules under this paragraph shall be exercisable by statutory instrument which shall be subject to annulment in pursuance of a resolution of either House of Parliament.

Interpretation

4. In this Schedule—

"escort arrangements" has the meaning given by paragraph 1 above; and

"offender" means an offender sentenced to secure training under section 1 of this Act.

"secure training centre" includes—

(a) a contracted out secure training centre;

(b) any other place to which an offender may have been committed or transferred under section 2 of this Act.

Definitions For "custody officer", see s 12(3); for "escort arrangements", see para 1(1), (3) above; for "escort monitor", see para 2(1)(a) above; for "offender" and "secure training centre", see para 4 above.
References See para 1.12.

SCHEDULE 2

Section 12

CERTIFICATION OF CUSTODY OFFICERS: ENGLAND AND WALES

Preliminary

1. In this Schedule—
"certificate" means a certificate under section 12(3) of this Act;
"the relevant functions", in relation to a certificate, means the escort functions or custodial duties authorised by the certificate.

Issue of certificates

2.—(1) Any person may apply to the Secretary of State for the issue of a certificate in respect of him.

(2) The Secretary of State shall not issue a certificate on any such application unless he is satisfied that the applicant—
(a) is a fit and proper person to perform the relevant functions; and
(b) has received training to such standard as he may consider appropriate for the performance of those functions.

(3) Where the Secretary of State issues a certificate, then, subject to any suspension under paragraph 3 or revocation under paragraph 4 below, it shall continue in force until such date or the occurrence of such event as may be specified in the certificate.

(4) A certificate authorising the performance of both escort functions and custodial duties may specify different dates or events as respects those functions and duties respectively.

Suspension of certificate

3.—(1) This paragraph applies where at any time—
(a) in the case of a custody officer acting in pursuance of escort arrangements, it appears to the escort monitor that the officer is not a fit and proper person to perform escort functions;
(b) in the case of a custody officer performing custodial duties at a contracted out secure training centre, it appears to the person in charge of the secure training centre that the officer is not a fit and proper person to perform custodial duties; or
(c) in the case of a custody officer performing contracted out functions at a directly managed secure training centre, it appears to the person in charge of that secure training centre that the officer is not a fit and proper person to perform custodial duties.

(2) The escort monitor or person in charge may—
(a) refer the matter to the Secretary of State for a decision under paragraph 4 below; and
(b) in such circumstances as may be prescribed by regulations made by the Secretary of State, suspend the officer's certificate so far as it authorises the performance of escort functions or, as the case may be, custodial duties pending that decision.

(3)   The power to make regulations under this paragraph shall be exercisable by statutory instrument which shall be subject to annulment in pursuance of a resolution of either House of Parliament.

Revocation of certificate

4.   Where at any time it appears to the Secretary of State that a custody officer is not a fit and proper person to perform escort functions or custodial duties, he may revoke that officer's certificate so far as it authorises the performance of those functions or duties.

False statements

5.   If any person, for the purpose of obtaining a certificate for himself or for any other person—
     (a)   makes a statement which he knows to be false in a material particular; or
     (b)   recklessly makes a statement which is false in a material particular,
he shall be liable on summary conviction to a fine not exceeding level 4 on the standard scale.

Definitions   For "custody officer", see s 12(3); for "contracted out functions", "contracted out secure training centre", "custodial duties", "directly managed secure training centre" and "escort functions", see s 15; for "escort arrangements", see Sch 1, para 1; for "escort monitor", see Sch 1, para 2(1)(a); for "certifcate" and "the relevant functions", see para 1 above.
References   See paras 1.9, 1.12.

SCHEDULE 3

Section 27

BAIL: SUPPLEMENTARY PROVISIONS

Bail Act 1976

1.   Section 5 of the Bail Act 1976 (supplementary provisions about decisions on bail) shall be amended as follows—
     (a)   in subsection (1)(d), after the words "a court" there shall be inserted the words "or constable"; and
     (b)   after subsection (10), there shall be inserted the following subsection—

"(11)   This section is subject, in its application to bail granted by a constable, to section 5A of this Act.".

2.   After section 5 of the Bail Act 1976 there shall be inserted the following section—

"5A   Supplementary provisions in cases of police bail

(1)   Section 5 of this Act applies, in relation to bail granted by a custody officer under Part IV of the Police and Criminal Evidence Act 1984 in cases where the normal powers to impose conditions of bail are available to him, subject to the following modifications.

(2)   For subsection (3) substitute the following—

"(3)   Where a custody officer, in relation to any person,—
     (a)   imposes conditions in granting bail in criminal proceedings, or
     (b)   varies any conditions of bail or imposes conditions in respect of bail in criminal proceedings,
the custody officer shall, with a view to enabling that person to consider requesting him or another custody officer, or making an application to a magistrates' court, to vary the conditions, give reasons for imposing or varying the conditions.".

(3)   For subsection (4) substitute the following—

"(4)   A custody officer who is by virtue of subsection (3) above required to give reasons for his decision shall include a note of those reasons in the custody record and shall give a copy of that note to the person in relation to whom the decision was taken.".

(4)   Subsections (5) and (6) shall be omitted.".

Magistrates' Courts Act 1980

3.   After section 43A of the Magistrates' Courts Act 1980 there shall be inserted the following section—

"43B   Power to grant bail where police bail has been granted

(1)   Where a custody officer—

    (a)   grants bail to any person under Part IV of the Police and Criminal Evidence Act 1984 in criminal proceedings and imposes conditions, or

    (b)   varies, in relation to any person, conditions of bail in criminal proceedings under section 3(8) of the Bail Act 1976,

a magistrates' court may, on application by or on behalf of that person, grant bail or vary the conditions.

(2)   On an application under subsection (1) the court, if it grants bail and imposes conditions or if it varies the conditions, may impose more onerous conditions.

(3)   On determining an application under subsection (1) the court shall remand the applicant, in custody or on bail in accordance with the determination, and, where the court withholds bail or grants bail the grant of bail made by the custody officer shall lapse.

(4)   In this section "bail in criminal proceedings" and "vary" have the same meanings as they have in the Bail Act 1976.".

Definitions   In the Bail Act 1976, for "bail" and "bail in criminal proceedings", see s 1 of that Act; for "the normal powers to impose conditions of bail", see s 3(6) of that Act, as amended by s 27(2)(b). In the Magistrates' Courts Act 1980, for "magistrates' court", see s 148 of that Act; for "bail in criminal proceedings", see, by virtue of s 43B(4) of that Act, as inserted by para 3 above, and s 150(1) thereof, the Bail Act 1976, s 1; for "vary", see, by virtue of s 43B(4) of that Act, as so inserted, s 2(2) of the 1976 Act.

SCHEDULE 4

Section 44

TRANSFER FOR TRIAL

PART I

PROVISIONS SUBSTITUTED FOR SECTIONS 4 TO 8 OF MAGISTRATES' COURTS ACT 1980

Transfer for trial

4   Transfer for trial: preliminary

(1)   Where—

    (a)   a person is charged before a magistrates' court with an offence which is triable only on indictment; or

    (b)   a person is charged before a magistrates' court with an offence triable either way and—

> (i) the court has decided that the offence is more suitable for trial on indictment, or
>
> (ii) the accused has not consented to be tried summarily,

the court and the prosecutor shall proceed with a view to transferring the proceedings for the offence to the Crown Court for trial.

(2) Where, under subsection (1) above or any other provision of this Part, a magistrates' court is to proceed a with view to transferring the proceedings for the offence to the Crown Court for trial, sections 5 to 8C below, or such of them as are applicable, shall apply to the proceedings against the accused, unless—

> (a) the prosecutor decides to discontinue or withdraw the proceedings;
>
> (b) the Commissioners of Customs and Excise decide, under section 152(a) of the Customs and Excise Management Act 1979, to stay or compound the proceedings;
>
> (c) the court proceeds to try the information summarily under section 25(3) or (7) below; or
>
> (d) a notice of transfer under section 4 of the Criminal Justice Act 1987 or section 53 of the Criminal Justice Act 1991 is served on the court.

(3) The functions of a magistrates' court under sections 5 to 8C below may be discharged by a single justice.

(4) A magistrates' court may, at any stage in the proceedings against the accused, adjourn the proceedings, and if it does so shall remand the accused.

(5) Any reference in this Part to a magistrates' court proceeding with a view to transfer for trial is a reference to the court and the prosecutor proceeding with a view to transferring the case to the Crown Court for trial and any reference to transferring for trial shall be construed accordingly.

5 Prosecutor's notice of prosecution case

(1) Where this section applies to proceedings against an accused for an offence, the prosecutor shall, within the prescribed period or within such further period as the court may on application by the prosecutor allow, serve on the magistrates' court a notice of his case which complies with subsection (2) below.

(2) The notice of the prosecution case shall—

> (a) specify the charge or charges the proceedings on which are, subject to section 6 below, to be transferred for trial;
>
> (b) subject to subsection (5) below, include a set of the documents containing the evidence (including oral evidence) on which the charge or charges is or are based; and
>
> (c) contain such other information (if any) as may be prescribed;

and in this Part a "notice of the prosecution case" means a notice which complies with this subsection.

(3) The accused and any co-accused shall be given an opportunity to oppose in writing within the prescribed period the grant of an extension of time under subsection (1) above.

(4) On serving the notice of the prosecution case on the magistrates' court, the prosecutor shall serve a copy of the notice on the accused, or each of the accused, unless the person to be served cannot be found.

(5) There shall be no requirement on the prosecutor to include in the notice of the prosecution case copies of any documents referred to in the notice as having already been supplied to the court or the accused, as the case may be.

(6) In this section "co-accused", in relation to the accused, means any other person charged in the same proceedings with him.

6 Application for dismissal

(1) Where a notice of the prosecution case has been given in respect of proceedings before a magistrates' court, the accused, or any of them, may, within the prescribed period, or within such further period as the court may on application allow, make an application in writing to the court ("an application for dismissal") for the charge or, as the case may be, any of the charges to be dismissed.

(2) If an accused makes an application for dismissal he shall, as soon as reasonably practicable after he makes it, send a copy of the application to—

(a) the prosecutor; and

(b) any co-accused.

(3) The prosecutor shall be given an opportunity to oppose the application for dismissal in writing within the prescribed period.

(4) The prosecutor and any co-accused shall be given an opportunity to oppose in writing within the prescribed period the grant of an extension of time under subsection (1) above.

(5) The court shall permit an accused who has no legal representative acting for him to make oral representations to the court when it considers his application for dismissal.

(6) An accused who has a legal representative acting for him and who makes an application for the dismissal of a charge may include in his application a request that, on the ground of the complexity or difficulty of the case, oral representations of his should be considered by the court in determining the application; and the court shall, if it is satisfied that representations ought, on that ground, to be considered, give leave for them to be made.

(7) The prosecutor shall be given an opportunity to oppose in writing within the prescribed period the giving of leave under subsection (6) above for representations to be made.

(8) If the accused makes the representations permitted under subsection (5) or (6) above, the court shall permit the prosecutor to make oral representations in response.

(9) Except for the purpose of making or hearing the representations allowed by subsection (5), (6) or (8) above, the prosecutor and the accused shall not be entitled to be present when the court considers the application for dismissal.

(10) The court, after considering the written evidence and any oral representations permitted under subsection (5), (6) or (8) above, shall, subject to subsection (11) below, dismiss a charge which is the subject of an application for dismissal if it appears to the court that there is not sufficient evidence against the accused to put him on trial by jury for the offence charged.

(11) Where the evidence discloses an offence other than that charged the court need not dismiss the charge but may amend it or substitute a different offence; and if the court does so the amended or substituted charge shall be treated as the charge the proceedings on which are to be transferred for trial.

(12) If the court permits the accused to make oral representations under subsection (6) above, but the accused does not do so, the court may disregard any document containing or indicating the evidence that he might have given.

(13) Dismissal of the charge, or any of the charges, against the accused shall have the effect of barring any further proceedings on that charge or those charges on the same evidence other than by preferring a voluntary bill of indictment.

(14) In this section "co-accused" has the same meaning as in section 5 above.

7 Transfer for trial

(1) Where a notice of the prosecution case has been served on a magistrates' court with respect to any proceedings and—

   (a)   the prescribed period for an application for dismissal has expired without any such application, or any application for an extension of that time, having been made; or

   (b)   an application for dismissal has been made and dismissed, or has succeeded in relation to one or more but not all the charges,

the court shall, within the prescribed period, in the prescribed manner, transfer the proceedings for the trial of the accused on the charges or remaining charges to the Crown Court sitting at a place specified by the court.

  (2) In selecting the place of trial, the court shall have regard to—

   (a)   the convenience of the defence, the prosecution and the witnesses;

   (b)   the expediting of the trial; and

   (c)   any direction given by or on behalf of the Lord Chief Justice with the concurrence of the Lord Chancellor under section 75(1) of the Supreme Court Act 1981.

  (3) On transferring any proceedings to the Crown Court the magistrates' court making the transfer shall—

   (a)   give notice of the transfer and of the place of trial to the prosecutor and to the accused or each of the accused; and

   (b)   send to the Crown Court sitting at the place specified by the court a copy of the notice of the prosecution case and of any documents referred to in it as having already been supplied to the magistrates' court on which it was served and (where an application for dismissal has been made) a copy of any other evidence permitted under section 6 above.

8   Remand

  (1) Where an accused has been remanded in custody, on transferring proceedings against him for trial a magistrates' court may—

   (a)   order that the accused shall be safely kept in custody until delivered in due course of law; or

   (b)   release the accused on bail in accordance with the Bail Act 1976, that is to say, by directing him to appear before the Crown Court for trial.

  (2) Where—

   (a)   a person's release on bail under subsection (1)(b) above is conditional on his providing one or more sureties; and

   (b)   in accordance with subsection (3) of section 8 of the Bail Act 1976, the court fixes the amount in which the surety is to be bound with a view to the surety's entering into his recognisance subsequently in accordance with subsections (4) and (5) or (6) of that section,

the court shall in the meantime make an order such as is mentioned in subsection (1)(a) above.

  (3) Where the court has ordered that a person be safely kept in custody in accordance with paragraph (a) of subsection (1) above, then, if that person is in custody for no other cause, the court may, at any time before his first appearance before the Crown Court, grant him bail in accordance with the Bail Act 1976 subject to a duty to appear before the Crown Court for trial.

  (4) The court may exercise the powers conferred on it by subsection (1) above in relation to the accused without his being brought before it if it is satisfied—

   (a)   that he has given his written consent to the powers conferred by subsection (1) above being exercised in his absence;

   (b)   that he had attained the age of 17 years when he gave that consent; and

   (c)   that he has not withdrawn that consent.

  (5) Where proceedings against an accused are transferred for trial after he has been remanded on bail to appear before a magistrates' court on an appointed day, the requirement that he shall so appear shall cease on the transfer of the proceedings unless the magistrates' court transferring the proceedings states that it is to continue.

(6) Where that requirement ceases by virtue of subsection (5) above, it shall be the duty of the accused to appear before the Crown Court at the place specified by the magistrates' court on transferring the proceedings against him for trial or at any place substituted for it by a direction under section 76 of the Supreme Court Act 1981.

(7) If, in a case where the magistrates' court states that the requirement mentioned in subsection (5) above is to continue, the accused appears or is brought before the magistrates' court, the court shall have the powers conferred on a magistrates' court by subsection (1) above and, where the court exercises those powers, subsections (2) and (3) above shall apply as if the powers were exercised under subsection (1) above.

(8) This section is subject to section 4 of the Bail Act 1976, section 41 below, regulations under section 22 of the Prosecution of Offences Act 1985 and section 25 of the Criminal Justice and Public Order Act 1994.

8A Reporting restrictions

(1) Except as provided in this section, it shall not be lawful—
   (a)   to publish in Great Britain a written report of an application for dismissal to a magistrates' court under section 6 above; or
   (b)   to include in a relevant programme for reception in Great Britain a report of such an application,
if (in either case) the report contains any matter other than matter permitted by this section.

(2) A magistrates' court may, on an application for the purpose made with reference to proceedings on an application for dismissal, order that subsection (1) above shall not apply to reports of those proceedings.

(3) Where in the case of two or more accused one of them objects to the making of an order under subsection (2) above, the magistrates' court shall make the order if, and only if, the court is satisfied, after hearing the representations of the accused, that it is in the interests of justice to do so.

(4) An order under subsection (2) above shall not apply to reports of proceedings under subsection (3) above, but any decision of the court to make or not to make such an order may be contained in reports published or included in a relevant programme before the time authorised by subsection (5) below.

(5) It shall not be unlawful under this section to publish or include in a relevant programme a report of an application for dismissal containing any matter other than matter permitted by subsection (9) below where the application is successful.

(6) Where—
   (a)   two or more persons are charged in the same proceedings; and
   (b)   applications for dismissal are made by more than one of them,
subsection (5) above shall have effect as if for the words "the application is" there were substituted the words "all the applications are".

(7) It shall not be unlawful under this section to publish or include in a relevant programme a report of an unsuccessful application for dismissal at the conclusion of the trial of the person charged, or of the last of the persons charged to be tried.

(8) Where, at any time during its consideration of an application for dismissal, the court proceeds to try summarily the case of one or more of the accused under section 25(3) or (7) below, while dismissing the application for dismissal of the other accused or one or more of the other accused, it shall not be unlawful under this section to publish or include in a relevant programme as part of a report of the summary trial, after the court determines to proceed as aforesaid, a report of so much of the application for dismissal containing any matter other than matter permitted by subsection (9) below as takes place before the determination.

(9) The following matters may be published or included in a relevant programme without an order under subsection (2) above before the time authorised by subsection (5) or (7) above, that is to say—

(a)   the identity of the magistrates' court and the names of the justices composing it;

(b)   the names, age, home address and occupation of the accused;

(c)   the offence, or offences, or a summary of them, with which the accused is or are charged;

(d)   the names of legal representatives engaged in the proceedings;

(e)   where the proceedings are adjourned, the date and place to which they are adjourned;

(f)   the arrangements as to bail;

(g)   whether legal aid was granted to the accused or any of the accused.

(10) The addresses that may be published or included in a relevant programme under subsection (9) are addresses—

(a)   at any relevant time; and

(b)   at the time of their publication or inclusion in a relevant programme.

(11) If a report is published or included in a relevant programme in contravention of this section, the following persons, that is to say—

(a)   in the case of a publication of a written report as part of a newspaper or periodical, any proprietor, editor or publisher of the newspaper or periodical;

(b)   in the case of a publication of a written report otherwise than as part of a newspaper or periodical, the person who publishes it;

(c)   in the case of the inclusion of a report in a relevant programme, any body corporate which is engaged in providing the service in which the programme is included and any person having functions in relation to the programme corresponding to those of the editor of a newspaper,

shall be liable on summary conviction to a fine not exceeding level 5 on the standard scale.

(12) Proceedings for an offence under this section shall not, in England and Wales, be instituted otherwise than by or with the consent of the Attorney General.

(13) Subsection (1) above shall be in addition to, and not in derogation from, the provisions of any other enactment with respect to the publication of reports of court proceedings.

(14) In this section—

"publish", in relation to a report, means publish the report, either by itself or as part of a newspaper or periodical, for distribution to the public;

"relevant programme" means a programme included in a programme service (within the meaning of the Broadcasting Act 1990); and

"relevant time" means a time when events giving rise to the charges to which the proceedings relate occurred.

8B Avoidance of delay

Where a notice of the prosecution case has been given in respect of proceedings before a magistrates' court, the court shall, in exercising any of its powers in relation to the proceedings, have regard to the desirability of avoiding prejudice to the welfare of any witness that may be occasioned by unnecessary delay in transferring the proceedings for trial.

8C Public notice of transfer

Where a magistrates' court transfers proceedings for trial, the clerk of the court shall, within the prescribed period, cause to be displayed in a part of the court house to which the public have access a notice containing the prescribed information.

Definitions   For "magistrates' court", see the Magistrates' Courts Act 1980, s 148; for "offence", see s 150(5) of the 1980 Act; for "proceeding with a view to transfer for trial" "transferred for trial", "transferring for trial", "tranfers proceedings for trial", see s 4(5) of the 1980 Act, as substituted above; for "legal representative" and "prescribed", see s 150(1) of the 1980 Act; for "notice of the prosecution case", see s 5(2) of the 1980 Act, as substituted above, and as to "co-accused", see, by virtue of sub-s (4), s 5(6) thereof, as so substituted; for "an application for dismissal", see s 6(1) of the 1980 Act, as substituted above; for the meaning of "bail" in the Bail Act 1976, see s 1 thereof, as repealed in part by s 168(3) of, Sch 11 to, this Act; for "age" see the Magsitrates' Courts Act 1980, s 150(4); for "publish", "relevant programme" and "relevant time", see s 8A(14) of the 1980 Act, as substituted above.

References   See para 3.17.

PART II

CONSEQUENTIAL AMENDMENTS

Preliminary

1.   In this Part of this Schedule—
  "the 1853 Act" means the Criminal Procedure Act 1853;
  "the 1878 Act" means the Territorial Waters Jurisdiction Act 1878;
  "the 1883 Act" means the Explosive Substances Act 1883;
  "the 1933 Act" means the Administration of Justice (Miscellaneous Provisions) Act 1933;
  "the 1948 Act" means the Criminal Justice Act 1948;
  "the 1952 Act" means the Prison Act 1952;
  "the 1955 Act" means the Army Act 1955;
  "the 1957 Act" means the Naval Discipline Act 1957;
  "the 1967 Act" means the Criminal Justice Act 1967;
  "the 1968 Act" means the Firearms Act 1968;
  "the 1969 Act" means the Children and Young Persons Act 1969;
  "the 1973 Act" means the Powers of Criminal Courts Act 1973;
  "the 1976 Act" means the Bail Act 1976;
  "the 1978 Act" means the Interpretation Act 1978;
  "the 1979 Act" means the Customs and Excise Management Act 1979;
  "the 1980 Act" means the Magistrates' Courts Act 1980;
  "the 1981 Act" means the Supreme Court Act 1981;
  "the 1982 Act" means the Criminal Justice Act 1982;
  "the 1983 Act" means the Mental Health Act 1983;
  "the 1984 Act" means the County Courts Act 1984;
  "the 1985 Act" means the Prosecution of Offences Act 1985;
  "the 1986 Act" means the Agricultural Holdings Act 1986;
  "the 1987 Act" means the Criminal Justice Act 1987;
  "the 1988 Act" means the Legal Aid Act 1988;
  "the 1991 Act" means the Criminal Justice Act 1991; and
  "the 1992 Act" means the Sexual Offences (Amendment) Act 1992.

Criminal Procedure Act 1853 (c 30)

2.   In section 9 of the 1853 Act (bringing up a prisoner to give evidence), for the words "under commitment for trial" there shall be substituted the words "pending his trial in the Crown Court".

Territorial Waters Jurisdiction Act 1878 (c 73)

3.   In section 4 of the 1878 Act (procedure under that Act), for the words "committal of" there shall be substituted the words "transfer of proceedings against".

Explosive Substances Act 1883 (c 3)

4.   In section 6(3) of the 1883 Act (inquiry by Attorney-General, and apprehension of absconding witnesses), for the words "committing for trial of" there shall be substituted the words "consideration of an application for dismissal under section 6 of the Magistrates' Courts Act 1980 made by such person for such crime or the transfer for trial of proceedings against".

Children and Young Persons Act 1933 (c 12)

5. In section 42 of the Children and Young Persons Act 1933 (deposition of child or young person), for subsection (2)(a) there shall be substituted the following paragraph—

"(a) if the deposition relates to an offence in respect of which proceedings have already been transferred to the Crown Court for trial, to the proper officer of the court to which the proceedings have been transferred; and".

6. In section 56(1) of the Children and Young Persons Act 1933 (powers of courts to remit young offenders to youth court)—

(a) for the words "the offender was committed" there shall be substituted the words "proceedings against the offender were transferred"; and

(b) for the words "he was not committed" there shall be substituted the words "proceedings against him were not transferred".

Administration of Justice (Miscellaneous Provisions) Act 1933 (c 36)

7.—(1) Section 2 of the 1933 Act (procedure for indictment of offenders) shall be amended as follows.

(2) In subsection (2)—

(a) for paragraph (a) there shall be substituted the following paragraph—

"(a) the proceedings for the offence have been transferred to the Crown Court for trial; or";

(b) for proviso (i) there shall be substituted the following proviso—

"(i) where the proceedings for the offence have been transferred to the Crown Court for trial, the bill of indictment against the person charged may include, either in substitution for or in addition to counts charging the offence in respect of which proceedings have been transferred, any counts founded on the evidence contained in the documents sent to the Crown Court by the magistrates' court on transferring the proceedings, being counts which may lawfully be joined in the same indictment;";

(c) in proviso (iA)—

(i) for the word "material" there shall be substituted the words "the evidence contained in the documents"; and

(ii) after the words "person charged" there shall be inserted the words "or which is referred to in those documents as having already been sent to the person charged"; and

(d) in proviso (ii), for the words "the committal" there shall be substituted the words "charge the proceedings on which were transferred for trial".

(3) In subsection (3), in proviso (b), for the words from "a person" to "for trial" there shall be substituted the words "proceedings against a person have been transferred for trial and that person".

Criminal Justice Act 1948 (c 58)

8.—(1) The 1948 Act shall be amended as follows.

(2) In section 27(1) (remand and committal of persons aged 17 to 20), for the words "trial or sentence" there shall be substituted the words "sentence or transfers proceedings against him for trial".

(3) In section 80(1) (interpretation of expressions used in the Act), in the definition of "Court of summary jurisdiction", for the words from "examining" to the end there shall be substituted the words "a magistrates' court proceeding with a view to transfer for trial;".

Prison Act 1952 (c 52)

9.—(1) Section 43 of the 1952 Act (remand centres, etc) shall be amended as follows.

(2) In subsection (1)(a)—
    (a)   the words "trial or" shall be omitted; and
    (b)   after the word "sentence" there shall be inserted the words "or are ordered to be safely kept in custody on the transfer of proceedings against them for trial".

(3) In subsection (2)—
    (a)   in paragraph (b)—
        (i)   the words "trial or" shall be omitted; and
        (ii)   after the word "sentence" there shall be inserted the words "or is ordered to be safely kept in custody on the transfer of proceedings against her for trial"; and
    (b)   in paragraph (c)—
        (i)   the words "trial or" shall be omitted; and
        (ii)   after the word "sentence" there shall be inserted the words "or ordered to be safely kept in custody on the transfer of proceedings against him for trial".

10. In section 47(5) of the 1952 Act (rules for the management of prisons, remand centres, etc), for the words "committed in custody" there shall be substituted the words "ordered to be safely kept in custody on the transfer of proceedings against them".

Army Act 1955 (c 18)

11. In section 187(4) of the 1955 Act (proceedings against persons suspected of illegal absence)—
    (a)   for the words from "courts of" to "justices" there shall be substituted the words "magistrates' courts proceeding with a view to transfer for trial"; and
    (b)   for the words "so acting" there shall be substituted the words "so proceeding".

Air Force Act 1955 (c 19)

12. In section 187(4) of the Air Force Act 1955 (proceedings against persons suspected of illegal absence)—
    (a)   for the words from "courts of" to "justices" there shall be substituted the words "magistrates' courts proceeding with a view to transfer for trial"; and
    (b)   for the words "so acting" there shall be substituted the words "so proceeding".

Geneva Conventions Act 1957 (c 52)

13. In section 5 of the Geneva Conventions Act 1957 (reduction of sentence and custody of protected persons)—
    (a)   in subsection (1), for the word "committal" there shall be substituted the words "the transfer of the proceedings against him"; and
    (b)   in subsection (2)—
        (i)   for the word "committal" the first time it occurs there shall be substituted the words "the transfer of the proceedings against him"; and
        (ii)   for the words "remand or committal order" there shall be substituted the words "court on remanding him or transferring proceedings against him for trial".

Naval Discipline Act 1957 (c 53)

14. In section 109(4) of the 1957 Act (proceedings against persons suspected of illegal absence)—
    (a)   for the words from "1952" to "justices" there shall be substituted the words "1980, that is to say the provisions relating to the constitution and procedure of magistrates' courts proceeding with a view to transfer for trial"; and
    (b)   for the words "so acting" there shall be substituted the words "so proceeding".

Criminal Justice Act 1967 (c 80)

15.—(1) The 1967 Act shall be amended as follows.

(2) In section 9 (general admissibility of written statements), in subsection (1), for the words "committal proceedings" there shall be substituted the words "proceedings under sections 4 to 6 of the Magistrates' Courts Act 1980".

(3) In section 11 (notice of alibi), in subsection (8), in the definition of "the prescribed period", for the words from "the end" to "or" there shall be substituted the words "the transfer of the proceedings to the Crown Court for trial, or".

Criminal Appeal Act 1968 (c 19)

16. In section 1(3) of the Criminal Appeal Act 1968 (limitation of right of appeal in case of scheduled offence), for the word "committed" there shall be substituted the words "transferred proceedings against".

Firearms Act 1968 (c 27)

17. In paragraph 3(3) of Part II of Schedule 6 to the 1968 Act (trial of certain offences under that Act)—
    (a) after the word "If" there shall be inserted the words ", under section 6 of the said Act of 1980,";
    (b) for the words from "determines" to "for trial" there shall be substituted the words "dismisses the charge against the accused";
    (c) in sub-subparagraph (a), for the words from "inquire" to "justices" there shall be substituted the words "proceed with a view to transferring for trial proceedings for the listed offence";
    (d) in sub-subparagraph (b)—
        (i) for the words "inquire into" there shall be substituted the words "proceed in respect of"; and
        (ii) for the words from "its inquiry" to "justices" there shall be substituted the words "a view to transferring for trial proceedings for that offence".

Theft Act 1968 (c 60)

18. In section 28(4) of the Theft Act 1968 (orders for restitution), for the words from ", the depositions" to the end there shall be substituted the words "and, where the proceedings have been transferred to the Crown Court for trial, the documents sent to the Crown Court by the magistrates' court under section 7(3)(b) of the Magistrates' Courts Act 1980.".

Children and Young Persons Act 1969 (c 54)

19. In section 23(1) of the 1969 Act (remands and committals to local authority accommodation)—
    (a) in paragraph (a), for the words "or commits him for trial or sentence" there shall be substituted the words ", transfers proceedings against him for trial or commits him for sentence"; and
    (b) for the words "the remand or committal shall be" there shall be substituted the words "he shall be remanded or committed".

Powers of Criminal Courts Act 1973 (c 62)

20. In section 21(2) of the 1973 Act (restriction on imposing sentences of imprisonment, etc, on persons not legally represented)—
    (a) for the words "or trial" there shall be substituted the words "or in respect of whom proceedings have been transferred to the Crown Court for trial"; and
    (b) after the words "committed him" there shall be inserted the words "or which transferred proceedings against him".

21. In section 32(1)(b) of the 1973 Act (enforcement, etc, of fines imposed and recognizances forfeited by Crown Court)—
    (a) the words "tried or" shall be omitted; and
    (b) after the words "dealt with" there shall be inserted the words "or which transferred proceedings against him to the Crown Court for trial".

Bail Act 1976 (c 63)

22. In section 3 of the 1976 Act (incidents of bail in criminal proceedings)—
    (a) in subsection (8) (variation and imposition of bail conditions by court), for the words from "committed" to "trial or" there shall be substituted the words "released a person on bail on transferring proceedings against him to the Crown Court for trial or has committed him on bail to the Crown Court"; and
    (b) in subsection (8A), for the words "committed on bail" there shall be substituted the words "released on bail on the transfer of proceedings against him".

23. In section 5 of the 1976 Act (supplementary provisions about decisions on bail)—
    (a) in subsection (6)(a)—
        (i) for the word "committing" there shall be substituted the words "transferring proceedings against"; and
        (ii) after the words "Crown Court" where they occur first, there shall be inserted the words "or has already done so"; and
    (b) in subsection (6A)(a), for sub-paragraph (i) there shall be substituted the following sub-paragraph—
        "(i) section 4(4) (adjournment when court is proceeding with a view to transfer for trial);".

24. In section 6(6)(b) of the 1976 Act (absconding by person released on bail), for the words from "commits" to "another offence" there shall be substituted the words "transfers proceedings against that person for another offence to the Crown Court for trial".

25. In section 9(3)(b) of the 1976 Act (agreeing to indemnify sureties in criminal proceedings), for the words from "commits" to "another offence" there shall be substituted the words "transfers proceedings against that person for another offence to the Crown Court for trial".

Sexual Offences (Amendment) Act 1976 (c 82)

26. In section 3 of the Sexual Offences (Amendment) Act 1976 (application of restrictions on evidence at trials for rape etc to committal proceedings etc), for subsection (1) there shall be substituted the following subsection—

    "(1) Where a magistrates' court considers an application for dismissal of a charge for a rape offence, then, except with the consent of the court, evidence shall not be adduced and a question shall not be asked at the consideration of the application which, if the proceedings were a trial at which a person is charged as mentioned in subsection (1) of the preceding section and each of the accused in respect of whom the application for dismissal is made were charged at the trial with the offences to which the application relates, could not be adduced or asked without leave in pursuance of that section.".

27. In section 4(6)(c) of the Sexual Offences (Amendment) Act 1976 (anonymity of complainants in rape etc cases), for the words "commits him for trial on" there shall be substituted the words "transfers proceedings against him for trial for".

Interpretation Act 1978 (c 30)

28. In Schedule 1 to the 1978 Act—
    (a) in the definition of "Committed for trial", paragraph (a) shall be omitted; and
    (b) after the definition of "The Tax Acts" there shall be inserted the following definition—
        ""Transfer for trial" means the transfer of proceedings against an accused to the Crown Court for trial under section 7 of the Magistrates' Courts Act 1980.".

Customs and Excise Management Act 1979 (c 2)

29.—(1) The 1979 Act shall be amended as follows.

(2) In section 147 (proceedings for offences under customs and excise Acts), in subsection (2), for the words from the beginning to "justices" there shall be substituted the words "Where, in England or Wales, on an application under section 6 of the Magistrates' Courts Act 1980 for dismissal of a charge under the customs and excise Acts, the court has begun to consider the evidence and any representations permitted under that section,".

(3) In section 155 (persons who may conduct proceedings under customs and excise Acts), in subsection (1), for the words "examining justices" there shall be substituted the words "magistrates' court proceeding with a view to transfer for trial".

Reserve Forces Act 1980 (c 9)

30. In paragraph 2(4) of Schedule 5 to the Reserve Forces Act 1980 (proceedings against persons suspected of illegal absence—
   (a) for the words "acting as examining justices" there shall be substituted the words "proceeding with a view to transfer for trial"; and
   (b) for the words "so acting" there shall be substituted the words "so proceeding".

Magistrates' Courts Act 1980 (c 43)

31.—(1) Section 2 of the 1980 Act (jurisdiction of magistrates' courts) shall be amended as follows.

(2) In subsection (3), for the words from "as examining" to "any offence" there shall be substituted the words "to proceed with a view to transfer for trial where the offence charged was".

(3) In subsection (4), for the words "as examining justices" there shall be substituted the words "to proceed with a view to transfer for trial".

(4) In subsection (5), for the words "as examining justices" there shall be substituted the words "to proceed with a view to transfer for trial".

32. In section 19 of the 1980 Act (court to consider mode of trial of either way offence), in subsection (4), for the words from "to inquire" to the end of the subsection there shall be substituted the words "with a view to transfer for trial.".

33. In section 20 of the 1980 Act (procedure where summary trial appears more suitable), in subsection (3)(b), for the words from "to inquire" to the end there shall be substituted the words "with a view to transfer for trial.".

34. In section 21 of the 1980 Act (procedure where trial on indictment appears more suitable), for the words from "to inquire" to the end there shall be substituted the words "with a view to transfer for trial.".

35.—(1) Section 23 of the 1980 Act (procedure where court proceeds to determine mode of trial in absence of accused) shall be amended as follows.

(2) In subsection (4)(b)—
   (a) for the words from "to inquire" to "justices" there shall be substituted the words "with a view to transfer for trial"; and
   (b) for the word "hearing" there shall be substituted the word "proceedings".

(3) In subsection (5)—
   (a) for the words from "to inquire" to "justices" there shall be substituted the words "with a view to transfer for trial"; and
   (b) for the word "hearing" there shall be substituted the word "proceedings".

36.—(1) Section 24 of the 1980 Act (trial of child or young person for indictable offence) shall be amended as follows.

(2) In subsection (1)—
   (a) in paragraph (b), for the word "commit" there shall be substituted the words "proceed with a view to transferring the proceedings in relation to"; and

(b)   for the words from "commit the accused" to the end there shall be substituted the words "proceed with a view to transferring the proceedings against the accused for trial.".

(3) In subsection (2), for the words from "commits" to "him for trial" there shall be substituted the words "proceeds with a view to transferring for trial the proceedings in relation to a person under the age of 18 years for an offence with which he is charged jointly with a person who has attained that age, the court may also proceed with a view to transferring for trial proceedings against him".

37.—(1) Section 25 of the 1980 Act (court's power to change from summary trial to committal proceedings and vice versa) shall be amended as follows.

(2) In subsection (2)—

(a)   for the words from "to inquire" to "justices" there shall be substituted the words "with a view to transfer for trial"; and

(b)   for the word "hearing" there shall be substituted the word "proceedings".

(3) For subsection (3) there shall be substituted the following subsection—

"(3)   Where on an application for dismissal of a charge under section 6 above the court has begun to consider the evidence and any representations permitted under that section, then, if at any time during its consideration it appears to the court, having regard to any of the evidence or representations, and to the nature of the case, that the offence is after all more suitable for summary trial, the court may—

(a)   if the accused is present, after doing as provided in subsection (4) below, ask the accused whether he consents to be tried summarily and, if he so consents, may (subject to subsection (3A) below) proceed to try the information summarily; or

(b)   in the absence of the accused—

(i)   if the accused's consent to be tried summarily is signified by the person representing him, proceed to try the information summarily or

(ii) if that consent is not so signified, adjourn the proceedings without remanding the accused, and if it does so, the court shall fix the time and place at which the proceedings are to be resumed and at which the accused is required to appear or be brought before the court in order for the court to proceed as provided in paragraph (a) above.".

(4) In subsection (5), in paragraph (b), for the words from "inquire" to "fall" there shall be substituted the words "consider the evidence and any representations permitted under section 6 above on an application for dismissal of a charge in a case in which, under paragraph (a) or (b) of section 24(1) above, the court is required to proceed with a view to transferring the proceedings to the Crown Court for trial,".

(5) In subsection (6)—

(a)   for the words from "to inquire" to "justices" there shall be substituted the words "with a view to transfer for trial"; and

(b)   for the word "hearing" there shall be substituted the word "proceedings".

(6) In subsection (7), for the words "the inquiry" there shall be substituted the words "its consideration of the evidence and any representations permitted under section 6 above.".

38. For section 26 of the 1980 Act (power to issue summons in certain circumstances) there shall be substituted the following section—

"26   Power to issue summons in certain circumstances

Where, in the circumstances mentioned in section 23(1)(a) above, the court is not satisfied that there is good cause for proceeding in the absence of the accused, the justice or any of the justices of which the court is composed may issue a summons directed to the accused requiring his presence before the court; and if the accused is not present at the time and place appointed for the proceedings under section 19(1) or 22(1) above, as the case may be, the court may issue a warrant for his arrest.".

39. In section 28 of the 1980 Act (use in summary trial of evidence given in committal proceedings)—

    (a) for the words from "inquire" to "justices" there shall be substituted the words "consider the evidence under section 6 above"; and

    (b) for the words from "then" to "any" there shall be substituted the words "any oral".

40. In section 29 of the 1980 Act (remission of person under 18 to youth court for trial), in subsection (2)(b)(i), for the words from "to inquire" to "discharges him" there shall be substituted the words "with a view to transfer for trial".

41. In section 42 of the 1980 Act (restriction on justices sitting after dealing with bail), in subsection (2), for the words "committal proceedings" there shall be substituted the words "proceedings before the court on an application for dismissal of a charge under section 6 above.".

42.—(1) Section 97 of the 1980 Act (summons to witness) shall be amended as follows.

    (2) In subsection (1)—

        (a) the words from "at an inquiry" to "be) or" shall be omitted; and

        (b) for the words "such a court" there shall be substituted the words "a magistrates' court for that county, that London commission area or the City (as the case may be)".

    (3) After subsection (1) there shall be inserted the following subsection—

"(1A) Where a magistrates' court is proceeding with a view to transferring proceedings against an accused for an offence to the Crown Court for trial, subsection (1) above shall apply in relation to evidence or a document or thing material to the offence subject to the following modifications—

        (a) no summons shall be issued by a justice of the peace after the expiry of the period within which a notice of the prosecution case under section 5 above must be served or the service of the notice of the prosecution case, if sooner; and

        (b) the summons shall require the person to whom it is directed to attend before the justice issuing it or another justice for that county, that London commission area or the City of London (as the case may be) to have his evidence taken as a deposition or to produce any document or thing.".

    (4) In subsection (2)—

        (a) after the words "subsection (1)" there shall be inserted the words "or (1A)"; and

        (b) after the word "court" there shall be inserted the words "or justice, as the case may be,".

    (5) In subsection (2A), after the words "subsection (1)" there shall be inserted the words "or (1A)".

    (6) In subsections (3) and (4), after the words "a magistrates' court" or "the court" wherever they occur there shall be inserted the words "or justice, as the case may be,".

43.—(1) Section 128 of the 1980 Act (remand in custody or on bail) shall be amended as follows.

    (2) In subsection (1)(b), for the words "inquiring into or" there shall be substituted the words "proceeding with a view to transferring the proceedings against that person for trial or is".

    (3) In subsections (1A), (3A), (3C) and (3E), for the words "section 5" there shall be substituted the words "section 4(4)".

(4) In subsection (4)—

    (a) for the words from "during an inquiry" to the words "committed by him" there shall be substituted the words "when it is proceeding with a view to transfer for trial"; and

    (b) in paragraph (c)—

        (i) for the word "hearing" there shall be substituted the word "proceedings"; and

        (ii) for the words from "person" to "committed" there shall be substituted the words "proceedings against the person so bailed being transferred".

44. In section 129 of the 1980 Act (further remand), in subsection (4)—

    (a) for the words from "commits" to "bail" there shall be substituted the words "transfers for trial proceedings against a person who has been remanded on bail"; and

    (b) for the words "so committed" there shall be substituted the words "in respect of whom proceedings have been transferred".

45. In section 130 of the 1980 Act (transfer of remand hearings), in subsection (1), for the words "section 5" there shall be substituted the words "section 4(4)".

46. In section 145(1)(f) of the 1980 Act (rules: supplementary provisions), for the word "committed" there shall be substituted the words "in respect of whom proceedings have been transferred".

47.—(1) Schedule 3 to the 1980 Act (corporations) shall be amended as follows.

(2) In paragraph 1(1), for the words "commit a corporation" there shall be substituted the words ", in the case of a corporation, transfer the proceedings".

(3) In paragraph 2(a), for the words from "a statement" to "to" there shall be substituted the words "an application to dismiss".

(4) In paragraph 6, for the words "inquiry into," there shall be substituted the words "transfer for trial".

48. In paragraph 5 of Schedule 5 to the 1980 Act (transfer of remand hearings), for the words "sections 5" there shall be substituted the words "sections 4(4)".

Criminal Attempts Act 1981 (c 47)

49. In section 2(2)(g) of the Criminal Attempts Act 1981 (application of procedural and other provisions to attempts), the words "or committed for trial" shall be omitted.

Contempt of Court Act 1981 (c 49)

50. In section 4(3)(b) of the Contempt of Court Act 1981 (contemporary reports of proceedings)—

    (a) for the words "committal proceedings" there shall be substituted the words "an application for dismissal under section 6 of the Magistrates' Courts Act 1980"; and

    (b) for the words from "subsection (3)" to "1980" there shall be substituted the words "subsection (5) or (7) of section 8A of that Act".

Supreme Court Act 1981 (c 54)

51. In section 76 of the 1981 Act (alteration of place of Crown Court trial)—

    (a) in subsection (1), for the words from "varying the decision" to the end there shall be substituted the words "substituting some other place for the place specified in a notice relating to the transfer of the proceedings to the Crown Court or by varying a previous decision of the Crown Court";

    (b) in subsection (3), for the words from the beginning to the words "varying the place of trial;" there shall be substituted the following words—

"If he is dissatisfied with the place of trial—

    (a)   the defendant may apply to the Crown Court for a direction, or further direction, varying the place of trial specified in a notice relating to the transfer of the proceedings to the Crown Court or fixed by the Crown Court, or

    (b)   the prosecutor may apply to the Crown Court for a direction, or further direction, varying the place of trial specified in a notice given by the magistrates' court under section 7 of the Magistrates' Courts Act 1980 or fixed by the Crown Court;"; and

    (c)   after subsection (4) there shall be inserted the following subsection—

"(5)   In this section any reference to a notice relating to the transfer of proceedings to the Crown Court is a reference to the notice given by the magistrates' court under section 7 of the Magistrates' Courts Act 1980 or by the prosecutor under section 4 of the Criminal Justice Act 1987 or section 53 of the Criminal Justice Act 1991.".

52.—(1) Section 77 of the 1981 Act (date of Crown Court trial) shall be amended as follows.

(2) In subsection (1), for the words from "a person's committal" to "beginning of the trial" there shall be substituted the words "the transfer of proceedings for trial by the Crown Court and the beginning of the trial;".

(3) In subsection (2)—

    (a)   for the words preceding paragraph (a) there shall be substituted the words "The trial of a person on charges the proceedings on which have been transferred for trial to the Crown Court—"; and

    (b)   in paragraph (a), for the words "his consent" there shall be substituted the words "the consent of the person charged".

(4) In subsection (3), for the word "committal" there shall be substituted the word "transfer".

(5) After subsection (3) there shall be inserted the following subsections—

"(4)   Where a notice of the prosecution case has been given in respect of any proceedings, the Crown Court before which the proceedings are to be tried shall, in exercising any of its powers in relation to the proceedings, have regard to the desirability of avoiding prejudice to the welfare of any witness that may be occasioned by unnecessary delay in bringing the proceedings to trial.

(5)   In this section references to the transfer of proceedings for trial are references to a transfer by a magistrates' court under section 7 of the Magistrates' Courts Act 1980 or by the prosecutor under section 4 of the Criminal Justice Act 1987 or section 53 of the Criminal Justice Act 1991 and the date of transfer for trial is the date on which the transfer is effected under the said section 7 or, where the transfer is by the prosecutor, the date specified in his notice of transfer.".

53. In section 80(2) of the 1981 Act (process to compel appearance before Crown Court), for the words from "the person" to "committed" there shall be substituted the words "proceedings against the person charged have not been transferred".

Criminal Justice Act 1982 (c 48)

54. In section 1(2) of the 1982 Act (restrictions on custodial sentences for persons under 21)—

    (a)   the words "trial or" shall be omitted; and

    (b)   after the word "sentence" there shall be inserted the words "or ordered to be safely kept in custody on the transfer of proceedings against him for trial".

55. In section 3(2) of the 1982 Act (restriction on imposing custodial sentences on persons under 21 not legally represented)—

(a) for the words "or trial" there shall be substituted the words "or in respect of whom proceedings have been transferred to the Crown Court for trial"; and

(b) after the words "committed him" there shall be inserted the words "or transferred proceedings against him".

Mental Health Act 1983 (c 20)

56.—(1) Section 52 of the 1983 Act (provisions relating to persons remanded by magistrates' courts) shall be amended as follows.

(2) In subsection (2), for the words from "accused" to "or" there shall be substituted the words "court, on transferring proceedings against the accused to the Crown Court for trial, orders him to be safely kept in custody, or commits the accused in custody to the Crown Court".

(3) In subsection (5), after the words "expired or that" there shall be inserted the words "proceedings against the accused are transferred to the Crown Court for trial or".

(4) In subsection (6), after the word "If" there shall be inserted the words "proceedings against the accused are transferred to the Crown Court for trial or".

(5) In subsection (7)—
(a) for the words from "inquire" to "into" there shall be substituted the words "proceed with a view to transferring for trial proceedings for"; and
(b) for the words from "commit" to "1980" there shall be substituted the words "transfer proceedings against him for trial".

County Courts Act 1984 (c 28)

57. In section 57(1) of the 1984 Act (evidence of prisoners), for the words "under committal" there shall be substituted the words "following the transfer of proceedings against him".

Police and Criminal Evidence Act 1984 (c 60)

58. In section 62(10)(a) of the Police and Criminal Evidence Act 1984 (power of court to draw inferences from failure of accused to consent to provide intimate sample), for sub-paragraph (i) there shall be substituted the following sub-paragraph—

"(i) whether to grant an application for dismissal made by that person under section 6 of the Magistrates' Courts Act 1980 (application for dismissal of charge in course of proceedings with a view to transfer for trial); or".

Prosecution of Offences Act 1985 (c 23)

59. In section 16 of the 1985 Act (defence costs)—
(a) in subsection (1), for paragraph (b) there shall be substituted the following paragraph—

"(b) a magistrates' court determines not to transfer for trial proceedings for an indictable offence;"; and

(b) in subsection (2)(a), for the word "committed" there shall be substituted the words "in respect of which proceedings against him have been transferred".

60. In section 21(6) of the 1985 Act (interpretation, etc), in paragraph (b), for the words from "the accused" to "but" there shall be substituted the words "proceedings against the accused are transferred to the Crown Court for trial but the accused is".

61. In section 22 of the 1985 Act (time limits for preliminary stages of criminal proceedings), in subsection (11)—
(a) in the definition of "appropriate court", in paragraph (a) for the words from "accused" to "or" there shall be substituted the words "proceedings against the accused have been transferred for trial or the accused has been"; and

(b) in the definition of "custody of the Crown Court", for paragraph (a) there shall be substituted the following paragraph—

"(a) section 8(1) of the Magistrates' Courts Act 1980 (remand of accused where court is proceeding with a view to transfer for trial); or".

62. In section 23 of the 1985 Act (discontinuance of proceedings in magistrates' courts), in subsection (2)(b)(i), for the words "accused has been committed" there shall be substituted the words "proceedings against the accused have been transferred".

Agricultural Holdings Act 1986 (c 5)

63. In paragraph 12(1) of Schedule 11 to the 1986 Act (procedure on arbitrations under the Act), for the words "under committal" there shall be substituted the words "following the transfer of proceedings against him".

Criminal Justice Act 1987 (c 38)

64.—(1) The 1987 Act shall be amended as follows.

(2) In section 4(1) (notices of transfer in serious fraud cases)—
   (a) in paragraph (b)(i), for the words from "person" to "trial" there shall be substituted the words "proceedings against the person charged to be transferred for trial"; and
   (b) in paragraph (c), for the words from the beginning to "justices" there shall be substituted the words "not later than the time at which the authority would be required to serve a notice of the prosecution case under section 5 of the Magistrates' Courts Act 1980,".

(3) In section 5 (procedure for notices of transfer)—
   (a) in subsection (9)(a), for the words "a statement of the evidence" there shall be substituted the words "copies of the documents containing the evidence (including oral evidence)"; and
   (b) after subsection (9) there shall be inserted the following subsection—

"(9A) Regulations under subsection (9)(a) above may provide that there shall be no requirement for copies of any documents referred to in the documents sent with the notice of transfer as having already been supplied to accompany the copy of the notice of the transfer.".

(4) In section 6(5) (applications for dismissal), for the words from "a refusal" to the end there shall be substituted the words "the dismissal of a charge or charges against an accused under section 6 of the Magistrates' Courts Act 1980.".

Criminal Justice Act 1988 (c 33)

65. In section 40 of the Criminal Justice Act 1988 (power to include counts for certain summary offences in indictment), in subsection (1), for the words from "an examination" to the end, there shall be substituted the words "the documents sent with the copy of a notice of the prosecution case to the Crown Court".

66.—(1) Section 41 of the Criminal Justice Act 1988 shall be amended as follows.

(2) In subsection (1)—
   (a) for the words preceding paragraph (a) there shall be substituted the words "Where a magistrates' court transfers to the Crown Court for trial proceedings against a person for an offence triable either way or a number of such offences, it may also transfer to the Crown Court for trial proceedings against a person for any summary offence with which he is charged and which—"; and
   (b) for the words from "appears" to "case" there shall be substituted the words "was sent to the person charged with the notice of the transfer of the proceedings".

(3) In subsection (2)—
   (a) for the words from "commits" to "indictment" there shall be substituted the words "transfers to the Crown Court for trial proceedings against a person"; and

(b) for the words "who is committed" there shall be substituted the words "in respect of whom proceedings are transferred".

(4) In subsection (4), for the words "committal of" there shall be substituted the words "transfer for trial of proceedings against".

Legal Aid Act 1988 (c 34)

67. In section 20 of the 1988 Act (authorities competent to grant criminal legal aid), in subsection (4), after paragraph (a) there shall be inserted the following paragraph—

"(aa) which proceeds with a view to transferring proceedings to the Crown Court for trial,".

68. In section 21 of the 1988 Act (availability of criminal legal aid)—
(a) in subsection (3)(a), for the words from "a person" to "his" there shall be substituted the words "proceedings against a person who is charged with murder are transferred to the Crown Court for trial, for that person's"; and
(b) in subsection (4), for the word "commits" there shall be substituted the words "transfers the proceedings against".

69.—(1) Schedule 3 to the 1988 Act (enforcement of contribution orders) shall be amended as follows.

(2) In paragraph 1(b)—
(a) for the words from "who" to "by a magistrates' court)" there shall be substituted the words "against whom proceedings were transferred for trial or who was committed for sentence"; and
(b) for the words "committed him" there shall be substituted the words "transferred the proceedings against him or committed him for sentence".

(3) In paragraph 9(b), for sub-subparagraph (i) there shall be substituted the following sub-subparagraph—

"(i) in theproceedings against the legally assisted person being transferred to the Crown Court for trial or in the legally assisted person being committed to the Crown Court for sentence, or".

(4) In paragraph 10(2)(b), for sub-subparagraph (i) there shall be substituted the following sub-subparagraph—

"(i) in the proceedings against the legally assisted person being transferred to the Crown Court for trial or in the legally assisted person being committed to the Crown Court for sentence, or".

Coroners Act 1988 (c 13)

70. In section 16 of the Coroners Act 1988 (adjournment of inquest)—
(a) in subsection (1)(b), for the words "examining justices" there shall be substituted the words "a magistrates' court which is to proceed with a view to transferring proceedings against that person for trial,"; and
(b) in subsection (8)—
(i) for the words "examining justices" there shall be substituted the words "a magistrates' court considering an application for dismissal under section 6 of the Magistrates' Courts Act 1980"; and
(ii) for the words from "person" to "committed" there shall be substituted the words "proceedings against the person charged are transferred".

71. In section 17 of the Coroners Act 1988 (supplementary provisions applying on adjournment of inquest)—
(a) in subsection (2)—
(i) after the word "Where" there shall be inserted the words "proceedings against"; and
(ii) for the words "is committed" there shall be substituted the words "are transferred"; and

(b) in subsection (3)(b), for the words "that person is committed" there shall be substituted the words "proceedings against that person are transferred".

War Crimes Act 1991 (c 13)

72. In the War Crimes Act 1991—
    (a) in section 1(4) (introducing the Schedule providing a procedure for use instead of committal proceedings for certain war crimes), the words "England, Wales or" shall be omitted; and
    (b) Part I of the Schedule (procedure for use in England and Wales instead of committal proceedings) shall be omitted.

Criminal Justice Act 1991 (c 53)

73.—(1) The 1991 Act shall be amended as follows.

(2) In section 53 (notices of transfer in certain cases involving children)—
    (a) in subsection (1)(a), for the words from "person" to "trial" there shall be substituted the words "proceedings against the person charged to be transferred for trial"; and
    (b) in subsection (2), for the words from "before" to the end, there shall be substituted the words "not later than the time at which the Director would be required to serve a notice of the prosecution case under section 5 of the Magistrates' Courts Act 1980,".

(3) In paragraph 4 of Schedule 6 (procedure for notices of transfer)—
    (a) in sub-paragraph (1)(a) for the words "a statement of the evidence" there shall be substituted the words "copies of the documents containing the evidence (including oral evidence)"; and
    (b) after sub-paragraph (1) there shall be inserted the following sub-paragraph—

"(1A) Regulations under sub-paragraph (1)(a) above may provide that there shall be no requirement for copies of any documents referred to in the documents sent with the notice of transfer as having already been supplied to accompany the copy of the notice of transfer.".

(4) In paragraph 5 of Schedule 6 (applications for dismissal), in sub-paragraph (7), for the words from "a refusal" to the end there shall be substituted the words "the dismissal of a charge or charges against an accused under section 6 of the Magistrates' Courts Act 1980.".

(5) In paragraph 6 of Schedule 6 (reporting restrictions), in sub-paragraph (8), for the words "sub-paragraphs (5) and (6)" there shall be substituted the words "sub-paragraphs (5) and (7)".

Sexual Offences (Amendment) Act 1992 (c 34)

74. In section 6(3)(c) of the 1992 Act, for the words "commits him" there shall be substituted the words "transfers proceedings against him".

Definitions For "magistrates' court" and "London commission area", see the Magistrates' Courts Act 1980, s 150(1); for "age", see s 150(5) of that Act; for "offence", see s 150(6) of that Act.
References See para 3.18.

SCHEDULE 5

Section 45

MAGISTRATES' COURTS: DEALING WITH CASES WHERE ACCUSED PLEADS GUILTY

Non-appearance of accused: plea of guilty

1. For section 12 of the Magistrates' Courts Act 1980 ("the 1980 Act") there shall be substituted the following section—

"12 Non-appearance of accused: plea of guilty

(1) This section shall apply where—
    (a) a summons has been issued requiring a person to appear before a magistrates' court, other than a youth court, to answer to an information for a summary offence, not being—
        (i) an offence for which the accused is liable to be sentenced to be imprisoned for a term exceeding 3 months; or
        (ii) an offence specified in an order made by the Secretary of State by statutory instrument; and
    (b) the clerk of the court is notified by or on behalf of the prosecutor that the documents mentioned in subsection (3) below have been served upon the accused with the summons.

(2) The reference in subsection (1)(a) above to the issue of a summons requiring a person to appear before a magistrates' court other than a youth court includes a reference to the issue of a summons requiring a person who has attained the age of 16 at the time when it is issued to appear before a youth court.

(3) The documents referred to in subsection (1)(b) above are—
    (a) a notice containing such statement of the effect of this section as may be prescribed;
    (b) a concise statement in the prescribed form of such facts relating to the charge as will be placed before the court by or on behalf of the prosecutor if the accused pleads guilty without appearing before the court; and
    (c) if any information relating to the accused will or may, in those circumstances, be placed before the court by or on behalf of the prosecutor, a notice containing or describing that information.

(4) Where the clerk of the court receives a notification in writing purporting to be given by the accused or by a legal representative acting on his behalf that the accused desires to plead guilty without appearing before the court—
    (a) the clerk of the court shall inform the prosecutor of the receipt of the notification; and
    (b) the following provisions of this section shall apply.

(5) If at the time and place appointed for the trial or adjourned trial of the information—
    (a) the accused does not appear; and
    (b) it is proved to the satisfaction of the court, on oath or in such manner as may be prescribed, that the documents mentioned in subsection (3) above have been served upon the accused with the summons,
the court may, subject to section 11(3) and (4) above and subsections (6) to (8) below, proceed to hear and dispose of the case in the absence of the accused, whether or not the prosecutor is also absent, in like manner as if both parties had appeared and the accused had pleaded guilty.

(6) If at any time before the hearing the clerk of the court receives an indication in writing purporting to be given by or on behalf of the accused that he wishes to withdraw the notification—
    (a) the clerk of the court shall inform the prosecutor of the withdrawal; and
    (b) the court shall deal with the information as if the notification had not been given.

(7) Before accepting the plea of guilty and convicting the accused under subsection (5) above, the court shall cause the following to be read out before the court by the clerk of the court, namely—
    (a) the statement of facts served upon the accused with the summons;

    (b)   any information contained in a notice so served, and any information described in such a notice and produced by or on behalf of the prosecutor;

    (c)   the notification under subsection (4) above; and

    (d)   any submission received with the notification which the accused wishes to be brought to the attention of the court with a view to mitigation of sentence.

(8)   If the court proceeds under subsection (5) above to hear and dispose of the case in the absence of the accused, the court shall not permit—

    (a)   any other statement with respect to any facts relating to the offence charged; or

    (b)   any other information relating to the accused,

to be made or placed before the court by or on behalf of the prosecutor except on a resumption of the trial after an adjournment under section 10(3) above.

(9)   If the court decides not to proceed under subsection (5) above to hear and dispose of the case in the absence of the accused, it shall adjourn or further adjourn the trial for the purpose of dealing with the information as if the notification under subsection (4) above had not been given.

(10)   In relation to an adjournment on the occasion of the accused's conviction in his absence under subsection (5) above or to an adjournment required by subsection (9) above, the notice required by section 10(2) above shall include notice of the reason for the adjournment.

(11)   No notice shall be required by section 10(2) above in relation to an adjournment—

    (a)   which is for not more than 4 weeks; and

    (b)   the purpose of which is to enable the court to proceed under subsection (5) above at a later time.

(12)   No order shall be made under subsection (1) above unless a draft of the order has been laid before and approved by resolution of each House of Parliament.

(13)   Any such document as is mentioned in subsection (3) above may be served in Scotland with a summons which is so served under the Summary Jurisdiction (Process) Act 1881.".

Application of section 12 procedure where accused appears

2.   After section 12 of the 1980 Act there shall be inserted the following section—

"12A Application of section 12 where accused appears

(1)   Where the clerk of the court has received such a notification as is mentioned in subsection (4) of section 12 above but the accused nevertheless appears before the court at the time and place appointed for the trial or adjourned trial, the court may, if he consents, proceed under subsection (5) of that section as if he were absent.

(2)   Where the clerk of the court has not received such a notification and the accused appears before the court at that time and place and informs the court that he desires to plead guilty, the court may, if he consents, proceed under section 12(5) above as if he were absent and the clerk had received such a notification.

(3)   For the purposes of subsections (1) and (2) above, subsections (6) to (11) of section 12 above shall apply with the modifications mentioned in subsection (4) or, as the case may be, subsection (5) below.

(4)   The modifications for the purposes of subsection (1) above are that—

    (a)   before accepting the plea of guilty and convicting the accused under subsection (5) of section 12 above, the court shall afford the accused an opportunity to make an oral submission with a view to mitigation of sentence; and

(b)   where he makes such a submission, subsection (7)(d) of that section shall not apply.

(5)   The modifications for the purposes of subsection (2) above are that—

(a)   subsection (6) of section 12 above shall apply as if any reference to the notification under subsection (4) of that section were a reference to the consent under subsection (2) above;

(b)   subsection (7)(c) and (d) of that section shall not apply; and

(c)   before accepting the plea of guilty and convicting the accused under subsection (5) of that section, the court shall afford the accused an opportunity to make an oral submission with a view to mitigation of sentence.".

Consequential amendments

3.—(1) In consequence of the amendments made by paragraphs 1 and 2 above the Magistrates' Courts Act 1980 shall be further amended as follows.

(2)   For section 13(4), there shall be substituted the following subsection—

"(4)   This section shall not apply to an adjournment on the occasion of the accused's conviction in his absence under subsection (5) of section 12 above or to an adjournment required by subsection (9) of that section.".

(3)   In section 13(5), for "12(2)" there shall be substituted "12(5)".

(4)   In section 155(2), for "12(8)" there shall be substituted "12(13)".

Definitions   For "clerk of the court", see the Magistrates' Courts Act 1980; for "magistrates' court", see s 148(1) of that Act; for "legal representative" and "prescribed", see s 150(1) of that Act; for "offence", see s 150(5) of that Act.
References   See para 3.18.

SCHEDULE 6

Section 114

CERTIFICATION OF PRISONER CUSTODY OFFICERS: SCOTLAND

Preliminary

1.   In this Schedule—
"certificate" means a certificate under section 114 of this Act;
"the relevant functions", in relation to a certificate, means the escort functions or custodial duties authorised by the certificate.

Issue of certificates

2.—(1) The Secretary of State may, on the application of any person, issue a certificate in respect of that person.

(2)   The Secretary of State shall not issue a certificate on any such application unless he is satisfied that the applicant—

(a)   is a fit and proper person to perform the relevant functions; and

(b)   has received training to such standard as he may consider appropriate for the performance of those functions.

(3)   Where the Secretary of State issues a certificate, then, subject to any suspension under paragraph 3 or revocation under paragraph 4 below, it shall continue in force until such date or the occurrence of such event as may be specified in the certificate.

(4)   A certificate authorising the performance of both escort functions and custodial duties may specify different dates or events as respects those functions and duties respectively.

Suspension of certificate

3.—(1) This paragraph applies where at any time—

    (a) in the case of a prisoner custody officer acting in pursuance of prisoner escort arrangements, it appears to the prisoner escort monitor for the area concerned that the officer is not a fit and proper person to perform escort functions;

    (b) in the case of a prisoner custody officer performing custodial duties at a contracted out prison, it appears to the controller of that prison that the officer is not a fit and proper person to perform custodial duties; or

    (c) in the case of a prisoner custody officer performing contracted out functions at a directly managed prison, it appears to the governor of that prison that the officer is not a fit and proper person to perform custodial duties.

(2) The prisoner escort monitor, controller or governor may—

    (a) refer the matter to the Secretary of State for a decision under paragraph 4 below; and

    (b) in such circumstances as may be prescribed by prison rules, suspend the officer's certificate so far as it authorises the performance of escort functions or, as the case may be, custodial duties pending that decision.

Revocation of certificate

4. Where at any time (whether on a reference to him under paragraph 3(2)(a) above or otherwise) it appears to the Secretary of State that a prisoner custody officer is not a fit and proper person to perform escort functions or custodial duties, he may revoke that officer's certificate so far as it authorises the performance of those functions or duties.

False statements

5. If any person, for the purpose of obtaining a certificate for himself or for any other person—

    (a) makes a statement which he knows to be false in a material particular; or

    (b) recklessly makes a statement which is false in a material particular,

he shall be guilty of an offence and liable on summary conviction to a fine not exceeding level 4 on the standard scale.

Definitions   For "contracted out functions" and "directly managed prison" see s 112(7); for "contracted out prison", see s 106(4); for "custodial duties" and "prison rules" see s 117(1); for "escort functions", see s 102(1); for "prisoner custody officer", see s 114(1); for "prisoner escort arrangements", see s 102(4). Note as to "certificate" and "the relevant functions", para 1 above.
References   See para 8.8.

SCHEDULE 7

Section 122(2)

CERTIFICATION OF PRISONER CUSTODY OFFICERS:
NORTHERN IRELAND

Preliminary

1. In this Schedule—

    "certificate" means a certificate under section 122 of this Act;

    "the relevant functions", in relation to a certificate, means the escort functions authorised by the certificate.

Issue of certificates

2.—(1) Any person may apply to the Secretary of State for the issue of a certificate in respect of him.

(2)   The Secretary of State shall not issue a certificate on any such application unless he is satisfied that the applicant—

(a)   is a fit and proper person to perform the relevant functions; and

(b)   has received training to such standard as he may consider appropriate for the performance of those functions.

(3)   Where the Secretary of State issues a certificate, then, subject to any suspension under paragraph 3 or revocation under paragraph 4 below, it shall continue in force until such date or the occurrence of such event as may be specified in the certificate.

Suspension of certificate

3.—(1)   This paragraph applies where at any time it appears to the prisoner escort monitor for the area concerned, that a prisoner custody officer is not a fit and proper person to perform the escort functions.

(2)   The prisoner escort monitor may—

(a)   refer the matter to the Secretary of State for a decision under paragraph 4 below; and

(b)   in such circumstances as may be prescribed by regulations made by the Secretary of State, suspend the officer's certificate so far as it authorises the performance of escort functions.

(3)   The power to make regulations under this paragraph shall be exercisable by statutory instrument which shall be subject to annulment in pursuance of a resolution of either House of Parliament.

Revocation of certificate

4.   Where at any time it appears to the Secretary of State that a prisoner custody officer is not a fit and proper person to perform escort functions, he may revoke that officer's certificate so far as it authorises the performance of those functions.

False statements

5.   If any person, for the purpose of obtaining a certificate for himself or for any other person—

(a)   makes a statement which he knows to be false in a material particular; or

(b)   recklessly makes a statement which is false in a material particular,

he shall be liable on summary conviction to a fine not exceeding level 4 on the standard scale.

Definitions   For "prisoner escort monitor", see s 118(3); for "prisoner custody officer", see s 122(1); for "escort functions", see s 122(3); for "certificate" and "the relevant functions", para 1 above.

SCHEDULE 8

Section 157

INCREASE IN PENALTIES

PART I

INCREASE OF FINES FOR CERTAIN SEA FISHERIES OFFENCES

(1) Enactment creating offence	(2) Penalty enactments	(3) Old maximum fines	(4) New maximum fines
SEA FISHERIES (SHELLFISH) ACT 1967 (c 83)			
Offences under section 3(3) (dredging etc for shellfish in contravention of restrictions etc or without paying toll or royalty)	Section 3(3)	Level 2	Level 5
Offences under section 5(7) (obstruction of inspector or other person or refusal or failure to provide information to inspector etc)	Section 5(7)	Level 3	Level 5
Offences under section 7(4) (fishing, dredging etc in area where right of several fishery conferred or private oyster bed)	Section 7(4)	Level 3	Level 5
Offences under section 14(2) (contravention of order prohibiting the deposit or taking of shellfish, or importation of shellfish, or non-compliance with conditions of licences)	Section 14(2)	Level 4	Level 5
Offences under section 14(5) (obstruction of inspector)	Section 14(5)	Level 3	Level 5
Offences under section 16(1) (selling etc of oysters between certain dates)	Section 16(1)	Level 1	Level 4
Offences under section 17(1) (taking and selling etc of certain crabs)	Section 17(4)	Level 3	Level 5
Offences under section 17(3) (landing and selling etc of certain lobsters)	Section 17(4)	Level 3	Level 5

PART II

INCREASE OF FINES FOR CERTAIN MISUSE OF DRUGS OFFENCEs

(1) Enactment creating offence	(2) Penalty enactments	(3) Old maximum fines	(4) New maximum fines
MISUSE OF DRUGS ACT 1971 (c 38)			
Offences under section 4(2) committed in relation to Class C drugs (production, or being concerned in the production of, a controlled drug)	Schedule 4, column 6	£500	£2,500
Offences under section 4(3) committed in relation to Class C drugs (supplying or offering to supply a controlled drug or being concerned in the doing of either activity by another)	Schedule 4, column 6	£500	£2,500
Offences under section 5(2) committed in relation to Class B drugs (having possession of a controlled drug)	Schedule 4, column 5	£500	£2,500
Offences under section 5(2) committed in relation to Class C drugs (having possession of a controlled drug)	Schedule 4, column 6	£200	£1,000
Offences under section 5(3) committed in relation to Class C drugs (having possession of a controlled drug with intent to supply it to another)	Schedule 4, column 6	£500	£2,500
Offences under section 8 committed in relation to Class C drugs (being the occupier, or concerned in the management, of premises and permitting or suffering certain activities to take place there)	Schedule 4, column 6	£500	£2,500
Offences under section 12(6) committed in relation to Class C drugs (contravention of direction prohibiting practitioner etc from possessing, supplying etc controlled drugs)	Schedule 4, column 6	£500	£2,500
Offences under section 13(3) committed in relation to Class C drugs (contravention of direction prohibiting practitioner etc from prescribing, supplying etc controlled drugs)	Schedule 4, column 6	£500	£2,500

PART III

INCREASE IN PENALTIES FOR CERTAIN FIREARMS OFFENCES

(1) Enactment creating offence	(2) Penalty enactments	(3) Old maximum term of imprisonment	(4) New maximum term of imprisonment
FIREARMS ACT 1968 (c 27)			
Offences under section 1(1) committed in an aggravated form within the meaning of section 4(4) (possessing etc shortened shot gun or converted firearm without firearm certificate)	Schedule 6, column 4	5 years	7 years
Offences under section 1(1) in any other case (possessing etc firearms or ammunition without firearm certificate)	Schedule 6, column 4	3 years	5 years
Offences under section 2(1) (possessing etc shot gun without shot gun certificate)	Schedule 6, column 4	3 years	5 years
Offences under section 3(1) (trading in firearms without being registered as a firearms dealer)	Schedule 6, column 4	3 years	5 years
Offences under section 3(2) (selling firearms to person without a certificate)	Schedule 6, column 4	3 years	5 years
Offences under section 3(3) (repairing, testing etc firearm for person without a certificate)	Schedule 6, column 4	3 years	5 years
Offences under section 3(5) (falsifying certificate, etc, with view to acquisition of firearm)	Schedule 6, column 4	3 years	5 years
Offences under section 4(1) (shortening a shot gun)	Schedule 6, column 4	5 years	7 years
Offences under section 4(3) (conversion of firearms)	Schedule 6, column 4	5 years	7 years

(1) Enactment creating offence	(2) Penalty enactments	(3) Old maximum term of imprisonment	(4) New maximum term of imprisonment
Offences under section 5(1) (possessing or distributing prohibited weapons or ammunition)	Schedule 6, column 4	5 years	10 years
Offences under section 5(1A) (possessing or distributing other prohibited weapons)	Schedule 6, column 4	(a) On summary conviction, 3 months (b) On conviction on indictment, 2 years	(a) On summary conviction, 6 months (b) On conviction on indictment, 10 years
Offences under section 19 (carrying loaded firearm other than air weapon in public place)	Schedule 6, column 4	5 years	7 years
Offences under section 20(1) (trespassing with firearm other than air weapon in a building)	Schedule 6, column 4	5 years	7 years
Offences under section 21(4) (contravention of provisions denying firearms to ex-prisoners and the like)	Schedule 6, column 4	3 years	5 years
Offences under section 21(5) (supplying firearms to person denied them under section 21)	Schedule 6, column 4	3 years	5 years
Offences under section 42 (failure to comply with instructions in firearm certificate when transferring firearm to person other than registered dealer; failure to report transaction to police)	Schedule 6, column 4	3 years	5 years

FIREARMS (NORTHERN IRELAND) ORDER 1981 (SI 1981/155 (NI 2))

(1) Enactment creating offence	(2) Penalty enactments	(3) Old maximum term of imprisonment	(4) New maximum term of imprisonment
Offences under Article 3(1) (possessing etc firearms or ammunition without firearm certificate)	Schedule 2, column 4	3 years	5 years
Offences under Article 4(1) (trading in firearms without being registered as a firearms dealer)	Schedule 2, column 4	3 years	5 years
Offences under Article 4(2) (selling firearms to person without a certificate)	Schedule 2, column 4	3 years	5 years
Offences under Article 4(3) (repairing, testing etc firearm for person without a certificate)	Schedule 2, column 4	3 years	5 years
Offences under Article 4(4) (falsifying certificate, etc, with view to acquisition of firearm)	Schedule 2, column 4	3 years	5 years

(1) Enactment creating offence	(2) Penalty enactments	(3) Old maximum term of imprisonment	(4) New maximum term of imprisonmen
Offences under Article 5(1) (shortening a shot gun)	Schedule 2, column 4	5 years	7 years
Offences under Article 5(3) (conversion of firearms)	Schedule 2, column 4	5 years	7 years
Offences under Article 6(1) (possessing or distributing prohibited weapons or ammunition)	Schedule 2, column 4	5 years	10 years
Offences under Article 6(1A) (possessing or distributing other prohibited weapons)	Schedule 2, column 4	(a) On summary conviction, 3 months (b) On conviction on indictment, 2 years	(a) On summary conviction, 6 months (b) On conviction on indictment, 10 years
Offences under Article 22(5) (contravention of provisions denying firearms to ex-prisoners and the like)	Schedule 2, column 4	3 years	5 years
Offences under Article 22(7) (supplying firearms to person denied them under Article 22)	Schedule 2, column 4	3 years	5 years
Offences under Article 43 (failure to comply with instructions in firearm certificate when transferring firearm to person other than registered dealer; failure to report transaction to police)	Schedule 2, column 4	3 years	5 years

243

SCHEDULE 9

Section 168(1)

MINOR AMENDMENTS

Poaching: increase in penalties

1.—(1) The Game Act 1831 shall be amended as follows.

(2) In section 30 (trespassing in search or pursuit of game)—
   (a) for the words "level 1" there shall be substituted the words "level 3"; and
   (b) for the words "level 3" there shall be substituted the words "level 4".

(3) In section 32 (searching for or pursuing game with a gun and using violence, etc), for the words "level 4" there shall be substituted the words "level 5".

(4) The Game (Scotland) Act 1832 shall be amended as follows.

(5) In section 1 (trespassing in search or pursuit of game)—
   (a) for the words "level 1" there shall be substituted the words "level 3"; and
   (b) for the words "level 3" there shall be substituted the words "level 4".

(6) In section 6 (penalty for assaults on persons acting under the Act), for the words "level 1" there shall be substituted the words "level 3".

(7) The amendments made by this paragraph shall not apply to offences committed before this paragraph comes into force.

Sexual offences: procurement of women

2. In sections 2(1) and 3(1) of the Sexual Offences Act 1956 (procurement of women to have unlawful sexual intercourse by threats or false pretences), the word "unlawful" shall be omitted.

Electronic transmission of obscene material

3. In section 1(3) of the Obscene Publications Act 1959 (definition of publication for purposes of that Act), in paragraph (b), after the words "projects it" there shall be inserted the words ", or, where the matter is data stored electronically, transmits that data.".

Poaching: forfeiture of vehicles

4. After section 4 of the Game Laws (Amendment) Act 1960 there shall be inserted the following section—

"4A Forfeiture of vehicles

(1) Where a person is convicted of an offence under section thirty of the Game Act 1831 as one of five or more persons liable under that section and the court is satisfied that any vehicle belonging to him or in his possession or under his control at the relevant time has been used for the purpose of committing or facilitating the commission of the offence, the court may make an order for forfeiture under this subsection in respect of that vehicle.

(2) The court may make an order under subsection (1) above whether or not it also deals with the offender in respect of the offence in any other way and without regard to any restriction on forfeiture in any enactment.

(3) Facilitating the commission of the offence shall be taken for the purposes of subsection (1) above to include the taking of any steps after it has been committed for the purpose of—
   (a) avoiding apprehension or detection; or
   (b) removing from the land any person or property connected with the offence.

(4) An order under subsection (1) above shall operate to deprive the offender of his rights, if any, in the vehicle to which it relates, and the vehicle shall (if not already in their possession) be taken into the possession of the police.

(5) Where any vehicle has been forfeited under subsection (1) above, a magistrates' court may, on application by a claimant of the vehicle, other than the offender from whom it was forfeited under subsection (1) above, make an order for delivery of the vehicle to the applicant if it appears to the court that he is the owner of the vehicle.

(6) No application shall be made under subsection (5) above by any claimant of the vehicle after the expiration of six months from the date on which an order in respect of the vehicle was made under subsection (1) above.

(7) No such application shall succeed unless the claimant satisfies the court either that he had not consented to the offender having possession of the vehicle or that he did not know, and had no reason to suspect, that the vehicle was likely to be used for a purpose mentioned in subsection (1) above.

(8) An order under subsection (5) above shall not affect the right of any person to take, within the period of six months from the date of an order under subsection (5) above, proceedings for the recovery of the vehicle from the person in possession of it in pursuance of the order, but on the expiration of that period the right shall cease.

(9) The Secretary of State may make regulations for the disposal of vehicles, and for the application of the proceeds of sale of vehicles, forfeited under subsection (1) above where no application by a claimant of the property under subsection (5) above has been made within the period specified in subsection (6) above or no such application has succeeded.

(10) The regulations may also provide for the investment of money and the audit of accounts.

(11) The power to make regulations under subsection (9) above shall be exercisable by statutory instrument which shall be subject to annulment in pursuance of a resolution of either House of Parliament.

(12) In this section, "relevant time", in relation to a person convicted of an offence such as is mentioned in subsection (1) above, means the time when the vehicle was used for the purpose of committing or facilitating the commission of the offence, or the time of the issue of a summons in respect of the offence.".

Magistrates' courts' jurisdiction in cases involving children and young persons

5. In section 18 of the Children and Young Persons Act 1963 (jurisdiction of magistrates' courts in certain cases involving children and young persons)—

    (a) in paragraph (a), for the words "the age of seventeen" there shall be substituted the words "the age of eighteen"; and

    (b) in paragraph (b), for the words "the age of seventeen" there shall be substituted the words "the age of eighteen".

Service of documents by first class post

6.—(1) In section 9(8) of the Criminal Justice Act 1967 (which relates to the service of a written statement to be admitted as evidence in criminal proceedings)—

    (a) in paragraph (c), after the word "service" there shall be inserted the words "or by first class post"; and

    (b) in paragraph (d), after the word "service" there shall be inserted the words "or by first class post".

(2) In section 11(7) of the Criminal Justice Act 1967 (which provides for the means by which a notice of alibi may be given), after the word "service" there shall be inserted the words "or by first class post".

(3) In section 1 of the Road Traffic Offenders Act 1988 (which requires warning of prosecution for certain offences to be given), after subsection (1), there shall be inserted the following subsection—

> "(1A) A notice required by this section to be served on any person may be served on that person—
>
> > (a) by delivering it to him;
> > (b) by addressing it to him and leaving it at his last known address; or
> > (c) by sending it by registered post, recorded delivery service or first class post addressed to him at his last known address.".

Transfers of proceedings

7. In section 11 of the Criminal Justice Act 1967 (notice of alibi), in subsection (8)—
   (a) in the definition of "the prescribed period" (as amended by paragraph 2 of Schedule 2 to the Criminal Justice Act 1987), for the words "section 4 of the Criminal Justice Act 1987" there shall be substituted the words "a relevant transfer provision"; and
   (b) after that definition there shall be inserted the following definition—

> ""relevant transfer provision" means—
> > (a) section 4 of the Criminal Justice Act 1987; or
> > (b) section 53 of the Criminal Justice Act 1991.".

Offences aggravated by possession of firearms

8. In Schedule 1 to the Firearms Act 1968 (which lists the offences to which section 17(2) (possession of firearms when committing or being arrested for specified offences) relates)—
   (a) in paragraph 4, after the word "Theft" there shall be inserted the word "robbery"; and
   (b) after paragraph 5, there shall be inserted the following paragraphs—

> "5A. An offence under section 90(1) of the Criminal Justice Act 1991 (assaulting prisoner custody officer).
>
> 5B. An offence under section 13(1) of the Criminal Justice and Public Order Act 1994 (assaulting secure training centre custody officer).".

Notice of proceedings

9. In section 34(2) of the Children and Young Persons Act 1969 (which requires notice of certain proceedings to be given to a probation officer), for the words "the age of seventeen" there shall be substituted the words "the age of eighteen".

Treatment of mental condition of offenders placed on probation

10.—(1) Paragraph 5 of Schedule 1A to the Powers of Criminal Courts Act 1973 (requirement in probation order for treatment of offender's mental condition) shall be amended as follows.

(2) In sub-paragraph (2)—
   (a) after the words "such part" there shall be inserted the words "or parts"; and
   (b) after the words "medical practitioner" there shall be inserted the words "or a chartered psychologist (or both, for different parts)".

(3) In sub-paragraph (3)(c), after the words "medical practitioner" there shall be inserted the words "or chartered psychologist (or both)".

(4) In sub-paragraphs (6) and (8), after the words "medical practitioner" (wherever they occur) there shall be inserted the words "or chartered psychologist".

(5) In sub-paragraph (10), after the words "In this paragraph" there shall be inserted the words "—

> "chartered psychologist" means a person for the time being listed in the British Psychological Society's Register of Chartered Psychologists; and".

Rehabilitation of offenders placed on probation

11.—(1) In section 5 of the Rehabilitation of Offenders Act 1974 (rehabilitation periods for particular sentences)—

    (a) in Table A in subsection (2), in the entry relating to fines or other sentences subject to rehabilitation under that Act, after the words "subsections (3)" there shall be inserted the words ", (4A)".

    (b) in subsection (4), the words "or placed on probation," and "or probation order" shall be omitted; and

    (c) after subsection (4), there shall be inserted the following subsection—

"(4A) Where in respect of a conviction a person was placed on probation, the rehabilitation period applicable to the sentence shall be—

    (a) in the case of a person aged eighteen years or over at the date of his conviction, five years from the date of conviction;

    (b) in the case of a person aged under the age of eighteen years at the date of his conviction, two and a half years from the date of conviction or a period beginning with the date of conviction and ending when the probation order ceases or ceased to have effect, whichever is the longer.".

(2) The amendments made by this paragraph shall apply only in relation to persons placed on probation after the date on which this paragraph comes into force.

Transfers of proceedings

12. In section 3 of the Bail Act 1976 (general provisions)—

    (a) in subsection (8A) (inserted by paragraph 9 of Schedule 2 to the Criminal Justice Act 1987), for the words "section 4 of the Criminal Justice Act 1987" there shall be substituted the words "a relevant transfer provision"; and

    (b) after subsection (9) there shall be inserted the following subsection—

"(10) In subsection (8A) above "relevant transfer provision" means—

    (a) section 4 of the Criminal Justice Act 1987, or

    (b) section 53 of the Criminal Justice Act 1991.".

Anonymity of victims of certain offences

13. In section 4 of the Sexual Offences (Amendment) Act 1976 (anonymity of victims in rape etc cases), after subsection (6) there shall be inserted the following subsection—

"(6A) For the purposes of this section, where it is alleged or there is an accusation that an offence of incitement to rape or conspiracy to rape has been committed, the person who is alleged to have been the intended victim of the rape shall be regarded as the alleged victim of the incitement or conspiracy or, in the case of an accusation, as the complainant.".

Execution of warrants for non-payment

14.—(1) In section 38A(6) of the Criminal Law Act 1977 (execution of warrants for imprisonment for non-payment of fine), for the words "the age of 17 years" there shall be substituted the words "the age of 18 years".

(2) In section 38B(6) of the Criminal Law Act 1977 (execution of warrants for commitment for non-payment of due sum), for the words "the age of 17 years" there shall be substituted the words "the age of 18 years".

Committals for sentence

15. In section 38 of the Magistrates' Courts Act 1980 (power of magistrates' court to commit offender to Crown Court for sentence), in subsection (2)(b)—

    (a) the words from "committed" to "21 years old" shall be omitted; and

    (b) for the words "sentence of imprisonment" there shall be substituted the words "custodial sentence".

Conditional or absolute discharge: appeal to Crown Court

16. In section 108(1A) of the Magistrates' Courts Act 1980 (right of appeal to Crown Court in case of conditional or absolute discharge), for the words "Section 13" there shall be substituted the words "Section 1C".

Transfers of proceedings

17. In section 76 of the Supreme Court Act 1981 (alteration by Crown Court of place of trial) (as amended by paragraph 10 of Schedule 2 to the Criminal Justice Act 1987)—

    (a) in subsection (1), for the words "section 4 of the Criminal Justice Act 1987" there shall be substituted the words "a relevant transfer provision";

    (b) in subsection (3), for the words "section 4 of the Criminal Justice Act 1987" there shall be substituted the words "a relevant transfer provision"; and

    (c) after subsection (4) there shall be inserted the following subsection—

"(5) In this section "relevant transfer provision" means—

    (a) section 4 of the Criminal Justice Act 1987, or

    (b) section 53 of the Criminal Justice Act 1991.".

The amendments made by this paragraph shall cease to have effect on the coming into force of the amendments made by paragraph 51 of Schedule 4 to this Act.

Transfers of proceedings

18. In section 77 of the Supreme Court Act 1981 (date of trial) (as amended by paragraph 11 of Schedule 2 to the Criminal Justice Act 1987)—

    (a) in subsection (1), for the words "section 4 of the Criminal Justice Act 1987" there shall be substituted the words "a relevant transfer provision";

    (b) in subsection (2), after the words "committed by a magistrates' court" there shall be inserted the words "or in respect of whom a notice of transfer under a relevant transfer provision has been given";

    (c) in subsection (3), after the words "committal for trial" there shall be inserted the words "or of a notice of transfer"; and

    (d) after subsection (3), there shall be inserted the following subsection—

"(4) In this section "relevant transfer provision" means—

    (a) section 4 of the Criminal Justice Act 1987, or

    (b) section 53 of the Criminal Justice Act 1991.".

The amendments made by this paragraph shall cease to have effect on the coming into force of the amendments made by paragraph 52 of Schedule 4 to this Act.

Transfers of proceedings

19. In section 81 of the Supreme Court Act 1981 (bail by Crown Court)—

    (a) in subsection (1)(a) (as amended by paragraph 12 of Schedule 2 to the Criminal Justice Act 1987), for the words "section 4 of the Criminal Justice Act 1987" there shall be substituted the words "a relevant transfer provision"; and

    (b) after subsection (6), there shall be inserted the following subsection—

"(7) In subsection (1) above "relevant transfer provision" means—

    (a) section 4 of the Criminal Justice Act 1987, or

    (b) section 53 of the Criminal Justice Act 1991.".

Electronic transmission of obscene material (Scotland)

20. In section 51(8) of the Civic Government (Scotland) Act 1982, after the words "otherwise reproducing" there shall be inserted the words ", or, where the material is data stored electronically, transmitting that data".

Fines for breach of attendance centre orders or rules

21. In section 19 of the Criminal Justice Act 1982 (breach of attendance centre orders or rules), for the subsection (3A) inserted by section 67(5) of the Criminal Justice Act 1991 there shall be substituted the following subsection—

"(3A) A fine imposed under subsection (3) above shall be deemed, for the purposes of any enactment, to be a sum adjudged to be paid by a conviction.".

Video recordings

22. In section 1 of the Video Recordings Act 1984 (which provides for the interpretation of, among other terms, "video work" and "video recordings")—
- (a) in subsection (2), in paragraph (a), the word "or" before the words "magnetic tape" shall be omitted and after those words there shall be inserted the words "or any other device capable of storing data electronically"; and
- (b) in subsection (3), the word "or" before the words "magnetic tape" shall be omitted and after those words there shall be inserted the words "or any other device capable of storing data electronically".

Standard period of validity of search warrants

23. In the following enactments there shall be omitted the words from "within" to "warrant" (which prescribe the period of validity of warrants under those enactments for which section 16(3) of the Police and Criminal Evidence Act 1984 prescribes a standard period of one month), namely—
- (a) section 4(2) of the Protection of Children Act 1978; and
- (b) section 17(1) of the Video Recordings Act 1984.

Transfers of proceedings

24. In section 62(10) of the Police and Criminal Evidence Act 1984 (power of court to draw inferences from failure of accused to consent to provide intimate sample), after paragraph (a) there shall be inserted the following paragraph—

"(aa) a judge, in deciding whether to grant an application made by the accused under—
- (i) section 6 of the Criminal Justice Act 1987 (application for dismissal of charge of serious fraud in respect of which notice of transfer has been given under section 4 of that Act); or
- (ii) paragraph 5 of Schedule 6 to the Criminal Justice Act 1991 (application for dismissal of charge of violent or sexual offence involving child in respect of which notice of transfer has been given under section 53 of that Act); and".

Transfers of proceedings

25. In section 16 of the Prosecution of Offences Act 1985 (defence costs)—
- (a) in subsection (2)(aa) (inserted by paragraph 14 of Schedule 2 to the Criminal Justice Act 1987), for the words "section 4 of the Criminal Justice Act 1987" there shall be substituted the words "a relevant transfer provision"; and
- (b) after subsection (11) there shall be inserted the following subsection—

"(12) In subsection (2)(aa) "relevant transfer provision" means—
- (a) section 4 of the Criminal Justice Act 1987, or
- (b) section 53 of the Criminal Justice Act 1991.".

Award of costs against accused

26. In section 18(5) of the Prosecution of Offences Act 1985 (award of costs against accused), for the words "the age of seventeen" there shall be substituted the words "the age of eighteen".

Transfers of proceedings

27. In section 22 of the Prosecution of Offences Act 1985 (time limits for preliminary stages of criminal proceedings), in subsection (11), in the definition of "custody of the Crown Court", after paragraph (c) (inserted by paragraph 104 of Schedule 15 to the Criminal Justice Act 1988), there shall be inserted the following paragraph, preceded by the word ", or namely—

> "(d) paragraph 2(1)(a) of Schedule 6 to the Criminal Justice Act 1991 (custody after transfer order in certain cases involving children).".

Confiscation orders in drug trafficking cases: variation of sentences

28. In section 1A of the Drug Trafficking Offences Act 1986 (inserted by section 8 of the Criminal Justice Act 1993) (power of court to postpone determinations required before a confiscation order can be made), after subsection (9) there shall be inserted the following subsection—

> "(9A) Where the court has sentenced the defendant under subsection (7) above during the specified period it may, after the end of that period, vary the sentence by imposing a fine or making any such order as is mentioned in section 1(5)(b)(ii) or (iii) of this Act so long as it does so within a period corresponding to that allowed by section 47(2) or (3) of the Supreme Court Act 1981 (time allowed for varying a sentence) but beginning with the end of the specified period.".

Transfer of fraud cases

29. In section 4 of the Criminal Justice Act 1987 (transfer of certain fraud cases to Crown Court), in subsection (1)(b)(ii), for the words "seriousness and complexity" there shall be substituted the words "seriousness or complexity".

Fraud cases: preparatory hearings

30. In section 7 of the Criminal Justice Act 1987 (preparatory hearings for certain fraud cases), in subsection (1), for the words "seriousness and complexity" there shall be substituted the words "seriousness or complexity".

Transfers of proceedings

31. In section 25(1) of the Criminal Justice Act 1988 (principle to be followed by court in certain proceedings), in paragraph (a), after head (iii) there shall be inserted the following—

> "(iv) on the hearing of an application under paragraph 5 of Schedule 6 to the Criminal Justice Act 1991 (applications for dismissal of charges in certain cases involving children transferred from magistrates' court to Crown Court); or".

Evidence through television links

32. In section 32 of the Criminal Justice Act 1988 (evidence through television links), in subsection (3B) (inserted by section 55(4) of the Criminal Justice Act 1991), for the words "subsection (3) above" there shall be substituted the words "subsection (3A) above".

Competence of children

33. In section 33A of the Criminal Justice Act 1988 (inserted by section 52(1) of the Criminal Justice Act 1991), after subsection (2) there shall be inserted the following subsection—

> "(2A) A child's evidence shall be received unless it appears to the court that the child is incapable of giving intelligible testimony.".

Reviews of sentencing

34. In section 35 of the Criminal Justice Act 1988 (kinds of case referable for review of sentence)—

(a) in subsection (3), for the words following "case" there shall be substituted the following words—

  "—
   (a) of a description specified in an order under this section; or
   (b) in which sentence is passed on a person—
      (i) for an offence triable only on indictment; or
      (ii) for an offence of a description specified in an order under this section"; and

(b) in subsection (4), after the word "case", there shall be inserted the words "of a description specified in the order or to any case".

Assaulting prisoner custody officer triable with indictable offence

35. In section 40(3) of the Criminal Justice Act 1988 (summary offences triable with indictable offences), after paragraph (a), there shall be inserted the following paragraphs—

   "(aa) an offence under section 90(1) of the Criminal Justice Act 1991 (assaulting a prisoner custody officer);
   (ab) an offence under section 13(1) of the Criminal Justice and Public Order Act 1994 (assaulting a secure training centre custody officer)".

Confiscation orders: va. iation of sentence

36. In section 72A of the Criminal Justice Act 1988 (inserted by section 28 of the Criminal Justice Act 1993) (power of court to postpone determinations required before a confiscation order can be made), after subsection (9) there shall be inserted the following subsection—

   "(9A Where the court has sentenced the defendant under subsection (7) above during the specified period it may, after the end of that period, vary the sentence by imposing a fine or making any such order as is mentioned in section 72(5)(b) or (c) above so long as it does so within a period corresponding to that allowed by section 47(2) or (3) of the Supreme Court Act 1981 (time allowed for varying a sentence) but beginning with the end of the specified period.".

Extradition from the United Kingdom

37.—(1) The Extradition Act 1989 shall be amended as follows.

(2) In section 2(4) (law of, and conduct in, parts or dependencies of foreign States)—
   (a) for the words "subsections (1) to (3) above" there shall be substituted the words "this Act, except Schedule 1"; and
   (b) at the end there shall be inserted the following paragraph preceded by the word "; but"—
      (d) reference shall be made to the law of the colony or dependency of a foreign state or of a designated Commonwealth country, and not (where different) to the law of the foreign state or Commonwealth country, to determine the level of punishment applicable to conduct in that colony or dependency.".

(3) In section 7 (procedure for making and implementing extradition requests)—
   (a) in subsection (1)—
      (i) after the word "made" there shall be inserted the words "to the Secretary of State";
      (ii) for paragraph (a) there shall be substituted the following paragraph—

      "(a) by—
         (i) an authority in a foreign state which appears to the Secretary of State to have the function of making extradition requests in that foreign state, or
         (ii) some person recognised by the Secretary of State as a diplomatic or consular representative of a foreign state; or" and

(iii) after paragraph (b), there shall be inserted the words—

"and an extradition request may be made by facsimile transmission and an authority to proceed issued without waiting to receive the original";

(b) in subsection (2)—

   (i) in paragraph (c), after the word "warrant" there shall be inserted the words "or a duly authenticated copy of a warrant"; and

   (ii) in paragraph (d), after the word "certificate" there shall be inserted the words "or a duly authenticated copy of a certificate"; and

(c) after subsection (6), there shall be inserted the following subsection—

"(7) Where an extradition request is made by facsimile transmission this Act (including subsection (2) above) shall have effect as if the foreign documents so sent were the originals used to make the transmission and receivable in evidence accordingly.".

Remands and committals of young persons to secure accommodation

38. In section 21 of the Children Act 1989 (provision of accommodation for children on remand, etc), in subsection (2)(c)(i), after the words "on remand" there shall be inserted the words "(within the meaning of the section)".

Non-intimate samples: samples of hair

39. In Article 63 of the Police and Criminal Evidence (Northern Ireland) Order 1989 (regulation of taking of non-intimate samples), at the end, there shall be inserted the following paragraph—

"(10) Where a sample of hair other than pubic hair is to be taken the sample may be taken either by cutting hairs or by plucking hairs with their roots so long as no more are plucked than the person taking the sample reasonably considers to be necessary (in point of quantity or quality) for the purpose of enabling information to be produced by means of analysis used or to be used in relation to the sample.".

Pre-sentence reports

40.—(1) The Criminal Justice Act 1991 shall be amended as follows.

(2) In section 3 (requirement to obtain pre-sentence reports before passing custodial sentences)—

(a) in subsection (2), the words from the beginning to "indictment," shall be omitted;

(b) after subsection (2), there shall be inserted the following subsection—

"(2A) In the case of an offender under the age of eighteen years, save where the offence or any other offence associated with it is triable only on indictment, the court shall not form such an opinion as is mentioned in subsection (2) above or subsection (4A) below unless there exists a previous pre-sentence report obtained in respect of the offender and the court has had regard to the information contained in that report, or, if there is more than one such report, the most recent report.";

(c) in subsection (4)—

   (i) the words from "which is" to "applies" shall be omitted;

   (ii) for the words "comply with that subsection" there shall be substituted the words "obtain and consider a pre-sentence report before forming an opinion referred to in subsection (1) above"; and

   (iii) in paragraph (a), after the word "shall" there shall be inserted the words ", subject to subsection (4A) below,"; and

(d) after subsection (4) there shall be inserted the following subsection—

"(4A) Subsection (4)(a) above does not apply if the court is of the opinion—

(a) that the court below was justified in forming an opinion that it was unnecessary to obtain a pre-sentence report, or

(b)   that, although the court below was not justified in forming that opinion, in the circumstances of the case at the time it is before the court, it is unnecessary to obtain a pre-sentence report.".

(3) In section 7 (requirement to obtain pre-sentence reports before passing certain community sentences)—

   (a)   in subsection (3), at the beginning, there shall be inserted the words "Subject to subsection (3A) below,";

   (b)   after subsection (3), there shall be inserted the following subsections—

"(3A)   Subsection (3) above does not apply if, in the circumstances of the case, the court is of the opinion that it is unnecessary to obtain a pre-sentence report.

(3B)   In the case of an offender under the age of eighteen years, save where the offence or any other offence associated with it is triable only on indictment, the court shall not form such an opinion as is mentioned in subsection (3A) above or subsection (5) below unless there exists a previous pre-sentence report obtained in respect of the offender and the court has had regard to the information contained in that report, or, if there is more than one such report, the most recent report.";

   (c)   in subsection (4)—

      (i)   for the words "comply with" there shall be substituted the words "obtain and consider a pre-sentence report before forming an opinion referred to in"; and

      (ii)   in paragraph (a), after the word "shall" there shall be inserted the words ", subject to subsection (5) below,";

   (d)   after subsection (4) there shall be inserted the following subsection—

"(5)   Subsection (4)(a) above does not apply if the court is of the opinion—

      (a)   that the court below was justified in forming an opinion that it was unnecessary to obtain a pre-sentence report, or

      (b)   that, although the court below was not justified in forming that opinion, in the circumstances of the case at the time it is before the court, it is unnecessary to obtain a pre-sentence report.".

Curfew orders

41. In section 12 of the Criminal Justice Act 1991 (curfew orders) after subsection (4) there shall be inserted the following subsection—

"(4A)   A court shall not make a curfew order unless the court has been notified by the Secretary of State that arrangements for monitoring the offender's whereabouts are available in the area in which the place proposed to be specified in the order is situated and the notice has not been withdrawn.".

Fines

42.—(1) Sections 18 and 20 of the Criminal Justice Act 1991 (which relate respectively to the fixing of fines and financial circumstances orders) shall be amended as provided in sub-paragraphs (2) and (3) below.

(2) In section 18—

   (a)   for subsection (1), there shall be substituted the following subsection—

"(1)   Before fixing the amount of any fine to be imposed on an offender who is an individual, a court shall inquire into his financial circumstances."; and

   (b)   in subsection (3), after the word "fine" there shall be inserted the words "to be imposed on an offender (whether an individual or other person)".

(3) In section 20, in subsections (1), (1A), (1B), (1C), (2) and (3) for the words "a person" and "any person" there shall be substituted the words "an individual" and "any individual".

(4) In section 57(4) of that Act (application to local authorities of power to order fines to be paid by a parent or guardian), paragraph (b) shall be omitted.

(5) The amendments made by this paragraph apply in relation to offenders convicted (but not sentenced) before the date on which this paragraph comes into force as they apply in relation to offenders convicted after that date.

False statements as to financial circumstances

43. After section 20 of the Criminal Justice Act 1991 there shall be inserted the following section—

"20A False statements as to financial circumstances

(1) A person who is charged with an offence who, in furnishing a statement of his financial circumstances in response to an official request—
   (a) makes a statement which he knows to be false in a material particular;
   (b) recklessly furnishes a statement which is false in a material particular; or
   (c) knowingly fails to disclose any material fact,
shall be liable on summary conviction to imprisonment for a term not exceeding three months or a fine not exceeding level 4 on the standard scale or both.

(2) For the purposes of this section an official request is a request which—
   (a) is made by the clerk of the magistrates' court or the appropriate officer of the Crown Court, as the case may be; and
   (b) is expressed to be made for informing the court, in the event of his being convicted, of his financial circumstances for the purpose of determining the amount of any fine the court may impose.

(3) Proceedings in respect of an offence under this section may, notwithstanding anything in section 127(1) of the 1980 Act (limitation of time), be commenced at any time within two years from the date of the commission of the offence or within six months from its first discovery by the prosecutor, whichever period expires the earlier.".

Effect of previous probation orders and discharges

44.—(1) Section 29 of the Criminal Justice Act 1991 (as substituted by section 66(6) of the Criminal Justice Act 1993) (effect of previous convictions and offending while on bail and treatment of certain orders as sentences and convictions) shall be amended as follows.

(2) In subsection (4), for the words "conditional discharge order" there shall be substituted the words "an order discharging the offender absolutely or conditionally".

(3) After subsection (4) there shall be inserted the following subsections—

"(5) A conditional discharge order made after 30th September 1992 (which, by virtue of section 1A of the Powers of Criminal Courts Act 1973, would otherwise not be a sentence for the purposes of this section) is to be treated as a sentence for those purposes.

(6) A conviction in respect of which an order discharging the offender absolutely or conditionally was made after 30th September 1992 (which, by virtue of section 1C of the Powers of Criminal Courts Act 1973, would otherwise not be a conviction for those purposes) is to be treated as a conviction for those purposes.".

(4) The amendments made by this paragraph shall apply in relation to offenders convicted (but not sentenced) before the date on which this paragraph comes into force as they apply in relation to offenders convicted after that date.

Sexual offences

45.—(1) In section 31(1) of the Criminal Justice Act 1991 (which defines, amongst other expressions, "sexual offence"), for that definition, there shall be substituted the following definition—
   ""sexual offence" means any of the following—
      (a) an offence under the Sexual Offences Act 1956, other than an offence under section 30, 31 or 33 to 36 of that Act;

(b) an offence under section 128 of the Mental Health Act 1959;

(c) an offence under the Indecency with Children Act 1960;

(d) an offence under section 9 of the Theft Act 1968 of burglary with intent to commit rape;

(e) an offence under section 54 of the Criminal Law Act 1977;

(f) an offence under the Protection of Children Act 1978;

(g) an offence under section 1 of the Criminal Law Act 1977 of conspiracy to commit any of the offences in paragraphs (a) to (f) above;

(h) an offence under section 1 of the Criminal Attempts Act 1981 of attempting to commit any of those offences;

(i) an offence of inciting another to commit any of those offences;".

(2) The amendment made by this paragraph shall apply in relation to offenders convicted (but not sentenced) before the date on which this paragraph comes into force as it applies in relation to offenders convicted after that date.

Discretionary life prisoners

46.—(1) In section 34 of the Criminal Justice Act 1991 (duty to release discretionary life prisoners after they have served the relevant part of their sentence and the Parole Board has directed their release)—

(a) in subsection (6), for the words after "sentence" there shall be substituted the following words—

"—

(a) account shall be taken of any corresponding relevant period; but

(b) no account shall be taken of any time during which the prisoner was unlawfully at large within the meaning of section 49 of the Prison Act 1952 ("the 1952 Act")."; and

(b) after that subsection, there shall be inserted the following subsection—

"(6A) In subsection (6)(a) above, "corresponding relevant period" means the period corresponding to the period by which a determinate sentence of imprisonment imposed on the offender would fall to be reduced under section 67 of the Criminal Justice Act 1967 (reduction of sentences to take account of police detention or remands in custody).".

(2) In paragraph 9(2) of Schedule 12 to that Act (application of early release provisions of the Act to existing life prisoners), after paragraph (b) there shall be inserted the following paragraph, preceded by the word "and"—

"(c) in section 34 of this Act, paragraph (a) of subsection (6) and subsection (6A) were omitted.".

Committals for sentence

47. In section 40(3) of the Criminal Justice Act 1991 (power of magistrates' court to commit offender convicted of new offence during currency of previous sentence to Crown Court for sentence), in paragraph (b), for the words from "in accordance with" to the end there shall be substituted the words "; and the Crown Court to which he has been so committed may make such an order with regard to him as is mentioned in subsection (2) above.".

Extradited persons: sentence of imprisonment to reflect custody

48.—(1) In section 47 of the Criminal Justice Act 1991 (computation of sentences of imprisonment of persons extradited to United Kingdom), in subsection (4), in the definition of "extradited to the United Kingdom", after paragraph (iv), there shall be inserted the following paragraph, preceded by the word "or"—

"(v) in pursuance of arrangements with a foreign state in respect of which an Order in Council under section 2 of the Extradition Act 1870 is in force;".

(2)   In each of sections 218(3) and 431(3) of the Criminal Procedure (Scotland) Act 1975 (corresponding provisions for Scotland), after paragraph (c) there shall be inserted the following paragraph—

> "(cc)   in pursuance of arrangements with a foreign state in respect of which an Order in Council under section 2 of the Extradition Act 1870 is in force;".

Transfers of proceedings

49.   In section 53 of the Criminal Justice Act 1991 (notices of transfer in certain cases involving children)—

(a)   in subsection (1), for the words "served" and "on" there shall be substituted the words "given" and "to";

(b)   in subsection (2), for the word "served" there shall be substituted the word "given";

(c)   in subsection (3), for the word "service" there shall be substituted the word "giving"; and

(d)   in subsection (4), for the word "serve" there shall be substituted the word "give".

Community sentences: binding over of parent or guardian

50.   In section 58(2) of the Criminal Justice Act 1991 (power of court to bind over parent or guardian of young offender), at the end, there shall be inserted the following paragraph—

> "Where the court has passed on the relevant minor a community sentence (within the meaning of section 6 above) it may include in the recognisance a provision that the minor's parent or guardian ensure that the minor complies with the requirements of that sentence.".

Confiscation orders in terrorist-related activities cases: variation of sentences

51.—(1)   In section 48 of the Northern Ireland (Emergency Provisions) Act 1991 (postponed confiscation orders etc), after subsection (3B) there shall be inserted the following subsection—

> "(3C)   Where the court has sentenced the defendant under subsection (2) or (3) above during the specified period it may, after the end of that period, vary the sentence by imposing a fine or making any such order as is mentioned in subsection (5)(b) or (c) below so long as it does so within a period corresponding to that allowed by section 49(2) or (3) of the Judicature (Northern Ireland) Act 1978 (time allowed for varying a sentence) but beginning with the end of the specified period.".

(2)   For the purposes of section 69 of the Northern Ireland (Emergency Provisions) Act 1991 (temporary provisions) the amendment made in that Act by this paragraph shall be treated, as from the time when this paragraph comes into force, as having been continued in force by the order made under subsection (3) of that section which has effect at that time.

Anonymity of victims of certain offences

52.—(1)   The Sexual Offences (Amendment) Act 1992 shall be amended as follows.

(2)   In section 2(1) (offences to which the Act applies), after paragraph (e) there shall be inserted the following paragraphs—

> "(f)   any conspiracy to commit any of those offences;
>
> (g)   any incitement of another to commit any of those offences.".

(3)   In section 6 (interpretation)—

(a)   after subsection (2) there shall be inserted the following subsection—

> "(2A)   For the purposes of this Act, where it is alleged or there is an accusation that an offence of conspiracy or incitement of another to commit an offence mentioned in section 2(1)(a) to (d) has been committed, the person against whom the substantive offence is alleged to have been intended to be committed shall be regarded as the person against whom the conspiracy or incitement is alleged to have been committed.

In this subsection, "the substantive offence" means the offence to which the alleged conspiracy or incitement related."; and

(b) in subsection (3), after the words "references in" there shall be inserted the words "subsection (2A) and in".

Application of 1993 Act powers to pre-commencement offences

53. Section 78(6) of the Criminal Justice Act 1993 (application of Act to pre-commencement offences) shall have effect, and be deemed always to have had effect, with the substitution, for the words from "or the powers" to the end, of the words "and, where it confers a power on the court, shall not apply in proceedings instituted before the coming into force of that provision.".

Definitions In the Rehabilitation of Offenders Act 1974, for "rehabilitation", see s 1 of that Act; in the Sexual Offences (Amendment) Act 1976, for "rape", see the Sexual Offences Act 1956, s 1, as substituted by s 142 of this Act; in the Criminal Justice Act 1988, s 33A, for "child" see sub-s (3) of that section; in the Extradition Act 1989, for "foreign state", see s 3(2) of that Act; for "designated Commonwealth country", see s 5(1) thereof; for "authority to proceed" and "extradition request", see s 7(1) thereof, as amended by para 37(1), (3)(a) above; for "warrant", see s 7(6) thereof; in the Northern Ireland (Emergency Provisions) Act 1991, for "defendant", see s 56(1) thereof; in the Criminal Justice Act 1991, for "pre-sentence report", see s 3(5) thereof; for "curfew order", see s 12(1) thereof; for "relevant minor", see s 58(1) thereof; for "the 1980 Act", see s 99(1) thereof.
References See para 12.16.

SCHEDULE 10

Section 168(2)

CONSEQUENTIAL AMENDMENTS

Bail: exclusion in homicide and rape cases

1. In section 2 of the Habeas Corpus Act 1679 (bail for persons released from custody under habeas corpus while awaiting trial), after the words "brought as aforesaid shall" there shall be inserted the words ", subject to section 25 of the Criminal Justice and Public Order Act 1994,".

Evidence of accused in criminal proceedings

2. In section 1 of the Criminal Evidence Act 1898 (competency of accused to give evidence in criminal proceedings), proviso (b) shall be omitted.

Evidence of accused in criminal proceedings

3. In section 1 of the Criminal Evidence Act (Northern Ireland) 1923 (competency of accused to give evidence in criminal proceedings)—

(a) after the words "Provided as follows:—" there shall be inserted the following proviso—

"(a) A person so charged shall not be called as a witness in pursuance of this Act except upon his own application;";

(b) proviso (b) shall be omitted.

Responsibility for fine for breach of requirements of secure training order

4. In section 55(1A) of the Children and Young Persons Act 1933 (power of court to order parent or guardian to pay fine imposed on child or young person), after paragraph (b) there shall be inserted the following paragraph—

"(c) a court would impose a fine on a child or young person under section 4(3) of the Criminal Justice and Public Order Act 1994 (breach of requirements of supervision under secure training order),".

Bail: exclusion in homicide and rape cases

5. In section 56(3) of the Children and Young Persons Act 1933 (powers of courts remitting young offenders to youth court), after the word "may" there shall be inserted the words ", subject to section 25 of the Criminal Justice and Public Order Act 1994,".

Bail: exclusion in homicide or rape cases

6. In section 37(1) of the Criminal Justice Act 1948 (power of High Court to grant bail on case stated or application for certiorari)—
   (a) in paragraph (b), after the word "may" there shall be inserted the words ", subject to section 25 of the Criminal Justice and Public Order Act 1994,"; and
   (b) in paragraph (d), after the word "may" there shall be inserted the words ", subject to section 25 of the Criminal Justice and Public Order Act 1994,".

Modernisation of "servant" in Prison Act

7. In section 3(1) of the Prison Act 1952 (officers and servants at prisons), for the word "servants" there shall be substituted the words "employ such other persons".

Use of young offender institutions as secure training centres

8. In section 37(4) of the Prison Act 1952 (prisons not deemed closed where used as remand centres etc), at the end, there shall be inserted the words "or secure training centre".

Young offenders absconding from secure training centres

9.—(1) Section 49 of the Prison Act 1952 (persons unlawfully at large) shall be amended as follows.

(2) In subsection (1), after the words "young offenders institution" there shall be inserted the words "or a secure training centre".

(3) In subsection (2), for the words between "detained in a" and "is unlawfully" there shall be substituted the words "young offenders institution or in a secure training centre".

(4) In subsection (2), in proviso (a), for the words after "prison" there shall be substituted the words "remand centre, young offenders institution or secure training centre".

Bail: exclusion in homicide and rape cases

10. In section 4(2) of the Administration of Justice Act 1960 (power of High Court to grant bail to persons appealing to the House of Lords), after the words "Divisional Court shall" there shall be inserted the words ", subject to section 25 of the Criminal Justice and Public Order Act 1994,".

Young offenders: application of prison rules

11. In section 23(4) of the Criminal Justice Act 1961 (which applies provisions relating to prison rules to other institutions), before the words "and remand centres" there shall be inserted the words "secure training centres".

Young offenders: transfer, supervision and recall within British Islands

12.—(1) Part III of the Criminal Justice Act 1961 (transfer, supervision and recall within British Islands) shall have effect with the following amendments.

(2) In section 29—
   (a) in subsection (1), for the words from "youth custody centre" to "young offenders institution" there shall be substituted the words "or institution for young offenders to which this subsection applies";
   (b) after subsection (2), there shall be inserted the following subsection—

"(2A) The institutions for young offenders to which subsection (1) above applies are the following: a remand centre, young offenders institution or secure training centre and, in Northern Ireland, a young offenders centre.".

(3) In section 30—

    (a) in subsection (3), for the words between "prison" and "in any part" there shall be substituted the words "or institution for young offenders to which this subsection applies";

    (b) after subsection (3), there shall be inserted the following subsection—

"(3A) The institutions for young offenders to which subsection (3) above applies are the following: a young offenders institution or secure training centre and, in Northern Ireland, a young offenders centre.".

(4) In section 32, in subsection (2), after paragraph (k), there shall be inserted the following paragraph—

"(l) sections 1 and 3 of the Criminal Justice and Public Order Act 1994.".

(5) In section 38(3), for paragraph (a), there shall be substituted the following paragraph—

"(a) the expression "imprisonment or detention" means imprisonment, custody for life, detention in a young offenders institution or in a secure training centre or detention under an equivalent sentence passed by a court in the Channel Islands or the Isle of Man;".

Payment of damages by police authority

13. In section 48(4) of the Police Act 1964 (payment by police authority of damages awarded against constables), after the words "section 14 of this Act" there shall be inserted the words "or section 141 of the Criminal Justice and Public Order Act 1994".

Cross-border enforcement: extension of protection

14. In section 51 of the Police Act 1964 (assaults on, and obstruction of, constables), after subsection (3), there shall be inserted the following subsection—

"(4) This section also applies to a constable who is a member of a police force maintained in Scotland or Northern Ireland when he is executing a warrant or otherwise acting in England or Wales by virtue of any enactment conferring powers on him in England and Wales.".

Bail: exclusion in homicide and rape cases

15. In section 22(1) of the Criminal Justice Act 1967 (power of High Court to grant bail), after the word "may", there shall be inserted the words ", subject to section 25 of the Criminal Justice and Public Order Act 1994,".

Young offenders: detention under secure training order

16. Section 67 of the Criminal Justice Act 1967 (computation of sentences of imprisonment or detention passed in England and Wales) shall be amended by the insertion in subsection (5), after paragraph (b), of the following paragraph—

"(c) to secure training orders under section 1 of the Criminal Justice and Public Order Act 1994;".

Payment of damages by Scottish police authority

17. In section 39(4) of the Police (Scotland) Act 1967 (payment by police authority of damages awarded against constables), after the words "section 11 of this Act" there shall be inserted the words "or section 141 of the Criminal Justice and Public Order Act 1994".

Assaults on constables etc

18. In section 41 of the Police (Scotland) Act 1967 (assaults on constables etc), after subsection (2), there shall be inserted the following subsection—

"(3)   This section also applies to a constable who is a member of a police force maintained in England and Wales or in Northern Ireland when he is executing a warrant or otherwise acting in Scotland by virtue of any enactment conferring powers on him in Scotland.".

Bail: exclusion in homicide and rape cases

19. In section 8(2)(a) of the Criminal Appeal Act 1968 (powers of Court of Appeal on retrial), after the words "custody or" there shall be inserted the words ", subject to section 25 of the Criminal Justice and Public Order Act 1994,".

Bail: exclusion in homicide and rape cases

20. In section 11(5) of the Criminal Appeal Act 1968 (powers of Court of Appeal on quashing interim hospital order), after the word "may" there shall be inserted the words ", subject to section 25 of the Criminal Justice and Public Order Act 1994,".

Bail: exclusion in homicide and rape cases

21. In section 16(3)(b) of the Criminal Appeal Act 1968 (powers of Court of Appeal on allowing an appeal against a finding that a person is under a disability), after the word "may" there shall be inserted the words ", subject to section 25 of the Criminal Justice and Public Order Act 1994,".

Bail: exclusion in homicide and rape cases

22. In section 19(1) of the Criminal Appeal Act 1968 (power of Court of Appeal to grant bail), after the word "may", there shall be inserted the words ", subject to section 25 of the Criminal Justice and Public Order Act 1994,".

Bail: exclusion in homicide and rape cases

23. In section 36 of the Criminal Appeal Act 1968 (power of Court of Appeal to grant bail on appeal by defendant), after the word "may" there shall be inserted the words ", subject to section 25 of the Criminal Justice and Public Order Act 1994".

Young offenders: possession of firearms

24.—(1) The Firearms Act 1968 shall be amended as follows.

(2) In section 21 (possession of firearms by persons previously convicted of crime)—

    (a)   in subsection (2), after the word "Scotland" there shall be inserted the words "or who has been subject to a secure training order"; and

    (b)   for subsection (2A) there shall be substituted—

"(2A) For the purposes of subsection (2) above, "the date of his release" means—

    (a)   in the case of a person sentenced to imprisonment with an order under section 47(1) of the Criminal Law Act 1977 (prison sentence partly served and partly suspended), the date on which he completes service of so much of the sentence as was by that order required to be served in prison;

    (b)   in the case of a person who has been subject to a secure training order—

        (i)   the date on which he is released from detention under the order;

        (ii)   the date on which he is released from detention ordered under section 4 of the Criminal Justice and Public Order Act 1994; or

        (iii)   the date halfway through the total period specified by the court in making the order,

whichever is the later.".

(3) In section 52(1) (forfeiture and disposal of firearms), in paragraph (a), after the word "Scotland" there shall be inserted the words "or is subject to a secure training order".

Cross-border enforcement: extension of protection

25. In section 7 of the Criminal Justice (Miscellaneous Provisions) Act (Northern Ireland) 1968 (assaults on, and obstruction of, constables), after subsection (3), there shall be inserted the following subsection—

"(4) This section also applies to a constable who is a member of a police force maintained in England and Wales or Scotland when he is executing a warrant or otherwise acting in Northern Ireland by virtue of any statutory provision conferring powers on him in Northern Ireland.".

Sexual offences: male rape

26. In section 9(2) of the Theft Act 1968 (offences which if intended by a trespasser constitute burglary), for the words "raping any woman" there shall be substituted the words "raping any person".

Payment of damages by Police Authority for Northern Ireland

27. In section 14(5) of the Police Act (Northern Ireland) 1970 (payment by Police Authority of damages awarded against persons serving with the Royal Ulster Constabulary), for the words "section 19" there shall be substituted the words "section 141 of the Criminal Justice and Public Order Act 1994".

Jury service: penalty for serving when not qualified

28. In section 20(5) of the Juries Act 1974 (offences in connection with jury service), at the end of paragraph (d) there shall be inserted ";or

(e) knowing that he is not qualified for jury service by reason of section 40 of the Criminal Justice and Public Order Act 1994, serves on a jury,".

Custody officers: ineligibility for jury service

29. In Part I of Schedule 1 to the Juries Act 1974, in Group B (ineligibility for jury service of certain persons concerned with the administration of justice), after the entry for prisoner custody officers within the meaning of Part IV of the Criminal Justice Act 1991, there shall be inserted the following entry—

"Custody officers within the meaning of Part I of the Criminal Justice and Public Order Act 1994".

Rehabilitation of offenders subject to secure training orders

30. In section 5(6) of the Rehabilitation of Offenders Act 1974 (rehabilitation periods for particular sentences), after paragraph (c), there shall be inserted the following paragraph, preceded by the word "or"—

"(d) a secure training order under section 1 of the Criminal Justice and Public Order Act 1994;".

Prisoner custody officers: ineligibility for jury service

31. In Schedule 2 to the Juries (Northern Ireland) Order 1974 (exemptions from jury service) in the group headed "Persons connected with the administration of justice", at the end there shall be inserted—

"Prisoner custody officers within the meaning of section 122(1) of the Criminal Justice and Public Order Act 1994.".

Bail: exclusion in homicide and rape cases

32. In section 4 of the Bail Act 1976 (entitlement to bail), after subsection (7), there shall be inserted the following subsection—

"(8) This section is subject to section 25 of the Criminal Justice and Public Order Act 1994 (exclusion of bail in cases of homicide and rape).".

Police bail: variation by magistrates

33. In section 4(2) of the Bail Act 1976 (occasions for implementation of right to bail), in paragraph (b), after the words "for bail" there shall be inserted the words "or for a variation of the conditions of bail".

Bail: no right for persons offending while on bail

34. In Part III of Schedule 1 to the Bail Act 1976, in paragraph 2, at the end, there shall be inserted the words "; and so as respects the reference to an offence committed by a person on bail in relation to any period before the coming into force of paragraph 2A of Part 1 of this Schedule.".

Sexual offences: male rape

35.—(1) The Sexual Offences (Amendment) Act 1976 shall be amended as follows.

(2) In section 1(2) (reasonable grounds for belief in consent to intercourse), after the word "woman" there shall be inserted the words "or man".

(3) In section 2(3) (restrictions on evidence at trials for rape etc), after the word "woman" there shall be inserted the words "or man".

(4) In section 7(2) (interpretation of terms used in the Act)—
    (a) the words from "references" to "only);" shall be omitted; and
    (b) for the words "and section 46 of that Act" there shall be substituted the words "section 46 of the Sexual Offences Act 1956".

Sexual offences: male rape

36.—(1) Section 4 of the Sexual Offences (Amendment) Act 1976 (anonymity of complainants in rape etc cases) shall be amended as follows.

(2) In subsection (1)—
    (a) in paragraph (a)—
        (i) after the word "woman" in both places where it occurs there shall be inserted the words "or man";
        (ii) for the words "woman's name nor her address" there shall be substituted the words "name nor the address of the woman or man";
        (iii) after the words "of her" there shall be inserted the words "or him";
        (iv) for the words "her lifetime" there shall be substituted the words "that person's lifetime"; and
        (v) for the words "identify her" there shall be substituted the words "identify that person"; and
    (b) in paragraph (b)—
        (i) after the word "woman" there shall be inserted the words "or man"; and
        (ii) for the words "her lifetime" there shall be substituted the words "that person's lifetime".

(3) In subsection (5A), after the word "woman" there shall be inserted the words "or man".

(4) In subsection (5B), for the words "woman's peace or comfort" there shall be substituted the words "peace or comfort of the woman or man".

(5) In subsection (6), in the definition of "complainant", after the word "woman" there shall be inserted the words "or man".

Indecent photographs etc

37.—(1) The Protection of Children Act 1978 shall be amended as follows.

(2) In section 2(3), after the words "proceedings under this Act" there shall be inserted the words "relating to indecent photographs of children".

(3) In section 4—

    (a) in subsection (1), after the word "photograph" there shall be inserted the words "or pseudo-photograph"; and

    (b) in subsection (2), after the word "photographs" there shall be inserted the words "or pseudo-photographs".

(4) In section 5(2), (5) and (6), after the word "photographs" there shall be inserted the words "or pseudo-photographs".

Indecent photographs etc (Northern Ireland)

38.—(1) The Protection of Children (Northern Ireland) Order 1978 shall be amended as follows.

(2) In Article 4(1)—

    (a) after the word "photograph" there shall be inserted the words "or pseudo-photograph"; and

    (b) after the word "photographs" there shall be inserted the words "or pseudo-photographs".

(3) In Article 5(3) and (5), after the word "photographs" there shall be inserted the words "or pseudo-photographs".

(4) In Article 6(1), after the word "photographs" there shall be inserted the words "or pseudo-photographs".

(5) In Article 7(1), after the word "Order" there shall be inserted the words "relating to indecent photographs of children".

Secure training orders: absence of accused

39. In section 11(3) of the Magistrates' Courts Act 1980 (certain sentences and orders not to be made in absence of accused), after the word "make" there shall be inserted the words "a secure training order or".

Procedure for young offenders in cases of grave crimes

40. In section 24(1)(a) of the Magistrates' Courts Act 1980 (exception to summary trial of children or young persons) the words "he has attained the age of 14 and" shall be omitted.

Bail: exclusion in homicide and rape cases

41. In section 29(4)(b) of the Magistrates' Courts Act 1980 (person under 18 remitted to youth court for trial), after the word "may" there shall be inserted the words ", subject to section 25 of the Criminal Justice and Public Order Act 1994,".

Bail: exclusion in homicide and rape cases

42. In section 37(1) of the Magistrates' Courts Act 1980 (committal to Crown Court for sentence), after the word "may" there shall be inserted the words ", subject to section 25 of the Criminal Justice and Public Order Act 1994,".

Police bail

43. In section 43(1) of the Magistrates' Courts Act 1980 (bail under the Police and Criminal Evidence Act 1984), after the words "bail under" there shall be inserted the words "Part IV of".

Bail: exclusion in homicide or rape cases

44. In section 113(1) of the Magistrates' Courts Act 1980 (power of magistrates' court to grant bail on appeal to Crown Court or by way of case stated), after the word "may" there shall be inserted the words ", subject to section 25 of the Criminal Justice and Public Order Act 1994,".

Prisoner custody officers: ineligibility for jury service

45. In Part I of Schedule 1 to the Law Reform (Miscellaneous Provisions) (Scotland) Act 1980 (which makes ineligible for jury service persons connected with the administration of justice), in Group B, after paragraph (o) there shall be inserted the following paragraph—

> "(oo) prisoner custody officers within the meaning of section 114(1) of the Criminal Justice and Public Order Act 1994;".

Young offenders: detention in the custody of a constable and others

46. In section 6 of the Imprisonment (Temporary Provisions) Act 1980 (detention in the custody of a constable)—
- (a) in subsection (1), after the words "remand centre" there shall be inserted the words "secure training centre";
- (b) in subsection (2), after the words "remand centre" there shall be inserted the words "secure training centre"; and
- (c) after the subsection (3) inserted by section 94 of this Act, there shall be inserted the following subsection—

> "(4) Any reference in this section to a constable includes a reference to a custody officer (within the meaning of section 12 of the Criminal Justice and Public Order Act 1994) acting in pursuance of escort arrangements (within the meaning of Schedule 1 to that Act).".

Detention by constables and officers of a prison etc: maximum period

47. In section 2 of the Criminal Justice (Scotland) Act 1980 (detention and questioning at police station etc)—
- (a) at the beginning of subsection (3A) there shall be inserted "Subject to subsection (3B) below,"; and
- (b) after subsection (3A) there shall be inserted the following subsection—

> "(3B) Subsection (3A) above shall not apply in relation to detention under section 41(3) of the Prisons (Scotland) Act 1989 (detention in relation to introduction etc into prison of prohibited article), but where a person was detained under section 41(3) immediately prior to his detention under subsection (1) above the period of six hours mentioned in subsection (2) above shall be reduced by the length of that earlier detention.".

Bail: exclusion in homicide and rape cases

48. In section 81(1) of the Supreme Court Act 1981 (power of Crown Court to grant bail), after the word "may", there shall be inserted the words ", subject to section 25 of the Criminal Justice and Public Order Act 1994,".

Young offenders: legal representation

49. In section 3(1) of the Criminal Justice Act 1982 (restriction on certain sentences where offender not legally represented), after paragraph (d) there shall be inserted the following paragraph, preceded by the word "or"—

> "(e) make a secure training order,".

Young offenders: early release

50. In section 32 of the Criminal Justice Act 1982 (early release by order of classes of prisoners and other persons), after subsection (7), there shall be inserted the following subsection—

> "(7A) Subsections (1) and (4) above shall apply in relation to secure training centres and persons detained in such centres as they apply, by virtue of section 43(5) of the Prison Act 1952, to young offenders institutions and to persons detained in such institutions.".

Bail: exclusion in homicide and rape cases

51. In section 51(4) of the Mental Health Act 1983 (power of court to remit or release on bail detained person), after the words "above or" there shall be inserted the words ", subject to section 25 of the Criminal Justice and Public Order Act 1994,".

Video recordings

52.—(1) The Video Recordings Act 1984 shall be amended as follows.

(2) In section 13, after subsection (2), there shall be inserted the following subsection—

"(3) A person guilty of an offence under this section shall be liable, on summary conviction, to a fine not exceeding level 5 on the standard scale.".

(3) For section 15 there shall be substituted the following section—

"15 Time limit for prosecutions

(1) No prosecution for an offence under this Act shall be brought after the expiry of the period of three years beginning with the date of the commission of the offence or one year beginning with the date of its discovery by the prosecutor, whichever is earlier.

(2) In Scotland, the reference in subsection (1) above to the date of discovery by the prosecutor shall be construed as a reference to the date on which evidence sufficient in the opinion of the Lord Advocate to warrant proceedings came to his knowledge.

(3) For the purposes of subsection (2) above—
   (a) a certificate signed by the Lord Advocate or on his behalf and stating the date on which evidence came to his knowledge shall be conclusive evidence of that fact;
   (b) a certificate purporting to be signed as mentioned in paragraph (a) above shall be presumed to be so signed unless the contrary is proved and
   (c) a prosecution shall be deemed to be brought on the date on which a warrant to apprehend or to cite the accused is granted provided that the warrant is executed without undue delay.".

Interim possession order: power of entry

53. In section 17 of the Police and Criminal Evidence Act 1984 (police powers of entry to effect arrest etc)—
   (a) in subsection (1)(c), after sub-paragraph (iii), there shall be inserted the following sub-paragraph—

   "(iv) section 76 of the Criminal Justice and Public Order Act 1994 (failure to comply with interim possession order);";

   (b) in subsection (3), after the words "subsection (1)(c)(ii)" there shall be inserted the words "or (iv)".

Bail: exclusion in homicide and rape cases

54. In section 38(1) of the Police and Criminal Evidence Act 1984 (duty of custody officer to release on bail or without bail after charge), after the word "shall" there shall be inserted the words ", subject to section 25 of the Criminal Justice and Public Order Act 1994,".

Searches of persons detained at police stations

55. In section 54(1)(b) of the Police and Criminal Evidence Act 1984 (searches of persons detained at police stations), for the words "under section 47(5) above" there shall be substituted the words ", as a person falling within section 34(7), under section 37 above".

Fingerprinting: speculative searches

56. In section 61 of the Police and Criminal Evidence Act 1984 (which regulates the taking of fingerprints)—
    (a)   after subsection (7) there shall be inserted the following subsection—

"(7A) If a person's fingerprints are taken at a police station, whether with or without the appropriate consent—
          (a)   before the fingerprints are taken, an officer shall inform him that they may be the subject of a speculative search; and
          (b)   the fact that the person has been informed of this possibility shall be recorded as soon as is practicable after the fingerprints have been taken."; and

    (b)   in subsection (8), after the word "them" there shall be inserted the words "and, in the case falling within subsection (7A) above, the fact referred to in paragraph (b) of that subsection".

Intimate samples: speculative searches

57. In section 62 of the Police and Criminal Evidence Act 1984 (which regulates the taking of intimate body samples)—
    (a)   after subsection (7) there shall be inserted the following subsection—

"(7A) If an intimate sample is taken from a person at a police station—
          (a)   before the sample is taken, an officer shall inform him that it may be the subject of a speculative search; and
          (b)   the fact that the person has been informed of this possibility shall be recorded as soon as practicable after the sample has been taken."; and

    (b)   in subsection (8), after the words "subsection (7)" there shall be inserted the words "or (7A)".

Non-intimate samples: speculative searches

58. In section 63 of the Police and Criminal Evidence Act 1984 (which regulates the taking of non-intimate body samples)—
    (a)   after the subsection (8A) inserted by section 55 of this Act, there shall be inserted the following subsection—

"(8B) If a non-intimate sample is taken from a person at a police station, whether with or without the appropriate consent—
          (a)   before the sample is taken, an officer shall inform him that it may be the subject of a speculative search; and
          (b)   the fact that the person has been informed of this possibility shall be recorded as soon as practicable after the sample has been taken."; and

    (b)   in subsection (9), after the words "(8A)" there shall be inserted the words "or (8B)".

Sexual offences: male rape and buggery

59. In Part I of Schedule 5 to the Police and Criminal Evidence Act 1984 (serious arrestable offences mentioned in section 116(2)(a) of that Act), for item 7 (buggery) there shall be substituted—

"7.   Buggery with a person under the age of 16.".

Trespassory assemblies

60. In section 15(1) of the Public Order Act 1986 (delegation of functions), for "14" there shall be substituted "14A".

Inferences from accused's silence

61.—(1) The Criminal Evidence (Northern Ireland) Order 1988 shall be amended as follows.

(2) In Article 3(1)(a), after the word "questioned" there shall be inserted the words "under caution".

(3) In Article 4—
    (a) in paragraph (1)—
        (i) for the words "to (7)" there shall be substituted the words "and (4)";
        (ii) in sub-paragraph (b), the words "be called upon to" shall be omitted;
        (iii) for the words from "if" onwards there shall be substituted the words ", at the conclusion of the evidence for the prosecution, his legal representative informs the court that the accused will give evidence or, where he is unrepresented, the court ascertains from him that he will give evidence";
    (b) for paragraphs (2) and (3) there shall be substituted the following paragraph—

"(2) Where this paragraph applies, the court shall, at the conclusion of the evidence for the prosecution, satisfy itself (in the case of proceedings on indictment conducted with a jury, in the presence of the jury) that the accused is aware that the stage has been reached at which evidence can be given for the defence and that he can, if he wishes, give evidence and that, if he chooses not to give evidence, or having been sworn, without good cause refuses to answer any question, it will be permissible for the court or jury to draw such inferences as appear proper from his failure to give evidence or his refusal, without good cause, to answer any question.";

    (c) in paragraph (4)—
        (i) at the beginning there shall be inserted the words "Where this paragraph applies,";
        (ii) in sub-paragraph (a), for the words "from the refusal as appear proper" there shall be substituted the words "as appear proper from the failure of the accused to give evidence or his refusal, without good cause, to answer any question";
    (d) in paragraph (5), for the words "refusal to be sworn" there shall be substituted the words "failure to do so"; and
    (e) paragraphs (9) and (10) shall be omitted.

(4) In Article 5(1)(b), for the words "the constable" there shall be substituted the words "that or another constable investigating the case".

(5) In Article 5(2), after sub-paragraph (a), for the word "and" there shall be substituted the following sub-paragraph—

        "(aa) a judge, in deciding whether to grant an application made by the accused under Article 5 of the Criminal Justice (Serious Fraud) (Northern Ireland) Order 1988 (application for dismissal of charge where a case of fraud has been transferred from a magistrates' court to the Crown Court under Article 3 of that Order); and".

(6) In Article 5, after paragraph 3, there shall be inserted the following paragraph—

"(3A) This Article applies in relation to officers of customs and excise as it applies in relation to constables.".

(7) In Article 6(1)(b), for the words "the constable" there shall be substituted the words "that or another constable investigating the case".

(8) In Article 6(2), after sub-paragraph (a), for the word "and" there shall be substituted the following sub-paragraph—

"(aa) a judge, in deciding whether to grant an application made by the accused under Article 5 of the Criminal Justice (Serious Fraud) (Northern Ireland) Order 1988 (application for dismissal of charge where a case of fraud has been transferred from a magistrates' court to the Crown Court under Article 3 of that Order); and".

(9) In Article 6, after paragraph 2, there shall be inserted the following paragraph—

"(2A) This Article applies in relation to officers of customs and excise as it applies in relation to constables.".

(10) In Article 6(3), for the words "do so" there shall be substituted the words "comply with the request".

Samples: application to terrorist suspects

62.—(1) The Prevention of Terrorism (Temporary Provisions) Act 1989 shall be amended as provided in sub-paragraphs (2) and (3) below.

(2) In section 15 (provisions supplementary to powers to arrest and detain suspected persons), after subsection (10), there shall be inserted the following subsections—

"(11) Section 62(1) to (11) of the Police and Criminal Evidence Act 1984 (regulation of taking of intimate samples) shall apply to the taking of an intimate sample from a person under subsection (9) above as if—
   (a) for subsection (2) there were substituted—

"(2) An officer may only give an authorisation under subsection (1) or (1A) above for the taking of an intimate sample if he is satisfied that it is necessary to do so in order to assist in determining—
   (a)   whether that person is or has been concerned in the commission, preparation or instigation of acts of terrorism to which section 14 of the Prevention of Terrorism (Temporary Provisions) Act 1989 applies; or
   (b)   whether he is subject to an exclusion order under that Act;
or if the officer has reasonable grounds for suspecting that person's involvement in an offence under any of the provisions mentioned in subsection (1)(a) of that section and for believing that an intimate sample will tend to confirm or disprove his involvement"; and

   (b)   in subsection (6), after the word "includes", there were inserted the words "where relevant".

(12)   In this section, "intimate sample" has the same meaning as in section 65 of the Police and Criminal Evidence Act 1984.

(13)   Section 63(1) to (9) of the Police and Criminal Evidence Act 1984 (regulation of taking of non-intimate samples) shall apply to the taking of a non-intimate sample from a person by a constable under subsection (9) above as if—
   (a)   for subsection (4) there were substituted—

"(4) An officer may only give an authorisation under subsection (3) above for the taking of a non-intimate sample if he is satisfied that it is necessary to do so in order to assist in determining—
   (a)   whether that person is or has been concerned in the commission, preparation or instigation of acts of terrorism to which section 14 of the Prevention of Terrorism (Temporary Provisions) Act 1989 applies; ;or
   (b)   whether he is subject to an exclusion order under that Act;
or if the officer has reasonable grounds for suspecting that person's involvement in an offence under any of the provisions mentioned in subsection (1)(a) of that section and for believing that a non-intimate sample will tend to confirm or disprove his involvement"; and

(b)   in subsection (7), after the word "includes" there were inserted the words "where relevant".

(14)   In this section, "non-intimate sample" has the same meaning as in section 65 of the Police and Criminal Evidence Act 1984.".

(3)   In Schedule 5, in paragraph 7 (provisions supplementary to powers to detain persons pending examination etc), after sub-paragraph (6), there shall be inserted the following sub-paragraphs—

"(6A)   Section 62(1) to (11) of the Police and Criminal Evidence Act 1984 (regulation of taking of intimate samples) shall apply to the taking of an intimate sample from a person under sub-paragraph (5) above as if—
(a)   for subsection (2) there were substituted—

"(2)   An officer may only give an authorisation under subsection (1) or (1A) above for the taking of an intimate sample if he is satisfied that it is necessary to do so in order to assist in determining—
      (a)   whether that person is or has been concerned in the commission, preparation or instigation of acts of terrorism to which paragraph 2 of Schedule 5 to the Prevention of Terrorism (Temporary Provisions) Act 1989 applies; or
      (b)   whether he is subject to an exclusion order under that Act; or
      (c)   whether there are grounds for suspecting that he has committed an offence under section 8 of that Act"; and

(b)   in subsection (6), after the word "includes", there were inserted the words "where relevant".

(6B)   In this paragraph, "intimate sample" has the same meaning as in section 65 of the Police and Criminal Evidence Act 1984.

(6C)   Section 63(1) to (9) of the Police and Criminal Evidence Act 1984 (regulation of taking of non-intimate samples) shall apply to the taking of a non-intimate sample from a person by a constable under sub-paragraph (5) above as if—
(a)   for subsection (4) there were substituted—

"(4)   An officer may only give an authorisation under subsection (3) above for the taking of a non-intimate sample if he is satisfied that it is necessary to do so in order to assist in determining—
      (a)   whether that person is or has been concerned in the commission, preparation or instigation of acts of terrorism to which paragraph 2 of Schedule 5 to the Prevention of Terrorism (Temporary Provisions) Act 1989 applies;
      (b)   whether he is subject to an exclusion order under that Act; or
      (c)   whether there are grounds for suspecting that he has committed an offence under section 8 of that Act"; and

(b)   in subsection (7), after the word "includes", there were inserted the words "where relevant".

(6D)   In this paragraph, "non-intimate sample" has the same meaning as in section 65 of the Police and Criminal Evidence Act 1984.".

(4)   In consequence of the foregoing amendments—
(a)   in section 62 of the Police and Criminal Evidence Act 1984 (which regulates the taking of intimate body samples), at the end there shall be inserted the following subsection—

"(12)   Nothing in this section, except as provided in section 15(11) and (12) of, and paragraph 7(6A) and (6B) of Schedule 5 to, the Prevention of Terrorism (Temporary Provisions) Act 1989, applies to a person arrested or detained under the terrorism provisions.";

(b) in section 63 of the Police and Criminal Evidence Act 1984 (which regulates the taking of non-intimate body samples), at the end there shall be inserted the following subsection—

"(10) Nothing in this section, except as provided in section 15(13) and (14) of, and paragraph 7(6C) and (6D) of Schedule 5 to, the Prevention of Terrorism (Temporary Provisions) Act 1989, applies to a person arrested or detained under the terrorism provisions."; and

(c) in section 28(2) of the Prevention of Terrorism (Temporary Provisions) Act 1989 (extent), in paragraph (b) (provisions extending only to England and Wales), after the words "section 15(10)" there shall be inserted the words "to (14)" and after the words "paragraph 7(6)" there shall be inserted the words "to (6D)".

(5) For the purposes of section 27 of the Prevention of Terrorism (Temporary Provisions) Act 1989 (temporary provisions), the amendments made by this paragraph shall be treated, as from the time when those amendments come into force, as having been continued in force by the order under subsection (6) of that section which has effect at that time.

Prevention of terrorism: consents for prosecutions etc

63.—(1) The Prevention of Terrorism (Temporary Provisions) Act 1989 shall be amended as follows.

(2) In section 17(1)(b) (purposes of investigations), for the words "section 21(4) of that Act" there shall be substituted the words "section 28(3) of that Act".

(3) In section 19(1) (consents required for prosecutions), after paragraph (a), there shall be inserted the following paragraph—

"(aa) in England and Wales for an offence under section 13A, 16A or 16B except by or with the consent of the Director of Public Prosecutions;".

(4) In section 28(2) (extent), in paragraph (a) (provisions not extending to Northern Ireland), for the words "and section 15(1)", there shall be substituted the words ", sections 13A and 15(1) and Part IVA".

(5) For the purposes of section 27 (temporary provisions), the amendments made by this paragraph shall be treated, as from the time when those amendments come into force, as having been continued in force by the order under subsection (6) of that section which has effect at that time.

Young offenders: powers to search and to test for drugs

64. In section 19(4) of the Prisons (Scotland) Act 1989 (remand centres and young offenders institutions), for the words "and 41" there shall be substituted the words "41, 41A and 41B".

Non-appearance of accused: plea of guilty

65. In section 20(1A) of the Criminal Justice Act 1991 (power of court to make financial circumstances order in absence of accused where guilty plea notified), for the words "section 12(2)" there shall be substituted the words "section 12(4)".

Young offenders: secure training order a custodial sentence

66. In section 31(1) of the Criminal Justice Act 1991 (which defines, amongst other expressions, "custodial sentence"), in paragraph (b) of that definition, after the words "1982 Act", there shall be inserted the words, "or a secure training order under section 1 of the Criminal Justice and Public Order Act 1994".

Bail: exclusion in homicide and rape cases

67. In section 40(3)(b) of the Criminal Justice Act 1991 (committal for sentence of offender convicted of offence during currency of original sentence), at the beginning, there shall be inserted the words "subject to section 25 of the Criminal Justice and Public Order Act 1994,".

Contracted out prisons: exclusion of search powers

68. In section 87(3) of the Criminal Justice Act 1991 (provisions of Prison Act 1952 not applying to contracted out prisons), after the word "officers)" there shall be inserted the words "and section 8A (powers of search by authorised employees)".

Testing prisoners for drugs: director's function

69. In section 87(4) of the Criminal Justice Act 1991 (certain functions as governor to be functions of director of contracted out prisons), after "13(1)" insert "16A".

The Parole Board

70. For Schedule 5 to the Criminal Justice Act 1991 (supplementary provisions about the Parole Board) there shall be substituted the following Schedule—

"SCHEDULE 5

THE PAROLE BOARD: SUPPLEMENTARY PROVISIONS

Status and capacity

1.—(1)The Board shall not be regarded as the servant or agent of the Crown or as enjoying any status, immunity or privilege of the Crown; and the Board's property shall not be regarded as property of, or held on behalf of, the Crown.

(2) It shall be within the capacity of the Board as a statutory corporation to do such things and enter into such transactions as are incidental to or conducive to the discharge of its functions under Part II of this Act.

Membership

2.—(1)The Board shall consist of a chairman and not less than four other members appointed by the Secretary of State.

(2) The Board shall include among its members—
    (a)   a person who holds or has held judicial office;
    (b)   a registered medical practitioner who is a psychiatrist;
    (c)   a person appearing to the Secretary of State to have knowledge and experience of the supervision or after-care of discharged prisoners; and
    (d)   a person appearing to the Secretary of State to have made a study of the causes of delinquency or the treatment of offenders.

(3) A member of the Board—
    (a)   shall hold and vacate office in accordance with the terms of his appointment;
    (b)   may resign his office by notice in writing addressed to the Secretary of State;

and a person who ceases to hold office as a member of the Board shall be eligible for re-appointment.

Payments to members

3.—(1)The Board may pay to each member such remuneration and allowances as the Secretary of State may determine.

(2) The Board may pay or make provision for paying to or in respect of any member such sums by way of pension, allowances or gratuities as the Secretary of State may determine.

(3) If a person ceases to be a member otherwise than on the expiry of his term of office and it appears to the Secretary of State that there are special circumstances that make it right that he should receive compensation, the Secretary of State may direct the Board to make to that person a payment of such amount as the Secretary of State may determine.

(4) A determination or direction of the Secretary of State under this paragraph requires the approval of the Treasury.

Proceedings

4.—(1)Subject to the provisions of section 32(5) of this Act, the arrangements relating to meetings of the Board shall be such as the Board may determine.

(2) The arrangements may provide for the discharge, under the general direction of the Board, of any of the Board's functions by a committee or by one or more of the members or employees of the Board.

(3) The validity of the proceedings of the Board shall not be affected by any vacancy among the members or by any defect in the appointment of a member.

Staff

5.—(1)The Board may appoint such number of employees as it may determine.

(2) The remuneration and other conditions of service of the persons appointed under this paragraph shall be determined by the Board.

(3) Any determination under sub-paragraph (1) or (2) shall require the approval of the Secretary of State given with the consent of the Treasury.

(4) The Employers' Liability (Compulsory Insurance) Act 1969 shall not require insurance to be effected by the Board.

6.—(1)Employment with the Board shall be included among the kinds of employment to which a scheme under section 1 of the Superannuation Act 1972 can apply, and accordingly in Schedule 1 to that Act (in which those kinds of employment are listed) at the end of the list of Other Bodies there shall be inserted—

"Parole Board.".

(2) The Board shall pay to the Treasury, at such times as the Treasury may direct, such sums as the Treasury may determine in respect of the increase attributable to this paragraph in the sums payable under the Superannuation Act 1972 out of money provided by Parliament.

Financial provisions

7.—(1)The Secretary of State shall pay to the Board—
    (a)   any expenses incurred or to be incurred by the Board by virtue of paragraph 3 or 5; and
    (b)   with the consent of the Treasury, such sums as he thinks fit for enabling the Board to meet other expenses.

(2) Any sums required by the Secretary of State for making payments under sub-paragraph (1) shall be paid out of money provided by Parliament.

Authentication of Board's seal

8. The application of the seal of the Board shall be authenticated by the signature of the Chairman or some other person authorised for the purpose.

Presumption of authenticity of documents issued by Board

9. Any document purporting to be an instrument issued by the Board and to be duly executed under the seal of the Board or to be signed on behalf of the Board shall be received in evidence and shall be deemed to be such an instrument unless the contrary is shown.

Accounts and audit

10.—(1) It shall be the duty of the Board—
    (a)   to keep proper accounts and proper records in relation to the accounts;

(b) to prepare in respect of each financial year a statement of accounts in such form as the Secretary of State may direct with the approval of the Treasury; and

(c) to send copies of each such statement to the Secretary of State and the Comptroller and Auditor General not later than 31st August next following the end of the financial year to which the statement relates.

(2) The Comptroller and Auditor General shall examine, certify and report on each statement of accounts sent to him by the Board and shall lay a copy of every such statement and of his report before each House of Parliament.

(3) In this paragraph, "financial year" means the period beginning with the date on which the Board is incorporated and ending with the next following 31st March, and each successive period of twelve months.

Reports

11. The Board shall as soon as practicable after the end of each financial year make to the Secretary of State a report on the performance of its functions during the year; and the Secretary of State shall lay a copy of the report before Parliament.".

Bail: exclusion in homicide and rape cases

71. In Schedule 6 to the Criminal Justice Act 1991 (procedure on notice of transfer in certain cases involving children), in paragraph 2(1), after the word "1976" where it occurs first there shall be inserted the words ", section 25 of the Criminal Justice and Public Order Act 1994".

Probation officers for offenders subject to secure training orders

72. In section 4 of the Probation Service Act 1993 (functions of probation committee)—
(a) in subsection (1), after paragraph (d), there shall be inserted the following paragraph—

"(dd) to make arrangements for the selection, from the probation officers appointed for or assigned to a petty sessions area within their probation area, of an officer to supervise any person subject to supervision by a probation officer under a secure training order (within the meaning of section 1 of the Criminal Justice and Public Order Act 1994) naming as that petty sessions area the petty sessions area within which the person to be supervised resides for the time being;"; and

(b) in subsection (4), for the words "paragraph (c) or (d)" there shall be substituted the words "paragraph (c), (d) or (dd)".

Secure training orders: cost of supervision by probation officer

73. In section 17 of the Probation Service Act 1993 (probation committee expenditure)—
(a) in subsection (1), for the words "and (5)" there shall be substituted the words "(5) and (5A)"; and
(b) after subsection (5) there shall be inserted the following subsection—

"(5A) Nothing in sections 18 or 19 requires there to be paid out of the metropolitan police fund or defrayed by a local authority any expenses of a probation committee which are defrayed by the Secretary of State under section 3(6) of the Criminal Justice and Public Order Act 1994.".

Definitions In the Children and Young Persons Act 1933, for "child" and "young person", see s 107(1) of that Act; in the Sexual Offences (Amendment) Act 1976, for "man", see (by virtue of s 7(2) thereof) the Sexual Offences Act 1956, s 46; in the Protection of Children Act 1978, for "pseudo-photograph", see s 7(7) of that Act, as amended by s 84(1), (3)(c) of this Act; in the Police and Criminal Evidence Act 1984, for "appropriate consent", "fingerprints", "intimate sample", "non-intimate sample" and "speculative search", see s 65 of that Act, as amended by s 58 of this Act. In the Bail Act 1976, for "bail", see s 2(1) of that Act.
References See paras 12.1, 12.16.

SCHEDULE 11

REPEALS

Chapter	Short title	Extent of repeal
1848 c 42	Indictable Offences Act 1848	Sections 12, 14 and 15
1898 c 36	Criminal Evidence Act 1898	In section 1, proviso (b)
1923 c 9 (NI)	Criminal Evidence Act (Northern Ireland) 1923	In section 1, proviso (b)
1925 c 86	Criminal Justice Act 1925	Section 13(3) Section 49(2)
1952 c 52	Prison Act 1952	In section 43(1)(a), the words "trial or" In section 43(1), the word "and" at the end of paragraph (b) In section 43(2)(b) and (c), the words "trial or"
1956 c 69	Sexual Offences Act 1956	In section 2(1), the word "unlawful" Section 2(2) In section 3(1), the word "unlawful" Section 3(2) Section 4(2) Section 22(2) Section 23(2)
1963 c 37	Children and Young Persons Act 1963	In section 57(2), the words "Section 49 of the principal Act and" and "an appeal by case stated or"
1965 c 45	Backing of Warrants (Republic of Ireland) Act 1965	In section 2(2)(a), the words from ", or an offence under an enactment" to "control"
1965 c 69	Criminal Procedure (Attendance of Witnesses) Act 1965	Section 1
1967 c 60	Sexual Offences Act 1967	In section 1(1), the words "but subject to the provisions of the next following section" Section 1(5) Section 2 Section 3
1967 c 77	Police (Scotland) Act 1967	Section 18
1967 c 80	Criminal Justice Act 1967	Section 7

Chapter	Short title	Extent of repeal
		In section 36(1), the definition of "committal proceedings"
		In section 67(5), the word "and" at the end of paragraph (a)
1968 c 19	Criminal Appeal Act 1968	In Schedule 2, paragraph 1, the words from "section 13(3)" to "but"
1968 c 52	Caravan Sites Act 1968	Sections 6 to 12
		In section 16, the definition of "gipsies"
1969 c 54	Children and Young Persons Act 1969.	Section 10(1) and (2). In section 57(4), the words "49 and the said sections"
1969 c 63	Police Act 1969	Sections 1, 3, 6 and 7
1970 c 9 (NI)	Police Act (Northern Ireland) 1970	Sections 19 and 20
1972 c 71	Criminal Justice Act 1972	In section 46(1), the following words—
		"Section 102 of the Magistrates' Courts Act 1980 and"; "which respectively allow";
		"committal proceedings and in other";
		"and section 106 of the said Act of 1980";
		"which punish the making of"; "102 or"; ", as the case may be".
		Section 46(2)
1973 c 62	Powers of Criminal Courts Act 1973	In section 32(1)(b), the words "tried or"
1974 c 23	Juries Act 1974	In section 10, the words "physical disability or"
1974 c 53	Rehabilitation of Offenders Act 1974	In section 5(4), the words "or placed on probation," and "or probation order"
1976 c 63	Bail Act 1976	Section 1(4)
		In section 3(6), the words "(but only by a court)"
1976 c. 82.	Sexual Offences (Amendment) Act 1976	Section 1(1) In section 7(2), the words from "references" to "only);"

Chapter	Short title	Extent of repeal
1977 c 45	Criminal Law Act 1977	Section 6(3) Section 38
1978 c 30	Interpretation Act 1978	In Schedule 1, paragraph (a) of the definition of "Committed for trial"
1978 c 37	Protection of Children Act 1978	In section 1(1)(a), the words following "child"
		In section 4(2), the words from "within" to "warrant"
1980 c 43	Magistrates' Courts Act 1980	In section 22(1), the words "subject to subsection (7) below"
		In section 24(1)(a) the words "he has attained the age of 14 and"
		In section 38(2)(b), the words from "committed" to "21 years old"
		In section 97(1), the words from "at an inquiry" to "be) or"
		Section 102
		Section 103
		Section 105
		Section 106
		Section 145(1)(e)
		In section 150(1), the definition of "committal proceedings"
		In Schedule 5, paragraph 2
1980 c 62	Criminal Justice (Scotland) Act 1980	In section 80, subsection (5); in subsection (7), paragraph (d) and the word "; or" immediately preceding that paragraph; and subsection (8)
1981 c 47	Criminal Attempts Act 1981	In section 2(2)(g), the words "or committed for trial"
1982 c 48	Criminal Justice Act 1982	In section 1(2), the words "trial or"
		Section 12(6), (7) and, in subsection (11), paragraph (b) and the word "and"
		Section 67(5)
		In Schedule 14, paragraph 8

Chapter	Short title	Extent of repeal
SI 1982/1536 (NI 19)	Homosexual Offences (Northern Ireland) Order 1982	In Article 3, in paragraph (1), the words "and Article 5 (merchant seamen)" and paragraph (4). Article 5
1984 c 39	Video Recordings Act 1984	In section 1, in subsection (2)(a), the word "or" and in subsection (3), the word "or" where it occurs first.
		In section 17(1), the words from "within" to "warrant"
1984 c 60	Police and Criminal Evidence Act 1984	Section 37(1)(b), together with the word "or" preceding it
		Section 47(5)
		In section 62(10), the words following "proper"
		In section 118(1), the definition of "intimate search"
1985 c 23	Prosecution of Offences Act 1985	In Schedule 1, paragraph 1
1986 c 64	Public Order Act 1986	Section 39
		In section 42(2), "39"
1987 c 38	Criminal Justice Act 1987	In Schedule 2, paragraphs 10 and 11
1988 c 33	Criminal Justice Act 1988	In section 25(1)(a)(ii), the word "or"
		Section 32A(10)
		In section 34(2), the words from "in relation to" to the end
		Section 126
		In section 160, in subsection (1), the words from "(meaning" to "16)" and subsection (5)
1988 c 34	Legal Aid Act 1988	In section 20(4)(a), the words "trial or"
		Section 20(4)(bb)
		Section 20(5)
SI 1988/1987 (NI 20)	Criminal Evidence (Northern Ireland) Order 1988	In Article 4, in paragraph (1)(b) the words "be called upon to" and paragraphs (9) and (10)
1989 c 45	Prisons (Scotland) Act 1989	Section 33

Chapter	Short title	Extent of repeal
1989 c 54	Children Act 1989	In Schedule 5, paragraph 7(2)(f)
		In Schedule 6, paragraph 10(2)(j)
1990 c 42	Broadcasting Act 1990	In Schedule 20, in paragraph 3(2), the words "and 49"
1991 c 13	War Crimes Act 1991	In section 1(4), the words "England, Wales or"
		Part I of the Schedule
1991 c 24	Northern Ireland (Emergency Provisions) Act 1991	In Schedule 7, paragraph 5(3)(c)
1991 c 53	Criminal Justice Act 1991	In section 3(2), the words from the beginning to "indictment,"
		In section 3(4), the words from "which is" to "applies"
		Section 50(4)
		Section 52(2)
		Section 57(4)(b), together with the word "and" preceding it
		Section 64
SI 1992/1829	Parole Board (Transfer of Functions) Order 1992	In Article 3, the words from "and 39" to "licence)" and the words "and (4)"
1993 c 24	Video Recordings Act 1993	Section 3
1993 c 36	Criminal Justice Act 1993	Section 67(2)

Note: The repeals that are to come into force on the passing of this Act are the following, namely, the repeals in the Sexual Offences Act 1967, the Caravan Sites Act 1968, the Sexual Offences (Amendment) Act 1976, the Public Order Act 1986, the Criminal Justice (Scotland) Act 1980 and the Homosexual Offences (Northern Ireland) Order 1982.

Definitions For "bail", see the Bail Act 1976, s 1(2); for "pseudo-photograph", see the Protection of Children Act 1978, s 7(7), as inserted by s 84(1), (3)(c) of this Act. In the Children and Young Persons Act 1933, for "child" and "young person", see s 107(1) of that Act. In the Police and Criminal Evidence Act 1984, for "appropriate consent", "fingerprints", "intimate sample", "non-intimate sample" and "speculative search", see s 65 of that Act, as amended by s 58 of this Act.
References See para 12.16.

Index